Ad Hominem Arguments

STUDIES IN RHETORIC AND COMMUNICATION
Series Editors:
E. Culpepper Clark
Raymie E. McKerrow
David Zarefsky

Douglas Walton

Ad Hominem Arguments

The University of Alabama Press   Tuscaloosa and London

Copyright © 1998
The University of Alabama Press
Tuscaloosa, Alabama 35487-0380
All rights reserved
Manufactured in the United States of America

∞

The paper on which this book is printed meets the minimum requirements of American National Standard for Information Science-Permanence of Paper for Printed Library Materials, ANSI Z39.48-1984.

Library of Congress Cataloging-in-Publication Data

Walton, Douglas, 1942–
    Ad hominem arguments / Douglas Walton.
        p. cm. — (Studies in rhetoric and communication)
    Includes bibliographical references and index.
    ISBN 0817309225 (cloth : alk. paper)
    1. Ad hominem arguments. 2. Persuasion (Rhetoric) 3. Reasoning.
    I. Title. II. Series.
    P301.5.P47 W347   1998
    808—ddc21   98-8889

British Library Cataloguing-in-Publication Data available

For Karen, With Love

Contents

Preface

The *ad hominem* or personal attack argument is frequently the immediate defensive response to any new and powerfully upsetting argument on a controversial and polarized issue, especially when interests are threatened, and emotions are running high on the issue.

When Rachel Carson's classic of environmental literature *Silent Spring* (1962) first appeared, agribusiness and pesticide interests reacted with the following ad hominem arguments (Proctor, 1995, p. 51). *Chemical World News* called the book "science fiction," comparing it to the television series *The Twilight Zone* and attacking Carson's capability and/or seriousness in collecting and using scientific evidence. A member of the U.S. Federal Pest Control Review Board replied: "I thought she was a spinster. What's she so worried about genetics for?"—using aspects of Carson's personal life in a snide attack suggesting that she should not be taken seriously as a person with any credibility. The director of New Jersey's Department of Agriculture replied that Carson's book was typical of that "vociferous, misinformed, group of nature-balancing, organic-gardening, bird-loving, unreasonable citizenry that has not been convinced of the important place of agricultural chemicals in our economy." Other representatives of the chemical industry called the book a "hoax" and called Carson a "fanatic defender" of a "cult" (Proctor, 1995, p. 51).

Silent Spring turned out to be ahead of its time in its prescient warnings about the dangers of pesticides in the ecosystem, a subject of much discussion and concern in subsequent years. But the agribusiness and pesticide interests, evidently because of the difficulty they had dealing with the evidence she presented, replied with these ad hominem attacks, evidently designated to silence her by discrediting her personally. Ultimately, in this case, the ad hominem attacks were not successful, but in many other instances they have been, as we will see in the case studies in this book.

Ad hominem arguments have become such a common tactic used in "attack ads" (negative campaigning) in election campaigns that they have reached the point of being an obsession in media reporting of political discourse in the late decades of the twentieth century. Personal attack arguments have often proved to be so effective, in election campaigns, for example, that even while condemning them, politicians have not been able to stop using them. Although ad hominem arguments have been around for a long time, now more than ever, the problem of how to deal with them in a critically balanced way is a matter of concern for public discourse in a democracy.

As far back as the 1860s, Northern newspapers attacked Abraham Lincoln's character in their political reporting of his policies (Bonevac, 1990, p. 48) by using the terms "drunk," "baboon," "too slow," "shattered, dazed and utterly foolish," and "craftiest and most dishonest politician that ever disgraced office in America," to discredit Lincoln personally.

In the 1990s candidates hesitate to step forward and run for high political office because they know how much time and money will be spent searching out character details and past accusations of any kind of alleged misconduct by the "oppo research" of the other party.

They know that in many recent cases, politicians have been forced to "confess" or endure other humiliations in public for behavior thought to be ethically questionable or inappropriate. The so-called character issue, as pursued in "attack journalism," has become central in American politics of the 1990s. There seems to be a consensus that character is all-important in political dialogue and that policy positions are of secondary importance, perhaps because they are more changeable. During this period, we have become very familiar indeed with the character attack type of ad hominem argument as a political instrument. The public has even, at certain times, indicated a revulsion at the excessive use of negative tactics in election campaigns, but the political media advisers still reserve it as a last-ditch powerful attack to be used if their side is behind in the polls and the election date is too close to retrieve a loss by other means.

Ad hominem arguments are easy to put forward as accusations, are difficult to refute, and often have an extremely powerful effect on persuading an audience to reject someone's argument, when used at an opportune moment in an exchange, even when little or no evidence has been brought forward to support the allegation. Indeed, personal attack on an arguer's character can make him look dishonest and untrustworthy or illogical and confused. The resulting lack of credibility can make it impossible for the person to carry on effectively to defend his side of the disputed issue at all. A reputation can be stained by a drastic and colorful allegation because the powerful stigma of the accusation itself is such that the critical faculties of the audience are suspended, leaving a residue of doubt and mistrust, even though little or no verifiable evidence supporting the charge was brought forward by the accuser.

The cases studied in this book illustrate the power of the ad hominem attack, the difficulty of dealing with it as an argument, and the mischief that it can cause. Regrettably, it is a negative tactic that the spin doctors, among others, have become adept at using. In one case (1.4) a U.S. presidential candidate was attacked on the basis that he was "trigger-happy" and not reliable as a potential officeholder by an ad showing a nuclear bomb exploding. In another case (3.5), the "wimp factor" was used to defeat a candidate for governor by ads suggesting he was not a strong enough leader. In another case, the CEO of a company was attacked unfairly as a ruthless person by the union side in a strike—the workers even calling him a "slimeball"—with the result that the negotiations were stalled, and the company eventually slid into bankruptcy.

Personal attack is such a subjective and emotional type of argument that one might wonder whether it is possible to discover objective logical criteria that would enable a rational critic to evaluate ad hominem arguments as justifiable (correct) or fallacious (incorrect) in given cases. It may seem that the only effective and available defense against such an attack is to insist that one is insulted by the accusation and to attack the character of the one who made such an allegation. But this reply is to counter one ad hominem attack with another. Although it may be an effective rebuttal in some cases, in other cases it is not effective, and in still other cases, it has the effect of turning a reasoned critical discussion of an issue into a personal quarrel. The alternative proposed by this book is to give an analysis of the logical structure of the ad hominem argument to show not only how this type of argument can be used fallaciously—as a sophistical tactic used deceptively to get the best of an opponent in an argument—but also how it can be used correctly to attack an argument by questioning the arguer's credibility. The aim then is not just to instruct the reader on how to attack someone using the ad hominem argument but how to do so in a rational manner, and how to reply in a rational way to such an attack.

The purpose of this book is to provide a normative and critical framework for identifying and evaluating personal attack (ad hominem) arguments. Although *argumentum ad hominem* has been traditionally treated as a fallacy in logic, recent research in argumentation has begun to indicate that, in many cases in conversational arguments, ad hominem arguments are not fallacious. This book concludes that while some personal attack arguments can definitely be judged fallacious, many others are quite reasonable (when evaluated in the appropriate context), while still others should be evaluated as weak (insufficiently supported) but not fallacious. The book shows that the real function of an ad hominem argument (when properly used) is to attack an arguer's credibility in order to criticize the argument she advocates.

In making the concepts of a person as arguer and the concept of the person's credibility (ethos) central to the analysis of the ad hominem, the new approach in this book overcomes the main weakness of the author's previous analysis of the ad hominem in Walton (*Arguer's Position*, 1985) and Walton (*Informal Logic*, 1989, chapter 5), which mainly stressed the structure of circumstantial ad hominem as the central focus of the analysis. This new analysis builds on that earlier work by providing a new and distinctively different analysis of the direct (or so-called abusive type of ad hominem argument) and provides a new, and much more carefully substantiated and detailed system of classification of all the various subtypes of the ad hominem argument. This new way of defining the ad hominem argument and distinguishing its subtypes leads to a new way of evaluating ad hominem arguments.

One of the most important aspects of this new and more advanced treatment of the ad hominem argument is the clarification of the terminological confusion in defining the ad hominem that has plagued this subject since the eighteenth century. Logic textbooks and philosophical writings on the ad hominem argument have systematically confused two distinct (but related) types of arguments—personal attack arguments and the kind of argument called "argument from commitment" in this book). This confusion has made a mess of any attempts to say anything meaningful about ad hominem arguments, and it was only after reading Nuchelmans's (1993) tracing of the two terminological roots of the ad hominem back to Aristotle that the scope and importance of this problem really became apparent to me—along with the need to do all the work necessary to solve it.

The realization of the full impact of this terminological confusion on all previous work on the ad hominem argument (including my own) led me to see that what was required at this stage in building the research program for the analysis of the ad hominem was a whole new approach of setting out, in a clear and precise structure, the distinctive forms of all the various types of ad hominem arguments, showing how each form of inference was related to each other related form of inference. What is provided by the new approach, by defining each form of inference clearly in a general way, is an objective basis for evaluating many different kinds of ad hominem arguments as used in particular cases (where they are often difficult to pin down and identify).

The method for identifying and evaluating ad hominem arguments presented in the book uses a set of argumentation schemes (forms of argument) for each distinctive subtype of ad hominem argument recognized and a set of appropriate critical questions matching each scheme. An ad hominem argument in a particular case is evaluated in relation to whether it meets the requirements of the scheme, in the first place, and in the second place, how the critical questions are managed in a dialogue exchange between the user of the ad hominem and her critical questioner. Thus the evaluation is *dialectical*, meaning that the argument is judged relative to the context and purpose of a communicative interaction between two participants in a dialogue.

The most innovative aspect of the method used in this book to evaluate ad hominem arguments is that the form of the argument is not the only basis for evaluating the correctness or incorrectness of how the argument was used in a particular case. The context of how the argument was used in a communicative exchange, as reconstructed from the text of discourse in a given case, will also play an important part in our method of evaluating ad hominem arguments.

Although the ad hominem argument is a part of the introductory logic curriculum, included under the heading of fallacies in most modern introductory logic textbooks that have a section or more on common fallacies, the textbook treatments are not very helpful. Not only do they disagree on basic terminology and on fundamental questions of how to evaluate the ad hominem argument, as indicated above, but also they contain a central ambiguity on how to define this type of argument. This ambiguity arises from the historical development of two conflicting but closely related views of the argumentum ad hominem, systematically confused throughout the history of philosophy, as noted above. The source of this pervasive ambiguity can even be traced back to Aristotelian origins, as Nuchelmans (1993) showed. Because current conceptions of the ad hominem continue to be so confused, and so confusing to both insiders and outsiders in the field of logic, disentangling this entrenched mass of disagreements and ambiguities in a helpful way requires a careful approach to the subject; chapter 3 carefully steers the readers through the intricacies of the closely related types of arguments at issue.

Chapter 1 begins with a consideration of some actual cases, which could be called classic or paradigm cases, that illustrate common kinds of uses of the ad hominem argument that have been and should be central items of concern for those who want to study the ad hominem as a type of argument that is both very common and also very powerfully persuasive (sometimes deceptively so). The only way to disentangle the mess of conceptual confusions that have grown into and around the current treatment of the ad hominem argument is to start with these paradigm cases to illustrate the argument for the reader and to have some kind of intuitive reference point.

Having tried to orient the reader to what is essentially at stake, and to give the reader an initial grip on the target subject matter of our analysis, the book then proceeds to chapter 2, where the modern textbook treatment of the ad hominem argument is surveyed. The survey is not meant to be a complete description of all the textbook accounts. It is meant to convey to the reader the general viewpoints adopted by the textbook accounts, the main conflicts between the accounts, and the evolution of the textbook accounts over the years toward an increased level of sophistication. Despite this increased level of sophistication, chapter 3 argues that there are fundamental problems in the textbook treatments that need to be cleared up before any real progress can be made on giving a useful way of identifying, analyzing and evaluating ad hominem arguments.

Chapter 3 delves into the subtleties in fundamental ambiguity inherent in the contemporary treatment of the ad hominem more deeply and resolves the ambiguity by introducing and bringing in a new vocabulary and new dialectical framework for evaluating how ad hominem arguments are used in a context of dialogue (conversational exchange) drawn from recent work in argumentation theory. This chapter is not easy for the beginner, but it is made necessary by the convoluted confusions of terminology that have been introduced by philosophical writings of previous (and present) generations on the ad hominem.

Chapter 4 offers a longer, very realistic case study of the ad hominem, which shows how powerful this type of argument is in political discourse, and illustrates the use of a clever defense against it. Luckily, this chapter is much easier to read and appreciate and is entertaining to anyone interested in the rhetoric of political argumentation.

Whereas chapter 3 analyzed one side of the fundamental ambiguity in the modern view of the ad hominem argument, the notion of argument from an arguer's commitments, chapter 4 analyzes the other side—the view of ad hominem as personal attack. The fundamental idea in the personal attack viewpoint is the notion of an arguer's character, and the problem to be addressed is how an arguer's character plays a role in deliberation and, in particular, in deliberation in political discourse, where the ad hominem is frequently such a powerful kind of attack. Personal attack arguments are always interesting, I find, not only to me but also to almost everyone. And the puzzle of trying to evaluate them in particular cases is one of the least dry and most entertaining tasks of logic. As the reader will see, however, even this type of ad hominem has a distinctive logical structure as an argument. And the job of evaluating instances of its use can be a lot more subtle, in many cases, than you might have thought.

Throughout the book, the analysis leads toward the goal of putting a theory into place that would enable a rational critic to evaluate ad hominem arguments used in particular cases. But the fundamental problem blocking any previous attempt to carry out such a project has been the ambiguities and plentiful confusions on even how to identify the varieties of ad hominem arguments as distinctive and identifiable types of arguments. Chapter 5 provides the theory that enables a user to carry out this task of identification by articulating forms of argument (argumentation schemes) for each subtype and developing a classification system for all these forms of ad hominem argument. Chapter 6 then gives the general method of evaluation that can be applied to any case.

Acknowledgments

I would like to thank the Social Sciences and Humanities Research Council of Canada for support in the form of a research grant and specifically to thank the following individuals for their help.

- Amy Merrett for word-processing the text and figures of the manuscript.
- Victor Wilkes for helping to collect materials that were used in the research for chapter 2.
- Alan Brinton, Erik Krabbe, Frans van Eemeren, and Rob Grooten-dorst for discussions that provoked thoughts and suggested some of the subjects and ideas pursued in the book.
- Lou Lépine for the initial word-processing of chapter 2 and the final draft.
- The readers for the University of Alabama Press, and particularly Tony Blair, for many helpful comments and criticisms that improved several of the formulations and corrected many errors and infelicities in this book.

In addition, I would like to thank the University of Winnipeg for granting me study leaves in 1996–97, the Department of Philosophy of the University of Western Australia for providing support and facilities while I was a Research Associate there in 1996–97, and the Oregon Humanities Center for inviting me to the University of

Oregon as a Distinguished Visiting Research Fellow in 1997 and for providing support and facilities for my work.

For help with the proofreading, I would like to thank Harry Simpson; for preparing the index, I would like to thank Rita Campbell. Staff members of The University of Alabama Press provided invaluable guidance in helping to find the right format and choice of styles to give the printed text an attractive and user-friendly appearance for the reader.

Ad Hominem Arguments

1

Classic Cases and Basic Concepts

When studying fallacies, it is useful to make a distinction among the three tasks of identification, analysis, and evaluation of the type of argument involved. Although the ultimate goal is evaluation (chapter 7), most of our efforts at this preparatory stage will be directed toward the task of identifying the ad hominem as a distinctive type of argument.

Before turning to the textbook treatments of the ad hominem—shown in chapter 2 to be an extraordinary mass of conceptual and terminological confusions—it will be very helpful, especially for the uninitiated reader, to attain a clear beginning grasp of how the five main types of ad hominem arguments work. In chapter 6, a much more refined classification and analysis of the various subtypes of these five basic types of ad hominem argument is given. But for now, to get some coherent initial point of departure in chapter 1, the reader is given a brief introduction to some classic cases that have already been studied in the scholarly literature.

The other goals of chapter 1 are: (a) to give a brief outline of the historical roots of the argumentum ad hominem; (b) to give a brief survey of leading developments in the recent scholarly literature on the ad hominem, or at least to introduce the reader to the basic logical concepts and leading theories needed to understand what follows; and (c) to make a statement of what the problems are that need to be resolved, at the current state of developments, to give us a better understanding of how the ad hominem argument fits into the current state of developments in dialogue logic.

Sections 1 through 4 of this chapter introduce the reader to the five classic types of ad hominem argument. Section 5 outlines three special cases that raise some problems of conceptualization and classification. Sections 6 and 7 outline the history of the ad hominem argument—especially its ancient origins, and how they developed into the modern treatment. Sections 8 and 9 introduce the reader to special problem areas, where the problems have to be carefully explained so that they can be later cleared up. Section 10 sketches out a provisional conclusion that states the understanding of the ad hominem argument achieved in the chapter, as a basis of going forward to a further analysis of it as a type of argument.

1. Abusive and Circumstantial

In what has come to be more or less accepted as the conventional treatment of the ad hominem argument in the scholarly literature (see Krabbe and Walton [1993] and van Eemeren and Grootendorst [1993]) five types or subcategories of ad hominem argument recur as being recognized as central most frequently—the abusive, the circumstantial, the bias, the tu quoque (or "you too"), and the poisoning the well. The abusive and the circumstantial subtypes are the most frequently emphasized ones and the ones that are usually accorded most importance in the scholarly accounts of the ad hominem fallacy.

The abusive type of ad hominem argument occurs where one party in a discussion criticizes or attempts to refute the other party's argument by directly attacking that second party personally. This argument has the form, "My opponent here is a bad person; therefore you (the audience) should not accept his argument." In this type of argument, the attack is centrally on the character of the opponent. Quite often it is bad character for veracity that is the focus of the attack.[1]

One of the most widely used logic textbooks has been Irving M. Copi's *Introduction to Logic.* This textbook is often cited as the leading paradigm on what a fallacy is taken to be in logical practices. The first edition was published in 1953. The ninth edition (1994) has a co-author, Carl Cohen. In the second edition (1961), the following illustration of the abusive ad hominem argument is given (p. 54).

Case 1.1

It may be argued that [Francis] Bacon's philosophy is untrustworthy because he was removed from his chancellorship for dishonesty.

Copi (p. 54) evaluates this ad hominem argument as fallacious on the grounds that "the personal character of a man is logically irrelevant to the truth or falsehood of what he says or the correctness or incorrectness of his argument." Copi's statement here is a questionable generalization, but one can appreciate the point he is driving at in case 1.1. Bacon's philosophy should be judged on its merits and not rejected simply because of an allegation about his bad character for veracity.

Whether or not the allegation made in case 1.1 is true or false is one factor that might be considered or further investigated. But either way, the ad hominem argument in case 1.1 should be subject to critical questioning. Although Bacon's character might be somewhat relevant to some parts of his philosophy, for example, his ethical views, nevertheless dismissing his philosophy as a whole as "untrustworthy"—without even looking at it, just on the premise of his dishonesty as suggested by this reported incident—would be too much of an inferential leap. Even if there were adequate grounds for questioning Bacon's honesty in his political dealings as chancellor, it hardly follows that his scientific and philosophical views should be rejected for this reason alone, without examining them on their merits.

A pair of examples cited more recently by Copi and Cohen (1994, pp. 122–23) are taken from a dispute on feminism between two American philosophers, Christine Sommers and Sandra Lee Bartky, in the *Proceedings of the American Philosophical Association*. Commenting on Sommers's views, Bartky (1992, p. 56) wrote as follows.

Case 1.2

It is one thing to be attacked by an honorable opponent in an honorable way. This happens all the time in philosophy. But in my view Sommers' intellectual methods are dishonest. She ignores the most elementary protocols of philosophical disputation.

Sommers (1992, p. 79), who was the target of this personal attack, replied as follows.

Case 1.3

One dishonest and unworthy tactic used by several of my detractors is to attribute to me complaints I never made and then to dismiss the "complaints" as "irresponsible" and evidence of my reckless unfairness.

Once again, the reason these arguments are classified under the heading of the ad hominem fallacy relates not to the truth or falsity of the allegations. Calling each other dishonest may be justified or not, but either way, these ad hominem attacks do not provide much of a basis for deciding on the issue of feminism the two parties are debating. As Copi and Cohen put it (p. 123), "the merits of the positions of the conflicting parties are not illuminated by arguments of this character." The problem seems to be that such personal attacks do not make any real contribution to the advancement of the discussion and may even pose a serious obstacle in this regard, if the quarrel escalates.

These textbook cases of the uses of the abusive ad hominem in philosophical disputations are relatively tame, however, compared to some of the uses of this type of argument as a devastating attack in political debate. Ever since the Gary Hart case, where a presidential aspirant was accused of marital infidelity, the lid came off the former "gentleman's agreement" not to report such matters in the media, and American politics since that time has been preoccupied with what are called "negative campaign tactics" or "going negative," referring essentially to abusive ad hominem attacks on a candidate's character and personal ethics. Even before this ascendancy of the abusive ad hominem into the mainstream of American political campaign argumentation, however, personal attack had long been a potent weapon in presidential campaigns.

What Jamieson (1992, p. 55) called the most famous ad in the history of political television attacked Barry Goldwater, the Republican candidate for president in the 1964 election campaign, by suggesting that Goldwater was trigger-happy.

Case 1.4

The Democrats juxtaposed a child plucking the petals from a daisy with the explosion of a bomb as Lyndon Johnson extolled the value of loving one another. A young girl is picking daisies in a field. "Four, five, six, seven," she says. An announcer's voice (actually the voice used to count down the space launches at Cape Canaveral) begins an ominous count. "Ten, nine, eight . . . " At zero the camera has closed on the child's eye. A nuclear bomb explodes. Lyndon Johnson's voice is heard: "These are the stakes. To make a world in which all of God's children can live. Or to go into the darkness. We must either love each other. Or we must die." Until the tag line appears, that ad has no explicit partisan content. "Vote for President Johnson on November 3. The stakes are too high for you to stay at home." (Jamieson, 1992, pp. 54–56).

What is fascinating about this particular ad is that no explicit ad hominem argument is stated at all. Instead, the argument is conveyed indirectly by suggestion and innuendo, giving it an element of plausible deniability.

Even so, the argument put forward is clearly an ad hominem attack to the effect that Goldwater's unstable character makes him an unsuitable and untrustworthy candidate for president. Goldwater was perceived as a candidate who was on the more extreme right of the Republican party and who was therefore highly susceptible to any attack suggesting he was not a moderate or careful and prudent person. Hence this ad hominem attack was a successful tactic in scaring voters away from him as a potential president.

In business as well as politics, the effective use of the abusive ad hominem can have awesome financial and social consequences. In a case described in Walton (*Plausible Argument*, 1992, pp. 148–50), the unions in the Eastern Airlines strike of 1980 portrayed Frank Lorenzo, the cost-cutting CEO of the company, as a ruthless and greedy person. The unions made Lorenzo's character the issue, and when striking workers saw his picture on television they shouted, "There's the slimeball." Even though, in fact, Lorenzo was not the robber baron type of person portrayed in the ad hominem attacks, the fight became personal as the workers became obsessed with getting the best of him. The dialogue was locked into an irretrievable quarrel, and Eastern went into bankruptcy when the strike could not be settled.

At any rate, these cases illustrate how abusive ad hominem attacks focus on the character of the person whose argument is attacked. Before examining a couple of classic cases that illustrate how the circumstantial ad hominem works, it is necessary to warn the reader about the broad scope of the term "circumstances," as used in connection with defining the circumstantial ad hominem argument.

The circumstantial ad hominem is distinguished from the abusive type by virtue of the feature that some "circumstances" of the arguer, other than his character, are used to attack his argument. The notion of 'circumstance' is quite broad, however, and could include many things. Accordingly, Whately (1870, p. 142) commented that the ad hominem has been described in logical usage as a fallacy in a "lax and popular language, . . . not scientifically," by those who have written about it: "The 'argumentum ad hominem,' they say, is addressed to the peculiar circumstances, character, avowed opinions, or past conduct of the individual, and therefore has a reference to him only, and does not bear directly and absolutely on the real question." But "circumstances" is a broad notion. For example, in case 1.1, supposed to be an abusive type of ad hominem, Bacon's removal from his chancellorship (or the actions that led to this removal) might come more under the heading of past actions that are his personal circumstances, rather than exclusively under the heading of character. The general problem is that the conceptual notion of "circumstances" is so broad here that it is difficult to pin down the circumstantial ad hominem type of argument in some fairly clear, well-defined, useful way.

A narrower type of approach to classifying these various subspecies of ad hominem arguments is the one outlined in Walton (*Informal Logic*, 1989, chapter 6). According to this account, the circumstantial type of ad hominem argument requires a contradiction or practical inconsistency between what an arguer says and some propositions expressed directly or indirectly by that arguer's personal circumstances. So, in other words, the circumstantial type of ad hominem argument requires some kind of practical inconsistency between the speaker's argument and something about the speaker's person or circumstances. This approach makes the circumstantial ad hominem more manageable and gives hope that it can be analyzed as a clear and recognizable type of argument for logic, as indicated in the next section.

In contrast to the circumstantial type (so defined), the abusive type of ad hominem can now be defined more precisely as a *direct* attack on the argument by questioning the arguer's veracity, normally by saying the arguer has a bad character. This type of argument is quite a direct attack in the sense that it does not require any kind of showing of pragmatic inconsistency or contradiction in the way that is characteristic of the circumstantial type of ad hominem argument. This approach offers a clear way of distinguishing between the abusive and the circumstantial.

The clearest way for the reader to get a better grip on the distinction being made here is to refer to the classic case of the circumstantial ad hominem argument—the smoking case—and a new case that illustrates the kind of argument at issue in a highly realistic actual case.

2. The Smoking and Tree Hugger Cases

The following case, from Walton (*Arguer's Position*, 1985, p. 67), also cited in Walton (*Informal Logic*, 1989, pp. 141–42), is a leading example of the circumstantial ad hominem type of argument. In this case, a parent cites evidence of the link between smoking and chronic obstructive lung disease as part of an argument to convince the child not to smoke.

Case 1.5

A parent argues to her child that smoking is associated with chronic disorders and that smoking is unhealthy, therefore the child should not smoke. The child replies "You smoke yourself. So much for your argument against smoking!"

What is at issue in this type of circumstantial ad hominem argument is not logical inconsistency, but what we could call pragmatic inconsistency, which means a kind of inconsistency between asserted statements and personal actions. Here the child observes the action of the parent (smoking) and cites this circumstance against her argument for not smoking. The parent advocates the policy of not smoking, but she herself smokes. She does not "practice what she preaches." Ergo, the child concludes, her argument is worthless.

The ad hominem fallacy comes in to the extent that the child may be "throwing out the baby with the bath water" by totally rejecting the parent's argument against smoking, once she sees the pragmatic inconsistency, instead of considering that the evidence against smoking given by the parent could be quite good.

These and some other considerations apart, however, the child may have a point worth considering. If the parent smokes but advocates nonsmoking, is not this pragmatic inconsistency a reasonable basis for criticism or at least for challenging the parent's personal advocacy of her own argument? It is as if the child is raising the question: "If you are really serious about your own argument, why don't you follow it yourself?" This seems to be basically a legitimate type of questioning or criticism to raise in this case.

Much depends on how you interpret the conclusion of the child's argument. If the child's conclusion is that the conclusion of the parent's argument is false and that her argument is totally refuted, then the child's argument is premature, weak, and flawed. If the child's conclusion is that the parent's position is open to question or challenge because of *prima facie* evidence of an inconsistency in that position, the child would seem to have a point worth considering, and his argument should not be rejected as fallacious or erroneous.

In judging this case, much depends as well on how good the evidence is that the parent has presented to the child. Perhaps the parent has presented findings brought forward by leading experts in the area of studies on the effects of smoking on health. It is possible that these are good arguments, worth serious consideration.

The context of dialogue of the smoking case is also significant. The parent may be basing good arguments on statistical or medical findings about smoking and health. But the child is no expert and may not be in a position to evaluate these arguments for himself. He is in the situation of having to operate on presumptions, based on an assumption that his parent can be trusted, and knows what she is talking about. Therefore, any perceived or apparent inconsistency between the parent's arguments and the parent's own personal conduct is a reasonable focus of concern for the child. And it seems reasonable and proper, even commendable perhaps, for the child to question the apparent inconsistency that is evident to him.

The reason for the legitimacy of the child's question of his parent's consistency derives from the context which indicates that the child does not know the facts of the issue and must judge on the basis of his plausible estimate of the sincerity and coherence of the parent's advice. Nevertheless, evidence of a possible inconsistency in the parent's position offsets the presumption that the parent's advice is acceptable and shifts the burden of proof back onto the parent to respond to the child's questioning. At least it should be said that the parent owes the child some sort of explanation concerning the possible inconsistency in the position she advocates.

These observations link the *argumentum ad hominem* with the *argumentum ad verecundiam*, the use of appeal to expert opinion to support an argument. In dialogue between two participants where one knows less and has to operate on a presumption that the other one (the "expert") knows what she is talking about, questioning what appears to the nonexpert to be a sign of inconsistency is a move in dialogue that is appropriate and acceptable. For after all, if the nonexpert has no direct access to the evidence or to the truth of the matter, what else can he do but to question the consistency and coherence of what the expert tells him, and the expert's consistency is a key aspect of her credibility.

Piaget (1959) showed that conflicts which place children in difficult argumentation situations are important to the child's learning cooperative skills of topical coherence and intellectual understanding. According to Eisenberg (1987, p. 114), conflicts between parents and children and the ways they are resolved are important for the development of many skills. Particularly important is how parents manage the child's freedom to disagree.

Psychological research on cognitive inconsistency might classify the situation of the child in this type of case as an instance of the double bind hypothesis. The child is caught in a situation where the adult's advice tells him to do one thing, but the adult's actual behavior guides him toward a line of conduct that is incompatible with the first directive. The child seems caught in a double bind, for any attempts to act in accord with this whole message must result in conflict and frustration. So what can the child do? Somehow, he must try to resolve the inconsistency in a helpful or constructive way. Otherwise, a coherent basis for action is lacking. What more appropriate way is there to proceed than to question the source of the apparent consistency to resolve the apparent contradiction?

Of course, questioning the parent's position is different from rejecting the parent's contention as completely worthless. Hence, in evaluating this case, it is well to repeat that much depends on reconstructing what the child's argument really is, judging from the given discourse and the context of dialogue.

Case 1.5 is especially compelling as an instance of the circumstantial ad hominem argument because there is a direct inconsistency involved. The parent decries the action of smoking while herself engaging in the action of smoking. More often in circumstantial ad hominem arguments, the pragmatic inconsistency cited is not so direct, as we can now see by considering another case.

The argument in this case was the main theme in an article on the opinion page of a newspaper (Wright, 1995) that took one side on the "green" issue—the critical discussion between those who advocate environmental restrictions on logging companies and those who oppose such restrictions. The argument in the article criticized "tree huggers" (a pejorative term for advocates on the environmentalist side—as we might call it, although both sides frequently claim to be "environmentalists"), using a circumstantial ad hominem argument. The argument was that the tree huggers criticize the logging companies, like MacMillan Bloedel, but they themselves live in buildings with wooden tables, wooden walls, wooden decks, and so forth, thus contributing to making profitable the very activities they criticize. During a trip to Vancouver Island, the author views clear-cut logging sites and concludes that they do not seem as ugly as the environmentalists or tree huggers so often tell us. During her stay, the author is drawn into a homey little bakery to eat a whole-wheat cinnamon bun and sees many posters and petitions on the walls that plead with everyone to save the trees. But then she notices that everything in the room is made of wood.

Case 1.6

As I sat eating my whole-wheat cinnamon bun, my eyes wandered around the large room. The walls were peppered with posters, petitions and other pleas for everyone to love the goddess, keep the karma and save the trees. As I grudgingly tried to remain sympathetic to all this peace and love, I noticed that this spiritual haven for all those who fight to make the world a better, greener place, was built almost entirely out of wood. The tables and chairs were made of rough-hewn logs. The walls were paneled in cedar. The roof was supported by massive exposed beams that could only have come from old-growth trees. Even the counters and shelving were made of wood, wood, wood. And, as the crowning touch, a huge wooden staircase spiraled up to the second floor.

The hypocrisy of it all suddenly struck me like a 200-year-old spruce succumbing to a chainsaw. Everyone wants to save the trees, but each one of us is as guilty as MacMillan Bloedel for their destruction. The demand for single-family homes with private driveways and yards leads developers to level woods and farmland for new suburbs. All these new homeowners insist on hardwood floors and wood-burning fireplaces. Gone are patios made with paving stones nestled into the grass. Now backyard lawns that rarely feel the tread of human feet are dominated by cedar decks, and the bigger the better. (Wright, 1995, A24)

The ad hominem argument in this case is based on a kind of connection cited between what the tree huggers advocate—indicated by the posters urging everyone to save trees—and a kind of action attributed to the tree huggers. The author in case 1.6 is not criticizing the tree huggers for themselves actually cutting down trees or being employed by a logging company but for engaging in a different type of action, consuming wood products, that makes the logging profitable and worth doing and thereby contributes to it.

Another aspect of case 1.6 worth noticing is that the author attacks the environmentalists or "tree huggers" as a group, rather than attacking a single person. This aspect ties the argument, in this particular case, in with the guilt-by-association type of argument, and in particular, in with the group attack version of this argument (classified in chapter 6, section 7).

The article cited in this case concludes on a positive note, suggesting "let's stop blaming the logging companies and start supporting new building materials for our homes and furniture, and cutting down on all the paper products we use so wastefully" (A24). But the central thrust of the argument in the article is the circumstantial ad hominem attack on the tree huggers—by citing their pragmatic inconsistency the argument concludes that they are hypocritical. The conclusion the reader is moved toward by this ad hominem argument is to give less credibility to the argument used by the tree huggers against their opponents in the dispute on logging.

A key difference between the ad hominem argument in the smoking case and the one in the tree hugger case is that in the smoking case, a direct inconsistency is alleged—the child claims that the parent argues against smoking, but at the same time, the parent admits that she herself smokes. In the tree hugger case, there is no direct contradiction alleged. The tree hugger is against clear-cutting, but nobody is alleging that he is actually cutting down trees himself. Instead, the connection is indirect. In chapter 1, section 8, more detailed consideration of this key difference is given. Before turning to these matters, however, the reader needs to be introduced to the other basic subtypes of ad hominem argument.

3. The Bias Ad Hominem

Another commonly problematic and widely cited type of ad hominem argument, the bias type, occurs where a critic questions the impartiality of an arguer. For example if a critic points out that a speaker on nuclear disarmament who spoke as a physician for peace during the cold war period is actually a member of the KGB, the critic has seriously attacked the speaker's argument through an ad hominem criticism by questioning the speaker's impartiality on the issue.[2] This type of ad hominem attack could be called "circumstantial," if being a member of the KGB is a "circumstance" of the physician. It might seem also that it could be included, in some respects, under the category of the abusive ad hominem because it attacks the personal motives of the arguer in a way that casts some suspicion on his honesty and sincerity. But the most distinctive element of this case is that the attack on the person of the physician is on the basis of an allegation that he has a bias. It is suggested in this case that the speaker cannot really be trusted because he has something to gain—he has a hidden agenda.

Nevertheless, there is a similarity between this type of ad hominem argument and the previous cases of the circumstantial ad hominem. In case 1.5 above, the speaker's ethics are somewhat brought into question by the child because her trustworthiness as an impartial or disinterested arguer on smoking in the argument is attacked. In this type of case of the circumstantial ad hominem, the allegation of pragmatic inconsistency also questions the ethics of the arguer by raising the question of whether the arguer who does not practice what he preaches may be hypocritical or insincere. This element relates to character.

In certain key respects, however, the bias type of ad hominem attack is distinctively different from either the abusive or the circumstantial types of ad hominem attack, as the cases below illustrate.[3]

Case 1.7

Bob and Wilma are discussing the problem of acid rain, in order to determine the extent and nature of the problem, and what steps, if any, should be taken to deal with the problem. Wilma cites evidence to show that newspaper reports on the problem are exaggerated and out of line with the true extent of the problem. She also argues that the price of taking action to offset the source of the problem, industrial pollutants, would be extremely costly, would have bad effects on U.S. and Canadian industries, and would mean severe layoffs and unemployment in both countries. Bob takes the opposite point of view, citing the widespread extent of damage to the environment, and stressing the severe consequences of this mounting damage.

In this critical discussion of the acid rain issue, the bias type of ad hominem attack might take one of two forms, represented by cases 1.8 and 1.9.

Case 1.8

Bob points out that Wilma is president of a Kentucky coal company, arguing that therefore she is biased.

Case 1.9

Bob points out that Wilma is chairperson of the U.S. coal industry Committee Against Government Regulation, arguing that therefore she is biased.

The initial problem with both case 1.8 and case 1.9 is to know what Bob's conclusion is. This is the same central problem indicated in the smoking case. How should we understand his statement that Wilma's point of view is biased? Consider case 1.8 first.

It could be that Wilma's arguments about the newspaper reports and the costs of taking action could be based on reasonable evidence. Even granted that Wilma is president of a Kentucky coal company, that is not necessarily a good reason for rejecting Wilma's arguments on the grounds that her evidence is faulty or weak. So to argue would be an instance of the ad hominem fallacy.

Perhaps that is not Bob's conclusion, however. It could be that Bob is conceding the worth of Wilma's arguments in themselves but is questioning whether Wilma is telling the whole story or taking a fair and balanced perspective. When Bob says that her point of view is biased, he could mean to suggest that Wilma may be concentrating on the arguments against taking action and ignoring the arguments for taking action because she is president of a Kentucky coal company and has a strong financial stake in the outcome.

Next consider case 1.9. The same initial remarks apply in case 1.9 as in case 1.8 about getting Bob's conclusion interpreted correctly. But in an important respect, this case is different. In case 1.9 Bob alleges that Wilma is chairperson of the Committee Against Government Regulation, a coal industry committee. Why is this affiliation significant in judging Wilma's arguments? Various reasons are possible. One important reason could be that Wilma, as a member of this committee, could be strongly committed to a particular position on the issue of acid rain.

Of course Bob's point may be similar to one interpretation of his allegation in case 1.8. Perhaps Bob is suggesting that by belonging to this committee, Wilma has shown that she has a particular interest, perhaps even a financial stake, in one side of the issue. But Bob could be making another type of criticism altogether. He could be arguing that Wilma is committed to a certain ideological position on the issue, worked out systematically by this committee to propound a particular interest they have collectively in influencing public opinion on acid rain and related issues where government regulation of industry is being considered.

What does the criticism "Your point of view is biased" come down to in these two cases? What is the thrust of this tactic in argumentation? In effect it functions as an announcement or allegation that the other party in the dialogue is engaged in self-interested advocacy or even negotiation—an adversarial, closed, interest-based advocacy rather than an open inquiry that takes all relevant evidence into account or a critical discussion that considers argumentation on *both sides* of the issue. The distinction between the interest-based negotiation and the critical discussion (for example) is a distinction between two different types of dialogue. Thus the criticism of bias above could be based on an alleged unilateral shift from one context of dialogue to another, concealing an interest or "ax to grind."

Both the quarrel and the negotiation are highly adversarial types of dialogue in which looking at both sides of an issue or trying to prove something by looking at the evidence for and against it tend not to be as important as pressing ahead aggressively for your own point of view. By contrast to these adversarial types of dialogue, in the inquiry, neither party is set to collect evidence to support only one side or the other of the issue. Here the objective is for all parties to examine all the evidence pro and con, on either side of the issue. Examples of an inquiry might include a commission report into the causes of an air accident, an investigative third-party inquiry into political charges of conflict of interest, or a scientific investigation by a team of researchers. In all these cases, bias is a serious failure.[4]

All of these types of dialogue are perfectly legitimate contexts of argument within the framework of their respective internal rules of procedure. There is nothing fallacious per se about them. The problem of concern in cases 1.8 and 1.9 comes in when a participant in argument seems to be and is supposed to be engaging in an inquiry when some grounds indicate that in fact this arguer is covertly engaged in shifting to an adversarial dispute. Such an allegation is at the bottom of the criticism in cases 1.8, 1.9, and similar cases that the arguer has a biased point of view. Nothing is intrinsically wrong with only presenting one side of a case, your own side, in a dispute. But in an inquiry, or even in a critical discussion, it does not serve the purpose of the dialogue to present only the reasons on one side while systematically ignoring or excluding all the reasons on the other side. Hence the basis of the bias type of ad hominem criticism is a dialectical shift of an illicit type, and the bias type can therefore be seen as a distinctive type of ad hominem argument in its own right, separate from the abusive and circumstantial subtypes.

Actually, two factors are involved in the ad hominem criticisms of bias advanced in cases 1.8 and 1.9. One is the allegation that the person criticized has something to gain and is negotiating to that end. The other is the suggestion that the person has attempted to conceal this hidden purpose, and therefore her argument is not what it purports to be. If Wilma had announced her affiliation overtly, in either case, the allegation of bias would have had less sting. By not making her purposes and affiliations known explicitly at the outset of the argument, she has put herself in a position of appearing to have a hidden agenda. This problem is a clue that with the bias type of ad hominem argument, the context of the talk exchange is the key. The goal in the type of dialogue supposedly being engaged in by the two parties is the key factor in assessing criticisms of that arguer's alleged bias.

4. Poisoning the Well and Tu Quoque

Another type of ad hominem argument known to be of central importance is the poisoning the well variety. In this type of ad hominem argument, the arguer claims that her opponent is espousing a particular cause, is an advocate of some point of view of a partisan kind, in such a way that he will always reflexively argue only from this particular interest or standpoint so that one can never take what he says seriously, or at face value, as an argument based on real evidence.

One way to fit the poisoning the well variety into the previous threefold classification is to see it as an extension of the bias ad hominem that is distinctively different from the abusive and circumstantial categories. By contrast to these two, the bias type of ad hominem argument is characterized by an allegation by the one party that the other party has a bias, that is, has some kind of interest at stake in the outcome and that, therefore, this party could not be believed or his argument or point of view should not be given much credibility. The bias type of ad hominem argument is a way of arguing that a speaker's credibility should be reduced because he cleaves to a prior interest or viewpoint. We should not take what this person says as having a high degree of credibility or as high as we might have initially thought, once we realize that this person has a bias, has something to gain, or has a special interest in the particular point of view that he or she is advocating. The poisoning the well type of argument, then, can be seen as an extension of the bias argument that suggests or implies that the person's bias is hardened. To say that a bias is *hardened* is to say that it is so fixed that we could never believe what this person says because he always adheres to this particular bias or this particular point of view in a routine way so that his arguments are never really based on independent evidence but simply on his advocacy of this point of view. The allegation is that we can never trust this person to be impartial or open-minded.

The example given to illustrate the poisoning the well type of ad hominem by Copi and Cohen (1994, p. 124) is of historical interest in its own right.

Case 1.10

The British novelist and clergyman Charles Kingsley, attacking the famous Catholic intellectual John Henry Cardinal Newman, argued thus: Cardinal Newman's claims were not to be trusted because, as a Roman Catholic priest (Kingsley alleged), Newman's first loyalty was not to the truth. Newman countered that this ad hominem attack made it impossible for him and indeed for all Catholics to advance their arguments, since anything that they might say to defend themselves would then be undermined by others' alleging that, after all, truth was not their first concern. Kingsley, said Cardinal Newman, had poisoned the well of discourse.

The strategy of the poisoning the well type of argument is to try to close off the argument by barring the other party as a suitable participant in a critical discussion that will adhere to the collaborative rules of the dialogue. The implication is that such a person cannot be trusted as a participant who is capable of sincere or cooperative participation in the dialogue. The imputation is that his mind is already made up, so there is no real point in trying to argue with him anyway—he is never really open to defeat by conceding any other point of view.

Another major category of ad hominem argument of central importance is the tu quoque type of argument. This expression (meaning "you too") is often appropriate because the ad hominem is commonly used with great effectiveness to reply to any sort of criticism suggesting that an arguer is to blame for some fault or has failed to meet some standard. The respondent can often retort, "You're just the same," or "You're just as bad," using one ad hominem to reply to another.

The primary case of the tu quoque type of ad hominem retort occurs where an ad hominem reply is used to respond to an ad hominem attack. Cases of this sort are not uncommon in political debate. Even more commonly, the expression "tu quoque" is used to cover the case of replying to any kind of argument by using the same kind of argument in rebuttal. This secondary type of case of the tu quoque is prevalent in many logic texts, as chapter 2 will show. Indeed, many of these cases of ad hominem argumentation cited in the textbooks can properly be called tu quoque arguments only in this secondary or wider sense of this phrase, as will be shown.

In some cases, one party blames another for some culpable act, and the other replies by counterblaming. But neither argument is necessarily ad hominem in the sense that the personal attack is being used to run down the other party's argument. Even so, these cases are traditionally classified as tu quoque arguments and typically taken as coming under the heading of ad hominem arguments.

For example, Kaminsky and Kaminsky (1974, p. 46) define the tu quoque type of argument as that in which "a person accused of wrongdoing answers the charge by accusing his accuser of wrongdoing." Kaminsky and Kaminsky give the following case to illustrate this subtype:

Case 1.11

Student No. 1: I saw you copying the answer to the exam question from your math book.
Student No. 2: At least it was my math book. Didn't you borrow John's term paper and hand it in as your own work?

Kaminsky and Kaminsky comment on this case by stating that the student's argument is fallacious because it does not deal with the issue of whether the second student was actually cheating (p. 46).

However, the problem with this type of argument, or the question it raises anyway, is that neither of the arguments really seems to be ad hominem. The charge of the one student is that the other student has committed some culpable action. This charge, in itself, is not necessarily an ad hominem argument because the student is not necessarily trying to run down the other student's argument by using any kind of concession or allegation of culpability or bad character or circumstances or anything of that sort. Moreover, when the second student replies by suggesting that the other student may have done something worse at some earlier point, this retort does not seem to be an ad hominem argument either. So, this example could be a tu quoque argument, in the sense that the one is replying by accusing the other of doing the same thing instead of really answering the charge or responding to it in a more relevant way. Nevertheless, neither argument seems to be an ad hominem argument. It is just a case of using the same kind of argument to reply to the other argument. So it is, in a sense, tu quoque, but it is questionable whether this type of argumentation should be classified under the general heading of ad hominem argument.

It seems then that on a more careful analysis, it is possible to distinguish between a broader and a narrower interpretation of what the tu quoque argument is. On the broader interpretation, it may not be a genuine ad hominem argument at all. This question of classification remains debatable, however. The same type of argument may come under the two wrongs fallacy, as characterized below, depending on how this type of argument is defined.

The tu quoque argument or "you too" argument, according to the broader account, can be described as the use of any type of argument to reply in like kind to a speaker's argument. In other words, if a speaker uses a particular type of argument, say in an argument from analogy, then the respondent can turn around and use that same kind of argument against the speaker, and this would be called a tu quoque argument, in the sense that the same kind of argument is used against the original speaker. So conceived, the tu quoque argument is quite a broad category that would include other types of argument as well as ad hominem arguments. Some sources think of the tu quoque as a subtype of the ad hominem argument. They, in effect, define the tu quoque in a narrower way and see it as the use of one ad hominem argument to reply to another ad hominem argument. In other words, the requirement here is that, for it to be a tu quoque argument, it has to be an ad hominem argument and not any other kind of argument— for example, an argument from analogy.

A middle-of-the-road definition of the tu quoque is also advanced by other sources, where the original argument is not (necessarily) ad hominem but the (tu quoque) reply is. The example given by Hurley (1994, p. 121) falls into this category.

Case 1.12

Child to parent: Your argument that I should stop stealing candy from the corner store is no good. You told me yourself just a week ago that you, too, stole candy when you were a kid.

Hurley's description (p. 121) of the tu quoque type of ad hominem argument in this case makes it seem a lot like the smoking case above (case 1.5), as a type of argument. "The second arguer attempts to make the first appear to be hypocritical or arguing in bad faith. The second arguer usually accomplishes this by citing features in the life or behavior of the first arguer that conflict with the latter's conclusion. In effect, the second arguer says, 'How dare you argue that I should stop doing X; why, you do (or have done) X yourself.' " This description of case 1.12 makes it sound so much like the type of argument characteristic of the smoking case that one begins to wonder what the difference is between the circumstantial ad hominem and the tu quoque. One can easily see, then, how these two categories tend to run in together, and are often confused with each other.

All five subcategories of ad hominem can begin to seem fuzzy around the edges, when you start carefully comparing the ten cases studied so far. The fuzziness increases even more when we look at some other fallacies that are generally (but not always) treated as separate from the ad hominem. It is incumbent upon us to try to get some sort of initial grip on how the traditions of logic supposedly conceive these related fallacies.

5. Genetic Fallacy, Two Wrongs, and Guilt by Association

Three other fallacies (normally treated as distinct fallacies from the ad hominem) are nevertheless often associated with the ad hominem and sometimes even identified with it. The first of these is the *genetic fallacy,* said to be the fallacy (Cohen and Nagel, 1934, pp. 388–90) of confusing the temporal order or origin of something with "the logical order in which elements may be put together to constitute existing institutions" (p. 389). Engel (1982, p. 170) classifies the genetic fallacy as a subspecies of ad hominem argument (of the non-abusive type):

A further variant of the nonabusive form of the personal attack fallacy is the genetic fallacy. It is an attempt to prove a conclusion false by condemning its source—its genesis. Such arguments are fallacious—because how an idea originated is irrelevant to its viability. Thus it would be fallacious to argue that, since chemical elements are involved in all life processes, life is therefore nothing more than a chemical process; or that, since the early forms of religion were matters of magic, religion is nothing but magic.

Other accounts see the relationship between the genetic fallacy and the ad hominem fallacy differently. Capaldi (1971, p. 73) sees the genetic fallacy as "the most sophisticated form of ad hominem." Kahane (1969, p. 250) writes that the argumentum ad hominem is "often called" the genetic fallacy. Byerly (1973, p. 45) classifies ad hominem as a subspecies of genetic fallacy. What the relationship really is appears to be unclear. Manicas and Kruger (1968, p. 342) define the genetic fallacy as "attacking the source rather than what is at issue," making this fallacy appear similar to the ad hominem type of argument generally.

The second fallacy of this group is called the *fallacy of two wrongs make a right* or simply the *two wrongs fallacy*, defined by Soccio and Barry (1992, p. 129) as the "argument that attempts to justify what is considered wrong by appealing to other instances of the same or similar action." The kind of example these sources have in mind is illustrated clearly by Groarke (1982, p. 10).

Case 1.13

Suppose, for example, that some government accuses another of subjecting dissenters to torture and other abuses that contravene the United Nations charter on human rights. In response to such charges, one can imagine the government in question replying that the nation which has leveled the charges employs similar—or worse—practices in its treatment of dissent. Here we have a clear case of two wrongs reasoning which illustrates why such reasoning is sometimes illegitimate, for the government in question does not deny such practices, but simply directs attention to other cases. In reply, it may be said that even if its charges could be substantiated, this doesn't make abusive practices acceptable, and does not excuse the acts in question. At most, it shows that both governments are guilty of the wrongs such acts entail.

One can see that this type of argument comes very close to the kind of argumentation we have already identified as being under one of the main subcategories of ad hominem argument—the tu quoque. For example, Kaminsky and Kaminsky's example of the tu quoque (case

1.11) seems that it could be an excellent paradigm case of the two wrongs fallacy. This seems like a serious overlap.

Kahane (1992, p. 60) defines the two wrongs fallacy in a way that makes it seem separate from the ad hominem fallacy, however. By his definition, the two wrongs fallacy is trying "to justify an apparently wrong action by charging their accusers with a similar wrong, on the grounds that if "they" do it, then it's all right for others to do so." But Kahane (p. 60) also acknowledges a connection between the two wrongs fallacy and hypocrisy, suggesting "most of the time, those who argue this way [using the two wrongs argument] are being hypocritical." But it is this element of being hypocritical—"not practicing what you preach" or saying one thing and doing another—that is characteristic of the circumstantial type of ad hominem argument. Hence it appears that the borderline between the two wrongs fallacy and some of the other subtypes of ad hominem fallacy is fuzzy and uncertain.

The third fallacy of this group, called *guilt by association*, is defined by Wheelwright (1962, p. 327) as weighing "evidence against a man . . . by reference to the alleged character of some of his relatives or friends." Wheelwright (1962) and Toulmin, Rieke, and Janik (1979, p. 173) see guilt by association as a subtype of ad hominem:

Case 1.14

> Another way of arguing against the person rather than against his or her claim, for instance, is sometimes referred to as attributing "guilt by association." Here we try to refute a claim by associating the claimant with a discredited *group* of persons; if the claimant is a Red, say, then he or she cannot be trusted to tell the truth. Smith's claim that unemployment is a graver problem than inflation, for example, may be countered on the grounds that Smith is a Communist. The presumed warrant is that the opinions of Communists on such matters are always biased.

The example cited here at first seems like a poisoning the well type of ad hominem, judging by our previous classification. But then, in their next sentence, Toulmin, Rieke, and Janik use the phrase "always biased," suggesting the bias type of ad hominem. Perhaps, then, guilt by association is supposed to be a subspecies of the bias type of ad hominem argument.

Several other sources define guilt by association as a separate category of fallacy from ad hominem. Johnson and Blair (1983, p. 84) define guilt by association as the kind of argument in which one party in a dialogue attacks the other on the basis of "some alleged association" between that party or his position "and some other person, group or belief." The distinctive aspect of the association between two parties or the one party and another group or belief seems to make two wrongs distinct from the ad hominem.

Little, Groarke, and Tindale (1989, p. 270) define the guilt by association type of argument in a similar way:

A person or group X is associated with another person or group Y.
Y has questionable beliefs or behaves in a questionable way.
Therefore, X's character and/or claims are questionable.

However, introducing the element of attack on a person's character as part of this type of argument makes it seem to be a kind of ad hominem attack.

The problem posed here is whether guilt by association is a subspecies of ad hominem fallacy or a distinct fallacy in its own right, apart from ad hominem. The competing classifications of the genetic fallacy—the two wrongs make a right argument and the guilt by association argument—and the various ways they are related to ad hominem show the conceptual morass involved here. Searching for firmer ground upon which to base some clearer fundamental notion of what the ad hominem is generally supposed to be, one might naturally look to the history of logic for guidance.

6. Historical Origins of the Ad Hominem

The historical origins of the argumentum ad hominem as a standard fallacy that began to appear in the logic textbooks were for a long time highly obscure. Hamblin (1970) emphasized the importance of the short passage in Locke's essay (1690), where Locke identified four kinds of arguments. The third one (Hamblin, 1970, p. 160) is the ad hominem: "A third way is to press a man with consequences drawn from his own principles or concessions. This is already known under the name of argumentum ad hominem." Locke contrasts the ad hominem type of argument with another type he calls *ad judicium*, "the using of proofs drawn from any of the foundations of knowledge or probability."[5] Hamblin notes (p. 161) that Locke's treatment of the ad hominem argument does not reject this type of argument as fallacious, but like Aristotle's treatment of dialectical arguments, it "stands poised between acceptance and disapproval." Also, Locke indicates he did not invent the term *argumentum ad hominem*, and this acknowledgment of its prior existence poses the problem of its origins.

Finocchiaro (1980, pp. 131–32) has cited the use of the argumentum ad hominem as an important methodological tool for Galileo in his dialogues. According to Finocchiaro (p. 131), Galileo defines an ad hominem argument as "one in which the arguer derives a conclusion not acceptable to an opponent from premises which are accepted by him." This account of the ad hominem as a type of argument is very similar to that given by Locke. In fact, the argumentum ad hominem so defined is a subspecies of the Lockean type of ad hominem argument. Both sources define an ad hominem argument as essentially an argument from premises that are commitments of the other party. This account of ad hominem is dialectical in nature because it involves a framework of two parties taking part in reasoning together. But is such an argument fallacious in the way that the modern textbooks commonly presume that it is? Here is where we run into problems. Locke, as we saw above, defines the argument in such a way that it is not necessarily fallacious and could be a reasonable type of argument. In addition, Locke's account does indicate how such a type of argument could be used in a fallacious way, and his account has perhaps influenced many of the textbooks that, when they define the fallacy of ad hominem, take their inspiration from Locke.

Finocchiaro also indicates that he takes Galileo's notion of an argument to have this aspect of relating to the ad hominem fallacy as well. For when Finocchiaro (1980, p. 131) defines the ad hominem argument as above, he adds that such an argument "may not be too well grounded," suggesting an aspect here of a weak argument or an aspect of some kind of error perhaps related to the ad hominem fallacy.

But where did the argumentum ad hominem originally come from? Hamblin (1970, p. 161) conjectured that it may possibly have come from some passages in Aristotle, and this hypothesis is borne out and proved by Nuchelmans (1993). Nuchelmans shows how there are two strands to the historical development of the argumentum ad hominem, both of which originate in passages from Aristotle. According to Nuchelmans's account, these two strands represent two distinct types of argumentation.

The ambiguity is nicely clarified by some remarks of Schopenhauer in his *Notes on Eristic Dialectic* cited by Nuchelmans (1993, p. 42). Schopenhauer draws a distinction between argumentum ad hominem in the sense of argument from the other party's commitment and personal attack argument. In this sense, the ad hominem argument may be described as a type of *ex concessis* argumentation. This is the Lockean type of ad hominem, in fact. In this sense, the argumentum ad hominem is not necessarily a fallacious argument. In fact, it is commonly quite a reasonable kind of argumentation. In this sense, argumentum ad hominem may be contrasted with the argumentum ad judicium, in Locke's sense, or with the argument against the "thing"—the matter or substance of a discussion—the *argumentum ad rem.* Now the other sense of argumentum ad hominem that Schopenhauer contrasts with this previous sense is described by Nuchelmans as "the artifice of attacking the adversary personally" (p. 42). Presumably, it is this second meaning of the argumentum ad hominem of personal attack that properly belongs in the textbook accounts under the heading of the fallacy of ad hominem.

Schopenhauer, as noted by Nuchelmans (p. 42), even offered a terminological suggestion for disambiguating between these two senses of argumentum ad hominem. Schopenhauer suggested that the first one, arguing from an opponent's conceptions or commitments, could continue to be considered argumentum ad hominem, whereas the second sort of argument, the artifice of personal attack, might be better called *argumentum ad personam.* The general problem in the history of this whole subject is that, especially with the effect of Locke's account on the textbooks, these two meanings of the expression argumentum ad hominem became fused together, or perhaps confused together, and the result is the standard treatment that we find in the current textbooks, surveyed in chapter 2.

In the sequel, let us call these two distinctive types of ad hominem arguments the *argument from commitment* (or *ex concessis*) type and the *personal attack* type. Of course, the two may be related at some deeper level but, as Nuchelmans has convincingly shown, there is a historical strand of development that makes it necessary and useful for us to distinguish between these two senses of argumentum ad hominem.

Aristotle, in *On Sophistical Refutations* (165 a 37 and following), distinguished four kinds of arguments: *demonstrative arguments, dialectical arguments, eristic arguments* and a fourth type of argument that he called *periastikoi logoi*, usually translated as "examination arguments" but sometimes also called "peirastic arguments." Guthrie (1981, p. 155) sees peirastic arguments as a subspecies of dialectical arguments. Citing *On Sophistical Refutations* (172 a 23) where Aristotle writes that dialectic is, in one of its uses, an art of examination, Guthrie (p. 155) distinguishes two types of argument use: *peirastic* ("testing or probing") and *exetastic* ("examining critically"). Aristotle (172 a 30) wrote, "Even the unskilled use dialectic or peirastic in some way, for everyone tries to test the pretensions to some extent" (quoted translation given in Guthrie, p. 155). This remark suggests that peirastic arguments are used to test out and probe the arguments of someone who pretends to be an authority or expert on some issue. But what are peirastic arguments, and are they different from or the same as dialectical arguments?

In *On Sophistical Refutations* (165 a 38–165 b 12), Aristotle defines them as two distinct arguments. Dialectical arguments (165 b 3) are those that have *endoxa* (generally accepted opinions) as premises and reason to establish a contradiction. Endoxa (Evans, 1977, p. 79, citing *Topics* 100 b 21–100 b 23) are opinions accepted as true, either by everybody or by the experts *(sophoi)*, or by "those with the most understanding" *(gnorimoi)*. Barnes (1980, p. 500) characterizes endoxa as the opinions that are "reputable" at a given time. Peirastic (examination) arguments (165 b 4–165 b 7) are "those which are based on opinions held by the answerer and necessarily known to one who claims knowledge of the subject involved." This description makes peirastic arguments appear to be different from dialectical ones. Peirastic arguments are evidently used in questioning an expert in a domain of knowledge or someone who claims to be an expert.

In fact, it is difficult to know what Aristotle meant by peirastic arguments. Hamblin (1970, p. 59) notes that Aristotle is not really sure whether dialectical and peirastic arguments are two types or one. Aristotle mentions (165 b 8) that the manner of use of peirastic arguments has been described elsewhere, but it is not known what other passage in his writings he refers to, or whether such a passage still exists or ever did exist.

According to Nuchelmans (p. 37), peirastic arguments are arguments based not on views that others hold but on the respondent's own views. According to Nuchelmans's account, such an argument, based on the other party's commitment, is used to correct that other party when it seems to us that his view is wrong. Nuchelmans traces out the history of this commitment-based type of argument telling us (p. 38) that, after Boethius, this way of arguing was called in Latin *disputatio temptativa*. This type of argument was also called a *tentative syllogism*, according to Nuchelmans (p. 38)—an argument that "proceeds from statements admitted by the adversary." It is based on premises that are propositions that appear true to this adversary and are conceded by him. Nuchelmans shows how this type of argument, which came to be characterized by the phrase argumentum ad hominem, is found in logic textbooks and manuals in a continuing thread from Aristotle through to the seventeenth century.

For example, according to Nuchelmans (p. 41), the *Logica Hamburgensis* of 1638 written by Joachim Jungius identified the argumentum ad hominem as occurring when "we draw a conclusion from assumptions that are perhaps not very probable but are conceded and accepted by the adversary." Many other logic textbooks continue to adopt this definition, and Nuchelmans (p. 42) also cites the passage from Isaac Watts's *Logic* of 1725—quoted by Hamblin (1970, pp. 163–64)—which describes argumentum ad hominem as being a type of argument based on the professed principles or opinions of the person with whom one is arguing. This argument from the other party's commitment, then, was one recurring meaning of argumentum ad hominem that continued to have a prominent place in logic textbooks and other writings on logic throughout the centuries. It is this ex concessis account of ad hominem that we find expressed in Locke and Galileo.

But did Aristotle mean by peirastic arguments commitment-based arguments, that is, arguments used by one party in a dialogue based on premises accepted by the other party? This interpretation (as an account of Aristotle's definition of peirastic arguments) seems highly questionable. Presumably the characteristic of being commitment-based is applicable to dialectical arguments as well as peirastic arguments (if these two categories are different). Evans (1977, p. 75) writes that in dialectical argument, success is achieved when one has secured the agreement of a particular opponent. Thus dialectical arguments are commitment-based, but that is not the only or defining characteristic of them. Nor does it seem to be the only characteristic of peirastic arguments, which seem also to have to do with arguing from premises put forward by experts (or pretended experts).

As the source of the other type of meaning of the argumentum ad hominem, Nuchelmans (p. 43) cites the passage in Aristotle's *On Sophistical Refutations* (178 b 17) in which Aristotle makes a contrast between two ways of handling sophisms. One way is directing a refutation at the argument "with methods which invoke factors that are less pertinent from a logical point of view such as the person of the questioner" (p. 43). Through the translation of Boethius, this way of arguing, which in Aristotle was contrasted with the proper way of handling a sophism, was identified with the expression ad hominem. According to Nuchelmans (p. 43), Boethius identified this way of handling an argument as ad hominem because, instead of attacking the real fault in the argument, it tried "to prevent the questioning person from achieving his aim by answering in a twisted or inappropriate manner." Hence, this type of argument, by its nature, has an element of inappropriateness attached to it. Given Aristotle's remarks, it can easily be interpreted as a species of failure of relevance and an inappropriate way of trying to refute someone else's argument. Thus, the tendency in the historical development of rhetoric concerning this type of ad hominem argument was to draw attention to the difference between the substantive issues of a case and the various personal aspects that may be involved in a debate (Nuchelmans, 1993, p. 43). Latin authors on the debate, according to Nuchelmans (p. 44) expressed this distinction by contrasting what they identified as the real issue of a debate with the aspect that they call *persona*.

Nuchelmans shows that in the subsequent development of logic and rhetoric, this second type of ad hominem argument was rejected by many authors as fallacious but accepted by other authors who were more willing to incorporate elements from rhetoric into their logic. These other authors were willing to accept the ad hominem argument of this second type as being reasonable in some cases. This second type seems to be the genesis of the modern notion of ad hominem as personal attack in argument, explaining where the so-called abusive type of ad hominem came from. But Aristotle was aware of the circumstantial and tu quoque subtypes as well.

It is historically interesting to note that Aristotle, in the *Rhetoric* (II, 1398a 7–8) recognized a type of argument he called "turning upon the opponent what has been said against ourselves." Although Aristotle did not use the label ad hominem to describe this type of argument and did not classify it as a fallacy, it seems quite clear from his account of it that it does come under the general heading of (what is nowadays called) the tu quoque argument. According to Aristotle's account of the situation giving rise to this type of argument, "in general the accuser aspires to be better than the defendant." So the argument cited by Aristotle, in effect the tu quoque argument, is for the defender to show that this aspiration is not met, by arguing that the accuser is just as bad as or worse than the person he accuses. Aristotle also shows an awareness of the connection of this tu quoque type of argument to the circumstantial type of ad hominem argument when he writes (1398 a 7), "generally, it is ridiculous for a man to reproach others for what he does or would do himself, or to encourage others to do what he does not or would not do himself." Here Aristotle shows clearly that he is aware of what a powerful kind of argument it can be to accuse someone of "not practicing what he preaches." Thus he is linking the tu quoque argument here with the circumstantial type of ad hominem argument. So Aristotle recognized the tu quoque type of ad hominem argument as a rhetorical argument. His discussion of this type of argument also definitely relates to the "two wrongs" type of ad hominem argument.

So, even though Aristotle did not include the argumentum ad hominem as one of the list of explicit fallacies given in his manual on fallacies, *On Sophistical Refutations*, if Nuchelmans is right, the origin of the concept of argumentum ad hominem as a fallacy is to be found in Aristotle's writings. But also, if Nuchelmans is right, the historical development of this concept shows a highly significant ambiguity that could and plausibly did result in confusion on the meaning of argumentum ad hominem and led to the conceptual disarray that one finds in the textbook treatments.

What has tended to happen, as will be shown in chapter 2, is that in many of the examples of ad hominem arguments presented in the logic textbooks, the central idea conveyed is that of ad hominem as the use of personal attack (in various forms) in argument. Nevertheless, when attempting to offer some abstract definition of what the ad hominem is generally, the textbooks express the ex concessis concept, often quoting Locke or using his words. This way of proceeding has also affected the scholarly treatments of the ad hominem argument to follow the same way of thinking.

Certainly the ad hominem argument, in precisely its modern meaning of use of personal attack on an arguer's character or circumstances to discredit his argument, was known in the rhetorical handbooks of the ancient world as a distinctive type of argument that can be used to persuade an audience. A quite accurate description of this type of argument is given in the *Rhetorica Ad Alexandrum*, a handbook once attributed to Aristotle but now widely thought to be the work of Anaximines, a contemporary of Aristotle who was, like Aristotle, a teacher of Alexander the Great. In the *Rhetorica Ad Alexandrum* (quoted from the Loeb Library edition, trans. H. Rackham, in the volume *Aristotle's Problems II*, Books 22–38), Anaximines defines evidence as "an admission voluntarily made by one who knows the facts" (1431 b 20–1431 b 21). According to Anaximines, when the thing stated is probable and the witness truthful, there is no need of further comment on the evidence. But if the thing stated is improbable, that is, it appears unlikely or implausible, or the witness is suspected to be untrustworthy, the citing either of these factors can be used as arguments to throw doubt on the evidence as questionable. In particular, if it can be shown that there is reason to think the witness untrustworthy, that can be used as an argument to contradict the evidence that has been offered by that witness.

When contradicting evidence we must run down the character of the witness if he is a rascal, or subject his evidence to examination if it is improbable, or even speak against both the person and his evidence together, collecting under one head the worst points in our adversaries' case. Another thing to consider is whether the witness is a friend of the man for whom he is giving evidence, or in some way connected with his act, or whether he is an enemy of the person against whom he is giving evidence, or a poor man; because witnesses in these circumstances are suspected of giving false testimony, from motives in the one case of favor, in the other of revenge, and in the other of gain. (1431 b 33–1432 a 2; Loeb ed., p. 345)

The kind of argument Anaximines describes is clearly meant to be used in a trial or court setting where one side is using the ad hominem argument to question critically or refute the argument of the other side by throwing discredit on the witness who has supported the argument of the other side.

7. The Contemporary Ex Concessis View

An excellent historical and systematic survey of the study of the argumentum ad hominem since the seventeenth century has been given by van Eemeren and Grootendorst (1993), but it will be useful to review briefly here the leading contemporary theories on the ad hominem. The leading theories of the ad hominem argument since Hamblin (1970) are clearly seen to be from the ex concessis view of this type of argumentation, based on the very clear expression of this viewpoint articulated by Whately (1870).

Perelman and Olbrechts-Tyteca (1969, p. 110) define argumentum ad hominem as the type of argument that uses premises based on what the respondent is prepared to concede. By this account, the ad hominem is an ex concessis type of argument, to be contrasted with what Perelman and Olbrechts-Tyteca (p. 110) call the *ad rem* type of argument "that is claimed to be valid for all rational beings." The ad hominem for them is an argument that is "valid" only with respect to the person (respondent, audience) to whom it was directed. It is relative to the person who is to be persuaded.

Perelman and Olbrechts-Tyteca (1969, p. 111) give the following example to illustrate an ad hominem argument.

> *Case 1.15*
>
> Here is a very simple example. There will be eleven people for lunch. The maid exclaims, "That's bad luck!" Her mistress is in a hurry, and replies, "No, Mary, you're wrong; it's thirteen that brings bad luck." The argument is unanswerable and puts an immediate end to the dialogue. This reply can be considered as a type of argument ad hominem. It does not question any personal interest of the maid, but is based on what she accepts. It is more immediately effective than a speech on the ridiculous character of superstitions and makes it possible to argue within the framework of the prejudice instead of opposing it.

This argument is said to be ad hominem because, instead of trying to challenge the maid's superstitious belief, the hostess bases her argument on what the maid accepts. It is quite a good example of an ex concessis argument.

This type of ex concessis analysis of the ad hominem is reminiscent of the account given by Richard Whately (1870, pp. 142–43):

> It appears then (to speak rather more technically) that in the *"argumentum ad hominem"* the conclusion which actually is established, is not the *absolute* and *general* one in question, but *relative* and particular; *viz.* not that "such and such is the fact," but that *"this man* is bound to admit it, in conformity to his principles of Reasoning, or in consistency with his own conduct, situation," &c. Such a conclusion it is often both allowable and necessary to establish, in order to silence those who will not yield to fair general argument; or to convince those whose weakness and prejudices would not allow them to assign to it its due weight.

It is clear that Whately, like Perelman and Olbrechts-Tyteca, see ad hominem argumentation of this argument from commitment type as reasonable (nonfallacious) in many cases. It is just arguing from the commitments of the other party, and this type of argumentation, for Whately and for Perelman and Olbrechts-Tyteca, is quite reasonable in principle. Indeed, as van Eemeren and Grootendorst (1993, p. 52) comment, for Perelman and Olbrechts-Tyteca, argumentum ad hominem is "a general characteristic of all successful argumentation." Whately (1870, p. 143), after describing the general type of argumentation he defines as ad hominem, calls it "perfectly fair," if carried out openly and without deception.

Johnstone (1959, p. 73) adopted the ex concessis interpretation of the ad hominem, basing his account of this type of argument explicitly on Whately's account of it. Johnstone (p. 73), however, emphasizes the nonfallaciousness of ad hominem argumentation by using this phrase "honorifically," instead of the more dominant practice of using it "pejoratively" to express "condemnation." Indeed, he takes this line so far as to argue for the thesis that all genuine philosophical argumentation is really of the ad hominem type. Needless to say, this thesis appeared paradoxical and even scandalous to the broad majority who were, at this point, well used to the tradition of classifying ad hominem arguments as fallacious. If one interprets the argumentum ad hominem as a species of ex concessis argument, the way Whately did, then Johnstone's thesis seems perfectly reasonable. In fact, Johnstone (1959) presented analyses of many famous philosophical arguments that convincingly backed up his thesis.

An important step in the analysis of the ad hominem argument was the use of formal structures of dialogue logic to analyze this type of argumentation by Barth and Martens (1977). They used a Lorenzen type of dialogue structure, of the type developed in Barth and Krabbe (1982), in which an argument is defined in the framework of an exchange of moves in a regulated dialogue game between a proponent and an opponent (respondent). The proponent has the goal of defending her thesis against critical attacks or questions posed by the respondent. A key aspect of this dialogue exchange is that each party uses the concessions of the other as a basis for his or her arguments. Thus the argumentation in the dialogue is essentially of an ex concessis type.

Within this framework, Barth and Martens give an analysis of the ad hominem fallacy. But as van Eemeren and Grootendorst (1993, p. 61) point out, they "do not undertake to analyze the abusive, circumstantial and tu quoque variants of the argumentum ad hominem" that the textbooks usually treat in their examples characteristic of ad hominem. Instead they define the fallacy in a way that is very reminiscent of Whately's treatment of it. Indeed, they quote Whately's account (Barth and Martens, 1977, p. 82) with approval, and use it as a target of their analysis. According to their account, nothing is inherently wrong with ad hominem arguments. Indeed, they note (p. 90) that in a formal Lorenzen dialogue, all of the proponent's arguments are ex concessis, and "hence they are argumenta ad hominem in the terminology of Perelman and Olbrechts-Tyteca" (Barth and Martens, p. 90). According to their account, however, such an argument commits the ad hominem fallacy where the proponent successfully argues for a proposition A in a dialogue, based on the concessions of her opponent, but then concludes (unjustifiably) that A is absolutely true, i.e. is defensible based on any set of concessions made by any opponent. In other words, the fallacy is concluding that just because A is relatively true (relative to this opponent's concessions), we can conclude that A is absolutely true.

This interpretation of the ad hominem fallacy does seem to fit the circumstantial variant used in the smoking case rather well. In fact, as shown earlier and supported in Walton (*Informal Logic,* 1989, p. 143), the child in the smoking case is said to be committing a basic type of ad hominem fallacy in this case if he is rejecting the (impersonal) conclusion 'Smoking is unhealthy' based on the relative conflict observed between this proposition and the parent's (personal) actions. This move could be a fallacy if the child is ignoring the good medical evidence of the harmfulness of smoking presented in the parent's argument.

Having now introduced the reader to the five classic types of ad hominem arguments, having considered some special cases that raised problems of classification, and having outlined the history of the ad hominem briefly, we pass on to two special problem areas that have to be cleared up, before the reader can get a good initial grasp of the ad hominem argument as a point of departure.

8. Actions, Circumstances, and Commitment

In the smoking case, the basis of the child's ad hominem argument is a perceived conflict between what the parent says and her actions (of smoking). Here the "circumstances" in the circumstantial ad hominem argument are actions of the one participant in the dialogue. But this aspect poses a problem because the actions of a participant in an argument are surely not a part of the argument, in the sense in which we evaluate the argument in logic.

To put the problem another way, the child is presuming that the parent's argument exhibits a conflict of commitments, on the grounds that the parent's actions represent some sort of commitment to smoking. So when the parent argues that she is against smoking, a conflict of commitments is revealed. But is this assumption justified? Can actions of a certain sort be taken to represent a commitment, an advocating or approving of a particular sort of action? The answer is—sometimes, but not necessarily.

Suppose the parent were to reply to the allegation of inconsistency by arguing as follows:

Case 1.16

Parent: Well, yes, I smoke. But I have tried hard to give it up. Nicotine is addictive, and once you start, it is hard to give up. However, I am still trying. But you yourself should not start smoking because it is addictive and because it is unhealthy.

In this continuation of the dialogue of the smoking case, the parent has explained her way out of the presumed inconsistency fairly well. She admits that she smokes and that this action does contravene her own advice on what the child should do. Yet she still maintains that this advice, as applied to the case of the child, is based on good evidence that smoking is unhealthy.

Suppose, however, that the parent had taken up a different line of argument, as indicated in the continuation of the dialogue postulated in Walton (*Arguer's Position*, 1985, p. 71).

Case 1.17

Child	Parent
1. You claim that smoking is unhealthy?	Correct.
2. But you yourself smoke.	Correct.
3. So you think it's all right to smoke?	Well, yes, I suppose.
4. Do you agree that health is a good thing?	Of course.
5. So you agree that any activity injurious to health is wrong.	Yes.
6. It follows from your concessions at 5 and 1 that smoking is wrong. Yet you conceded at 3 that it is all right, i.e. not wrong to smoke. You're inconsistent!	Well, just a minute. I don't think smoking is always all right. But I'm a lot older than you, and anyway I've tried to quit but haven't succeeded yet.

This further analysis of the smoking case indicates that actions of a certain type may suggest certain commitments, but this suggestion may be either confirmed or refuted by a continuation of the dialogue. Typically, actions defeasibly suggest commitment to a general policy or proposition, but only in a tentative way that is subject to further questioning, clarification, and possible defeat.

This general problem of how to interpret actions as expressing commitments in dialogue was pointedly revealed by the tree hugger case (1.6) above. This case should be compared to another classic circumstantial ad hominem case called the sportsman's rejoinder. The version below is from Walton (*Informal Logic*, 1989, p. 145).

Case 1.18

A hunter is accused of barbarity for his sacrifice of innocent animals to his own amusement or sport in hunting. His reply to his critic: "Why do you feed on the flesh of harmless cattle?"

Let's say that it is in fact true that the critic is a meat-eater and does not deny eating meat. But what exactly does this admitted action or personal circumstance commit him to? Is he inconsistent if, as an acknowledged meat-eater, he scolds the hunter for "barbarity for his sacrifice of innocent animals to his own amusement or sport in hunting"? The short answer is no—because the critic is (presumably) not himself a hunter, and he criticizes the hunter for engaging in cruel sports for amusement. As DeMorgan (1847, p. 265) put it: "The parallel will not exist until, for the person who eats meat, we substitute one who turns butcher for amusement." The same failure of inconsistency was true in the tree hugger case, where the tree hugger is presumably not a tree cutter.

Nevertheless, the hunter does have some basis for his rejoinder because of the connection between meat-eating and hunting. The action of eating meat does support and does require the killing of animals. So the action of eating meat could be taken to be a condoning or an indirect support of the killing of animals. Similarly, in the tree hugger case, being a consumer of wood products does support the felling of trees.

But what sort of commitment to a policy of killing animals does meat-eating imply? This is the key question in evaluating the worth of the sportsman's rejoinder as a circumstantial ad hominem argument. Certainly meat-eating does not necessarily imply a commitment to or approval of hunting as sport. In this respect, at least, the sportsman's argument is misleading. So, too, consuming wood products does not necessarily imply an approval of clear-cutting or of cutting down trees generally.

The sportsman's rejoinder case has proved complex to sort out as a circumstantial ad hominem argument. Extensive analyses of it are given in Walton (*Arguer's Position*, 1985, pp. 53–59; *Informal Logic*, 1989, pp. 145–47) and in Lagerspetz (1995). Useful discussions of it can also be found in DeMorgan (1847, p. 265) and Whately (1870, p. 142, footnote 41). Further analysis and discussion of this case will be taken up in chapter 7. For now it is enough to see that although reports or allegations of actions do play an important role in circumstantial ad hominem arguments, what an action specifically implies as an arguer's commitments in a given case is problematic. A confessed action may commit a person to a certain policy, as something he supports or advocates generally. But, again, it may not. There can be different levels of involvement in a practice, and these different levels imply different kinds of commitment.

Actions, in the right circumstances, can be a basis for attributing goals or motives to the agent. And goals or motives can reveal important aspects of a person's character and commitments. So cases of alleged pragmatic inconsistency used to attack someone's argument, as in the smoking case, can be classified as ad hominem arguments. But the deeper logic of how such cases work as arguments remains a deep mystery not well penetrated by the accounts of ad hominem given in the current logic textbooks, as will become evident in chapter 2.

9. Person and Commitment

The next problem area that needs to be clarified is the relationship between the concept of a person, so vital to understanding the ad hominem argument, and the concept of commitment, so central to the dialectical framework of argument. The general question confronted in this section is: What is the concept of person to be used in the dialectical framework of argument? No attempt to study the ad hominem argument and to evaluate it as a distinctive type of argument used in a dialectical framework can avoid addressing this question.

The textbooks mostly agree in defining ad hominem as personal attack—that is, as attacking the person with whom you are engaged in dialogue as a means of attacking or attempting to refute that person's argument. But this definition raises sweeping theoretical questions that have not yet been clearly confronted in the literature on argumentation or informal logic so far. One important question is how to define what constitutes a "person" for purposes of argumentation. A secondary question also raised is the extent to which the concept of person should be part of the concept of argument appropriate for logic. We normally think of an argument as being a set of propositions, and in recent times a dialectical concept of argument has become more popular whereby an argument is thought of as a sequence of reasoning taking the form of a verbal exchange between two parties—that is, where the two parties are reasoning together. According to this dialectical concept of argument, we think of argument not just as a set of propositions, but as a goal-directed sequence of verbal exchanges between two parties who take turns making moves so that, in effect, they are arguing with each other. This is a dynamic and social concept of argument. What role then does the concept of person play in this dialectical framework of argument?

Hamblin (1970) discussed the concept of argument in chapter 7 of his book on fallacies and introduced the dialectical notion of argument as a way of providing a framework for analyzing fallacies. Even Hamblin did not explicitly raise this question of whether or how the concept of person is legitimate as a part of the concept of argument appropriate for logic. One important concept that Hamblin did define and introduce, however, that does play an important role in analyzing the argumentum ad hominem is that of commitment. Hamblin (1970, pp. 256–57) defined the concept of argument as an exchange of moves within the framework of a dialectical system. This dialectical system is like a game in which two partners take part, and each one takes turns making moves. Among the important kinds of moves in such a framework are arguments. As an alternative to the concept of belief that plays such a large role in modern epistemology and logic, Hamblin introduced a form of acceptance that he called *commitment*. As a speaker takes part in a Hamblin dialectical game, he will make certain moves—for example, asking questions, making observations, or putting forth arguments. By making these moves, the speaker will insert propositions into a set or store that Hamblin calls a *commitment set*. According to Hamblin, "The store represents a kind of *persona* of beliefs: it need not correspond to his real beliefs, but it will operate, in general, approximately as if it did" (p. 257). Hamblin calls such a set of propositions a *commitment store*, and the function of a commitment store, according to Hamblin (p. 257), is to "keep a running tally of a person's commitments." For example, when a person makes an assertion in response to a question of the other party, the proposition contained in that assertion will go into his commitment set. And, when a person retracts a proposition or indicates that he no longer accepts it or wishes to reject it, then it will be deleted from his commitment store. So, commitment stores fulfill the function of keeping track of the various propositions an arguer is committed to in virtue of the different moves he makes within a Hamblin dialectical system.

Walton and Krabbe (1995) base their analysis of commitment in dialogue on Hamblin's idea of commitment. The Walton and Krabbe analysis of commitment begins with Hamblin's concept but goes on to study several types of dialogue that function as normative models in which commitment operates somewhat differently in each different context. Walton and Krabbe (pp. 186–87) give an analysis of three different types of commitment in a special type of dialogue called *persuasion dialogue*. The first type is represented by assertions that are analyzed as commitments that a participant in dialogue is obliged to defend if challenged. The essential characteristic of this type of commitment is that it has a burden of proof attached. Commitments of a second type are concessions that a participant agrees to take on only for the sake of argument or for the sake of expediting an argument. But characteristic of this second type is that the arguer is not obliged to defend it—that is, no burden of proof is attached to it. The commitment is only accepted temporarily, as it were, as a means of getting the argument to go a little further. The participant is not bound to the obligations in the stronger sense of the first type of commitment where he accepts it in a sense of taking on an obligation to defend it if challenged. The third type of commitment is called by Walton and Krabbe (1995) the *dark side* type of commitment. These are propositions that are central to an arguer's underlying position as expressed implicitly by the moves he has made in the sequence of dialogue. It is characteristic of these dark side commitments, however, that neither party in the dialogue may be fully aware of what these obligations are as explicit commitments. Nevertheless, dark side commitments are important because we often base arguments in everyday conversation on presumed commitments, that is, commitments that we think the other party plausibly has by virtue of some position—perhaps an abstract position—that the other party has taken without it being clearly defined in these particular circumstances.

Case 1.19

> We may know that George is a communist because he has often advocated communist views and called himself a communist and so forth. If we're talking about a particular issue, say some aspect of financing in the universities, or something of the sort, we may have a pretty good idea that George will take a communist type of position, where he will advocate government control instead of free enterprise as a way of approaching the problem. But, we may not know that he is in fact committed to such a solution exactly or have any clear evidence that this position is exactly the one George would take.

Of course, if we ask George, we could find out exactly what position he *has* taken and then he would be committed to the particular proposition in the sense of the first type of commitment—that is, it would be an assertion, and he would be committed to it as a light side proposition that everyone would be clearly aware of, and he would be obliged to defend it. Everyday conversation has many instances of participants in argument who are only committed in their dark side sets for which we can conjecture on the basis of textual and contextual evidence that, given what we do know about their position, we can infer that they are likely to be committed to this particular proposition or to its opposite. But, we cannot say that we definitely know that they are committed to it in a sense that they have actually gone on record as saying so or have responded to a question by indicating that, yes, they are definitely committed to that proposition in Hamblin's sense. So, to deal with these "fuzzy" cases, in which we often have to deal with arguments that are enthymemes that have nonexplicit premises and the like, Walton and Krabbe introduce this notion of the dark side commitment set.

Now this notion of commitment, defined in the sense of Walton and Krabbe (1995), is precisely the concept that we need for analyzing the Lockean type of ad hominem argument. Locke (Hamblin, 1970, p. 160) defined argumentum ad hominem as a way of arguing whereby a participant in a dialogue presses the other party with consequences drawn from that other party's "principles or concessions."

Presumably, these principles or concessions can be analyzed fairly well as commitments in what Hamblin calls an arguer's commitment store. The arguer's concessions are the second type of commitment defined in Walton and Krabbe—those propositions conceded for the sake of argument. And the notion of the arguer's principles could be analyzed as his dark side commitment set—the things he is basically committed to in virtue of his general position. Or, in other instances, they could represent specific propositions that are clearly in his commitment set—the first type of explicit commitments identified by Walton and Krabbe.

So the use of the concept of commitment in dialogue to analyze the Lockean argumentum ad hominem could be quite a plausible type of analysis once we have defined the notion of commitment in dialogue. Then it would be quite clear how we could go ahead to use that concept as a framework to analyze the Lockean ad hominem.

Moreover, if we define the circumstantial type of ad hominem as involving a pragmatic inconsistency, then, as shown in Walton (*Arguer's Position*, 1985), we could use the concept of commitment to analyze this type of argumentation. For the pragmatic inconsistency is the kind of case in which an arguer puts forward a particular proposition that is thus clearly in his light side commitment store. Also, he implicitly concedes some other proposition or advocates it through his personal circumstances, as expressed perhaps by his actions or some other kind of indirect means by which we can infer that, for him, this is a dark side commitment. So, this method of analysis of commitment—distinguishing between the light side and dark side commitments—provides us with an attractive way of analyzing the circumstantial type of ad hominem argument involving a pragmatic inconsistency.

The crucial problem, the missing link, in this analysis is how to define the abusive or personal direct type of ad hominem that involves a direct attack on character but is presumably not based on an allegation of pragmatic inconsistency or some sort of Lockean argument from commitment. In other words, there seems to be a necessity here to distinguish between an arguer's commitment set, which as Hamblin says, does represent in some sense his *persona* of beliefs and the arguer's person or character as an individual person. In Walton and Krabbe (1995) the commitment set represents the set of propositions he is committed to, as judged by the sequence of dialogue and the text and context of the given case as we know it. But, does the arguer's commitment set represent the arguer's person or the arguer as a person? In personal attack, what would be attacked: the arguer's person? The answer seems to be "no," although it is possible to identify an arguer with this commitment set. Nevertheless, in the sense of 'person' represented by the personal or direct, abusive type of ad hominem attack, basically the focus of the attack is the arguer's character—his person in the sense of his personal character—and especially character for veracity. Now, to what extent can we identify an arguer's character—his personal character—with his set of commitments in a dialogue? There seems to be no reason to believe that any one-to-one correspondence exists between these two things. In general, the concept of character—the notion of the arguer's person—does seem to be separate from the Hamblin-style notion of the arguer's commitment set. As stated above, the whole question of how the concept of person, that is, the concept of an arguer's character, fits into the concept of argument appropriate for logic, has not really been asked by anyone yet, much less answered.

10. Conclusion

The account given (in section 6) is not the end of the story on tracing back the origins of the argumentum ad hominem to its sources in passages in Aristotle. Brinton (1985; 1986; 1995) and Wisse (1989) trace an important aspect of the argumentum ad hominem back to a concept in Aristotle called ethotic argument. Ethotic argument is defined by Brinton (1986, p. 246) as "the kind of argument or technique of argument in which *ethos* is invoked, attended to, or represented in such a way as to lend credibility to or detract credibility from conclusions which are being drawn." According to Wisse (1989, p. 5), the Greek word *ethos* means 'character,' and Wisse shows how both Aristotle and Cicero saw the use of a speaker's character as a means to help persuade an audience. According to Brinton (1986, p. 245), the most appropriate use of the term *ethos* in argumentation theory is to refer to an arguer's character used to support his argument. In this sense, Aristotle presented the idea in *Rhetoric* (1356 a 4–5) that an arguer's character is important in lending credibility to his argument. According to Aristotle, in this passage, the orator persuades not just in virtue of his speech but also in virtue of the extent to which the audience feels confidence in him as a person of worth. Aristotle writes that to the extent we feel confidence in a speaker to a greater degree, we are thus more inclined to have confidence in or to think credible what he advocates. Aristotle notes (1356 a 5) that such confidence is especially true when the proposition the speaker advocates is not one for which we have enough information to be absolutely certain that it is true or false, so there is room for doubt about its truth or falsity. In such a situation of uncertainty, the speaker's character is a strong influence on how credible we take the speaker's argument to be.

Wisse (1989) has shown how Cicero in his *De Oratore* followed Aristotle in stressing ethos, the presentation of the character of the speaker as a means of persuasion when that speaker's argument has the goal of persuading an audience. Both Aristotle and Cicero contrasted ethos and pathos (playing on the feelings of an audience) with rational argument (Wisse, 1989, p. 5), suggesting that both ethos and pathos could be associated with less than perfectly rational argumentation. Both Aristotle and Cicero were concerned with ethotic and pathetic arguments as used rhetorically for persuasion in a basically legitimate way, however, and it would be a mistake to see them as condemning such arguments as inherently fallacious.

Brinton (1985) and Wisse (1989) show how this rhetorical conception of ethos had an important influence in ancient rhetorical handbooks. Brinton (p. 57) goes on to identify ethotic argument with the concept of argumentum ad hominem as found in modern logic textbooks. Nevertheless, Brinton claims that if we view argumentum ad hominem in this way, it is not necessarily a fallacious argument. That is, in some cases, the speaker's ethotic argument could be backed up by his being a person of genuinely good character, and if this character is correctly perceived by the audience, then this perception could be a reasonable kind of consideration toward the audience's rightly attaching greater credibility to his argument. In such a case, the ethotic argument, according to Brinton (p. 56), would involve a reasonable and not necessarily fallacious type of argumentum ad hominem. Brinton (1995), in particular, sees the ethotic ad hominem argument as having a legitimate function in deliberation.

Indeed, as Brinton shows (1985, pp. 57–59), this ethotic type of argumentum ad hominem could be abused as well in some cases and could be the basis of the argumentum ad hominem as fallacy of the kind we are familiar with in the standard logic textbooks. In particular, Brinton (1995) suggests that the abusive or direct type of argumentum ad hominem might profitably be analyzed using the concept of the ethotic argument. Brinton (1986, pp. 250–53) goes on to show how the concept of ethotic argument was also used in the Stoics— particularly Seneca and Marcus Aurelius and also in Cicero. This Aristotelian notion of ethos will ultimately serve as the conceptual basis for the analysis of the concept of an arguer's character given in chapter 5 and for my own theory that perception of character in a dialogue exchange is the basis of the ad hominem argument.

It appears, then, that the argumentum ad hominem did not just pop into logic after Locke. There was a long tradition of the use of the phrase argumentum ad hominem in logic textbooks, manuals, and other writings on logic going back at least to Aristotle. The problem revealed is that several important ambiguities exist in the expression *argumentum ad hominem* as evolved into the modern informal logic as a term of art to stand for one of the traditional informal fallacies. Students could easily recognize that, once the ad hominem was identified as personal attack, it was a form of argumentation that is both common and powerful. They could also realize that, because of the power of this type of argumentation, it can be deceptive. Therefore, it was clearly evident to the writers of logic books and their students that the argumentum ad hominem was well worth including under the head of fallacies or sophistical refutations.

The problem of defining, analyzing, and clarifying this distinctive type of argumentation was impeded not just by the neglect, within logic, of the whole field of fallacies, when it came to giving any kind of theoretical analysis of the types of argumentation associated with the fallacies. It was also hampered by underlying ambiguities within the very concept of the argumentum ad hominem itself. A few astute commentators like Johnstone (1952; 1959) saw that if you define ad hominem in the Lockean way as argumentation from the other party's commitment, then this was not only *not* a fallacious type of argument in all cases but also a common type of argument that is often reasonable in everyday conversational exchanges and in other contexts like argumentation in academic disciplines. This aspect, no doubt, seemed hugely puzzling especially when Johnstone (1952; 1959) ventured the provocative thesis that all philosophical argumentation is essentially ad hominem in nature. This thesis makes sense when one defines the argumentum ad hominem in Lockean fashion as argumentation from the other party's commitment. Much philosophical argumentation is based on carefully taking premises from the writings or expressed statements of the philosopher whom you hope to criticize or interact with argumentatively; therefore, in the Lockean sense, philosophy is a kind of argumentum ad hominem. This reasoning seems appropriate. But, because of the historical ambiguity, the expression "argumentum ad hominem" was identified with the logical fallacy found in the standard treatment of informal fallacies in the logic textbooks. So, Johnstone's thesis then had the shocking implication that all philosophical argumentation is inherently fallacious. Thus, we could interpret Johnstone's provocative thesis, from one point of view, as an impetus to call upon the field of philosophy generally to begin to work toward analyzing the concept of argumentum ad hominem and disambiguating it.

In reconstructing or rehabilitating the concept of the argumentum ad hominem in a fashion that can make it a useful category of argument for modern logic, we need to look back to the historical roots of development of this phrase and, especially, we need to be careful not to trip over the historical ambiguities that have plagued the development of the subject so far.

Two hypotheses stand out as representing fruitful lines of future inquiry. One is that the so-called circumstantial ad hominem of the standard treatment can be analyzed as a subspecies of the Lockean type of argumentum ad hominem or argument from the other party's commitment. But, so analyzed, the circumstantial ad hominem argument is not precisely identical with the Lockean kind of argument. Rather, it is a special subspecies of it which involves a pragmatic inconsistency between the speaker's argument and some aspect of the speaker's circumstances as expressed in his commitment store in a context of dialogue. So the Lockean approach to the ad hominem does indicate a kind of avenue for the future analysis of the circumstantial ad hominem. In contrast, the abusive, the direct or personal type of ad hominem, which is generally distinguished as separate from the circumstantial subtype, can be analyzed with reference to the concept of ethotic argument developed by Brinton and found originally in Aristotle's *Rhetoric*. In the scholarly literature on the argumentum ad hominem over the past twenty years, the vast bulk of the analytical literature that has been successful has concentrated mainly on the circumstantial and the Lockean types of argument. These types of arguments are admittedly easier to analyze, once we introduce Hamblin's notion of the commitment set; after we have the notion of the commitment set in a context of dialogue in place as a tool of analysis, we can then use this tool to analyze the notion of pragmatic inconsistency. In fact, this program has already been followed out to some extent in Walton (*Arguer's Position*, 1985).

Nevertheless, there has been much less progress toward developing any kind of analytical exegesis of the abusive or direct personal type of argumentum ad hominem. In some ways, this type of argumentum ad hominem poses a much larger puzzle because it raises the general question of what role the person or the character of the person plays in the concept of argument appropriate for informal logic. In fact, an important clue is to be found in Brinton's analysis of ethotic argument building on Aristotle's remarks in the *Rhetoric*. The clue is that character does play a role in our assessment of arguments because we do give greater credibility to the argument of a speaker where we perceived that the speaker is a worthy person who has what we perceive as a good character. It is this avenue that is explored and developed in chapter 5.

The problem, however, is also partly one of relevance. The question posed is just exactly when is the character of a speaker relevant as a line of argument in evaluating that speaker's argument. Thus the problem is that, in many cases, for example in political discourse, a case can be made for saying that character is relevant. Political discourse being what it is, the character—especially of an elected official—is relevant, to some extent, in our political deliberations on how to vote and which policies to support. So we cannot exclude ethotic argument or the aspect of character entirely as being irrelevant. Indeed, it is all too evident (as the standard treatment of the textbooks outlined in chapter 2 will make clear) that, too often, attacking an arguer's character in the form of the abusive ad hominem personal attack does digress from the issue that is supposed to be the subject of discussion in a particular case; such a case has a fallacy of relevance. So, the problem of the analysis of the abusive type of ad hominem is clearly tied to the question of relevance.

The key fact to note initially, as abundantly observed by the standard treatment of ad hominem in the textbooks, is that, in one case in particular, in the cross-examination of a witness in court, character is a relevant issue. In this context, the ad hominem move of attacking the speaker's character for veracity or honesty and so forth does represent a type of argument that is acceptable within the law of evidence and, moreover, does seem to be a relevant and legitimate line of argument generally, even though it can be abused in some cases. So, the problem then for the analysis of the abusive type of ad hominem argument is this: What conditions distinguish between the fallacious and nonfallacious use of this type of argument? In such a project of analysis, as shown in chapter 7, Brinton's concept of ethotic argument, involving the character of the arguer and its link with the arguer's credibility, turns out to be central. Before we can get to these questions of how to evaluate ad hominem arguments as fallacious or not in particular cases, the prior problem is to give some clear and useful basis for identifying the ad hominem as a distinctive type of argument and clearly defining its basic subtypes.

The initial classification of the subtypes of ad hominem argumentation given above as a point of departure is by no means universally accepted and, in fact, a system of classification directly different from it is advocated by van Eemeren and Grootendorst (1984, pp. 190–91). According to van Eemeren and Grootendorst's classification (p. 190), the abusive variant of the ad hominem argument is a direct personal attack in which the opponent is made out to be "stupid, dishonest, unreliable or otherwise negative" in personal characteristics. This abusive category broadly agrees with our own classification given above, but in defining the circumstantial and tu quoque variants, van Eemeren and Grootendorst have it the other way around. They define the circumstantial variant as "an attempt to undermine the opponent's position by suggesting that his only motive is *self-interest.*" So, what van Eemeren and Grootendorst call the "circumstantial variant" is in fact identical to what was called, in the above account, the "bias" type of ad hominem argument.

Van Eemeren and Grootendorst (1984, p. 190) define the tu quoque variant as "calculated to show up the contradiction that the other party in this discussion is attacking (or defending) a point of view that he himself earlier defended (or attacked)." This description of what they call the tu quoque variant is, in fact, very close to what was described above as the circumstantial type of ad hominem argument. In other words, it is the type of ad hominem argument that requires a contradiction between what the party said and some personal circumstances or some point of view that he defended, perhaps on another occasion.

Such striking conflicts of opinion in the scholarly literature on how to define the basic subtypes of ad hominem argument show that what is needed next is a survey of the leading textbook accounts. We need to see what are the most important differences of opinion on how to define the ad hominem argument and to classify its main subtypes and also to determine if there is some underlying basis for a common underlying target conception of this type of argument that could help point the way to consensus.

2

The Textbook Treatment

This survey of the treatment of the ad hominem fallacy in logic textbooks and critical thinking manuals covers sixty-six such textbook accounts ranging from 1883 through 1994. In some cases, these logic textbooks have gone through many editions, and it is not always the first edition that has been cited here. For example, as noted in chapter 1, the widely used logic textbook *Introduction to Logic* (Copi and Cohen) is now in its ninth edition (1994). In some cases, I have taken multiple editions into account, but, in most cases, I have only cited the edition that was available. Most of these textbook accounts of the ad hominem fallacy are fairly short. They range from the majority of instances where the treatment is one-half page or shorter to other cases where the treatment may be as long as three or four pages, or even, in rare instances, a whole chapter. All the textbooks cited are ones that do explicitly treat the ad hominem fallacy as a distinct type of fallacy. Many other logic textbooks do not include treatment of this fallacy, either because they do not treat of fallacies at all or because they treat some fallacies but omit the ad hominem. The ad hominem fallacy is generally regarded as a major fallacy, however, and it seems to be treated by most textbooks that include consideration of fallacies at all.

I have not attempted any systematic survey of comparing instances of textbooks that included ad hominem versus those that did not. It would seem from my survey that most logic textbooks that do treat of fallacies do include the ad hominem fallacy. All of the sixty-six books chosen to be included in this account were selected because each did have a section on the ad hominem fallacy. Nevertheless, I know that this account is not complete because I did omit from consideration some textbooks that did have some remarks on the ad hominem fallacy. Even so, I think that this sample is reasonably representative of the standard treatment of the ad hominem fallacy in twentieth-century logic textbooks and that it probably includes most or a very good number of these textbooks—especially the ones that have been popular or are currently being used in university teaching.[1] The survey takes a broadly temporal approach, starting from the earliest texts first, but it makes some exceptions to an exact temporal sequence in order to group some textbook accounts on the basis of common themes.

1. The Early Accounts

The early accounts surveyed here cover the period from around the turn of the century to just after World War II (1948). These accounts tend not to discriminate very well (if at all) between the abusive and circumstantial subtypes, and they tend to presume that the ad hominem argument is generally fallacious. Indeed, several state that ad hominem arguments are always fallacious. Black (1946) stands out as a text that states that the ad hominem argument can be used nonfallaciously in some cases, and Creighton (1929) and Werkmeister (1948), as noted below, also concede the nonfallacious use of ad hominem arguments in some instances. These early textbooks also tend not to mention other subtypes, such as bias or poisoning the well. Also, their treatments of the ad hominem argument are generally quite brief.

Jevons (1883) has a half page on the argumentum ad hominem, which he describes as a fallacy that is committed when "an argument . . . rests, not upon the merits of the case, but the character or position of those who engaged in it." As one of his three examples (p. 172), Jevons cites the legal case of an attorney who hands his barrister a brief marked "No Case: Abuse the Plaintiff's Attorney." Subsequent textbooks have quoted this same example over and over again in many instances. Jevons recognized that the ad hominem argument is both powerful and common as a tactic in everyday reasoning. Nevertheless, he does not acknowledge it as a reasonable argument in some cases, instead describing it as being fallacious. He makes this clear (p. 172) in describing a type of case that would generally be considered an instance of the circumstantial type of ad hominem argument but does not make the distinction between the abusive and circumstantial types of ad hominem argument.

Case 2.1

Every one who gives advice lays himself open to the retort that he who preaches ought to practice, or that those who live in glass houses ought not to throw stones. Nevertheless there is no necessary connection between the character of the person giving advice and the goodness of the advice.

In dismissing this type of ad hominem argument as fallacious on the grounds that no necessary connection exists between the character of the person and the worth of the advice he gives, Jevons is revealing a kind of deductivist bias by making it a requirement of a good argument that there be a necessary connection between the premise and the conclusion. Hence, we see in Jevons's textbook a clear case in which the ad hominem argument is dismissed as generally being fallacious on the grounds that it fails to meet a requirement for an argument to be a good one.

A sharply contrasting treatment of the argumentum ad hominem is given by Read (1901, p. 399), who describes this type of argument generally in Lockean terms and who sees it as a type of argument that can be either fallacious or nonfallacious. According to Read (p. 390), the argumentum ad hominem "consists in showing not that a certain proposition is true but that the [respondent] ought to accept it in consistency with his other opinions." This is essentially Locke's ex concessis analysis of the ad hominem argument as cited in Hamblin (1970, pp. 159–60). Read, like Locke, sees the ad hominem argument as a type of argument that can be nonfallacious in some instances even though it is possible for it to be fallacious in other cases. Read cites an argument that would nowadays be classified as a circumstantial type of ad hominem (p. 399), but he adds that whether or not the argument should be evaluated as fallacious depends on what its proponent is trying to prove by using the argument. Citing Whately (p. 399), Read writes that whether or not the circumstantial ad hominem is fallacious in a given case depends "upon whether it is urged as actually proving the point at issue, or merely as convicting the opponent of inconsistency." Thus, we see that even as early as 1901, some textbook accounts did recognize that, in principle, the ad hominem could be a reasonable type of argument in some cases.

Like the treatment of ad hominem given by Jevons and Read, that of Creighton (1904; first edition, 1898) makes no explicit distinction between the abusive and circumstantial varieties, although it does describe the argumentum ad hominem broadly enough so that it can include both these subtypes. Creighton (p. 168) defines the argumentum ad hominem as "an appeal to the character, principles, or former profession of the person against whom it is directed." Such a broad description of this type of argument would seem to suggest that it might not be fallacious in all cases, but Creighton describes it as a type of argument that "has reference to a person or persons, not to the real matter under discussion." Thus he sees the argumentum ad hominem as always being fallacious on grounds of irrelevance. In fact (p. 169), he explicitly describes it as an irrelevant argument, writing that, in all of the cases he considers, the "real pointed issue" is "evaded." In a later edition, Creighton (1929) conceded that ad hominem could be admissible and relevant when "the known bad character or untrustworthiness of some person is appealed to in order to impeach the evidence he may give" (p. 185). Creighton somewhat grudgingly concedes that this instance could be a reasonable type of ad hominem argument in the sense that it "at least assists us to exclude what is false" (p. 185). He concedes therefore that in such a case it could be a relevant argument even though he describes it as being one that has a "merely negative character" (p. 185). Here we have an account that generally presumes the argumentum ad hominem to be fallacious but by way of exception concedes the presence of some cases in which it could have some force as a negative type of argument that would make it relevant and nonfallacious.

Mellone (1913, p. 353) gives a brief account of the argumentum ad hominem that is similar to that of Jevons. Quoting Jevons, Mellone dismisses the ad hominem as being always a fallacious type of argument on grounds of irrelevance. The justification he gives (p. 353) is to quote Jevons's explanation that, in the argumentum ad hominem, there fails to be a necessary connection between the character of the person giving a piece of advice and the worth of that advice. Here is an instance of something generally noted in Hamblin's account of the standard treatment, that is, one textbook essentially copying the remarks of another on a given fallacy.

Cohen and Nagel (1934), in their popular textbook on logic and scientific method, describe the argumentum ad hominem (p. 380) as being a fallacious type of argument. They note that this type of argument has become popular with the rise of psychoanalysis and add "any argument whatsoever can be refuted in this way [by an ad hominem argument], inventing some unfavorable psychogenetic account of how or why the proponent of the argument came to hold that view" (p. 380). Then they add that it would be highly fallacious to try to refute a philosopher's arguments on grounds of citing some of his personal characteristics or biographical facts about how he lived. They cite the case (p. 380) that it would be fallacious to try to refute some of Spinoza's arguments on the nature of substance, for example, by arguing that he was a man who lived alone and had an intellectualist temper.[2] Cohen and Nagel do concede (p. 380) that arguing from the existence of personal motives in ad hominem fashion can be relevant to determining the credibility of a witness who testifies on what he has observed. But they add that this type of argument is one in which the premises are not meant to be sufficient to demonstrate the conclusion and that, in all cases for which the premises are supposed to be sufficient to demonstrate the conclusion, using an ad hominem argument would be fallacious.

But the individual motives of a writer are altogether irrelevant in determining the logical force of his argument, that is, whether certain premises are or are not sufficient to demonstrate a conclusion. If the premises are sufficient, they are so no matter by whom stated. The personal history of Gauss is entirely irrelevant to the question of the adequacy of his proof that every equation has a root; and the inadequacy of Galileo's theory of the tides is independent of the personal motives that led Galileo to hold it. The evidences for a physical theory are in the physical facts relevant to it, and not in the personal motives that led anyone to take an interest in such questions.

It is especially interesting to observe that Cohen and Nagel use the case of scientific reasoning, citing the cases of Gauss's proof a mathematical equation and Galileo's arguments and hypotheses concerning his theory of the tides. In such a context of scientific argument within a specialized discipline like mathematics or physics, for example, the argumentum ad hominem does indeed tend to be inappropriate and generally irrelevant. Citing this context supports Cohen and Nagel's contention that the argumentum ad hominem can be described generally as a fallacy. They take this view because their textbook is an introduction both to logic and to scientific method and also because, as the quotation above makes clear, they have a preference for arguments that are sufficient to demonstrate a conclusion. This view represents a kind of deductivist or perhaps inductivist bias that would tend to exclude ad hominem arguments because they generally tend to be presumptive in nature. Hence Cohen and Nagel's textbook represents a kind of point of view that sees the ad hominem argument as being generally fallacious, even though they do concede, by way of exception, that it could be nonfallacious type of argument in evaluating eyewitness testimony.

Black (1946, p. 216) gives a Lockean account of the argumentum ad hominem, describing this type of argument as occurring when "we may try to use the propositions already accepted by our adversary as a way of disproving his position." Black also concedes that the ad hominem argument "may be justifiably used, provided its limitations are recognized" (p. 216). When it is used in this justifiable way, Black adds, it can properly serve to shift the burden of proof to the other party in an argument. Thus, even though Black sees the ad hominem argument as being "formally irrelevant" in proving that a conclusion is true, nevertheless, he gives a balanced account by conceding that it can be used in some cases to shift a burden of proof.

To illustrate his point, Black cites the sportsman's rejoinder case from DeMorgan, the case analyzed briefly in chapter 1 above, and in greater detail in Walton (*Informal Logic*, 1989, pp. 145–47). In this case, classified in chapter 1 as a circumstantial type of ad hominem argument, one party argues that the taking of all life is evil and the other party replies, "but you don't object to killing animals for food" meaning that this party is implicitly committed to the policy of killing animals by virtue of his eating meat. In this kind of case, then, the second party is apparently caught in a circumstantial inconsistency by not practicing what he preaches, by advocating a certain principle but in his own personal practice carrying out actions that appear to run counter to that principle. Black (p. 216) cites this case as a typical ad hominem argument and classifies it as a fallacy on the grounds that the claim of inconsistency by the one party is "formally irrelevant to the question whether the conclusion is actually true." This case is actually quite complex and a difficult one to analyze, and yet it does require analysis in detail before we can make much sense of any claim that the ad hominem argument in it is fallacious or not. One reason is the number of ambiguities implicit in the argument, so students who used Black's popular textbook no doubt were somewhat perplexed by this complex case. Although this case is clearly an example of the circumstantial type of ad hominem argument, Black makes no distinction between the circumstantial and abusive varieties.

Werkmeister (1948) gives an account of the argumentum ad hominem (pp. 56–57) that also combines the abusive and circumstantial types, or at any rate, fails to make a distinction between them. He (p. 56) defines the argumentum ad hominem as "essentially an appeal involving the personal circumstances of the opponent, usually in an abusive way." Werkmeister compares the ad hominem argument to the genetic fallacy, writing that in both types of arguments "the merits of the point at issue are disregarded while attention is focused upon the source" (p. 57). Thus, he sees the ad hominem argument as being generally fallacious and describes it as "an irrelevant attack upon the person arguing on the opposite side" (p. 57). Werkmeister does go on to add, however, that the ad hominem argument can be "used in court to impeach the testimony of a witness" (p. 57).

He allows that, in such cases, the ad hominem argument is "not irrelevant" because "the witness' credibility is at issue." Werkmeister concedes (p. 57) that the ad hominem argument is "not irrelevant" when it is used in court to impeach the testimony of a witness, but he goes on to add that he judges that it is irrelevant "insofar as the logical force of the argument is concerned." So, as he sees it, the "personal history of a man, his character and economic or social position are irrelevant to the validity of his reasoning" (p. 57). It seems then that Werkmeister, like some of the other texts, has set up a certain standard for an argument to be reasonable as evidence for a proposition and sees the ad hominem argument as failing to be relevant to validity of an argument in this sense. His treatment of the argumentum ad hominem is comparable to that of Cohen and Nagel in that it does concede a certain kind of relevance of the ad hominem argument in the case of the impeachment of eyewitness testimony, but he sees this kind of relevance as not strong enough to bear on arguments that are supposed to be valid as based on objective evidence.

As noted, in the textbook treatments up to the late 1940s, the abusive and circumstantial versions of the ad hominem arguments tend not to be distinguished, other subtypes are not mentioned, although some of them are in effect described, and with a few exceptions the authors, perhaps displaying a deductivist bias, regard the ad hominem argument as inherently fallacious.

2. Growing Recognition of Nonfallacious Aspect

The next group of textbook accounts introduce the tu quoque and poisoning the well subtypes as features. We also see increasing recognition of the thesis that ad hominem arguments can sometimes be reasonable. Curiously, one textbook even puts forward the radical, go-it-alone thesis that ad hominem is generally a reasonable kind of argument that does not deserve to be categorized as a fallacy. Little evidence suggests that other textbook authors paid much or any attention to this unsettling line of argument.

In fact, we see two streams here. Following Black and Beardsley, some textbooks began to acknowledge more openly that ad hominem arguments can be reasonable in some cases. However, another stream of textbook accounts continued to condemn them as being generally fallacious.

Beardsley (1950, p. 135) defines the ad hominem argument as the kind of argument in which "the speaker seeks to discredit the character, motives, family, friends, pronunciation, grammar, or some other characteristic of the person who disagrees with him." Beardsley (p. 134) also equates the ad hominem argument with the phrase "poisoning the well," claiming that the ad hominem argument is sometimes called "poisoning the well." To illustrate it, Beardsley gives the following case:

Case 2.2

My opponent says that we should return the municipal garbage-disposal plant to private hands. But why does he say this? What are his underlying motives? Could it be that he and his friends want to get in on a profitable little monopoly?

Two observations about the preceding case are relevant. One is that it seems to be a bias type of ad hominem argument because the speaker discredits the other party's argument by suggesting that the other party and his friends "want to get in on a profitable little monopoly." The other observation is that this accusation of bias is put in the form of a question, which indicates perhaps that the ad hominem argument in the case might be a reasonable argument. After all, if the speaker is just raising critical questions, rather than definitely claiming that his opponent's opinion must be wrong, then this could be a reasonable ad hominem argument.

Beardsley is aware of the difficulty of making discriminations between reasonable and fallacious ad hominem arguments. He acknowledges, as we have seen so many textbooks do already, that an ad hominem argument could be nonfallacious in the case where it is used to throw doubt on the testimony of a witness in a trial. Beardsley attempts to explain the difference between this kind of case and the fallacious type of ad hominem argument by giving the following explanation:

Now, obviously, the most villainous and despicable character in the world can say that fire is hot and that statement will still be true. But by arousing mistrust in the *source* of the statement, the *ad hominem* arguer hopes to make us reject the statement itself. That is his technique. Of course, when a witness is giving *testimony* in a trial, the question at issue is, precisely, the reliability of the witness. Here it is legitimate to impeach the evidence by raising doubts about its source. The appeal is *ad hominem* when the question at issue is the *truth* of a statement, but we are asked to disbelieve it because we do not approve of the person who uttered the statement. (p. 135)

The distinction Beardsley makes is that, in the case of the witness giving testimony, the issue is supposedly the reliability of the witness, whereas, in the case where the ad hominem argument is fallacious, the issue is supposed to be the truth of the statement. This is a valiant attempt to sort out the problem of distinguishing between fallacious and nonfallacious ad hominem arguments. But it is not successful, for, in the case of the witness giving testimony, we are interested in the truth of the proposition in the testimony and not just in the reliability of the witness. We are judging the reliability of the witness in order to arrive at some estimate of the truth or falsity of the testimony that he or she is giving. So, the truth of a statement is the issue here, and therefore this is a kind of ad hominem argument as well. Hence it seems that Beardsley's attempt to give us a basis for distinguishing between the fallacious and nonfallacious uses of the ad hominem argument is not successful. Nevertheless, his account of the ad hominem argument is unusually good, in that he is sensitive to the importance of this distinction and, at least, makes an attempt to try to give us a basis for sorting out the problem.

Ruby (1950, p. 131) describes the argumentum ad hominem as a fallacy on the grounds that an attack that directs its force against the speaker is insufficient to prove that a proposition is false because such a proof requires evidence that the proposition is false. Thus, generally, Ruby sees the argumentum ad hominem as fallacious because it is a failure to provide adequate evidence required to prove a proposition. Citing a case of mathematical reasoning similar to the kind of cases cited by Cohen and Nagel, Ruby writes, "Euclid's geometry stands or falls on its own merits, whether or not Euclid was a kind husband and father" (p. 133). Ruby does acknowledge, however, that in the case of a trial in which an attorney for the defense prevents a character witness who testifies that another witness is a liar or has been previously convicted of perjury, the ad hominem argument is, or could be, not fallacious. As Ruby puts it (p. 133), this testimony of bad character is a kind of evidence that proves the witness is untrustworthy and therefore his testimony has little credibility. Ruby adds that liars do sometimes tell the truth; therefore, there is a sense of the word 'proof' in which we have not proved that what the witness says is false. Ruby identifies this form of attack that seeks to discredit a witness in court by throwing doubt on his character as the "poisoning the wells" argument (p. 133). He calls this "poisoning the wells" a special variety of the ad hominem argument and adds that it is sometimes a legitimate procedure provided we do not treat it as a disproof of the proposition that the witness had claimed.

So Ruby's treatment is similar to that of other textbooks where he draws a line between what he calls proof, meaning proving that a proposition is true or false, and the ad hominem type of argument in which doubt is thrown on a witness's credibility—that is, a witness who has vouched for the truth of a particular proposition. It seems then that Ruby, like Black and some other textbooks, has a high standard of what constitutes a proof, implying a kind of deductivism or the idea that the notion of proof requires objective evidence; therefore discrediting a witness could never count as a kind of proof or disproof in this sense.

Ruby (1950, p. 135) has some interesting points about the tu quoque type of ad hominem argument. He gives an example, which he classifies as a tu quoque argument, that is strikingly similar to a comparable case studied by Krabbe and Walton (1993).[3] Ruby describes the tu quoque or "You're another" argument as being the kind of argument in which one ad hominem argument is directed in reply against another one. He gives the following illustration (p. 135):

Case 2.3

X, a forty-year-old professor argued in favor of a military draft in 1941. He stated that it was necessary for the defense of the nation. A student interposed, "You favor the draft because you are in the higher age bracket and are not in danger of being drafted." The professor responded with the *tu quoque,* "By the same token, you are against the draft merely because you are afraid that you will be drafted."

In his commentary on this case, Ruby (p. 135) writes that the tu quoque argument "settles nothing" because the issue is whether the draft is or is not necessary for the welfare of the country and the tu quoque argument simply evades this issue. Consequently, Ruby describes the tu quoque as an argument that is fallacious.

In a textbook entitled *Fundamentals of Logic* (Hartman, 1949, p. 247), the author defines the tu quoque or "you too" argument as characterized by the expression "You do not practice what you preach." Hartman (p. 247) even gives the following interesting example of this type of argumentation:

Case 2.4

Christ employed this argument against the Pharisees when they accused Him of breaking the Sabbath by healing a man who had the dropsy: "Which of you shall have an ass or an ox fall into a pit, and will not immediately draw him up on the Sabbath?" (Luke 14:5)

Although this use of the argument would seem to be reasonable, Hartman classifies it (p. 247) as a fallacy on the grounds that it is a psychological substitute for proof.

One textbook on formal logic (Fitch, 1952, pp. 222–25) advocates the surprising thesis that the ad hominem argument is often quite a reasonable argument that does not deserve its bad reputation as a fallacy. Fitch even advocates the thesis that the use of the ad hominem argument in philosophical speculation and in the criticism of systems of philosophy is a characteristic that distinguishes philosophy from the empirical sciences (p. 222). This thesis is very similar to that of Henry W. Johnstone, Jr. (1952), who (as noted in chapter 1) argued that the argumentum ad hominem is a reasonable, that is, nonfallacious type of argument in many instances and, indeed, that this type of argumentation is generally characteristic of philosophical argumentation. Fitch gives the example of someone who formulates a theory about all theories. Such a theory, he says (p. 223), "may be said to have attained the level of maximum theoretical generality." Note in the case of a theory about all theories a certain element of self-reference; it is this element of self-reference that is characteristic, according to Fitch, of ad hominem arguments. Fitch uses the example (p. 223) of an arguer who denies the existence of a theory of all theories. Thus the arguer denies that there can be a theory at the level of maximum theoretical generality: "To deny that there is such a level is already to be proposing a theory about all theories and, hence, to be presenting a theory that is itself of the level of maximum theoretical generality." In other words, Fitch is pointing out that this argument that denies any such level can be found refutes itself because it itself is a theory at the level of maximum theoretical generality; it itself represents a kind of theory about all theories—that no such theory exists. So this negative criticism, that no such maximum level is to be found, is quite susceptible to an ad hominem argument. Indeed, Fitch concludes (p. 223) that it is characteristic of philosophy to reach this maximum level of generality and to use self-referential sorts of reasoning that are possible only on this level.

Fitch's account of the ad hominem argument is surprising among the textbook treatments, most of which routinely assume that the ad hominem argument is a fallacy. Fitch even has an explanation of why this assumption is made. According to Fitch's account (p. 222), the ad hominem argument is likely to stir up the resentment of an opponent because it has the appearance of being directed at the opponent himself as well as against the proposition he has advocated and, therefore, it may often appear to such a person to be a personal insult involving ridicule or irony. The ad hominem argument is such a strong form of attack and is or appears to be directed at the arguer himself, so a very real danger exists that an arguer to whom it has been directed may feel that he looks like a fool or is being made to look a fool. It is this upsetting aspect, according to Fitch (p. 222) that makes the ad homi-

nem argument tend to be regarded as generally unfair and even fallacious.

3. Wild Variations

In the next wave of treatments, we see the contradiction between
the two types of evaluations emerge quite explicitly. Some stress the
reasonable aspects of the ad hominem argument while others describe or even define it as inherently fallacious. Also, in this wave,
we see the bias type of ad hominem begin to be more prominently
featured. The tu quoque and the poisoning the well subtypes are also
recognized prominently by name, in Chase (1956).

Wide differences in ways of defining argumentum ad hominem
are evident in this group. Defining it in terms of the character of
the person who is attacked by the argument seems to be a common
thread. But there are variations on and deviations from this central
theme. "Origins," "history," and "motivation" are cited as what is
attacked in an ad hominem argument, instead of or in addition to the
character of person of the arguer.

Another textbook that stresses the reasonable aspect of argumentum ad hominem is Chase (1956, p. 59) who argues that the ad hominem can be a reasonable type of argument in political debate. According to Chase (p. 59), "When a man is running for office or being
chosen for any position in government or elsewhere, his personal behavior is always relevant." Thus, he emphasizes that not every personal attack should rightly be classified as an ad hominem fallacy.
Chase (p. 62) proposes that the phrase "poisoning the well" is "another name for the ad hominem fallacy." He (p. 154) treats the tu
quoque argument as a separate type of argument from the ad hominem argument even though (p. 65) he does classify tu quoque as a
subspecies of ad hominem. The example that he offers of the tu quoque argument makes it, in certain respects, different from the typical
type of case of ad hominem argument that is normally given in textbooks.

Case 2.5

The story runs that when the Moscow underground was first opened
to visitors in the 1930's, an American tourist was invited to inspect
one of the stations. He was shown the self-registering turnstiles and
the spotless washrooms. "Fine," he said; then looking down the
tracks, "How about the trains?" They showed him the safety devices
and the excellent tile frescos on the tunnel walls. He was again impressed, but continued to look anxiously down the tracks. "How

about the trains?" snapped his guide. "How about the trains? How about the sharecroppers in Alabama?"

In this case, the Russian replies to the American by asking a comparable kind of question, but this question about the sharecroppers in Alabama does imply a kind of guilt that he attributes to the American political system. Thus, there could be a sort of ad hominem argument implicit in his use of this question to reply to the American tourist. It is not exactly clear that, in this case, the tu quoque is a case of one ad hominem argument being used against another. Rather, the American tourist asks a question about the trains, and it appears to be a reasonable question, but the guide then replies with this guilt-imputing question about the sharecroppers in Alabama, which could be interpreted as containing a kind of ad hominem attack. Chase is quite condemnatory about this argument. He calls it an irrelevant counterattack and, in this case, the evaluation does seem reasonable. But it certainly is a case that represents the problems we addressed with respect to the tu quoque category in chapter 1.

Latta and MacBeath (1956) only have a couple of sentences on the argumentum ad hominem, which they dismiss as a fallacious kind of argument that is a subspecies of irrelevant conclusion. They make no comments about subclassifications of the argumentum ad hominem.

Blyth (1957, p. 39) describes the ad hominem as a generally fallacious type of argument in which an attempt is made to arouse doubt about a statement by discrediting the person who made the statement. Blyth (pp. 39–40) emphasized the bias type of ad hominem argument, especially writing, "a person arguing for something in which he has a personal interest is always open to the charge of bias" (p. 39).

Case 2.6

For example, a home-owner arguing for a reduction in real-estate taxes may be greeted with the remark "Of course you would be in favor of reduced real estate taxes because you would benefit personally by such a reduction." The appropriate reply would be "Of course you are against such a reduction because you own no real estate. Now let's get down to the relevant facts of the matter."

Blyth provides interesting comments on this case, pointing out that it is not "altogether irrelevant to take note of the bias" (p. 40), but he adds that such a charge of bias does not establish or disprove the correctness of an arguer's conclusion. Hence, Blyth does concede that the bias form of ad hominem argument can be reasonable in some cases, but, as in many textbooks, he adds that such an argument does not establish or disprove the proposition that is at issue. Blyth also goes on to say (p. 45) that, in a case of evaluating eyewitness testimony in a legal trial, the ad hominem argument can be reasonable.

Huppé and Kaminsky (1957) also emphasize the bias type of ad hominem. They characterize the argumentum ad hominem generally (p. 196) as attempting to argue by attacking the personal character of an opponent. They offer the following case:

Case 2.7

> For example, in a discussion on higher wages, if the proponent of higher wages is a union official, his opponent may be strongly tempted to resort to the argument *ad hominem* by pointing out that the union official's argument must be discounted because he is an "interested party," a member of the union.

This argument seems to be an instance of the bias ad hominem type of argument because the criticism is that the speaker, being a member of the union, is an "interested party" who has something to gain in the negotiations. Also, it could be classified as a circumstantial type of ad hominem argument because the speaker is being criticized in reference to something in his personal circumstances, so a kind of conflict could be involved here. What is even clearer is that this case involves an alleged bias because the speaker is said to have something to gain by a particular outcome of the negotiations.

Huppé and Kaminsky (1957, p. 197) treat the genetic fallacy separately from the argumentum ad hominem. They describe the genetic fallacy as involving "the attempt to destroy the value of an argument by criticizing its origin" and give the example of some persons who have argued that religion is no more than a superstition because it originated from superstition. They comment that even if this remark about the origin of religion is true, it does not follow that religious views are still to be equated with superstition. Although they see the genetic fallacy and the ad hominem fallacy as being separate, they add (p. 197) that attempts to discredit an argument by reflecting on the proponent's background can combine both fallacies.

Brennan (1957, p. 196) defines the argumentum ad hominem in terms of the character and motives of an arguer: "We argue *ad hominem* when we try to refute an argument by arguing against the character of the man who brings it forward or his dubious motives in so doing." This definition of the ad hominem is a little bit unusual in that it includes the concept of motive along with that of character in defining the argumentum ad hominem. Brennan has only a short section on the argumentum ad hominem but does include a statement to the effect that this type of argumentation can be reasonable in some circumstances. As an example, he cites (p. 196) the case of the argument of Jesus, related in John 8:7, against the crowd who were prepared to stone a woman who was accused of adultery.

Case 2.8

He that is without sin among you, let him first cast a stone at her.

This example might perhaps suggest the tu quoque classification of the ad hominem argument but, at any rate, Brennan cites it as an instance of the use of an ad hominem argument that would not be fallacious. Because it refers to past actions, implying a possible pragmatic inconsistency on the part of the accusers, the argument could also possibly be classified as a circumstantial ad hominem.

Schipper and Shuh (1959, p. 33) define the ad hominem in such a way that it is a fallacy. According to their account, the argumentum ad hominem "consists in an irrelevant appeal to the person being addressed, or against a third person, instead of an appeal to the matter at issue." This makes the ad hominem argument always a fallacy of irrelevance. Schipper and Shuh distinguish between the abusive and the circumstantial type of ad hominem argument. In the case of the abusive type, the argument contends that "There is something disreputable about the character or background of the man who is proposing the argument" (p. 33). In contrast, in the circumstantial type of ad hominem argument, "A man's special circumstances are taken as a reason for his accepting the truth of some belief" (p. 33). Interestingly, the examples that Schipper and Shuh give of the circumstantial type of ad hominem argument, which they call the "constructive" type, are Lockean ex concessis arguments in form. They give the example of a case in which the person to whom the argument is addressed is a Presbyterian and the other party claims that this person ought to believe that all events are predetermined by God. The assumption here appears to be that because this person is a Presbyterian there is no room for him to deny some belief or proposition that the other party takes to be in the Presbyterian position.

Fearnside and Holther (1959) emphasize, in their account of the ad hominem argument, that it is a common and powerful type of argumentation that is difficult to combat. Nevertheless, they contend that the ad hominem argument is not always fallacious. According to Fearnside and Holther (p. 99), "There is no argument easier to construct or harder to combat than character assassination." In addition, they explain that personal considerations can be relevant for judging whether or not a person is telling the truth in a given case. They add, however, that a difference exists between "taking into account the reliability of the witness and blindly assuming that personalities dispose of issues" (p. 99).

Emmet (1960) classifies the argumentum ad hominem under the larger category of misrepresentation of an opponent's case. Such a classification would seem to make the argumentum ad hominem a subspecies of the straw man philosophy. Emmet defines the argumentum ad hominem as "attacking the man instead of what he is arguing about" (p. 166). Emmet sees this as a fallacy of irrelevance as well as one of misrepresentation, but he concedes that it may not be irrelevant and may be justifiable as a species of argument when used to cast doubt on the reliability of a witness in a legal trial.

4. Elaboration of Subtypes

In this group, some of the textbooks begin to pay attention to classifying the subtypes in a more careful way, but considerable disagreement and confusion are in evidence. What one describes as the bias type is described by others as the circumstantial type. What some describe as the circumstantial type fits the description by others covering the bias type or the tu quoque type.

Copi (1961, second edition, pp. 54–57) distinguishes between two subtypes of argumentum ad hominem—the abusive and the circumstantial. The abusive is said to be committed (p. 54) "when, instead of trying to *disprove the truth* of what is asserted, one attacks the man who made the assertion." Copi gives the example (p. 54) of arguing that Bacon's philosophy is untrustworthy because he was removed from his chancellorship for dishonesty (case 1.1). Copi writes that this argument is fallacious because "the personal character of a man is logically irrelevant to the truth or falsehood of what he says or the correctness or incorrectness of his argument." Thus, Copi classifies the abusive ad hominem as a fallacy of relevance.

Copi defines the circumstantial variety (p. 55) as having to do with "the relationship between a person's belief and his circumstances." Thus, when two parties are disputing, rather than trying to prove an opponent's contentions true or false, one may "seek instead to prove that his opponent ought to accept it because of his opponent's special circumstances." Copi gives the following example:

Case 2.9

> If one's adversary is a clergyman, one may argue that a certain con-
> tention *must* be accepted because its denial is incompatible with the
> Scriptures.

So, this case has a kind of Lockean interpretation of the circumstantial ad hominem similar to case 2.8, because the adversary in this
case is the clergyman who presumably has the official position of
advocating or upholding the doctrines represented in the Scriptures.
Therefore, it is argued, he must accept a particular proposition because it is in the Scriptures or follows from what is expressed in the
Scriptures. But then Copi follows this up (p. 56) by citing the famous
sportsman's rejoinder case, a somewhat different case from 2.9 and a
more complicated type of case, which we will discuss subsequently.

In the eleventh edition of this same textbook, Copi and Cohen
(1994) add to the circumstantial and abusive ad hominem an account
of another variety they call "poisoning the well." The case they give
(p. 124) to illustrate this poisoning the well type of fallacy is the
dispute of intrinsic historical interest between Kingsley and Newman (case 1.8). Copi and Cohen classify this poisoning the well type
of argument as a subcase of the circumstantial ad hominem argument. Curiously, however (p. 124), they add some comments that are
relevant to the general question of how to classify these various subspecies of ad hominem argument. They write that, when a circumstantial ad hominem argument is used, an arguer is charging his
opponent with inconsistency of a certain kind, for example, inconsistency among a set of beliefs or "between what they profess and what
they practice" (p. 124). Nevertheless, they also include, within the
category of circumstantial ad hominem argument, the kind of argument that was classified above as poisoning the well, that is, charging
somebody with a lack of trustworthiness by virtue of their belonging
to some group or having some particular type of conviction. Copi and
Cohen (p. 124) claim that, in this kind of case, "there is an accusation
of prejudice in defense of self-interest." So, it seems then that, although they do not use this term, they include the bias type of ad hominem under the heading of the circumstantial type. In other words,
they think of the circumstantial type as being very broad and as including the poisoning the well type of argument as one subspecies
and the bias type of argument as another subspecies. This is an interesting approach that is somewhat unusual.

In addition, to fill out their system of classification, Copi and Cohen (p. 124) use the term tu quoque to characterize the type of argu-

mentation used in the sportsman's rejoinder case. But, they add that this tu quoque type of argument is a variety of circumstantial ad hominem argument. So, the long and the short of this account is that Copi and Cohen think of the circumstantial category as quite broad in that it includes the tu quoque, the poisoning the well, as well as the bias type of ad hominem argument under this umbrella. So, it is only the abusive type of ad hominem argument that stands outside of the circumstantial classification for Copi and Cohen.

Wheelwright (1962) defines the ad hominem argument broadly as any argument that "shifts from the point at issue to the opponent himself." This shift is said to include any "smudging of the argument by vilification" as well as "all recriminations, sarcasm, and references to incidental characteristics of the opponent" (p. 327). This broad characterization of the ad hominem argument would allow it to include any vilification of an opponent even though that vilification is not necessarily to try to detract from that person's argument for a specific proposition. Conceived in such a broad way, the fallacy of the argumentum ad hominem is also taken by Wheelwright to include a form of vilification called *guilt by association* when "perhaps in a court or an investigating committee, the evidence against a man may be waived by reference to the alleged character or activities of some of his relatives or friends" (p. 327). This account is really a broad characterization of the ad hominem argument so that it would include virtually any form of vilification of a person in speech. Wheelwright also recognizes the tu quoque as a more precise form of the ad hominem typified by the retort "But you yourself do the same kind of thing that you accuse me of doing" (p. 327). This characterization is also quite broad because the tu quoque reply could be addressed to any kind of accusation, making it seem more like the two wrongs fallacy (see chapter 1).

Clark and Welsh (1962) define the argumentum ad hominem as a fallacious type of argument as a species of irrelevant conclusion that tries "to refute the contentions of a man by proving something about his personal character or history or motivation" (p. 142). They also admit that the argumentum ad hominem need not be fallacious in the case of a lawyer attacking the credibility of a witness in a trial. So, curiously, even though they define the ad hominem as a fallacious type of argument, they are willing to admit the existence of some cases in which the argumentum ad hominem is nonfallacious.

Rescher (1964, p. 81) also describes the argumentum ad hominem as fallacious. He defines this type of argument as one in which the premises address themselves "to the man" instead of to the issue. Rescher distinguishes three categories of ad hominem: abusive, circumstantial, and tu quoque. The abusive one is characterized as making a personal attack on an opponent instead of trying to disprove what he says. Rescher gives the example of Nietzsche's views on ethics being attacked because he was an unhappy, bitter, and neurotic man who eventually became insane. Rescher adds, "Any argument of this sort is, of course, highly improper and thoroughly fallacious: the personal or moral character of the man has nothing whatever to do with the correctness or incorrectness of the argument he advances" (p. 81). Van Eemeren and Grootendorst (1993, p. 56) call this statement of Rescher's "rather apodictic."

What Rescher describes as the circumstantial ad hominem, we would classify as the bias type of ad hominem. He classifies this type as the ad hominem argument that "does not directly abuse the opponent but undercuts his position by suggesting that he is serving a personal interest in advancing his views but does not adhere to them for properly evidential reasons." This is quite a good account of the bias type of ad hominem argument, so it is a bit surprising that Rescher defines this as the circumstantial argumentum ad hominem though, certainly, as we noted above, there is precedent for this type of classification. Rescher gives the following example (p. 82).

Case 2.10

Somebody supports a rent control bill and a critic accuses him for sponsoring it because he is a tenant, where the critic adds that all the people who have joined this person in supporting this bill are tenants and renters and they don't include a single landlord.

This case is quite a good illustration of the bias type of ad hominem argument, so it is interesting to see Rescher classifying it under the heading of circumstantial and giving it as the only example of this type of ad hominem argument.

Finally, what Rescher describes as the tu quoque form of argumentum ad hominem (p. 82) is the type of argument that would normally be classified by the majority of textbooks as the circumstantial type. Rescher defines this type as the kind of case in which an arguer "contends that the opponent has also on some other occasion held the view he now opposes or adopted the practice he now condemns . . . instead of trying to show by actual evidence that the view or practice is correct." Again, we can see that Rescher defines this form of ad hominem argument as inherently fallacious.

Barker (1974) also defines the ad hominem argument as being inherently fallacious: it is the type of argument that "is directed at an opponent in a controversy, rather than being directly relevant to proving the conclusion under discussion" (p. 190). Barker gives the example of someone attacking the social and economic arguments of Karl

Marx by describing him as a failed man who could not even earn enough money to support his family. Barker describes this argument as fallacious on the grounds that it attacks Marx personally instead of offering reasons why his views are incorrect (p. 190). Barker classifies this type of case as the abusive form as contrasted with the circumstantial form, which he defines in a Lockean fashion: the circumstantial form occurs "if a speaker produces reasons why his opponent might be expected to believe the conclusion rather than reasons why the conclusion is true" (p. 190). He gives the example of a debate (p. 190):

> *Case 2.11*
>
> Members of Congress are discussing funding promotion of birth control in underdeveloped countries. One senator happens to be a Catholic but supports the proposal and another one, who is not a Catholic, opposes it. So the one might argue "This birth control proposal is contrary to your religious principles so that it ought to prove to you that it's a bad proposal."

According to Barker (p. 190), the critic here, instead of offering a direct reason why the proposal is bad, is merely providing a reason why this particular person, given his religious affiliation, might be expected to regard the proposal as bad and reject it. This is a Lockean conception of the ad hominem argument, and Barker identifies it with the circumstantial subtype.

Finally, Barker identifies a third form of ad hominem argument (p. 191) that he calls the tu quoque, in which a speaker, "trying to show that he is not at fault, argues that his opponent has said or done things just as bad as those of which he, the speaker, is accused." He gives the following example (p. 191).

> *Case 2.12*
>
> One person accuses another person of driving a car that's unsafe because it has bad brakes, whereupon the second person turns around and aims a refutation at his accuser saying, "On your car, the doors won't even shut."

Barker adds, however (p. 191), like so many of the texts, that not all ad hominem arguments are fallacious, because, in some cases, information about an arguer's personality may not be irrelevant to the question of whether his views are incorrect. So, Barker admits exceptional cases in which ad hominem arguments are not logically fallacious even though his definition of the ad hominem as a type of argumentation is quite a strong one in that it defines it as being generally or inherently fallacious.

5. Justifying the View That It Is Fallacious

In this next set of treatments, the authors return to the view that the ad hominem argument is generally fallacious. In fact, most of these authors define it in a way that makes it (by definition) an inherently fallacious type of argument. Despite this general agreement, the authors have considerable disagreement on how the argumentum ad hominem should be defined. Some highly unusual classifications of subtypes are evident.

There appears to be a growing recognition of the idea that the ad hominem argument is nonfallacious in some cases and at the same time a resistance to this potentially troublesome view. To deal with the perceived problem, some novel strategies are adopted.

In this collection, the group attack (guilt by association) type of ad hominem gets recognition. Beardsley (1966, p. 216), like many of the textbooks, describes the ad hominem argument generally as fallacious, "a form of distraction" when "attention is no longer directed to the matter at hand *(ad rem)* but to the person *(ad hominem)*." Nevertheless, he recognizes that, in some cases, the ad hominem argument, of a kind he identifies with the bias type, can be reasonable. Beardsley writes, "When the question at issue concerns precisely the legitimacy of an alleged authority, it will be relevant to point out evidences of his bias" (p. 216). He describes the ad hominem (p. 217) as a powerful kind of distraction that can easily divert people away from the issue of a discussion, but he concedes that, in some cases, it can be a reasonable type of argument. However, Beardsley, with others, gives us no firm method for judging, in a particular case, whether the ad hominem we are confronted with is reasonable or fallacious. We are told only that it is a tactic of irrelevance, and we are not given any method of determining whether, in a given case, it might be one of those instances for which it is a relevant argument.

Manicas and Kruger (1968) have a novel way of dealing with the problem that some ad hominem arguments do not appear to be fallacious. They define the ad hominem (p. 342) as the type of argument that "attacks a man's character rather than his argument." They evaluate this type of argumentation as a fallacy but add, as many texts do, that there can be the exceptional kind of case, for example, in court, when attacking the credibility of an arguer—such as a witness—could be a reasonable way of casting doubt on his argument: "If, for instance, [a person] is known to be a chronic liar or a convicted perjurer, it is prudent to have reservations about whether he is now telling the truth, even though he may be" (p. 343). Manicas and Kruger deal with such a case by adopting the hypothesis that "to voice such a doubt under these circumstances would not be considered an ad hominem attack" (p. 343). So, they take this novel strategy of saying that, in the impeachment of the witness type of case, the argument is not a genuine ad hominem argument. Thus they use the somewhat nonstandard approach that ad hominem arguments can be defined as fallacious except in certain legitimate types of arguments (that is, in the eyewitness testimony types of cases in court) that are not classified as ad hominem. Unfortunately, it is difficult to accept this solution because the argument in the impeachment of the witness case does seem to fit the general characterization of the argumentum ad hominem that Manicas and Kruger provide, and they give us no further grounds for excluding this case from their definition. So, it is not clear in this case why the raising of doubts about the eyewitness testimony of the witness is not really an ad hominem argument.

Manicas and Kruger don't distinguish between the abusive and circumstantial subtypes, but they do distinguish (p. 343) the tu quoque subtype of the ad hominem argument. They give the example (p. 343):

Case 2.13

A man criticizes his wife for baking a soggy cake and she replies, "Can you do any better?"

In this case, Manicas and Kruger claim that the wife is committing the tu quoque fallacy on the grounds that the issue is not whether the husband can bake such a cake; therefore the wife's argument can be categorized as a diversionary tactic (p. 343). This case is actually a curious and interesting one and is difficult to classify other than (perhaps) as an instance of the two wrongs fallacy. It could also possibly be considered in relation to some of the unusual types of ad hominem arguments recognized in Krabbe and Walton (1993), but it may not even be an ad hominem argument and may be better classified as an irrelevant reply, an instance of the *ignoratio elenchi* fallacy.

Vernon and Nissen (1968) describe the ad hominem argument as a fallacy that "consists in attacking a proposition on the basis of its source rather than its merit" (p. 146). Vernon and Nissen formulate a basic pattern or form of the ad hominem argument (p. 146) as follows: *Premise 1 — X says p; Premise 2 — X is bad; Conclusion — p is false (or bad)*. In this form of argument, presumably *X* is a person or arguer

and p is a proposition. What is especially interesting about this treatment is that the authors mention the group attack form of ad hominem argument, proposing that the ad hominem fallacy is committed
(p. 147). If one argues that a measure is unsound because "it is advocated by such a group or class [like the American Medical Association or organized labor], who are then accused, by declaration or innuendo, of being incompetent, or of having sinister designs, etc." (p.
147), then the argument is said to be ad hominem. To identify this
type of ad hominem argument is interesting because it refers to a
specific subtype in which an arguer's proposition is attacked on the
grounds that the arguer belongs to some group or class. It could be
guilt by association, or it could be a kind of ex concessis argument
from the group policies or commitments. It could also possibly refer
to bias because of the interests of the group. Vernon and Nissen do
not distinguish between the abusive and circumstantial varieties of
the ad hominem argument, instead focusing on this notion of group
attack or attack on the group to whom the arguer belongs.

Kilgore (1968) does distinguish, in a fairly standard way, between
the abusive and circumstantial variants of the ad hominem argument, and he (p. 60) defines the argumentum ad hominem in a way
that makes it intrinsically fallacious: "the fallacy of the appeal to
the man seeks to prove a conclusion false by attacking the character,
reputation, associations, or social situations of the person proposing
it." This type of ad hominem argument is described as fallacious on
the grounds that it shifts the point at issue from evidence onto the
person making the opposed argument. The abusive ad hominem type
of argument is said to be the type that "seeks to discredit the person
proposing an argument by an attack upon his character," and under
this heading is included guilt by association (p. 60). The circumstantial type of ad hominem argument is described as including the class
of arguments that "discredit the person advancing opposing arguments by claiming that his circumstances or groups with which he
is identified warrant rejection of his views." Thus, Kilgore, like Vernon and Nissen, emphasizes the group attack type of ad hominem,
but Kilgore puts the group attack together with the attack on the circumstances of an arguer as being two subspecies of the circumstantial type of ad hominem argument.

Kilgore also (1968, p. 61) adds the tu quoque as a subspecies of circumstantial ad hominem. According to Kilgore (p. 61), the tu quoque
"seeks to discredit views of an opposing party by pointing to discrep-
ancies between his circumstances and views he is advocating or between a previous and present position." Curiously, this characterization of the tu quoque argument would make it coextensive with

the category normally called circumstantial ad hominem argument in most textbooks.[4] So, we could say that the system of classification proposed by Kilgore is broadly in keeping with the standard type of classification of ad hominem arguments of the majority. Nevertheless, in certain respects, it is different, particularly in seeing the circumstantial type of ad hominem as specifically including the group attack and the tu quoque as closer to what most textbooks would identify with the circumstantial type.

Olson (1969) also defines the argumentum ad hominem as a fallacious type, generally, and he defines the circumstantial ad hominem as a subfallacy of another popular fallacy of relevance called the *fallacy of wishful thinking* (p. 185). The circumstantial ad hominem fallacy is defined as "playing upon the interests of the persons to whom an argument is addressed in order to win favor for the conclusion." The example is given of the politician who argues that a given group ought to support a specific measure because that measure is in the group's best interest (p. 185). This case is curious because it seems to be a kind of reverse or obverse of the bias type of ad hominem argument. Instead of critically attacking an argument on the grounds that the proponent is only arguing this way because it is in his best interests, this type of argument tries to get somebody to follow a given policy because it is in his best interests to do so. This odd argument seems to be a kind of shift from a critical discussion, or truth-oriented type of discussion, toward a negotiation type of dialogue in which the parties' interests are appealed to as a basis for accepting the truth or falsity of a particular proposition. Indeed, this is a curious interpretation of the circumstantial ad hominem. Olson does not mention the abusive type of ad hominem or any other types and gives only one paragraph (about half a page) to this type of ad hominem fallacy.

Kahane (1969) identifies the argumentum ad hominem with the genetic fallacy, defining both as fallacious (p. 250). The genetic fallacy or argumentum ad hominem "consists in an attack on the man argued against, rather than on his arguments" (p. 250). Although Kahane defines this type of argument as fallacious, he does admit that not all ad hominem arguments are fallacious (p. 251), citing the usual case of the impeachment of the testimony of a witness in court by questioning the witness's moral character. Kahane, to his credit (p. 251), notes that the question of determining when an ad hominem argument is fallacious and when it is not is a complex problem. He also treats the tu quoque fallacy as a separate category but identifies it as a species of argumentum ad hominem. According to Kahane, the tu quoque fallacy is committed (p. 251) "when someone argues that his opponent holds or held the view he now attacks, or engages in or engaged in the kind of activity he now attacks." This, like many accounts of the tu quoque argument, is quite broad.

A highly nonstandard classification of the subtypes of ad hominem argument is given by Michalos (1970, pp. 53–57). Michalos defines the tu quoque as being separate from the ad hominem and also distinguishes a separate type of fallacy that he calls *faulty motives.* Michalos begins (p. 53) by defining the fallacy of *abusing the man,* which he equates with the argumentum ad hominem as being "committed when the defender of an issue is attacked instead of the issue of itself." Even more curiously, the first example that Michalos gives of this fallacy is that of the eyewitness to a crime whose testimony is attacked in court by the defense attorney on the grounds that the witness happens to be an ex-convict. Oddly, Michalos seems to presume that this argument is fallacious whereas most of the textbooks that cited this particular type of example use it as an illustration of the claim that the argumentum ad hominem can be nonfallacious in some cases.

At any rate, Michalos has quite a novel classification of the different subtypes of ad hominem and related fallacies. He distinguishes another fallacy he calls the fallacy of the *bad seed* (p. 54) that is committed "when it is argued that the views of some descendent of a bad man must be false." Michalos classes this type of argument as a subspecies of the fallacy of abusing the man, but he adds that it has particular characteristics of its own (p. 54). Yet another fallacy Michalos classifies as a subspecies of the fallacy of abusing the man is what he calls *bad connections,* "The fallacy of appealing to *bad connections* is committed when it is argued that the views of some person must be false because he has certain nefarious, unsavory, or evil connections" (p. 54). An additional fallacy related to this group is one Michalos calls *faulty motives.* "The fallacy of appealing to *faulty motives* is committed when it is argued that, because someone's motives for defending an issue are not proper, the issue itself is unacceptable" (p. 55). This type is not said by Michalos to be a subspecies of ad hominem argument, but because it is treated right behind the other types of ad hominem arguments, it appears that it could be in Michalos's view related to ad hominem.

Finally, Michalos distinguishes the tu quoque fallacy (p. 55) as "committed when a person's inconsistent position with respect to some issue is used as an argument against it." The example of this fallacy he gives (p. 56) is the case in which some people claim that President Johnson's views on integration must be false because, earlier in his career, he had an opposite view. This curious way of defining the tu quoque fallacy differs from the way most textbooks define it. This account resembles what most textbooks would probably classify as a species of circumstantial ad hominem. At any rate, the classification of the various subtypes of ad hominem argument and related arguments given by Michalos is quite nonstandard.

6. Fundamental Disagreements

The next wave of treatments exhibits several fundamental disagreements. Some of them treat the ad hominem in a balanced way, whereas others define it in a one-sided way that ensures, by definition, that it always has to be fallacious.

Moreover, basic disagreements continue on how to classify the subtypes. In particular, the bias type is classified as circumstantial, and the Lockean type is classified also, by other texts, as circumstantial. The tu quoque is characterized as a kind of argument that does not seem to be an ad hominem argument at all. In other texts, the generic category of ad hominem arguments is equated with the genetic fallacy.

Kreyche (1970) classifies the argumentum ad hominem under the heading of fallacies, but he does not define it in such a way that it necessarily has to be fallacious. He (p. 30) defines the argumentum ad hominem or *appeal to the man* as "trying to discredit an argument by discrediting the opponent himself." Kreyche does not use the terms "abusive" or "circumstantial" at all but does distinguish between two subtypes of ad hominem argument. First, he says (p. 31) that the argumentum ad hominem often assumes the form of name-calling, which he sees as a practice involving the use of labels such as "thief," "murderer," "good-for-nothing," and other epithets used to attack a person. The other form of ad hominem mentioned by Kreyche (pp. 31–32) is the tu quoque. He uses the following example (p. 31):

Case 2.14

Someone is accused of stealing apples, and then turns around and says to his accuser, "Well, didn't you admit that when you were a boy, you too used to steal your neighbor's apples?"

Kreyche sees this tactic as a failure of relevance that "attempts to distract attention from the issue by putting the blame on someone else who is presumed guilty of the same thing." Judging by the criteria of chapter 1, it would be a case of the two wrongs fallacy, but Kreyche classifies it as a tu quoque. Finally, Kreyche adds (p. 32) that the argumentum ad hominem can be nonfallacious in some cases and cites the case of a witness who is lawfully discredited in court on the grounds that he is a habitual liar or is insufficiently informed.

Fischer (1970) classifies the argumentum ad hominem into four subcategories. First, he cites the abusive ad hominem, defined as being the type of ad hominem argument that "directly denounces an opponent" (p. 291). The second variety of ad hominem cited by Fischer is the circumstantial. The third is an unusual one that he calls the "associative" ad hominem argument, which attempts "to undercut an opponent by reference to the company he keeps" (p. 291). This so-called associative type of ad hominem seems similar to what other textbooks, especially the more recent ones, frequently call guilt by association (chapter 1). The fourth type of ad hominem argument recognized by Fischer is the tu quoque, defined as one "in which it is suggested that an opponent has sometimes held the view he now opposes, or that he has adopted the practice which he now condemns" (pp. 291–92). This category is broad, judging from the perspective of chapter 1.

Capaldi (1971, p. 72) defines the ad hominem attack as against "the man who presents an argument rather than the argument itself." Capaldi sees the genetic fallacy as a subtype of ad hominem argument (p. 73) and represents it as a kind of genetic explanation that describes the origin of an event used as a kind of argument. Capaldi (p. 74) cites, as the two most famous cases of genetic explanation, Freudian psychoanalysis and some forms of Marxism. According to these views, Capaldi writes (p. 74), "Different varieties of anxieties and neuroses are identified with traumatic experiences that began in childhood." One difficulty here is distinguishing a difference between an explanation and an argument, and certainly a difference is evident between a genetic explanation and an ad hominem argument.

Byerly (1973, p. 45) defines an ad hominem argument as "an attack on a person's assertion by means of an attack on the person himself." He defines this type of argument in a balanced way and makes it clear at the outset that, in the case of undermining the credibility of a witness's testimony by attacking his character in court, this type of argument could be quite reasonable. Byerly sees the degree to which an ad hominem argument is fallacious as depending upon the relevance of the personal attack to the issue in question (p. 45). He has quite an interesting nonstandard classification of the subtypes of ad hominem argumentation. What he describes as the tu quoque would, in more conventional treatment, be defined by many texts as the circumstantial type of ad hominem. Further, what Byerly describes as the circumstantial type corresponds to what we would define as the bias type.

Byerly divides the ad hominem argument into three subcategories. The first is the abusive type, defined (p. 45) as those kinds of arguments that cite a connection between a person's character and the truth of his statements. According to Byerly (p. 46), the circumstantial type of ad hominem argument occurs when "an opponent's claim is attacked by referring to circumstances likely to prejudice him." He gives the following example of this second type of ad hominem argument:

Case 2.15

We cannot trust Dr. Technak's views on smelter pollution. After all, he is a member of the board of Smoganda Copper Co.

On this case Byerly comments that we generally assume that someone who has an interest in a matter is less likely to speak without bias. So, he seems to be suggesting that this type of bias ad hominem argument can be a reasonable way of evaluating someone's argument. Nevertheless, he adds (p. 46) that this type of argument, which he classifies as circumstantial, is "not at all conclusive." The third type of ad hominem identified by Byerly (p. 46) is the tu quoque, which is said to apply "when someone argues against a practice of which he himself is guilty." The example he gives of this is the following case (p. 46):

Case 2.16

Mr. Lipperty advocates immediate desegregation of the schools, yet he himself sends his son to a private school to avoid the integrated school in his neighborhood.

Byerly describes this case (p. 46) by saying that there is an apparent inconsistency between Mr. Lipperty's advocacy and his deeds. This type of case would normally be classified in textbooks, at least according to the leading standard type of treatment described in chapter 1, under the heading of a circumstantial ad hominem, because of a conflict between the arguer's arguments and his own practices, a pragmatic inconsistency. It is curious, however, that Byerly calls this the tu quoque type of ad hominem argument. We seem to have come full circle here—the circumstantial, tu quoque, and bias classifications are in complete confusion, as we go from text to text.

The third type of ad hominem identified by Byerly (p. 46) is the tu quoque, as noted in chapter 1. Another type of argument treated is called "poisoning the wells," but it is not treated as a subcategory of ad hominem fallacy. Instead, it is treated as a special type of genetic fallacy.

The classification of subtypes of ad hominem arguments given by Carney and Scheer (1974, pp. 22–24) is somewhat similar to that of Byerly. Carney and Scheer distinguish between a type of ad hominem used to criticize an arguer's character and another type defined as appealing to the special circumstances of an arguer. They do not use the terms "abusive" and "circumstantial" to make this distinction. Also, the examples they give of the special circumstances type seem to be cases in which biases are involved. A good instance is the following case (p. 23):

> *Case 2.17*
>
> Air Force General "Flip-Flop" Herbert has testified in favor of our starting to manufacture the new RS-1099E. In fact it is his view that it would be absolutely disastrous to our defenses if we do not immediately start building these bombers in great quantity. But his views are ridiculous and are nothing more than the expression of ruthless self-interest. For in two months General Herbert will retire and become a high-level executive and stockholder in the bomber division of General Juggernaut Corporation—the very people who will build the RS-1099E.

In this case, it is argued that General Herbert's views about this particular project are "ridiculous" because of his financial connection with the company that makes a profit out of this particular item. Carney and Scheer note that this would be a reasonable type of argument in the sense that "this knowledge about the General's new job would certainly be a good reason to examine the evidence for and against his views." So, this type of argument, which they call the *special circumstances* subtype of ad hominem argument, seems to be really the bias type. It is interesting that Carney and Scheer see it as, in some but not all cases, a reasonable type of argument that can be used nonfallaciously in evaluating a person's views.

Kaminsky and Kaminsky (1974) describe argumentum ad hominem in a way that makes it fallacious and that distinguishes three subtypes. They also treat the fallacy of poisoning the well but treat it separately from ad hominem. According to Kaminsky and Kaminsky (p. 45), the argumentum ad hominem "is a fallacious kind of reasoning employed by the speaker or writer who is *solely* concerned with attacking his opponent rather than with the argument required to prove the truth of his conclusion." Note that the word "fallacious" actually occurs right in the definition, making it absolutely clear and leaving no doubt that this type of argument is fallacious.

Kaminsky and Kaminsky define the abusive type of ad hominem in the usual way but define the circumstantial ad hominem in an unusual way. According to their definition (p. 45), when the circumstantial ad hominem occurs, "an individual gives reasons why his opponent should accept a conclusion rather than reasons that prove the conclusion to be true." The fallacy here seems to be that of giving an argument that is not conclusive enough. No mention at all is made of any kind of pragmatic inconsistency that would normally be the criterion of the circumstantial type of ad hominem argument. The example Kaminsky and Kaminsky give (p. 45) is a Lockean case of the ex concessis type of ad hominem, but it may also have elements of poisoning the well and guilt by association.

Case 2.18

Priest: I do not believe that the state should provide public aid to parochial schools.
Congressman: But you are a Catholic and your schools need money, and certainly your religion requires you to support the bill for financial aid to Catholic schools.

In this type of case, there seems to be no circumstantial inconsistency of the type normally held to be characteristic of the circumstantial ad hominem. Instead, it is simply a case in which the congressman is trying to use the priest's position or religious affiliation in order to claim that he should take a particular view; the congressman is using this view to try to get the priest to agree on or to undertake a certain course of action. As Kaminsky and Kaminsky put it (p. 46), the congressman "uses the personal circumstance of the priest's religion to coerce him into acceptance of the bill." The description is perhaps why Kaminsky and Kaminsky classify this case as circumstantial. However, we would use the word "position" here in the sense of the arguer's position or commitments rather than the term "circumstance" (Walton, *Arguer's Position*, 1985).

Kozy (1974) distinguishes two subtypes of ad hominem argument: the abusive and the circumstantial (pp. 210–14). An interesting aspect of Kozy's treatment of argumentum ad hominem, however, is that he explicitly states that not all ad hominem arguments are fallacious. Some ad hominem arguments are described by Kozy (p. 215) as "valid" or reasonable.

Annis (1974) does not use the terms "abusive" or "circumstantial" but distinguishes three subtypes of ad hominem argument, two of which would correspond to these traditional categories. The first type he distinguishes (p. 89) is when one arguer attacks another's character. The second type (p. 90) is when one arguer attacks the proposal of another on the basis of the first party's interests, that is, something that the first party has to gain by the acceptance of this proposal. Annis does not use the term "bias" or call this the bias type of ad hominem, but it is clear from his example and his use of the word "interest" that this is the subtype to which he refers. Then, third, Annis distinguishes (p. 90) a type of ad hominem characterized by the claim that an arguer's actions are inconsistent with his beliefs. This subtype would correspond to what is normally called the circumstantial type in other textbooks, according to chapter 1.

The ad hominem argument is described as generally fallacious by Barry (1976, p. 236) and is defined as the type of argument in which "we attack someone's personality rather than his argument." In such a case, we are said by Barry (p. 236) to be "guilty of an *ad hominem* appeal." One common variation of the ad hominem fallacy cited is the fallacy of guilt by association. Barry (p. 237) cites this fallacy as occurring in the use of such political labels as "liberal," "conservative," "radical," "progressive," "revisionist," and so forth.

Munson (1976, p. 286) describes the ad hominem as definitely a fallacious type of argument. According to Munson, the ad hominem is a "sophistical" argument that "consists in attributing unfavorable characteristics to the person who has made an assertion and, on this ground, rejecting the assertion" (p. 286). He goes even further in making clear that the ad hominem is generally fallacious by stating its fallaciousness in the form of the following general principle: "It's a fundamental principle of rational argument that a claim must be evaluated on the basis of the reasons and evidence offered for its support and not on the basis of the characteristics of the person who makes it" (p. 287). Note that Munson, as do some of the others, labels as the circumstantial ad hominem the type of argument we would call the bias type. As an example of the circumstantial ad hominem argument, Munson (p. 287) gives the following case:

Case 2.19

You have heard Clore tell you that the oil industry is doing all it can to preserve and protect the environment. To put the lie to this statement, I need only tell you something you probably don't know: Clore is an employee of the American Petroleum Institute, an organization supported by the oil companies.

This is a clear case of the bias type of ad hominem argument, by the standards of chapter 1, but Munson classifies it as circumstantial. By now the reader must be thoroughly confused. It seems that every classification, even in clear cases, is contradicted by the classification of some other textbook.

Thomas (1977, p. 201) describes the argumentum ad hominem as a subcase of the genetic fallacy: "This fallacy occurs when someone argues against a claim or position by attacking its holder(s) in logically irrelevant ways." This description of the argumentum ad hominem makes it clear that Thomas defines it specifically as a fallacy. Even so, he (p. 201) acknowledges exceptions to this rule and states that the argumentum ad hominem can be a nonfallacious type of argument in some cases, citing the usual type of case of someone who is testifying as a witness but whose credibility is questioned on the grounds that he or she may be motivated, for example, by prospects of personal gain (p. 201).

Runkle (1978, p. 285) describes the argumentum ad hominem as "attacking one's opponent instead of his argument," and writes that an alternative term for this type of argument is "poisoning the well." This is highly unusual because Runkle is identifying the generic category of ad hominem argument with the label of poisoning the well. Under the heading of a second type of ad hominem argument, according to Runkle (p. 285), "a speaker does not directly attack his opponent but points out the circumstances that his opponent is in and suggests that his views are a product of those circumstances." This subtype sounds as if it could be the circumstantial ad hominem argument but, in fact, the example Runkle gives (p. 286) makes it clear that it is the bias type of ad hominem argument to which he refers.

Case 2.20

A school teacher argues for increased pay for school teachers and a critic attacks his argument by replying, "Sure! It's easy to see why *you're* in favor of a raise!"

Runkle describes this case (p. 286) by noting that the respondent is "suggesting that the teacher's point of view is simple bias." Although Runkle does not explicitly call this bias type of argument the circumstantial species of ad hominem, nevertheless, by using the word 'circumstances' to describe the defining feature of this subtype, he identifies this particular subtype as relating to the circumstances of the arguer.

7. Nonstandard Systems of Classification

This group shows a much more serious effort to classify subtypes. However, not only do the proposed systems flatly disagree with each other, but many of them are go-it-alone, nonstandard schemes. Classification seems to be going from bad to worse.

Toulmin, Rieke and Janik (1979) define the argument against the person as "the fallacy of rejecting the claims a person advances simply on the basis of derogatory facts (real or alleged) about the person making the claim." They describe three forms of this fallacy. The first, they call "name calling" (p. 173). The second type of ad hominem, they call "guilt by association" in which "we try to refute a claim by associating the claimant with a discredited *group* of persons" (p. 173); they use the example of discrediting someone's view by calling him a Communist. The third type is the instance of assuming "that all members of any group are interchangeable . . . so that it is assumed that by the very nature of the group, anyone who belongs to it simply cannot—with all the good will in the world—treat the given question objectively" (p. 173). This description sounds as if it could be the bias type of ad hominem or the poisoning the well type, or perhaps it could be a combination of both—a poisoning the well type of argument that is a species of bias argument. Their example (p. 173) certainly resembles a case in which bias is a central feature.

Case 2.21

It is argued that a historian's interpretation of Luther is incorrect "merely by virtue of the fact that the historian happens to be Roman Catholic."

According to Toulmin, Rieke, and Janik (p. 173), "This argument assumes that Roman Catholics are incapable of viewing the Protestant Reformation (more specifically, Luther) without bias." So this clearly is a case of bias allegation, and the use of the word "incapable" suggests also that it could be a poisoning the well type of bias that is alleged. Yet the authors classify it as a case of the guilt by association type of ad hominem.

Despite the way Toulmin, Rieke, and Janik classify these various subspecies of ad hominem, the poisoning the well or bias type (their third type) is really a special case or subspecies of their second type, which is the guilt by association or group ad hominem attack subtype. This is a novel system of classification and does point to an interesting kind of link between the poisoning the well type of ad hominem argument and the group attack type.

Crossley and Wilson (1979) have a simple two-part classification of the ad hominem argument—abusive and circumstantial. They define the abusive ad hominem (p. 42) as involving "personal attacks on an opponent's character, ethnic origins, or other irrelevant features, rather than investigations into and evaluations of the truth and logical coherence of the argument presented by that person." This definition automatically makes it a fallacious type of argument. The second category of ad hominem argument they describe (p. 43) is called the circumstantial ad hominem, but the cases that illustrate this type make it clear that elements of bias are involved, in that a strong element of interest or having something to gain is included. Crossley and Wilson (p. 43) define the circumstantial type as the kind of case in which "the opponent's personal or professional standing is cited as a reason for discounting his or her argument," and they give the following example:

Case 2.22

It is clearly fallacious to argue that we ought to reject the union negotiators' proposal for a shortened work week simply on the grounds that this is the type of proposal one might expect from the union's representatives.

Crossley and Wilson describe this type of argument as fallacious because the proposal might be supported by good reasons and, by discounting it, we are disregarding these reasons (p. 43). What is notable about this case, however, is that the union negotiators' proposal is being rejected or its credibility is being lessened or questioned at least partly on the grounds that they have something to gain or an interest at stake with respect to the proposal in question. Hence, it would seem natural, or more natural perhaps, to classify this type of case as an instance of the bias type of ad hominem.

Damer (1980) has quite a standard classification in that he distinguishes four types of arguments: the abusive ad hominem, the circumstantial ad hominem, the poisoning the well type of argument, and the tu quoque argument. He appears to treat the latter two as separate fallacies, however, so that his two subclassifications of the ad hominem would be the abusive and circumstantial. He defines the abusive ad hominem as a fallacy of relevance (p. 79), and he explicitly defines it as a fallacy. The circumstantial ad hominem fallacy (p. 80) is defined as consisting in "urging an opponent to accept a particular position by appealing to his or her special circumstances or self-interest." The inclusion of the notion of interest here is somewhat curious and nonstandard. It is not the bias type of ad hominem argument that is involved because it is not a kind of case in which one party is attacking the argument of the other party by claiming that the other has some kind of interest at stake that would constitute a bias. Instead, what Damer has in mind is the kind of case in which one party is trying to get the other party to agree to some policy or conclusion by arguing that it is in that first party's interest to do so, as in the following (p. 80):

> *Case 2.23*
>
> Example: "I really don't see how you can favor no-fault automobile insurance. A large part of your law firm's business comes from cases involving auto accidents. In fact, I wouldn't be surprised if it weren't accident-related cases that are keeping us lawyers in business." One lawyer is here attempting to appeal to another on the basis of the other's self-interest. No consideration at all is given to the worth of the program of no-fault insurance itself.

The problem with this kind of case is that it does not really seem to be an ad hominem argument or certainly not one of the standard type. In an ad hominem argument, the normal pattern is that the critic is attacking an arguer by appealing to some negative aspect of that arguer's circumstances or character. In this case, it is quite a different sort of argument in which one lawyer is trying to get the other to agree to a kind of policy by pointing out that it would be in that other lawyer's best interest to do so. This is a kind of appeal to self-interest and therefore is related in a way to the bias type of ad hominem argument, but it seems somewhat questionable to classify it as an ad hominem argument at all.

Damer (p. 81) describes the poisoning the well fallacy as "rejecting a claim defended by another because of that person's special circumstances or improper motives or because of a negative evaluation of that person." This broad category perhaps would be more indicative of what would usually be called the circumstantial type of ad hominem argument, but it would include characteristics of what many textbooks classify under the abusive type of ad hominem argument as well. Damer does add (p. 82) that a characteristic of the poisoning the well type is that it "damns the source" so that "nothing that comes from that source will be or can be regarded as worthy of serious consideration." His example (p. 82) does clearly bring out this feature of the special characteristic of the poisoning the well subtype of ad hominem argument.

> *Case 2.24*
>
> "You're not a woman, so anything you might say about abortion is of no significance." The special circumstance of not being a woman should not preclude a male from presenting a position on the question of abortion that is worthy of serious consideration.

In this case, the special characteristic of the poisoning the well type is clearly indicated because of some feature of the person that this person cannot change—the feature of gender. This feature is taken as excluding the person from having any right to say anything at all so that, in effect, anything this person says is automatically discounted. The source is damned or discredited, as it were, which is the characteristic of this type of argument.

Finally, Damer distinguishes the tu quoque subtype as "responding to an attack on one's ideas or actions by accusing one's critic or others of thinking or acting in a similar way or a way that is equally hard to defend" (p. 83). This seems to be a fairly standard account of the tu quoque argument except that under this heading Damer also treats cases in which a critic points out inconsistencies between what a person says and what he or she does (p. 83). Although this type of argument is highly characteristic of what is normally called the circumstantial type of ad hominem, Damer includes it under the heading of the tu quoque argument—definitely a nonstandard approach to a system of classifying ad hominem arguments.

Fearnside (1980, p. 8) classifies the ad hominem argument under the heading of "psychological fallacies." Fearnside's definition of the ad hominem argument makes it clear that this is a fallacious type of argument: "A personal attack seeks to discredit the source of argument by charging personal shortcomings that are irrelevant to the issue to be decided." Thus, Fearnside defines ad hominem argument or personal attack—the two are said to be equivalent (p. 8)—as an inherently fallacious type of argumentation. He classifies the ad hominem argument as a subspecies of a fallacy he calls "damning the origin," defined (p. 9) as follows: "Damning the origin is to claim that the origin of an argument is unimpressive, with the suggestion that it should not be accepted for this reason." This type of argument would be what other texts call the genetic fallacy.

In a somewhat nonstandard type of classification of the ad hominem argument, Engel (1982) distinguishes between the abusive and nonabusive categories, and then, under the nonabusive, he has three subcategories: the circumstantial ad hominem, the tu quoque, and the genetic fallacy. When Engel defines the circumstantial type of ad hominem (p. 169), it is clear that it would come under the heading of what is normally (see chapter 1) called the bias type of argument, as Engel defines it in terms of vested interests. Engel's definition (p. 169) of the circumstantial form of the nonabusive ad hominem, or personal attack, is the "attempt is made to undercut an opponent's position by suggesting that, in advancing the views in question, that individual is merely serving his or her own interests." He gives the following case (p. 169) to illustrate this type of argument:

Case 2.25

Someone making use of the circumstantial form might point out, for example, that a manufacturer's argument in favor of tariff protection should be rejected on the ground that, as a manufacturer, the individual would naturally favor a protective tariff; or that a proposed rent increase must be unjustified because no tenant supports it.

Engel classifies this as a fallacy (p. 169) because it offers only "reasons for expecting that one's opponent might view" a conclusion in a certain way rather than offering reasons for the conclusion as being true or false. He classifies the genetic fallacy (p. 170) as "a further variant of the nonabusive form of the personal attack fallacy." The tu quoque species of ad hominem argument is defined (p. 171) as the type of fallacious personal attack "in which the person advocating a position is charged with acting in a manner that contradicts the position taken." So, what Engel calls the tu quoque fallacy would normally be taken according to the more standard treatment of the ad hominem as the paradigm case of the circumstantial type of ad hominem that has a pragmatic inconsistency. In fact, the case Engel gives of this is a classic type of case that has been typified in Walton (*Informal Logic*, 1989, pp. 141–42) as being the circumstantial ad hominem subtype—the classic smoking case discussed in chapter 1. Engel's version of it (p. 171) is the following:

Case 2.26

Look who's telling me to stop smoking? You smoke more than I do.

As we have seen, this example is the typical type of case having a practical inconsistency: the person says one thing, but his critic, using the circumstantial type of ad hominem attack, points out that his personal practice in fact contradicts what he is saying. Indeed, as clear evidence that it is this sort of ad hominem attack that Engel has in mind, he uses the phrase "practice what they preach" to describe this type (p. 171).

Cederblom and Paulsen (1982, p. 108) distinguish between the abusive and the circumstantial forms of the fallacy of attacking the person. In this respect, their treatment of the ad hominem fallacy is standard and straightforward. In describing the fallacy generally, however, they make an interesting link between the ad hominem argument and the quarrel. According to their account (p. 105), the ad hominem fallacy is an effective type of argumentation because "it identifies a person as a common enemy—someone it would be satisfying to defeat—and it associates a certain point of view with this enemy" (pp. 105–6). This account suggests the group attack type of ad hominem, but it also indicates the presence of an element of the quarrel implicit in ad hominem argumentation; this element is what makes the ad hominem effective as a tactic in persuading another party.

Johnson and Blair (1983) have quite a different analysis of the ad hominem fallacy and define it as attacking a wrong or incorrect version of the other party's position. This account makes the ad hominem argument comparable to the straw man fallacy in that both are based on the concept of the arguer's position and both are fallacies in virtue of their misrepresentation of the other party's position in a dispute. Johnson and Blair (p. 79) characterize the argumentum ad hominem by two conditions. The first condition is that two parties are engaged in argumentation and one responds to a position the other has taken by attacking the person rather than by attacking that position. The second is that the attack on the person is not relevant to the assessment of that position. What this analysis implies is that the argumentum ad hominem is a fallacy of relevance because the arguer, when he commits this fallacy, attacks the other party personally instead of attacking the other party's position, the latter being what he should really be doing. Johnson and Blair add, however (p. 80), that it is "difficult to come up with a rule of thumb for distinguishing legitimate from illegitimate criticisms of a person when the dispute is over a position." They concede that not all ad hominem arguments are fallacious. It depends on whether or not the argument is relevant—that is, whether or not the person's character or something about him that has been personally criticized is relevant to the position in the case in dispute. Johnson and Blair conclude that in evaluating ad hominem arguments one has to judge each case on its merits (p. 80).

Halverson (1984) describes the ad hominem argument as the fallacy that "occurs when someone who wishes to oppose a certain view attempts to discredit the person who holds the view rather than assessing the merits of the view itself." This way of defining the argumentum ad hominem makes it generally fallacious and makes it a fallacy of relevance. Halverson distinguishes three subspecies of the ad hominem: the abusive, the circumstantial, and the tu quoque. Also, the genetic fallacy is said to be similar to the ad hominem argument. The abusive form is defined (p. 58) as a kind of attack on character that attempts to arouse negative feelings to transfer these negative feelings to the view held by the arguer. The description of the circumstantial type of ad hominem argument given by Halverson (p. 59) makes it sound more Lockean in nature. He maintains that a circumstantial argument against a person occurs if "the object is to discredit a person's views by suggesting that the circumstances of that person's life are such that he or she could be expected to hold exactly those views." This account of the circumstantial type makes no mention of an inconsistency, but it does sound at least similar to the ex concessis type of ad hominem. However, the leading example given by Halverson (p. 59) appears to fit more into the category of the bias type of ad hominem argument.

Case 2.27

Suppose, for example, that a researcher, Dr. X, claims to have found evidence that, contrary to the findings of other researchers, there is no causal link between cigarette smoking and lung cancer. To argue against this finding on the grounds that "Dr. X's family has been in the tobacco-growing business for many years; moreover, his research was financed by the tobacco industry" would be to present an argument containing this kind of fallacy.

In this case, the argument is supposedly fallacious. The basis of the ad hominem allegation is presumably that Dr. X has something to gain by promoting the thesis that there is no causal link between cigarette smoking and lung cancer because his family has been in the tobacco-growing business for many years and because his research is financed by the tobacco industry. Both these reasons suggest that Dr. X advocates a particular thesis partly because he has something to gain by doing so. So, this would normally be classified as a bias type of ad hominem argument, even though Halverson classifies it as circumstantial.

The account given by Halverson of the tu quoque variant is also, in certain respects, nonstandard. Halverson defines the tu quoque as the form of ad hominem argument that "consists in an attempt to defend oneself against some accusation by making a countercharge against one's accuser, the purpose being to shift the discussion from one's own alleged misdeeds to those of one's accuser" (p. 59). This interpretation of the tu quoque fallacy makes it essentially similar to what is typified in chapter 1 as the two wrongs fallacy. The example that Halverson gives is also interesting (p. 59):

Case 2.28

Mary: Oh, John, have you started smoking again? You know that before your surgery the doctor said that your system just couldn't stand any more nicotine.

John: *You're* a fine one to talk! Why, I'll bet you're forty pounds overweight. What does the doctor think about that?

Halverson diagnoses the fallacy here by commenting that "Mary's weight problem has nothing to do with whether or not it is inadvisable for John to resume smoking" (p. 60). The failure, so conceived, is one of irrelevance. This is quite a different interpretation of the tu quoque argument because usually the tu quoque argument is characterized as the kind of counteraccusation in which one person puts forward a particular type of argument and then a second person replies with the same type of argument. Nevertheless, in this case, although it is the same type of argument, what seems to characterize the you-too aspect of it is that both of the criticisms relate to health problems, and in both cases the upshot of the argument is to make the person criticized appear to be guilty for some action that is supposed to be culpable or unhealthy. So, when Mary attacks John on the subject of smoking, he turns around and attacks her on the somewhat unrelated problem of her being overweight. What is similar here, or what makes it a tu quoque, is not just that the same type of argument is used but that the subject matter is somewhat parallel and that the nature of the culpability in both cases—the failure to live a healthy life—is analogous. The account given of the tu quoque here is also somewhat nonstandard because it is described as essentially being a fallacy of irrelevance whereas the purpose is to shift the discussion from one's own alleged misdeeds to those of the other party.

The classification of ad hominem arguments given by Wesley Salmon (1984) differs from most texts and is unusual. He describes the ad hominem argument as a kind of converse of appeal to authority, and he also describes another type of ad hominem as a type of argument from negative consensus. Salmon defines the argument against the person (p. 101) as "a type of argument that concludes that a statement is false because it was made by a certain person." According to this definition, the argument against the person is not necessarily a fallacious type of argument.

Salmon goes on to define the argument against the person as related to the argument from authority—a negative type of argument as contrasted to the argument from authority that is positive in nature. According to Salmon (pp. 101–2), in the argument from authority, the fact that a particular person asserts a proposition is taken as evidence that this proposition is true. In contrast (p. 102), in the argument against the person, the fact that a certain person asserts a particular proposition is taken as evidence that this is false. So, the argument against the person is a kind of negative variant of the argument from authority. Salmon carries this contrast even further (p. 102) by introducing the concept of a *reliable anti-authority*: "A reliable anti-authority about a given subject is a person who almost always makes false statements about that subject." Using this definition, Salmon gives the following form of the argument against the person. *Premise 1:* Person X is a reliable anti-authority concerning proposition P; *Premise 2:* X asserts P; *Conclusion:* Not P, i.e., P is false. Salmon sees this as an inductively correct argument form. In other words, he does not see the ad hominem argument as inherently fallacious—quite the opposite. He sees it as a form of argument that is generally reasonable.

Salmon goes on to add, however (p. 103), that the argument against the person is frequently misused and, when this happens, the failure is a fallacy of relevance in which a critic attempts to arouse negative feelings instead of showing that the person who made the argument really is an anti-authority in Salmon's sense. Salmon sees another variant of the argument against the person as taking the form of a negative argument from consensus (p. 104). In Salmon's account of this type of argument, it starts from a premise that a group has negative prestige and then infers that a conclusion is to be rejected because it is attributed to this group. This appears to be what we have generally classified as the group attack type of ad hominem argument.

Merrilee Salmon (1984) describes the ad hominem fallacy in similar terms. She also (p. 80) sees the ad hominem fallacy as a kind of converse of the argument from authority. According to her analysis, the ad hominem argument starts with an initial premise that states that most of what an individual says about some subject matter is false. It proceeds to a second premise that this individual asserts some proposition in that subject matter, and then it moves to the conclusion that this proposition is false. Essentially, this outline of the form of the argument is indeed similar to the account given by Wesley Salmon (1984). Both these accounts are interesting in that they do attribute a specific form of reasoning as the schema of the argumentum ad hominem and that they share the unusual feature of treating it as a kind of converse of the appeal to authority type of argument.

8. Increased Sophistication

In the next group of treatments, there is an increased level of sophistication, both in awareness of the possibility that the ad hominem can be reasonable and in the familiarity with various sub-types. Nevertheless, this increased sophistication is not matched by any growth of agreement in how to name or classify the subtypes or in how to evaluate ad hominem arguments. The same problems and contradictions persist.

Hoaglund (1984) criticizes the standard treatment of the ad hominem fallacy, and he (p. 98) states that ad hominem fallacies are often analyzed as fallacies of relevance but points out that this analysis is misleading because, in many cases, information about a person can be relevant to evaluating testimony. Hoaglund also warns us (p. 101) that, in some cases, the abusive and circumstantial ad hominem arguments are closely related so that it may be difficult to decide in a particular case which type of ad hominem argument is involved.

Pirie (1985) distinguishes between the abusive and circumstantial categories in fairly standard fashion. According to Pirie, the abusive type of ad hominem argument consists in the use of an insult "calculated to undermine an opponent's argument, and to encourage an audience to give it less weight than it merits" (p. 92). In contrast, the circumstantial ad hominem argument is described (p. 94) as the appeal "to the special circumstances of the person one argues with." This is said to be a fallacy by Pirie because such an argument appeals to the position or interests of the audience instead of trying to prove that the proposition is true or false on the basis of the evidence. This classification combines the usual categories of circumstantial and bias types of ad hominem argument. The examples given by Pirie of the circumstantial ad hominem make it appear that it is the Lockean ex concessis type that he has in mind. For example, in the case below, the appeal is to try to get an opponent to accept a proposition on the grounds that he is somehow committed to that proposition already in virtue of his position or some fact that is already known about his position.

Case 2.29

As an opera lover, you will be the first to agree that we need more subsidy for the arts.

This case appears to have no inconsistency, and the argument is not used to attack the other party by showing that the other party is somehow wrong or guilty of something. Instead, it is an attempt to get the other party to agree to something by appealing to his previous commitments.

Davis (1986, p. 60) describes the argumentum ad hominem in a way that makes it generally fallacious, defining it as the "non sequitur" argument "in which the premises describe someone's personal characteristics, from which the conclusion is drawn that his opinions or reasoning about matters unrelated to himself are fallacious." This definition makes the ad hominem fallacy one of irrelevance and, by using the expression "non sequitur," ensures that such arguments are inherently fallacious. The concept of bias is prominent in Davis's treatment (pp. 61–62). He describes the fallacy of poisoning the well as a separate type of fallacy, as follows: "Forestalling disagreement by positively characterizing those who would agree with the speaker's position or negatively characterizing those who would disagree is called "poisoning the well" (p. 62). According to this account, the fallacy of poisoning the well appears to be closely related to the ad hominem with the added aspect that the element of forestalling disagreement is enhanced.

Waller (1988) emphasizes that ad hominem arguments are not always fallacious. He (p. 97) notes, however, many dangers, confusions, and temptations associated with this type of argumentation. He puts this distinction judiciously in describing the ad hominem fallacy: "The ad hominem fallacy is committed when one fallaciously attempts to discredit an argument by attacking the source of the argument" (p. 98). Here it is clear that the fallacy is being described only as the misuse of the ad hominem argument, and the ad hominem argument itself is not being generally condemned as fallacious. Waller goes on to add (p. 98) that not all uses of the ad hominem argument are fallacious, and he shows in detail (pp. 99–101) how legitimate, relevant, and nonfallacious cases of ad hominem can occur in legal cross-examination of a witness.

Dauer (1989), like Engel, distinguishes between abusive and non-abusive types of ad hominem argument. The abusive subtype is characterized (p. 258) by the use of negative appellations in order to urge rejecting someone's view. The nonabusive form (p. 259) is described as the kind of case in which a party presents a view, but then some other party urges an audience to reject that view because the first party had also accepted some other view compatible with the first view. This account of the nonabusive type of ad hominem argument clearly involves an inconsistency between two views of a speaker. Although one might be generally inclined to typify this as the circumstantial type of ad hominem argument, Dauer does not use the term 'circumstantial' to describe it. He adds, however, that this nonabusive form of the ad hominem argument can be legitimate in some cases (p. 259) and only becomes fallacious when one goes from the criticism of inconsistency to the view that the arguer's conclusion should be rejected. This account is reminiscent of the Barth and Martens analysis.

The account of the ad hominem argument given by Little, Groarke, and Tindale (1989) is similar to that of Salmon in that the ad hominem is described as a negative form of argument from authority (p. 265). One interesting and novel aspect of the account given by Little, Groarke, and Tindale, however, is that the ad hominem argument is described as having a positive form called the *pro homine* (p. 266), in which the positive personal characteristics of a speaker are used as evidence to add to the credibility of his view. They also stress that ad hominem arguments can be reasonable in cases in which an arguer's bias or characteristics do provide some evidence that leads to a legitimate conclusion that his or her views are unreliable. Little, Groarke, and Tindale (p. 269) treat guilt by association as a separate type of fallacy from the argumentum ad hominem.

Bonevac (1990) has an unusual way of classifying the subtypes of ad hominem arguments. He defines the abusive type of ad hominem argument in terms of the concept of insult (p. 47). Then he gives a contrasting definition of the circumstantial type of ad hominem that is quite wide, and under the circumstantial type he includes the tu quoque as a subspecies. Bonevac defines the ad hominem generally (p. 46) as the argument that attempts to "refute positions by attacking those who hold or argue for them." The subspecies called the abusive ad hominem is defined as the kind of case in which the attack consists of "an assault on a person's integrity, moral character, psychological health, or intellectual ability" (p. 46). By contrast, the ad hominem argument is classified as circumstantial if "the attack may consist of a charge of inconsistency or unreliability due to a person's special circumstances" (p. 46). More specifically, Bonevac gives a definition of the abusive ad hominem (p. 47) as one that "purports to discredit a position by insulting those who hold it." This linking the notion of the abusive ad hominem to the concept of an insult is somewhat unusual. One wonders how the concept of an insult might be defined, for purposes of logic. But Bonevac offers no guidance, and the question is left hanging.

The specific definition of the circumstantial ad hominem given by Bonevac (p. 49) is broad: the argument that "purports to discredit a person by appealing to the circumstances or characteristics of those who hold it." In fact, the leading example that Bonevac gives (p. 49) would normally be classified as a case of the bias type of ad hominem.

Case 2.30

People tend to advance arguments of this sort against lobbying groups. The Tobacco Institute, for example, frequently releases reports raising questions about the link between smoking and disease and routinely denounces reports claiming to establish such links. Critics of the Institute often dismiss its statements on the grounds that the tobacco industry funds its research. This is a circumstantial *ad hominem:* The critics charge that the motives of those who pay for the institute's work suffice to discredit it.

In this case, the basis of the criticism is that the Institute is getting funding from the tobacco industry and therefore has a vested interest or something to gain by coming up with a particular conclusion. Although this would normally be classified as the bias type of ad hominem, Bonevac's definition of circumstantial ad hominem is broad enough that it can include this type of case.

Govier (1992) characterizes the ad hominem argument as concluding that a person's position is faulty based on criticizing "a person's personality, background, actions, or situation" (p. 160). According to Govier, this type of argument is "almost always mistaken as far as logic is concerned." Govier distinguishes (p. 161) between the abusive and circumstantial varieties of the ad hominem argument. The abusive type of argument attacks a person "on the basis of the some characteristic" and commits a fallacy of relevance. The circumstantial type of ad hominem, according to Govier, is the kind in which "people are attacked not so much because of their personal traits, but because of their actions or circumstances." She cites the famous smoking case as an example of the circumstantial type: somebody rejects a doctor's argument against smoking on the grounds that the doctor herself is a smoker (p. 161). Although Govier does not demand, in her definition of the circumstantial ad hominem, that there be an inconsistency involved in such an argument, the examples she gives suggest that, generally, an inconsistency is characteristic of this type of argument.

Harrison (1992, p. 507) distinguishes between the abusive and the circumstantial subtypes: an abusive ad hominem "attacks the personal character of the presenter of the original argument," and a circumstantial ad hominem argument "brings into question some particular condition or situation in which the presenter finds herself." This definition of the circumstantial ad hominem is certainly broad enough to include the bias type of argument as well; in fact, Harrison (p. 508) classifies the poisoning the well type of ad hominem argument as a subspecies of the circumstantial type. He describes the poisoning the well variant as a type of argument that "cites some condition or situation of the presenter of an argument in an attack against the proposed argument" (p. 508). He adds, however, that "Often special or vested interests of the presenter are mentioned." It is clear that Harrison includes the bias type of ad hominem argument as at least partly coming under the heading of the poisoning the well.

According to the account given in Hughes (1992, p. 139), the ad hominem fallacy is defined as "committed when the premise of an argument provides information about the author of some statement in an attempt to show that this statement is false, when this information is irrelevant to the truth of falsity of the statement." This account suggests that the ad hominem argument need not always be fallacious; in fact, Hughes (p. 140) does add that not all attacks upon a person's personal qualities are fallacious. Hughes (p. 141) cites the case of assessing the reliability of the testimony of a witness in court as a type of argument that does not commit the ad hominem fallacy, and he also cites the kind of case in which a conflict of interest is used as a basis in politics for arguing against somebody's arguments.

Kahane (1992, p. 57) defines the ad hominem argument as that of attacking an opponent rather than the opponent's evidence and arguments. Although he does not define the ad hominem argument as inherently fallacious, Kahane does treat it under the heading (p. 57) of fallacious reasoning. He recognizes that attacks on character or credentials of a courtroom witness may be cogent, but he does not classify such arguments as being ad hominem: "Lawyers who attack the testimony of courtroom witnesses by questioning their character or expertise are not necessarily guilty of ad hominem argument" (p. 58). According to Kahane, testimony that an expert who testifies in court has been convicted of perjury, or is a professional witness, would be good reason to prefer the opposed opinion of the expert who testifies for the other side. In such a case, Kahane suggests that we do not prove that the expert opinion is incorrect. Instead, the character attack provides grounds only for canceling or disregarding the expert opinion, and that tactic is different from inferring that such an opinion is false (p. 58). So it may be that what Kahane is saying is that, in the case of questioning eyewitness testimony on grounds of character, the argument is not really an ad hominem argument in his sense. Yet, it does seem to fit this definition because, in such a case, one is attacking the opponent (that is, the expert who testifies) rather than the evidence the opponent is presenting. It is not exactly clear what Kahane is saying. Is he saying that, in the case of impeachment of eyewitness testimony, it is not really an ad hominem argument? Or, is he saying that it could be an ad hominem argument, but it is not used to prove that the eyewitness's testimony is false, so it is not really a fallacious ad hominem argument? His view is not too clear from his presentation of this question.

Kahane does not distinguish between the abusive and circumstantial types of ad hominem argument. But he does cite what he calls an important variation on the ad hominem argument: guilt by association (p. 58), which he defines as judging people by the company they keep. Kahane defines the fallacy he calls "two wrongs make a right" as being separate from the ad hominem fallacy. He defines the fallacy of two wrongs make a right (p. 60) as the kind of case in which those who attempt to justify a wrong action charge their accusers with a similar wrong on the grounds that, if the accuser does it, then it must be all right for others to do it. Kahane gives the following example to illustrate the fallacy of two wrongs make a right:

Case 2.31

For example, in 1989, when British Foreign Secretary Sir Geoffrey Howe accused the Soviet Union of selling long-range supersonic bombers and refueling equipment to Libya, Soviet Foreign Minister Edward Shevardnadze committed this fallacy when he tried to justify these dealings by pointing out that Britain had sold arms to Middle Eastern countries. His reasoning was fallacious because Britain's actions did not excuse the Soviet arms sales.

Kahane makes no further comment on this example, but Shevardnadze's reasoning is supposed to be fallacious, presumably because instead of justifying the Soviet arms sales, he merely hit the ball back into the court of his opponents by accusing the British of having done something comparable in the past. It is difficult to distinguish between the two wrongs make a right fallacy in this case and what is usually called the tu quoque type of ad hominem argument, and this appears to be a serious problem. Are there two fallacies here, or are they two aspects of the same kind of argument, or are they really just the same kind of fallacy with two different names? Or was Shevardnadze's reply even an ad hominem fallacy at all? Was it a personal attack on Howe or merely an irrelevant reply, a red herring used to shift the discussion onto a different issue?

Kahane goes on to point out that the two wrongs fallacy seems plausible because it does resemble another kind of argument that is reasonable in many cases. He calls this type of argument "fighting fire with fire" (p. 60). He gives the following example:

Case 2.32

A good example is the killing of someone in self-defense: We're justified in fighting one evil (the taking of our own life) with what would otherwise be another evil (the taking of our attacker's life).

Kahane concludes that the fallacy of two wrongs is not automatically committed every time one apparent wrong is justified by citing an opponent's comparable wrong; he adds that the key question in separating out the fallacious from the nonfallacious types of cases is "whether the second wrong indeed is necessary to fight or counteract the first" (p. 60). However, there are serious questions about this approach.

One problem is whether what is described is really a logical fallacy or some sort of ethical problem. Indeed, it is well known that the problem of self-defense is a very difficult type of case because whether or not self-defense is justified by citing a comparable case is something that can be decided only in a case-by-case basis using a complicated set of criteria. In fact, the problem of self-defense is quite a serious legal problem in criminal defenses, just because of all these ethical ramifications. So, some problems may occur here in defining or attempting to define this type of argument as a logical fallacy.

The general problem with this way of construing the two wrongs fallacy is that it is not clear whether it is an ad hominem argument at all. In case 2.32, the reply based on self-defense appears to be a denial that the act was blameworthy. Is that an ad hominem argument? It does not seem to be. It seems much more care is needed if the two wrongs fallacy is to be analyzed as being a species of ad hominem argument. This lesson will need to be kept in mind when the two wrongs argument is analyzed in chapter 6.

Another serious problem with Kahane's account concerns the connection between the two wrongs fallacy and the circumstantial ad hominem fallacy. Kahane adds (p. 60) that the fallacy of two wrongs often seems plausible because it also bears a similarity to a kind of argument that is used to imply that one's opponent is being hypocritical. The example he gives (p. 60) is that the town drunk is not the appropriate person to tell us that we have had one too many drinks. In other words, Kahane is saying here that sometimes such allegations of inconsistency in citing the hypocrisy of an arguer are reasonable kinds of arguments. Calling this case an instance of the two wrongs fallacy, however, is a nonstandard approach because, normally, this type of argumentation would be the classic case of the circumstantial type of ad hominem argument (following the paradigms set out in chapter 1, adhered to by many of the texts cited above). It would seem, judging from this example at any rate, that Kahane thinks somehow that the two wrongs fallacy is closely related to the ad hominem argument and, in particular, the circumstantial type.

9. Persistence of the Problems

One might hope that the most recent textbook accounts would include some movement toward consistency in the treatment of the ad hominem and would have at least a convergence toward some sort of consistency in terminology and classification of subtypes. However, this movement forward has not taken place.

In fact, we see the problems and disagreements becoming even more exacerbated. The circumstantial subtype is defined in terms of bias. A paradigm case normally classified as circumstantial (according to the sketch of classic cases outlined in chapter 1) is repeatedly labeled a tu quoque. Nonstandard concepts such as "insult" are used to define the abusive subtype. Some texts persist in defining argumentum ad hominem as inherently fallacious.

Soccio and Barry (1992, p. 125) define the personal attack or ad hominem type of argument as occurring "whenever we attack a person instead of his or her argument." They define this as a fallacy, writing that whenever we so attack a person, we commit a form of fallacy known as personal attack or ad hominem. So, then, they specifically define a fallacious personal attack (pp. 125–26) as "an argument that claims to be a refutation of an opponent's argument when it in fact attacks the person." What this kind of definition appears to deny is the possibility that attacking an opponent can be a way of attacking or even refuting that opponent's argument. This denial seems a little dubious, especially in cases like that cited by Fitch where the ad hominem attack does in fact seem to be quite a decisive and conclusive refutation of an opponent's argument as stated.

Soccio and Barry distinguish between the character assassination type of ad hominem and circumstantial personal attack (p. 126), but in their treatment they emphasize the group attack type of ad hominem argument as well as the bias type of ad hominem (p. 127). They treat the tu quoque as yet another category of personal attack (p. 128).

The account by Soccio and Barry (1992) is one of those interesting cases of a textbook that defines the circumstantial type of ad hominem argument in terms of bias. What we would call the bias type of ad hominem argument is classified by them or identified with them as being the circumstantial type. According to their account (p. 126), "A circumstantial personal attack is an argument that rejects an opponent's argument solely on the basis of possible bias due to some aspect of the opponent's personal life." It is curious, however, that they define this type of fallacy as a kind of reverse false authority fallacy (p. 127) in a way very similar to that of Salmon. Their comments on the fallacy do stress the group attack type of ad hominem, as noted: "Whenever we uncritically reject others' arguments *only on the basis of their membership in a group*, we are in danger of committing a circumstantial personal attack" (p. 127). So, this is definitely a case of what we would normally call the group attack type of ad hominem, usually covered under the category of guilt by association (as identified in the paradigms set out in chapter 1 and as will be classified in the analysis in chapter 6).

Finally, their treatment of the circumstantial ad hominem also stresses the aspect of bias as you might expect inasmuch as they define the whole ad hominem category in terms of bias. They give the following example (p. 127):

> *Case 2.33*
>
> Someone rejects a teacher's argument for an increased allotment of funds for education *because he or she is involved in education.*

Soccio and Barry write that this form of circumstantial attack is based on the observation that people are often biased so that they do favor what is to their advantage (p. 127). Presumably, then, when a critic observes this bias, he takes it as an indicator that we ought to reduce the degree of credibility that we should attach to such a person's opinion because if that person has something to gain, he or she is probably inclined to be biased and to give that opinion more credibility than should really be attached to it.

Interestingly, Soccio and Barry (pp. 128–29) treat the tu quoque and the two wrongs make a right fallacies as being two separate categories. They define the tu quoque personal attack (p. 128) as "an argument that rejects advice or criticism solely on the grounds that those giving it don't follow it." The example they give of the tu quoque is in fact the famous smoking case: "How dare you tell me not to smoke! *You* do!" What Soccio and Barry classify here as the tu quoque type of personal attack would be, in the more conventional treatment, the paradigm case of the circumstantial ad hominem argument.

Soccio and Barry (p. 129) describe the fallacy of two wrongs make a right as "an argument that attempts to justify what is considered wrong by appealing to other instances of the same or similar action." They give the example of one person scolding another for ripping the funnies out of the newspaper, and the other party replies that the first person tears the sports section out of the paper. Soccio and Barry see the fallacy here as introducing a premise that is irrelevant to the conclusion because they say "the fact is that two wrongs *don't* make a right" (p. 129). Soccio and Barry (p. 129) give the following case to illustrate the two wrongs make a right fallacy:

Case 2.34

Defenders of President Jimmy Carter's Administration were quick to point out in the wake of Bert Lance's forced resignation as manager of the budget because of banking improprieties (is that doublespeak?) that other presidents had had their "Lances." For example, Lyndon Johnson had Bobby Baker and Dwight Eisenhower had Sherman Adams. So what? That's irrelevant to what Lance did or didn't do and to the aspersions his behavior cast on the Carter Administration.

This case illustrates what they mean when they say that the fallacy here is that of introducing a premise that is irrelevant to the conclusion that is supposed to be proved. Is citing what happened with previous presidents in this case irrelevant, though? It does not seem to be completely irrelevant. It is just a weak kind of argument to cite precedent in this way. So, it may be that the explanation Soccio and Barry give of the two wrongs make a right fallacy is not ultimately satisfactory.

Moore (1993, p. 255) distinguishes between the abusive and tu quoque subtypes of ad hominem fallacy and defines the argumentum ad hominem thus: "The fallacy called *argumentum ad hominem* urges that a claim is false because it came from the lips of a scoundrel." This definition of argumentum ad hominem explicitly defines it as a fallacy. Moore goes on to write that the ad hominem fallacy is "exactly the opposite of the fallacious appeal to authority." Moore's analysis of this type is similar to that of Salmon. Moore explains the fallaciousness of the abusive ad hominem (p. 257) by appealing to the concept of an insult: "In abusive ad hominem arguments, angry insults substitute for reasons." Moore defines the tu quoque type of ad hominem (p. 258) as having the following pattern: "A says to B, you are guilty of C. Instead of responding to the charge directly, B says to A, you are also guilty of C." Moore describes this fallacy as one of irrelevance, claiming that whether the charge is true of one person is logically independent of the question of whether it is true of the other person (p. 258). What Moore defines as the tu quoque type of ad hominem argument would be normally classified or defined in more standard textbook treatments as being the two wrongs make a right fallacy (as indicated in chapter 1).

Kelley (1994) defines the ad hominem argument as the type of argument that "rejects or dismisses another person's statement by attacking the person rather than the statement itself" (p. 139). This definition does make the ad hominem appear to be generally fallacious and, in fact, Kelley explicitly (p. 140) gives an account of the form of the argument as follows: *Premise 1: X* says *p; Premise 2: X* has some negative trait; *Conclusion: p* is false. Here, *X* presumably is a person and *p* is a proposition. Kelley describes this form of argument as "a fallacy because the truth or falsity of the statement itself, or the strength of an argument for it, has nothing to do with the character, motives, or any other trait of the person who makes the statement or argument" (p. 140).

This account, then, makes the ad hominem a fallacy of irrelevance. Is it really true, however, that truth or falsity of the statement itself or the strength of an argument for a proposition has nothing to do with the character, motives, and so forth of the person who makes the statement or argument? In general, this claim does not seem to be true because if the argument in fact was about the person who put forward the argument (and this is possible), then the argument and the strength of the argument would have something to do with the character and so forth of the person who made the argument. In other words, the account of the fallacy given by Kelley claims that all ad hominem arguments of the general form he identifies are irrelevant arguments. This claim is not persuasive because sometimes ad hominem arguments can be relevant and, of course, the kind of case that would normally be cited here would be that of the use of an ad hominem argument in impeachment of a witness's testimony in court by attacking the character of that witness.

Kelley, however, does recognize this difficulty (p. 140) and argues that in such a case "discrediting witnesses or authorities does not provide evidence that what they say is actually false; it merely eliminates any reason for thinking that what they say is true." Kelley's way of dealing with the potential counterexample of the eyewitness testimony type of case is similar to that of Kahane. Kelley simply does not see that in the impeachment of the witness type of case the allegations of character that discredit the witness provide any evidence that what the witness says is false. This reasoning does not seem persuasive either, for when one attacks the character of a witness in court in order to impeach his or her testimony, according to legal principles of evidence, this attack does qualify legally as a type of evidence to the effect that what the witness is saying is not true. At any rate, it gives evidence for doubting the credibility of the witness and presents some reason for conjecturing or thinking that in fact the proposition on behalf of which the witness is testifying may not be true. In other words, it functions as a kind of evidence that is a reason or justification for retracting commitment or reducing credibility in favor of the witness's proposition.

So the eyewitness testimony type of case here, in conjunction with the ad hominem argument as a fallacy, does seem to be a bone of contention in the textbooks. Most textbooks do recognize the problem. They recognize that we have here what appears to be an ad hominem argument that attacks the character of an arguer that is a reasonable kind of argument, but various textbooks have different ways of dealing with this case.

Kelley (1994) links the ad hominem argument to the concept of insult: "In its crudest form, the ad hominem fallacy involves nothing more than insults" (p. 140). He (p. 141) distinguishes the tu quoque argument as a species of ad hominem characterized by the kind of case in which someone who is criticized (for being a notorious liar, for example) turns around and says to his critic, "Look who's talking!" Kelley explains that this is a fallacy because: "The fact that someone else is guilty of an accusation doesn't prove that you are innocent" (p. 141). So this account of the tu quoque fallacy seems to come close to what other textbooks have defined as the two wrongs make a right fallacy.

Kelley also identifies the poisoning the well subspecies of ad hominem fallacy, which he defines as the kind of case in which one person attacks the other by arguing that she has "a nonrational motive for supporting a position" (p. 141). He suggests that having such a non-rational motive does not mean that the position advocated is false so that it would be inappropriate to dismiss such an argument ahead of time once it is discovered that a person has such a motive. Kelley sees the poisoning the well type of fallacy as based on and closely related to allegations of bias. When he describes the type of argument characteristic of the poisoning the well ad hominem fallacy, he uses the expression "vested interest" and also writes about one's judgment being "biased by subjective factors" (p. 142). He sees such allegations of bias as being fallacious because the soundness of an argument "is unaffected by the existence of other motivations" like bias or self-interest (p. 142).

Hurley (1994) distinguishes three subtypes of ad hominem argument: the abusive, the circumstantial, and the tu quoque. He defines the argument against the person generally (p. 120) as the kind of dialogue situation involving two arguers when one of them advances a certain argument "and the other then responds by directing his or her attention not to the first person's argument but to the first person *himself*." Hurley defines the abusive variant of the ad hominem argument (p. 120) as the kind of case where the second person in the dialogue "responds to the first person's argument by verbally abusing the first person." This is interesting because it defines the abusive subtype of ad hominem in terms of a category called "verbal abuse," which is presumably a sort of ethical category of language. When

Hurley gives his explanation of what is wrong with a particular case, however, he describes the abusive ad hominem as a fallacy of irrelevance, claiming (p. 121) that the personal characteristics cited are "irrelevant to whether the premises of his arguments support the conclusion." On these grounds, Hurley describes the abusive ad hominem argument as a fallacy. This is the dubious "apodictic" claim of irrelevance once again.

Hurley (p. 121) defines the circumstantial ad hominem argument as the kind of case in which "instead of heaping verbal abuse on his or her opponent, the respondent attempts to discredit the opponent's argument by alluding to certain circumstances that affect the opponent." The illustration Hurley gives of the circumstantial ad hominem argument is interesting because it definitely does cite a factor we could call circumstances, yet it could also function as an illustration of the bias type of ad hominem argument.

Case 2.35

Bill Gates has argued at length that Microsoft Corporation does not have a monopoly on computer disc operating systems. But Gates is chief executive officer of Microsoft, and he desperately wants to avoid antitrust action against his company. Therefore, we should ignore Gates's arguments.

Hurley explains the fallacy in this case by citing the irrelevance of the fact that Gates is affected by the given circumstances to the question of whether his premises support a conclusion. Thus, Hurley sees the circumstantial ad hominem argument as a fallacy of relevance.

This system of classification is especially interesting in light of the fact that he cites as his primary example of the tu quoque argument the classic case of a kind normally cited as the paradigm of the circumstantial type. According to Hurley, the characteristic of the tu quoque subtype is that "the second arguer attempts to make the first arguer appear to be hypocritical or arguing in bad faith" by "citing features in the life or behavior of the first arguer that conflict with the latter's conclusion" (p. 121). So, his description of the tu quoque subtype in fact involves a conflict or practical inconsistency between what the arguer says and what the arguer does. This definition is reflected quite accurately in the example that Hurley gives.

Case 1.12

Child to parent: Your argument that I should stop stealing candy from the corner store is no good. You told me yourself just a week ago that you, too, stole candy when you were a kid.

Hurley comments (p. 122) that the fallacy here is one of relevance because "whether the parent stole candy is irrelevant to whether the parent's premises support the conclusion that the child should not steal candy." His citing of this case is interesting because it is the exact kind of case (for example, the smoking case) that is the paradigm of what is normally called the circumstantial ad hominem argument, yet he defines it as the tu quoque type of ad hominem.

10. General Problems Posed

The variety of treatments, definitions, and classifications of the ad hominem outlined above indicates a serious lack of direction. What is indicated is the lack of basic agreement of a kind based on a body of research on the ad hominem as a distinctive type of argument. Out of the general chaos, however, several distinct, fundamental, theoretical problems are raised.

Because the presumption has emerged from chapter 1 that the ad hominem argument is reasonable in some cases, the first problem is to define its form as a distinctive, reasonable type of argument. The second problem is to devise independent criteria to show, in a given case, where this type of argument has been misused or used fallaciously.

On defining the ad hominem argument, we see that the textbook accounts do generally fit the outline, broadly speaking, of the various subtypes identified in chapter 1—the abusive, the circumstantial, the bias, poisoning the well, and the tu quoque. But a serious problem is posed by the fact that many of them define ad hominem as an inherently fallacious type of argument, while others cite instances of what appear to be ad hominem arguments that are not fallacious. In general, the textbook accounts fall into three categories.

The first category portrays the ad hominem argument as always fallacious. This kind of account either defines ad hominem as a fallacious (or irrelevant) kind of argument or indicates to readers that it is inherently fallacious. Textbooks in this category are Jevons (1883), Mellone (1913), Latta and MacBeath (1956), Schipper and Schuh (1959), Copi (1961), Wheelwright (1962), Rescher (1964), Vernon and Nissen (1968), Kilgore (1968), Olson (1969), Michalos (1970), Kaminsky and Kaminsky (1974), Barry (1976), Munson (1976), Toulmin, Rieke, and Janik (1979), Crossley and Wilson (1979), Damer (1980), Fearnside (1980), Engel (1982), Halverson (1984), Pirie (1985), Davis (1986), Soccio and Barry (1992), Moore (1993), and Kelley (1994).

Contradicting this first group of textbooks, a second group explicitly states that ad hominem arguments are nonfallacious in some cases, for example, in impeachment of a witness during cross-examination in court. These texts include Whately (1870), Read (1901), Black (1946), Beardsley (*Practical Logic*, 1950), Fitch (1952), Chase (1956), Brennan (1957), Fearnside and Holther (1959), Byerly (1973), Carney and Scheer (1974), Kozy (1974), Cederblom and Paulsen (1982), Johnson and Blair (1983), Salmon (1984), Hoaglund (1984), Waller (1988), Dauer (1989), Little, Groarke, and Tindale (1989), and Hurley (1994).

A third group of textbooks treats the ad hominem as a generally fallacious type of argument but somewhat grudgingly admits in passing that ad hominem arguments may not be fallacious in certain special cases. These cases include Creighton (1904), Cohen and Nagel (1934), Werkmeister (1948), Ruby (1950), Blyth (1957), Emmet (1960), Barker (1974), Beardsley (1966), Manicas and Kruger (1968), Kahane (1969), Kreyche (1970), Thomas (1977), Runkle (1978), Bonevac (1990), Govier (1992), Harrison (1992), Hughes (1992), and Copi and Cohen (1994).

These differences pose a fundamental conflict. Clearly part of the problem is that of separating the tasks of defining and evaluating the ad hominem argument. Before approaching the evaluation problem, the ad hominem needs to be identified and defined so it is recognizable as a common type of argument.

To solve this identification issue, the problem of the subtypes must also be tackled. How is the circumstantial subtype supposed to be defined, for example? Generous clues have been supplied in chapter 1, but the textbooks, for the most part, come nowhere near this level of sophistication and clarity.

Because the adjective "circumstantial" can be interpreted in such a broad way, the term can include virtually anything in relation to an arguer and the background of his or her argument. So, this broad interpretation is one major problem. Should we restrict the circumstantial ad hominem to just those cases in which there exists a pragmatic inconsistency or, at least, an allegation that can be analyzed as one turning on a presumption of pragmatic inconsistency? Or, should we allow the concept of circumstantial ad hominem to be interpreted in a much broader way, which could include all kinds of personal circumstances of the arguer? Of course, one broad way—perhaps the broadest way—to characterize ad hominem argumentation generally is the Lockean way of defining an ad hominem argument as any kind of argument in which two parties are engaged in dialogue and one puts forward an argument based on premises that are commitments of the other. The problem with the Lockean definition, as applying to the analysis and evaluation of the ad hominem fallacy as we typically identify it in the logic textbooks, is that it is so broad that it would include all kinds of arguments that normally we would not intuitively classify as ad hominem. It is much broader than the idea of personal attack and also inherently different, it seems.

The ad hominem notion seems to have as its basis in the textbook treatment the idea of personal attack, as noted in chapter 1. That is, this type of argumentation focuses on the person of the other party (paradigmatically, that would be the character of the other party) or something about the personal circumstances of the other party. The Lockean account, which requires only that the premises of an argument be commitments of the other party, does broadly relate to the notion of personal attack because the arguer's commitments do represent the position, that is, the personal position, of the arguer. But yet, the notion of ad hominem attack or ad hominem argument of the kind that generates the sort of fallacy we are concerned with in the textbooks does seem narrower than this account. It seems to be a requirement of this type of personal attack that the argument should focus on the person—that is, centrally the character of the other party—or on something about the personal circumstances of the other party that are related to some kind of personal culpability or relationship to the person. This requirement is not necessarily characteristic of the broad type of Lockean ad hominem argument, in which the other party's commitments that are used as premises in an argument could be propositions on anything—not necessarily anything related to the person or the person's character or anything of that sort but any sort of propositions that the person has previously conceded in the argument.

Judging from the treatment of the ad hominem in the logic textbooks, one can see the pervasive influence of the Lockean account. In fact, many of the textbooks not only gave a Lockean account or used Lockean terms in describing the ad hominem argument broadly but also quoted Locke as their source for defining this type of argumentation. So, this first theoretical problem of the definition of the circumstantial ad hominem is how broad or narrow this category should be. Should it be the broad type of Lockean ad hominem argument that defines the circumstantial? Or, should we add the requirement that a pragmatic inconsistency must be involved, making the circumstantial category much narrower?

The second problem is how to fit in the bias and the tu quoque subcategories. Because the term "circumstance" contained within the term circumstantial ad hominem argument is very broad, it is quite possible to include the bias and the tu quoque variants as subspecies of the same circumstantial type of ad hominem argument. It is clear, for example, that bias, because it is often identified as vested interest or something to gain, does relate to the personal circumstances of an arguer. Consequently, it is possible, it seems, to include the bias subspecies under the category of the circumstantial subspecies and also to include the tu quoque type of argument under the circumstantial category. So, should these two other types of arguments be included as subtypes of the circumstantial ad hominem, or are they separate categories in addition to the circumstantial ad hominem? If we define the circumstantial ad hominem in the narrower way of requiring a pragmatic inconsistency, then both the bias and the tu quoque subtypes would fall outside the circumstantial category as being separate and distinctive types of ad hominem arguments in their own right. But this, too, in view of the treatment of the textbooks seems to be a fairly radical approach because, in particular, the bias type of argument is so often treated as a subspecies of circumstantial ad hominem. In fact, in many of the textbooks, the bias ad hominem is not even identified as a separate category but merely included under the circumstantial ad hominem argument, either as being the circumstantial ad hominem type generally or as being a special subclass of it.

The same problem here applies to the poisoning the well argument, for if poisoning the well is a subspecies of the bias type of ad hominem argument, then the question is whether or not both of these (that is, the bias type and the poisoning the well type) are subcategories of the circumstantial type. Consider the Bob and Wilma case (1.8) as an example. Bob points out that Wilma is on the board of directors of a U.S. Coal Company. In this case then, Bob's claim is that Wilma is biased because she has a vested interest. At any rate, that is one way of describing the ad hominem argument in this case. By this description, it is clear that it is a bias type of ad hominem and, certainly, bias seems to be a central factor in the basic type of ad hominem criticism of Wilma that is being made here in the dialogue. To describe it a different way, however, one could say that Bob is citing some circumstances of Wilma; in fact, the circumstance is in this case that Wilma is on the board of directors of this U.S. Coal Company. Something in her personal circumstance, Bob is saying, should be weighed in relation to her argument that the problem of acid rain is gravely exaggerated. Bob is pointing out this "circumstance" and then using it to suggest that we ought to give less credibility to Wilma's argument because of this "personal circumstance" of hers. Although our inclination is to treat this case as essentially a bias type of ad hominem argument, one can see why this type of argument has generally been classified under the circumstantial heading in the standard treatment in the textbooks. It does seem natural to put this argument in with a lot of others, when the notion of the circumstances of the arguer seems to be the important factor in distinguishing the type of argument involved.

But the concept of circumstance is a broad one. Citing the "circumstances" of an arguer in a given case could involve any kind of pragmatic factor of the argument. This is obviously an extremely inclusive category. But what distinguishes the particular type of argument characteristic of the ad hominem in the Bob and Wilma case is that Bob is citing this particular "circumstance" because it makes evident to the audience that Wilma has something to gain, that she is biased, and that this bias ought to affect how we judge the argument she has put forth on the issue of acid rain.

Another theoretical problem that is made evident by considering the standard treatment of the logic textbooks is the radical inconsistency between two subgroups of types of treatments in the textbooks. These two approaches conflict sharply with each other. The problem here could be called one of the reversal tendency. What some of the textbooks identify as the circumstantial type of ad hominem argument is precisely what others identify as the tu quoque type and vice versa. For example, take a case of the classic type of circumstantial ad hominem argument like the smoking case studied in chapter 1. Many of the textbooks would classify this as a circumstantial type of ad hominem argument, but others identify it as being the example of the tu quoque type. There is definitely a serious terminological confusion, and this failure of consistency of treatment must be confusing indeed to more advanced students, who see that the very same type of case that is classified as circumstantial by one textbook is classified as a leading or illustrative example of the tu quoque by another. This variance needs to be ironed out, resolved, or at least recognized as being a serious theoretical problem.

Another theoretical problem is the definition of the tu quoque type of ad hominem argument itself and the relationship of it to the two wrongs fallacy (which some textbooks call tu quoque). Others would classify the same kind of argument as being two wrongs. In fact, the same fundamental and direct type of conflict is clearly evident here. Some of the leading types of cases were classified as tu quoque by some textbooks and classified by others as instances of the two wrongs fallacy. Considerable confusion generally is evident about the tu quoque category: how it is different from the circumstantial category and the two wrongs category and how these three categories are related or exactly how they should be defined.

These seem to be pervasive general problems, and it is evident from the survey of the textbook treatments that sharp conflicts and flat terminological disagreements are in evidence. In the case of argumentum ad hominem, plenty of evidence suggests an abandonment of Hamblin's term "the standard treatment" in favor of the expression, "the current disarray."

Having gained an orientation from chapters 1 and 2, the reader has now acquired the preparatory historical and critical background for the positive analysis beginning with chapter 3.

3

Commitment and Personal Attack

The textbook treatment poses a dilemma that seems to block further pursuit of the ad hominem as a clearly definable type of argument. On the one side is the ex concessis (Lockean) conception of the ad hominem, which holds a strong place in philosophical tradition as expressing the real nature of ad hominem and which is possible to analyze, along the lines of Barth and Martens. But the realistic cases of the ad hominem argument for the most part stressed in the textbook treatments seem to be a different type of argumentation and treat the ad hominem argument primarily as the use of personal attack in argumentation. On the other side of the dilemma is the apparently insurmountable problem of giving an analysis of personal attack in a form that would be useful for the evaluation of arguments in logic. For, notoriously, in philosophy, attempting to define 'person' has proved difficult and has seemed to take us into the area of ethics and values.

According to Lomasky (1992, p. 953), definitions of 'person' typically display one or more of the following properties:

1. Persons are all and only human beings.
2. Persons are all and only those beings who possess moral standing (or who possess the highest moral standing).
3. Persons are all and only those beings who display attribute F (where F signifies some suitably elevated cognitive ability).

For our purposes of defining the concept of a person that would be useful in identifying ad hominem arguments, property 1 is merely accidental. A participant in a dialogue in which reasoned argument occurs could be a machine (for example, a computer) as well as a human. But properties 2 and 3 are important. Property 2 comes in because ad hominem arguments are based on a premise that the arguer is a dishonest or bad person, that is, a person who cannot be trusted to tell the truth or otherwise to argue in a fair and reliably collaborative way. Property 3 comes in as well because ad hominem arguments also attack an arguer's cognitive skills, for example, the person's ability to handle information intelligently, to draw conclusions where warranted, and to deal with contradictions in a reasonable manner. The concept of person appropriate for understanding ad hominem arguments, therefore, combines a moral and social element with a cognitive element. *Person* in this sense means a participant in argument who is capable of arguing in a coherent, consistent sequence of reasoning and who has commitments and obligations to other persons by virtue of a role that the person has in these relationships. A person who has these properties is someone entitled to respect. The assumption is that a person is a participant in dialogue with another person and can be judged as a credible advocate for his or her argument on the basis of his or her moral standing and cognitive ability, as a credible source who stands behind his or her argument. It seems then that the ad hominem argument involves the idea of an arguer's qualities giving him or her a certain standing or credibility with other persons.

This development poses a problem because the concept of a credible person contained in the concept of personal attack takes us beyond (and is quite different from) the concept of argument from an opponent's commitment as described in the Lockean ex concessis type of argument. The two streams, identified by Nuchelmans so clearly, pose a dilemma that blocks further progress.

Two steps need to be taken to sort out this problem and to give us a useful analysis of the ad hominem argument. One step is to see how far the concept of commitment can take us toward analyzing the concept of a person needed to give a clear account of the structure of the personal attack type of argument. Because this step takes us only so far, a second step will be required. This step, undertaken in chapter 5, is to give an analysis of the concept of a person that is suitable to capture the idea of personal attack as a distinctive type of argument described in the various cases cited in chapters 1 and 2.

The first step taken in this chapter is to utilize Hamblin's concept of commitment, as developed in Walton (*Arguer's Position*, 1985) and Walton and Krabbe (1995), to define a form of argument called *argu-*

ment from commitment that approximates the Lockean ex concessis kind of argumentation (except that the Lockean phrase of the arguer's "own principles or concessions" is replaced by the more precise—and perhaps somewhat different—concept of an arguer's set of commitments in a dialogue). With this definition, we can see that argument from commitment is not the same type of argument as the textbook ad hominem.

The second step is to try to define the form of argument corresponding to the use of personal attack in argumentation, using the cases of ad hominem in chapters 1 and 2 as presenting a target of analysis. This project is carried out in chapter 6. A reconsideration of the three main recognized forms of personal attack—the abusive, the circumstantial, and the bias type—shows that all attempts to capture this concept in the usual frameworks of formal dialogue logic are hopelessly outrun by pragmatic and contextual complications inherent in real cases of ad hominem in arguments. The idea of a person being an entity with a character (including character traits like veracity and prudence) has to be introduced in such a way that an arguer's perceived character in a dialogue affects her credibility to others, which in turn affects how these others ought to evaluate her argument.

1. Argument from Commitment

In using argument from commitment a proponent cites the commitment of the respondent as a reason why he (the respondent) should accept a certain proposition that can be inferred from that commitment. In the following case, Ed has often advocated the communist position in the past.

Case 3.1

Bob: Ed, you are a communist, aren't you?
Ed: Of course. You know that.
Bob: Well, then you ought to be on the side of the union in this recent labor dispute.

In this case, Bob verifies that Ed is committed to the communist position by asking him directly whether or not he is so committed. When Ed answers in the affirmative, Bob goes on to use this concession as a premise in his argument from commitment. The conclusion that Bob draws, and puts to Ed, is that he (Ed) ought to be on the side of the union in a recent labor dispute.

One can see in this case that the argument from commitment is based on a defeasible inference. For it could be that, for some reason, Ed does not side with the union in the case of this particular dispute. Bob is presuming the premise, 'Communists generally side with the union in labor disputes.' It would be fair to say that this generalization is reasonably reliable, but it could be that for some reason this case is the exception to the rule.

In response to the use of the argument from commitment in case 3.1 then, the burden would be on Ed to explain why, in this particular case, even though he admits he is a communist, Ed does not side with the union. He could reply, "Well, yes, normally I support the union, but in this case their demands are unreasonable for such-and-such a reason." By making this type of response, Ed would have replied appropriately to the use of the argument from commitment by Bob.

According to the account given in Walton (*Pragmatic Theory*, 1995, p. 101), the argumentation scheme for the argument from commitment has the following structure, where a is an arguer, and A is a proposition.

AC

a is committed to proposition A (generally, or in virtue of what she said in the past).
Therefore, in this case, a should support A.

In the account given in Walton (*Pragmatic Theory*, 1995, p. 101), three critical questions are cited as matching the argument from commitment.

CQ1

Is a really committed to A, and if so, what evidence supports the claim that she is so committed?

CQ2

If the evidence for commitment is indirect or weak, could there also be contrary evidence, or at least room for the rebuttal that this case is an exception?

CQ3

Is the proposition A, as cited in the premise, identical to the proposition A as cited in the conclusion? If not, what exactly is the nature of the relationship between the two propositions?

Each of these critical questions represents important ways that the argument from commitment could fail to be reasonable as an argument.

With respect to cq1, it is important to note that the evidence to support the claim of commitment could be remote and subject to questioning, in various ways. It could be based on an incident that supposedly happened long ago. It could be based on a second-hand report of this incident. It could be based on an action that may or may not suggest a commitment to *A*, subject to interpretation of the action.

Case 2.29 is an example of argument from commitment, where the premise is that *a* is an "opera lover," implying a commitment to support opera in the form (expressed by the proponent of the argument in case 2.29), "you will be the first to agree that we need more subsidy for the arts." Case 2.29 is an instance of the circumstantial ad hominem, as classified by Pirie. But on the method of classifying these arguments advocated here, case 2.29 will not be classified as an ad hominem argument at all.

2. Relation to Circumstantial Ad Hominem

In case 3.1, Bob might try to make his use of argument from commitment even stronger by closing off (in advance) Ed's possible reply that in this case (for some reason) he does not side with the union, even though he is a communist. Bob might argue as follows.

Case 3.2

Bob: "You admit you are a communist, and you have always supported communism very strongly in the past. Yet, in this case you are not supporting the union cause? Come on, Ed! You can't have it both ways."

In this argument, Bob implies that Ed is inconsistent if he does not follow the communist line by supporting the union. Bob is suggesting that communism is prounion, and therefore if Ed votes against the union, he is in conflict with his commitment to communism.

In the case as outlined above, Bob is using the allegation of inconsistency as a preemptive attack against the possibility that Ed may not side with the union. Nevertheless, this argument from allegation of inconsistency is even more likely to be used in a case in which Ed has in fact taken this course. For example, suppose Ed argues as follows.

> **Ed:** Well, yes, of course I am a communist. But in this case I do not support the union's position because it has gone too far. And that is a bad thing for collective negotiation and for unions generally because the public can see that the union's position is excessive and makes unreasonable demands.

In this case, Ed has actually put forth a justification for his not supporting the union. As a response to this argument, Bob could now bring out his allegation of inconsistency, in order to try to counter Ed's move.

One can begin to see, in a case like this, the relationship between the argument from commitment and the circumstantial ad hominem argument. Bob's argument in case 3.2 seems as if it could be classified as a circumstantial ad hominem argument and would no doubt be so classified by many of the textbook accounts. But is it a circumstantial ad hominem argument? It depends on how this subtype should best be defined. Two approaches are possible. First, the approach that does not classify Bob's argument in case 3.2 as circumstantial ad hominem is outlined.

Bob is implying that Ed is inconsistent or that he would be inconsistent if he persists—as an avowed communist—in being against the union side. But in the case as presented, Bob is not using personal attack to argue that Ed is dishonest, by attacking his character or personal integrity. Is Bob arguing to a third-party audience, "Ed has a bad character for veracity or integrity, so don't believe what he says as credible!" It seems that he is not (although there may be some implicit suggestion of this line of argument in case 3.2). Hence, we can conclude that the argument in case 3.2 is not a personal attack—not a circumstantial ad hominem argument.

Notice also that by the same criterion the child's argument in the smoking case is not an ad hominem either—at least not necessarily, as case 1.5 was presented. The reason is that (at least, as far as we are told, from the information in case 1.5) the child is not making a personal attack against the parent, that is, arguing that the parent's argument is not credible because she is a bad person.

Of course it is possible in both these cases that the allegation of pragmatic inconsistency could be a lead-in to a personal attack ad hominem argument—for example, on the grounds that the proponent is dishonest, hypocritical, confused, illogical, insincere, or whatever. But as things stand, in these cases, there is no definitive evidence that such a personal attack is being made.

The general implications of this viewpoint are quite radical, with respect to the conventional wisdom on the argumentum ad hominem, suggesting that an alternative, less radical approach should also be considered as a possibility.

According to this second viewpoint, any case in which one party in an argument criticizes the other party by claiming that the other party exhibits a conflict or inconsistency in his commitments makes one of two implications: (a) the second party has committed an error that he needs to correct, or (b) he is a kind of hypocrite, or he lacks integrity, because what he advocates in his argument conflicts with what he is really committed to himself, as far as his own personal convictions are concerned. According to this approach, any allegation of inconsistency of commitments by one party against another in an argument exchange like that of a critical discussion does imply, at least indirectly, a personal attack by the one party against the other.

On this second viewpoint, the argument in the smoking case would automatically be a circumstantial ad hominem because the child's allegation of pragmatic inconsistency suggests, by shifting a weight of presumption toward the parent's side in the argument, that the parent either does not know what she is talking about or is deceitful, pronouncing one course of conduct as suitable for someone else but following the opposite course herself. According to this viewpoint, the child's argument in the smoking case does indirectly contain a personal attack, even if the parent's argument is only being questioned rather than repudiated by the child.

Case 3.2 can also be classified as a circumstantial ad hominem, by this viewpoint, insofar as we take it to be part of Bob's argument that Ed has allegedly revealed an inconsistent set of commitments by being for the communist position generally but against it in the particular argument he advocated in this case. Of course, Ed resolved the alleged conflict in his reply, in case 3.3. But in case 3.2, on this view, Bob's citing of an apparent or presumptive inconsistency in Ed's commitments surely does suggest or indirectly imply personal attack, raising questions whether Ed might be confused or dishonest. It could be the source of our problem with case 3.2 that a third viewpoint also needs to be considered. Perhaps Bob is only requesting that Ed clarify his commitments. We could say then that Ed is not really arguing against Bob or against Bob's argument. Instead, he is only trying to get clarification from Bob on what Bob's argument is, prior to arguing against it. This interpretation makes case 3.2 different from the smoking case, with respect to the ad hominem.

This third viewpoint, in turn, suggests a fourth. According to this fourth viewpoint, Bob is arguing that because Ed has committed himself to a contradiction, his justification for his decision not to support the union cause could not possibly be right. According to this viewpoint on case 3.2, what Bob has said is an ad hominem argument of the circumstantial type because Bob is attacking Ed's argument on the basis that it is (or appears to be) inconsistent. Even on this interpretation, however, there is a lingering doubt that Bob's argument is really an ad hominem argument because it is unclear that Bob is alleging that Ed is a bad person as part of the argument. It could be, however, that Bob's argument can be taken to imply that Ed lacks veracity, on the grounds that Ed has contradicted himself. If so, the argument in case 3.2 would qualify as a circumstantial ad hominem.

Whatever decision is taken on case 3.2, it is clear from our analysis of case 3.1, in which no conflict of commitments is cited, and no personal attack is made, that the Lockean ex concessis argument is not an ad hominem argument. This in itself is quite a radical conclusion, going against many of the textbook accounts. What Locke describes is (in our terms) simply use of argument from commitment by one party in a dispute with another party. Moreover the so-called ad hominem type of fallacy described by Barth and Martens is not an ad hominem argument at all. It should be more accurately described as a fallacious use of argument from commitment.

Van Eemeren and Grootendorst (1987, p. 291) describe a fallacy called *absolutizing the success of a defense,* seen by them as a separate fallacy from ad hominem:

concluding that a standpoint is true because it has been successfully defended against the opposition of the antagonist	'You can't have any objections anymore, so what I said is true' *(absolutizing the success of a defence)*

The fallacy defined by Barth and Martens would be the opposite type of move, which could be called *absolutizing the success of a refutation.* In their account (see chapter 1, section 7) the ad hominem fallacy is concluding that just because one party in a dialogue shows that a proposition is true relative to her opponent's concessions (ex concessis), she concludes that this proposition is absolutely true.

By the new viewpoint, however, the fallacy of absolutizing the success of a refutation should no longer be classified (correctly) as being the ad hominem fallacy. These two fallacies should be treated as separate and distinct. But absolutizing the success of a refutation is the key fallacy, or at least the danger, in the smoking case. So absolutizing the success of a refutation is an important ingredient in the circumstantial ad hominem fallacy, even if it is not an essential ingredient in defining the ad hominem as a distinctive type of argument.

Finally, note that the fourth viewpoint on case 3.2 suggests regarding the smoking case in such a way that the child's argument can correctly be seen as a circumstantial ad hominem. When the child sees the parent smoking and sees the clash between this act and what the parent is preaching, the child rejects the parent's argument against smoking on the grounds that the parent lacks credibility—in this sense the child sees it as lacking veracity of the kind that, in the child's eyes, is necessary for the parent to have a plausible argument. The key to this interpretation is the idea that in order to have a plausible argument the arguer must be in some sense credible as a proponent of that argument. But the idea of the proponent's credibility as a necessary requirement for an argument to be plausible is quite a novelty in logic. What could be meant by an arguer's credibility? And how should such a factor be determined, or evaluated, in a given case? This fundamental question will be taken up in chapter 7, section 4.

3. Form of Personal Attack

Once we adopt the viewpoint that the argumentum ad hominem is interpreted to be the use of personal attack in argument, of the kind supported by textbook accounts, an initial form of the argument (indicated at the beginning of chapter 1) can be sketched out as follows. The context of dialogue is a dispute between two parties, a and b, in which a has already put forward and advocated a particular argument α, and then b replies, at his next move, with an argument of the following form.

GENERIC AH

a is a bad person.
Therefore a's argument α should not be accepted.

In matching this form to real cases, two complications should be noted. First, the argument having the form GENERIC AH is generally directed to a third-party audience who plays the role of the judge or evaluator of the outcome of the dispute and the argumentation in it. Second, the conclusion of GENERIC AH generally takes the more complex form: you, the audience, should not take α as being as credible (plausible) an argument as you would have otherwise. In other words, arguments of the form GENERIC AH are designed to reduce the credibility of an argument in the evaluation of some third-party audience.

The first question to ask about arguments of the form GENERIC AH is why they should, in general, ever be acceptable or persuasive.

For, in general, the conditional warrant GENERIC AH is based on this form:

WPP

If x is a bad person, then (generally) x's argument should not be accepted.

Such a form is not plausible or generally acceptable. One would normally reply to an argument of the form GENERIC AH, based on the warrant WPP, "The argument α should be evaluated on its merits, that is, on the evidence for and against it, so whether a is a bad person or not is not a good (relevant) basis for rejecting α." This reply leads to the reasonable question: Why should a's being a bad person be, in general, a good reason for rejecting a's argument or assigning it a reduced degree of credibility?

It is interesting that in the range of examples of ad hominem arguments studied in chapters 1 and 2, the answer is always to be sought in the context of dialogue in which the argument was used. Take the example in which an ad hominem argument of the form GENERIC AH is used in court by the cross-examining attorney to attack the testimony of a witness. Here, an argument of the form GENERIC AH can, with good reason, be a powerfully persuasive argument to a judge or jury. The reason is basically that the witness is testifying on oath about matters on which the jury (or judge) does not have direct access to the facts. The jury (or judge) has to "take the witness's word for it" and evaluate what the witness has said as plausible or not in relation to the body of evidence presented in the case as a whole.

Thus, the context of dialogue in which the ad hominem is used in this type of case is complex, in certain respects, in a way that makes it deviate from the straightforward use of GENERIC AH we have been contemplating so far. In the latter type of case, a and b were the two opposed parties arguing in the dispute, and b was using the GENERIC AH type of argument to throw doubt on the argument α of a. In the courtroom case, however, the principal opposed arguers are the attorneys for the prosecution and defense. The witness is a third party who is brought in to provide information (testimonial evidence) for the jury (or judge), the party who evaluates the arguments and the outcome of the case. True, the cross-examining attorney is attacking the argument of the other side, who has brought this witness in to support their side. But the individual attacked by the GENERIC AH argument is not the attorney for the other side. It is the witness.

In such a courtroom case of cross-examination of a witness, it is not difficult to see why arguments of the form GENERIC AH are generally credible. Because the jury members do not have direct access to the facts or because what circumstantial evidence they do have may not be decisive, they have to depend on the sayso of witnesses. But witnesses can be bribed or can have various reasons for lying. Hence witness testimony is fallible. The assumption is that if the witness is honest and is generally a good person, then he or she would not lie or otherwise give false or unfounded testimony. Hence wpp is a plausible or generally acceptable warrant, in this context of dialogue, to support GENERIC AH as generally being an applicable and plausible type of argumentation.

What is meant by saying that an arguer is a "bad person" in the premise of an ad hominem argument? Does it mean that the person is said to be morally bad or ethically deficient in regard to some duty or ethical standard? Although morality is frequently the focus of the ad hominem attack, "bad person" in this sense is not perfectly equivalent to "morally bad person." Instead, the focus of an ad hominem argument is on the role the person is supposed to be playing in some conventional type of dialogue exchange he and his critic are taking part in when they argue with each other.

The following case, summarized from Cragan and Cutbirth (1984) will illustrate this point.

Case 3.4

In the 1982 Illinois election for governor, Adlai E. Stevenson (son of the presidential candidate, Adlai E. Stevenson) enjoyed a comfortable lead over James Thompson. During the campaign, Stevenson was criticized for being a member of an all-male Chicago club, so he resigned, explaining that he had only joined it to find a place to eat lunch in downtown Chicago. A number of reporters commented on this minor issue, and one in particular belittled Stevenson's famous father as a "sissy-type, cookie-cutter State Department type" (Cragan and Cutbirth, p. 234). In reaction, Stevenson (the son) said that this reporter had talked about him as if he were "some kind of wimp" and that he resented this characterization (p. 234). Then another reporter wrote a satirical column headed "A No-Wimp Situation" that triggered an avalanche of public debate on the so-called wimp factor. In the public debate between the two candidates just before the election, Thompson, in his closing statement, attacked Stevenson using an ad hominem argument to the effect that Stevenson claimed he wanted to hold the line on taxes, but had voted thirty-three times in the past to increase taxes.

The outcome of the election was that Stevenson lost, and the perception was that he lost because the "wimp factor" had become such a prominent issue, even getting national coverage and outweighing Stevenson's lead on the substantive issues (p. 236).

In this case, the focus of the ad hominem attack was on Stevenson as a fussy patrician type who got upset because he could not find a decent place to eat lunch. The implication drawn by the voters, after the various ad hominem attacks on Stevenson, was that Thompson would provide stronger leadership than would Stevenson.

The ad hominem argument in this case was not based on the premise that Stevenson was a morally bad person. Instead, it was based on the premise that Stevenson showed that he was deficient in the qualities of character needed to show to the voters that he was the best candidate for the office of governor. The ad hominem argument was that he was a "bad person" with respect to his role as a participant in an election campaign. As Cragan and Cutbirth (1984) put it (p. 230): "Fitness for office is a major issue in a political campaign and *ad hominem* is the argument that speaks directly to this issue." A person who is not a strong leader is not (necessarily) a morally bad person. But this deficiency is relevant to the issue in a political campaign.

4. Person and Participant

When it is alleged that *a* is a bad person in an ad hominem argument, of the kind encountered in chapters 1 and 2, it is meant that *a* is deficient in fulfilling some obligations or commitments appropriate for his role in the kind of argumentative exchange in which the two parties (the arguer and his critic) are taking part. What is meant here is a person who is said to be "bad" or deficient in some way—in respect to a role that he is supposed to be playing in the case in point.

It could be alleged for example that this person is a liar, or has a criminal record, or something of the sort, which indicates he may not be a trustworthy witness. Or it could be alleged that he does not practice what he preaches and is a hypocrite, and therefore his political rhetoric as a leader (or would-be leader) is not credible. Or it could be argued that he has a concealed bias and therefore is not to be trusted as taking a balanced view in some discussion that requires a participant to weigh the evidence fairly on both sides of an issue.

In the formal dialogue structures of Hamblin (1970; 1971)—and also in the Lorenzen formal dialogue logics in Barth and Krabbe (1982)—there are two participants, called the *proponent* and the *respondent* (or *opponent*), who take turns making moves. But both participants are defined only by their roles in the dialogue—meaning that each party has a certain designated goal or objective in taking part in the dialogue—and therefore, according to the dialogue rules, each party is required or allowed to make certain types of moves at the various points in the dialogue. Nothing beyond that is known or defined about either participant as a "person" or as a distinct individual with a personal history.

As indicated in chapter 1, section 9, the closest thing to defining either party as a person is the commitment set of that party, as that set builds up over the course of the dialogue into a body of propositions that may have some internal coherence or "shape"; this internal cohesiveness is called the *arguer's position* in Walton (1985). Again, in many cases, the commitment set of an arguer need not generally be of this kind: it could be empty, or contain only a scattering of apparently unrelated propositions, or even contain an inconsistent set in some cases.

Although, as noted in chapter 1, Hamblin does write that the arguer's commitment set is meant to correspond roughly to his or her persona of beliefs, he did not mean this literally. In fact, as Hamblin (1970) makes clear consistently, the commitment set is not meant to represent the actual belief set of an arguer. Hamblin sees this sort of assumption as psychologistic and defines commitment as meaning, precisely, acceptance in a structure of dialogue, as defined by the arguer's moves in a given case and the rules (in particular, what Hamblin calls the commitment rules) of the game of dialogue.

In this framework, the notion of "person" is thin and minimal. A "person" is conceived of as a "participant" in a regulated game, or formal structure of dialogue, defined only by his or her role as a maker of moves in the game. In any of the Hamblin or Lorenzen dialogue games, there is no place for using an argument of the type GE-NERIC AH. Such a move would simply not have any function and would be an illegal move.

Much the same kind of remarks would seem to apply to the normative model of argumentation defined as the critical discussion by van Eemeren and Grootendorst. The purpose of a critical discussion is to resolve a conflict of opinions by bringing arguments to bear on the propositions at issue on either side of the conflict. The arguments used are supposed to present evidence that counts for or against the propositions at issue (pro and contra argumentation in the sense of van Eemeren and Grootendorst, 1984, pp. 43–44). Personal attack has no real place, generally, in this type of dialogue exchange of argumentation. In fact, van Eemeren and Grootendorst (1987, pp. 284–85) see "performing personal attack on an opponent" as against their rule 1 for a critical discussion: "Parties must not prevent each other from casting doubt on standpoints."

The only exception to these exclusions of the GENERIC AH type of argument in such dialogue structures seems to be the unusual type of case in which the issue (the conflict of opinions the dialogue is supposed to resolve) is in fact whether one or both of the participants is a bad person or not (or somehow relates in an appropriate way to that issue). Normally, in one of these disputes, the issue would be some fairly abstract topic of controversy, such as "Is tipping generally a good practice or not?" An argument of the form GENERIC AH used by one of the participants in a discussion of this type would not be relevant as a contribution to the goal of the dialogue.

The basic problem is that the concept of a bad person in GENERIC AH makes no sense in the familiar formal dialogue structures of argumentation theory, such as those of Hamblin and Lorenzen. The concept of a participant is not robust enough to sustain any definition of the concept of a person, of the sort that would be rich enough to define the constant "bad person" in GENERIC AH. In everyday conversational dialogue, arguments of the form GENERIC AH have considerable force. They are powerful arguments. But no explanation of why they are powerful is given by defining the concept of a person in GENERIC AH as being equivalent to the concept of a participant in a formal dialogue structure of the current types.

The use of the concept of a bad person as a reason for giving less credibility to that person's argument in a dialogue would, of course, make sense as a powerful kind of argument if the person were giving personal or ethical advice to the respondent on how to live his life. But in this type of advice-giving dialogue, the goal would not be simply to resolve a conflict of opinions about some issue (which could be quite abstract and have little to do with personal or ethical questions of how the participants should live their lives), as it is in a critical discussion. Instead, the goal would be for one party to give the other party wise and sensible advice on some personal matter. However, this dialogue framework of personal advice-giving has not yet been given much recognition in the literature on argumentation (except mainly in Walton [*Practical Reasoning,* 1990; *Pragmatic Theory,* 1995, pp. 116–18]).

So far GENERIC AH is hard to make sense of, as a commonly used and effective type of argument, by placing it in a well-studied context of use, other than by moving to a deliberation type of dialogue different from the usual models of dialogue found in either Hamblin or van Eemeren and Grootendorst. This lack of clear use seems to lend support to the Lockean ex concessis analysis, for those who are unfamiliar with or are reluctant to admit the deliberation as a normative framework of dialogue.

5. Ways Out of the Dilemma

One way out of the dilemma is to give up the GENERIC AH form as defining the ad hominem argument and go back to the Lockean model. One attraction of this approach is that the circumstantial type of ad hominem argument can plausibly be cast as a species of argumentation from commitment. In the circumstantial cases examined so far, the pragmatic inconsistency is generated from a clash between what an arguer advocates as his explicit argument and certain commitments (propositions he also appears to advocate), judging from his avowed opinions, past conduct, or other personal circumstances. Of course, these commitments are not explicitly incurred by the arguer, but perhaps they can be reconstructed as implicit or darkside commitments (see chapter 1, section 9).

Once having started to see ad hominem from this viewpoint, it is tempting to extend it to the abusive type of case as well, by absorbing the concept of bad person into the concept of commitment—a return to the Lockean model, by redefining morally "bad person" in a narrower way.

Perhaps any alternative approach has seemed to be blocked by the substantial problem of defining "bad person" in a general way, a task that would seem to require developing an ethics of personal responsibility. For it does seem as if many ad hominem attacks are so powerfully effective precisely because they attack the moral character of the person (so-called smear tactics).

In the fallacious cases of ad hominem arguments, the attack is effective precisely because the moral character of the person is attacked, and the audience rejects any argument from this person because he is perceived as morally bad. But what is the logical link between such perceived moral badness of the person and rejecting the argument put forward by this bad person? After all, it might be a good argument, in the senses that the premises are supported by the facts and the conclusion follows from the premises. The link is that if the arguer is "smeared" as a bad person, his credibility is reduced or removed, and this reduction of credibility reduces the plausibility of the argument in a dialogue. So the core notion of "bad person" is not broadly moral in nature in ad hominem arguments but is more narrowly focused on an arguer's credibility as a sincere and reliable participant in a dialogue exchange of arguments. The best approach then might be to restrict this notion, for the purposes of logic, to accord with the types of ad hominem arguments that are the central concern. What seems rightly to be the principal focus of concern exhibited by the textbook treatment is the kind of case in which one party to a dispute attacks the argument of a second party on the grounds that the second party is a bad person in the sense that he is not a credible advocate or believable spokesperson for that argument. The general imputation in these attacks seems to be: "Yes, he is advocating that conclusion on the surface, but under the surface, he does not really follow that line of thinking or way of behaving." The focus of the attack is not the whole person, or all aspects of the person who advocates the argument, but only certain aspects that throw doubt on the sincerity or wholeheartedness of that advocacy and then use that doubt to undermine the credibility of the person as an advocate of her argument.

Judging from the cases in chapters 1 and 2, these aspects are the character of the arguer and certain types of circumstances: his past conduct (actions), his previous avowed opinions on the subject, his interests (especially financial) on one side of the argument, his ideology or general position (if known, for example, being a communist or a Catholic), and his group affiliations or associations that may be relevant to his concerns on the subject. The general program of research suggested by this way of thinking about ad hominem requires reducing all these aspects of the person to some sort of conflict of commitments in a Hamblin or Lorenzen formal dialogue structure. The different types of conflicts or pragmatic inconsistencies would represent different types of insincerity that would be a basis for the various kinds of personal attacks used in ad hominem arguments.

Given the dominance of the Lockean model of the ad hominem in scholarly and textbook attempts to provide a theory of ad hominem arguments, this program would no doubt seem highly promising to a majority of researchers in this field. Indeed, this program could be seen as the basis of the analysis of Barth and Martens (1977) as well as that of Walton (*Arguer's Position*, 1985).

Nevertheless, there may be a limit to how far this program of research can go as a general account of ad hominem arguments of the kind sketched out as the target of analysis in chapters 1 and 2. The basic reason is that in some cases, particularly in the abusive category, the ad hominem argument is not based primarily on an allegation that the proponent of an argument is insincere because of an underlying conflict of commitments. The allegation in these cases is more simple and straightforward, simply alleging that the proponent is a bad person and therefore that you (the audience) should not accept his argument as credible.

Another limit to this program is that ad hominem arguments, examined carefully, tend to reveal themselves as context-sensitive arguments that cannot be adequately evaluated by viewing them as a critical discussion or a Lorenzen type of dialogue exchange. The dialectical complexity of one kind of case of this sort—that of personal attack in cross-examination of a witness in court—has already been indicated. But even in some of the leading kinds of cases of ad hominem arguments cited by the textbooks, the context-sensitive nature of the arguments is easily revealed by a little examination. Subsequent cases will bear out this limitation, and eventually they will show that a purely commitment-based approach is inadequate to capture the logic of ad hominem arguments. Ultimately, in chapter 7, the concept of an arguer's credibility will be introduced, and joined to the concept of a person's character (as analyzed in chapter 5).

The problem with many of these cases under consideration is that the context of dialogue is not that of a critical discussion. Nor is the structure of the dialogue of the kind modeled by the Hamblin or Lorenzen dialogues. Also, what is characteristic of many of these cases is a shift from one type of dialogue to another, called a *dialectical shift* in Walton ("Commitment," 1993) and Walton and Krabbe (1995). Yet another problem is that some cases involve a comparison of two situations in certain respects. All of these problems indicate that (a) either the ad hominem argument is not a Lockean ex concessis type of argument at all or (b) if it is, it is a subspecies of ex concessis argument that has many special characteristics in its own right as a distinctive type of argument.

6. The Direct Ad Hominem Revisited

In some cases, questions of character and personal conduct have little or no legitimate place as a proper issue of the dialogue, yet in other cases, character is highly relevant to the argumentation of a dialogue. Particularly on a contentious issue for which knowledge is difficult to obtain, personal reliability or reputation for veracity of a source of information, testimony or advice may be a reasonable factor in shifting a presumption.

It is true that logic textbooks have traditionally castigated the temptations, errors, and fallacies of overreliance or uncritical reliance on matters of personality and character in argumentation. For example, as noted in chapter 2, according to Cohen and Nagel (1934, p. 217), "the individual motives of an arguer are altogether irrelevant in determining the logical force of his argument." One can easily appreciate that considerations of personal motives, background, or personality should not be held relevant to the question of the adequacy of a scientist's arguments or proofs in such fields as physics and mathematics. The context of a scientific inquiry in such a case is not well cast as a critical discussion or as a Lorenzen or Hamblin-style dialogue exchange.

If the subject of the dialogue is, say, ethics, politics, or biography, for which character and personal integrity may be part of the topic of the dialogue, it is by no means clear that the motives of a writer must always be altogether irrelevant to determining the force of his argument. If a biographer is studying the sincerity of Rousseau's convictions on marriage as expressed in his philosophical writings on the subject, then facts about Rousseau's own personal motives or his personal conduct (for example, his extramarital affairs) might be highly relevant. Indeed, they may be the main focus of the argumentation, and these matters of character and personal motives may be important evidence in reaching the conclusions in the biography.

The book *Intellectuals* (Johnson, 1988) is a biographical study of the personal lives of several secular intellectuals, over the past two hundred years, who proclaimed it their task in their writings to give advice to humanity on how to solve social problems and live better lives. The whole book is a prolonged ad hominem argument, showing that each person studied ran his or her own life badly in their sexual and financial dealings, were cruel to their friends, and were dishonest. Karl Marx is shown to have exploited a woman who worked as a nursery maid and house servant for him (pp. 79–80). Bertrand Russell, who took the "general position that the ills of the world could be largely solved by logic, reason and moderation" (p. 203), showed in his personal life that at moments of crisis logic was disregarded, and decisions were made emotionally: "At every great juncture, his views and actions were as liable to be determined by his emotions as by his reason." The basis of these ad hominem arguments by Johnson against Marx, Russell, and other intellectuals is that these intellectuals purported to give the mass of humanity advice on how to live their lives, and therefore it is reasonable to ask how they managed their own personal affairs—to ask about their respect for truth in their personal conduct and about how they applied their public principles to their private lives.

In his biographical essay on Rousseau, Johnson (p. 18) shows in detail how Rousseau's writings are full of distortions and falsehoods, how he consistently lied to his friends, colleagues, and sexual partners, and in particular how he exploited an illiterate servant girl and "despised himself for consorting with her." Even during his lifetime, Rousseau's personal reputation among his colleagues was bad. Hume called him "a monster, who saw himself as the only important being in the universe" (Johnson, 1988, p. 26). These allegations can certainly be classified as being of the abusive ad hominem type, as arguments. But they also seem to be relevant and appropriate as arguments for Johnson to consider in his book because Rousseau and the other intellectuals studied in the book were engaging in a kind of advice-giving dialogue with the people they addressed in their writings. They were claiming to give advice to these people on how to make better choices in their personal lives.

If the validity of Rousseau's arguments on some abstract subject was the issue of a philosophical inquiry into the strength of his arguments for his conclusions on that subject, it could be quite reasonable to hold biographical matters of Rousseau's own personal conduct and personality aside as irrelevant to the inquiry. Here it is not the sincerity of Rousseau's commitments that are the issue, in the context of his giving advice on how to conduct personal deliberations, but only the internal strength or validity of the arguments he set down as a theoretician.

The dangers of getting personal at all in argumentation are rightly emphasized and warned against by the logic textbooks. For any discussion of personal matters in arguments has a well-known way of generating more heat than light. But excluding all matters of character or personal intentions and conduct as completely irrelevant to the real issue in all contexts of dialogue is going too far in one direction, barring any argumentative discussion of personal matters.

The interesting question remains whether allegations of good moral character, or good character for veracity, could be used as a way of supporting an arguer to build up his argument positively as more credible. As cited in the textbooks, the abusive ad hominem always seems negative. But, as noted in chapter 1, section 10, there is the possibility of a positive counterpart.

Brinton (1985, 1986, 1987) cites Aristotle's remarks in the *Rhetoric* and *Nicomachean Ethics* explaining that persuasion can be achieved by a speaker's personal character because the good person's speech is more credible, especially if opinions are divided, and exact certainty is impossible. Building on these remarks, Brinton cites *ethos* (character) as a positive factor in argumentation credibility. According to Brinton, ethos can be used in either a positive or a negative way in argumentation. As defined in chapter 1, an ethotic argument is one in which ethos (character) is used to transfer credibility (either positively or negatively) from the person who is a proponent of an argument to the conclusion of that argument.

The negative use of ethotic argumentation can be identified with the traditional abusive ad hominem argument (Brinton, 1985). But the positive use of ethotic argumentation could be a new kind of direct type of ad hominem argumentation that is not "abusive" but is used positively to build up the credibility of an argument by citing the good moral character or veracity of the speaker. This is no longer an argument *against* the person (attack on the arguer) but an argument for the person—or, at any rate, an argument to support another argument by appealing to positive factors of the person's character that make his argument more plausible.

A complication in this proposal is the logical backing of positive ethotic ad hominem arguments. Whereas it is undoubtedly true that character plays a strong role in rhetorically supporting argumentation (in political speeches, for example), it is less clear whether character should correctly be treated as a form of *evidence* (say, of the kind used properly in a critical discussion) that supports a person's argument positively. Brinton acknowledges the problem (1985, p. 63) but seems to think that it is important to treat ad hominem arguments from a rhetorical rather than more narrowly from a "logical" point of view. Nevertheless, if a positive, direct type of ad hominem argument exists, one of the most important questions about it is whether or how it can be logically justified as a good or correct type of argumentation, in those instances when it is positive. Here, the argument does not seem to be treated adequately as just an inference from the speaker's set of commitments (ex concessis). Instead, her argument is argued to be more credible because she is a good person.

In such a case, the character of the speaker—that is, the perceived moral goodness of the speaker's personal qualities—is significant. In other contexts of dialogue, however, questions of character can rightly be dismissed as irrelevant. Hence, the logical justifiability of ethotic argumentation is highly dependent on the context of dialogue and, in particular, on the type of dialogue in a certain case.

For example, a lecturer on a scientific subject may make an aside or digression about the character of a famous scientist. Clues to the dialectical shift from the context of a scientific inquiry to that of a personal discussion may be found in changes in tone of voice, humor, and other factors of discourse. In this type of case, the personal allegations made by the speaker about the scientist may have no relevance to the scientific validity or verification of the scientific theories discussed in the talk. But these personal matters may be relevant to a discussion of the personal difficulties that scientists can face in their careers. In short, the context of dialogue is important, and it is not always that of a critical discussion.

Another important factor is that in contexts of personal deliberation and advice giving, the character of the advice giver can be an important and legitimate factor for the advice taker to weigh in arriving at a conclusion. According to Aristotle, in the *Nicomachean Ethics* (1094b–95a), it may be easier to recognize wisdom and virtue in a person than to recognize the best course of action in a difficult situation. Here we verge on the *ad verecundiam* with the suggestion that it may be a good source of advice to look to the person of wisdom and virtue for help in arriving at a personal decision on what course of action to take when confronted by a personal problem. The smoking case has already been cited as an example. Factual or scientific evidence may not be decisive in a case of personal deliberation of this sort, hence appealing to a subjective source of advice may be a reasonable way of altering a burden of proof that is not at odds with or in conflict with relevant objective evidence. In such a case, then, the character of the advice giver, insofar as it is known by the advice recipient, could be a positive kind of ad hominem evidence to support the plausibility of the conclusion pointed to by the advice given. Character might not be a determining factor in weighing up advice on personal deliberation, but it could be a positive factor to be accorded some weight as ethotic argumentation.

Another factor is that in certain contexts of argumentation it can be legitimate that part of the reason for accepting or rejecting an argument is trust or a presumption that the proponent of the argument is a trustworthy source. In the smoking example (case 1.5), the child may be trying to decide whether or not to take the parent's advice largely on trust or on the presumption that the parent is an honest, sincere, and reliable source. Trust and reliability are important parts of the context of political argumentation because of the nature of political decision making as a democratic institution. Where trust and reliability of a source are part of the argumentation basis for accepting a proposal, ethotic considerations can be highly relevant. In these kinds of cases, the reputation and character of the speaker, for morality and veracity, could be legitimate parts of the total body of evidence for deciding whether or not to accept a speaker's proposal.

It is at this point that the ad hominem and the ad verecundiam come closest together. For to take the advice of a wise and experienced authority, an expert, would seem to be essentially similar to the kind of ethotic argumentation involved in finding an argument more credible because its proponent has a good character or reputation for veracity. These situations are not the same, however, even if they may approach each other in some cases.

Although the argumentum ad hominem and the argumentum ad verecundiam are in principle different kinds of argumentation,[2] in fact often significant overlap is evident between them. For example, if one party cites an expert to back up his opinion, and the other party can give good evidence to show that this person cited as an expert has a bad reputation for veracity, then such an objection might be legitimate argumentation. In such a case, we have the use of an ad hominem (ethotic) to counter an argumentum ad verecundiam. Hence, the two types of argumentation can be connected in significant ways in their underlying argumentation schemes.

Our conclusion is that the ad hominem argument, in either of the forms represented by the abusive or positive ethotic versions, is neither a fallacious nor a nonfallacious argument per se. It can be a reasonable kind of argumentation, as used in some cases, and it can be fallacious when abused or used as a sophistical tactic of attack, in other cases. The difference between the two kinds of cases depends on the context of dialogue in which the argument was used.

7. Context Sensitivity of the Circumstantial Ad Hominem

One factor the sportsman's rejoinder case reveals is that an action attributed to one person may be the same kind of action also attributed to another person (or at least to a related or parallel action), yet the precise descriptions of the pair of actions may differ in significant details.[3] Hence what appears to be a circumstantial inconsistency may not be one at all, when the precise descriptions of the actions are carefully compared. But every action is carried out in a context or background of familiar circumstances, of reasonably expectable outcomes and known connections. In the language of artificial intelligence, every action is only comprehensible as an action in relation to its *script*, the story that lies behind it. For example, if I say "Bob burned his finger by touching the stove," we reasonably infer from the script of this action that it was the heat of the stove that relates the touching to the burning.[4]

This context-sensitive aspect of actions leads to some interesting cases of circumstantial ad hominem criticisms because the parallel between the pair of actions cited is characteristically based on a presumption that the two sets of situations or scripts are similar. If it can be reasonably argued by the defender that the two cases are not similar, the ad hominem criticism can be refuted. But a presumption of similarity can shift a burden of proof onto the defender to show that the two cases are not similar.

Case 3.5

Rodney Smith, of the President's Commission on organized crime, testified before a House subcommittee that he thought there were good reasons why drug tests should be mandatory for federal workers. A critic at the subcommittee meeting asked whether Mr. Smith would himself be now willing to give a urine sample. He replied that he would not.[5]

The presumption at work here is to favor legal principles that are fair in the sense that they apply the same legal restrictions on anyone in a similar situation. Thus any suggestion of differential restrictions places a burden of proof on the advocate of the law being proposed. In case 3.5, it appears that the lawmaker is proposing a rule that would not apply to himself. The appearance of having proposed an inequitable law is a challenge to Smith that shifts a serious burden of proof against his argument.

This case is an instance of the circumstantial ad hominem because the critic is arguing that Smith is pragmatically inconsistent in advocating a new law but not being ready to apply it to his own personal practices or situation. This allegation shifts a burden of proof against Smith, opening his argument for drug tests to critical questioning. This ad hominem appears to be nonfallacious, but Smith does have a way of countering it.

Mr. Smith described the demand for a urine sample from him by the critic as "a cheap stunt." Why might he have thought the demand to be open to criticism? Perhaps he may have reasoned that his present situation was not similar, in an important respect, to the situation of a federal worker who might be affected by his proposal, should it come to be legislated and enforced. Once the proposal becomes law, all federal workers would have to follow it. But until it does go into effect—if it does—there is no good reason why anyone should now give a urine sample to this subcommittee. Whatever else one might say about the critic's ad hominem question, Smith's reply would make a good point if it made clear that the two cases of himself and that of a federal worker affected (possibly, in the future) by the proposal are not similar.

In some cases, evaluating the ad hominem criticism can be open to significant and interesting kinds of further disputation, turning on the question of how similar the two allegedly parallel cases may be argued to be. The following case may serve to illustrate how each argument must be evaluated on its merits or demerits.

Case 3.6

A news program investigated evidence that the deaths of several schoolchildren in a small town could have been due to toxic chemicals that came to be in the water system through industrial waste disposal. The interviewer asked a corporate representative about the possibility that his company had violated the law by dumping toxic chemicals. The representative replied that the interviewer was "an interesting person to raise that question" in relation to the fact that his network was recently cited for some contamination problems. The interviewer countered to this reply by pointing out that, unlike the corporation's case that is the subject of the program, in the case of the network citation no deaths or illnesses were reported, no lawsuits resulted, and no criminal investigation occurred.[6]

Here the corporate representative is using the classical tu quoque circumstantial ad hominem rejoinder: he alleges that the interviewer's own television network has committed the same type of act that the interviewer criticizes this corporation for committing. The implied conclusion is that the interviewer's contention can be rejected as of no serious value evidentially. But the interviewer's reply is especially interesting. He alleges the presence of several key differences between the two cases. The network case resulted in no deaths or illnesses, no lawsuits, and no criminal investigation. Thus, he rebuts the parallel between the two cases. This is a relatively constructive type of reply—a cool tactic that helps to prevent a shift to the quarrel from destroying the original discussion.

In case 3.6, both the attacking circumstantial ad hominem argument and the defender's reply can be judged as powerful and also relatively reasonable moves in the argument, as far as we can judge from the given information. But another case will reveal that the merits of the attack and the reply can be highly dependent on our interpretation of the circumstances.

Case 3.7

Parliamentarian A: Can you assure the people that no increase in interest rates will take place tomorrow?
Parliamentarian B: This is a ludicrous question coming from the honorable member who was a minister when his previous government was pushing interest rates up to 20 and 25 percent *per annum.*[7]

B's reply is a circumstantial ad hominem attack on *A*'s request for assurance of no raise in interest rates, given the enormous raise in interest rates when *A*'s party was in power. It is a classical tu quoque reply, which sets the stage for further abusive attacks and takes the first steps in that direction. It also has elements of the guilt by association or group attack type of ad hominem because *A* is attacked on the grounds of having been one of the ministers in the previous government, who were (allegedly) collectively responsible for raising interest rates.

The novel aspect of this case is that the ad hominem argument is used to reply to a question. The suggestion is that Parliamentarian *A* had no right to ask the question. The conclusion of the ad hominem argument is that the contention of blame in the question should be rejected, on the grounds that the questioner himself is responsible for the same outcome he criticizes in others (inflation). The use of ad hominem replies to questions is a technique studied in depth in Walton (*Informal Logic*, 1989, chapter 5).

Is *B*'s reply fallacious or reasonable? One might argue that *B* should answer the question and that his ad hominem reply is evasive. If a question contains a loaded presupposition or is unduly aggressive, it should be reasonable for the answerer to reply other than by giving a direct answer.

This case has much for consideration, but especially note that it could be open to *A* to reply to *B*'s ad hominem attack by giving evidence that the fiscal situation was different when his party was in power. He might argue, for example, that in those days high interest rates were evident all over the world, whereas now the world economic situation has changed significantly, and interest rates are much lower. By arguing that his own situation was therefore different from that of *B* in a crucial respect, *A* can undermine the parallel that *B* has drawn as the basis of his ad hominem criticism. This would be a constructive and relevant reply.

But this case has room for considerable dispute about how similar the circumstances of the one parliamentarian are, or were, to the circumstances of the other. How much control a governing party has over interest rate fluctuations at any particular time is a circumstantial factor that may be highly subject to change and interpretation.

In general, the personal circumstances of every arguer are different from the personal circumstances of any other arguer. This factor may be discouraging for anyone who tries to use a criticism of circumstantial inconsistency to try to undermine or refute argument.

Nevertheless, resources of logical reasoning can be used to help analyze the argumentation in cases of the circumstantial ad hominem (cases 3.6 and 3.7) on the assumption that actions do express commitments. Defeasibly, it can be argued that if arguer *a* admittedly carried out action α, then this admission may reveal that *a* is committed to a certain proposition and that this implied commitment is inconsistent (or questionably consistent) with *a*'s argument. For example, in analyzing case 3.6, it may be (defeasibly) inferred that if someone works for a company that has been cited for "contamination problems," a question of that person's consistency of commitments is posed if he attacks someone else for working for a company that has been responsible for industrial pollution. The nature of the defeasible use of practical reasoning as a method of analysis for cases of this sort is explored in chapter 5.

8. The Bias Attack Explored

The bias type of ad hominem argument has been classified by some—for example, van Eemeren and Grootendorst (1984, p. 190)—as a species of circumstantial ad hominem. This is the type of argument in which the critic questions the personal trustworthiness of an arguer by showing that circumstances indicate that this arguer has something to gain by adopting his position on an issue. By this means, the critic suggests that the motives of the person he criticizes may be open to suspicion. Although the use of the term 'circumstances' indicates why it is plausible to classify this type of argument as a circumstantial ad hominem, in some respects it resembles the abusive category, for it centers on the motives and veracity of a person.

Actually, this type of ad hominem argument is a special one. What is really going on at a deeper level in this type of criticism is that an arguer is being accused of bias. This argument amounts to a criticism to the effect that such an arguer has a vested interest. Rather than being concerned with conviction, truth, or reasoned persuasion, as he purports to be, such an arguer is said to be covertly engaged in a different type of dialogue altogether. Hence bias is connected to a dialectical shift. In many of the cases studied in chapters 1 and 2, the allegation is that the proponent is negotiating in an interest-based bargaining type of dialogue. Thus the problem underlying this type of case involves a dialectical shift from a critical discussion context of dialogue to that of a negotiation. It is not a pragmatic inconsistency that is involved but a personal attack on personal reliability and integrity, as a person who can be relied on to give fair weight to the arguments on both sides of the issue. It is an allegation of a concealed, unilateral shift—an illicit shift. In case 2.7, for example, the union official's argument for higher wages is discounted because he is an "interested party" who stands to gain by a wage increase.

Although this third type of ad hominem argument could be (and often is) called "circumstantial," it is more closely related to the direct ad hominem argument because the arguer's sincerity and concern for the truth is directly the focus of challenge. This third type, therefore, does not fit squarely into either category and merits special mention in its own right as a separate type of ad hominem argument. It should properly be called the bias or *something to gain* type.

The bias type of argumentum ad hominem attack on an arguer's impartiality has the argumentation scheme: *a* is biased; therefore the proposition *A* advocated by *a* should be rejected. But the argumentation theme is crucial because it is a form of attack that alleges a dialectical shift from one context of dialogue to another. For example, if an arguer is ostensibly engaged in a supposedly objective type of dialogue such as an inquiry but is covertly engaging in a more partisan type of dialogue such as negotiation or persuasion dialogue, this type of allegation of bias could be appropriate, reasonable, and justified.[8] Basically, the reason is that each type of dialogue has its own specific aims and rules of procedure, which should be agreed to by all participants at the confrontation stage (the stage at which the dispute is identified, according to van Eemeren and Grootendorst, 1984, p. 154). If one party is playing by a different set of rules—and especially if this action is covert or concealed—then an important type of insincerity and deception has taken place through the use of a tactic concealing an illicit shift. All types of reasoned dialogue (except the eristic) are cooperative types of undertaking that presuppose the good faith and honesty of the participants in working collaboratively together toward a common goal, according to Gricean maxims.

In particular cases of ad hominem arguments of the sort cited in chapters 1 and 2, we may not have enough evidence to tell what type of dialogue engages the participants. They may not have agreed on the type of dialogue in advance, but even if there is evidence that they have or that the dialogue is supposed to be of a particular type, the textual evidence given in the case, especially in a brief textbook example, may be insufficient to make such a firm determination. In such cases, the best that can be done is to give a conditional analysis and evaluation, based on an assumption about the type of dialogue applicable to the case. Such conditional analyses are often useful and illuminating, even though longer case studies (to supplement the short ones typical in the textbooks) should be encouraged as well.

Although it is true, as shown in chapter 1, that critical discussion is partly adversarial, an element of cooperativeness must also exist in adhering to basic procedural rules. These rules may be quite different for another type of dialogue, such as a negotiation. Hence, dialectical shifts can be crucial. If a participant has agreed to engage in a critical discussion at the opening stage of a dialogue but then shifts to a negotiation or quarrel during the ongoing sequence of argumentation, the shortcoming can be identified as an illicit dialectical shift. On shifts generally, see Walton and Krabbe (1995) and Walton (*Pragmatic Theory*, 1995).

Bias is not in itself fallacious or harmful in a critical discussion. In fact, it is normal in a critical discussion for both participants to have a point of view (standpoint) and to use partisan (advocacy) proargumentation to support that point of view as strongly as possible. Bias becomes a problem when there is a dialectical shift, however, because advocacy appropriate in one type of dialogue may be inappropriate for or contrary to the goals of another type of dialogue.

Holland (1919) in his *Memoir of Kenelm Henry Digby* makes the following comment in evaluating a critic's claim that Digby depicts only the beautiful, showing advocacy of a point of view, and passes over the reverse side of medieval life and religion. Whether or not Digby's writing is biased therefore depends on the goal of dialogue of the type he was supposedly engaging in.

Case 3.8

[A] writer should be judged according to his professed aims. Kenelm Digby never pretended to be a judicial, scientific historian like the German Ranke, or the French Guizot, exactly weighing with cold deliberation the merits and demerits of men and times, but rather as an advocate who wished to set forth the good of his cause.

There is nothing wrong with presenting only one side of an argument, if that is your professed goal in advocating a partisan point of view. But if the goal of the dialogue is to have a critical discussion that weighs the arguments on both sides of an issue or to conduct an inquiry that collects all the relevant evidence, it is a different matter.

It is surprising how many of the examples of ad hominem arguments from the textbook treatments presented in chapters 1 and 2 are the bias type. Such examples include (at least) cases 1.8, 1.9, 2.2, 2.6, 2.7, 2.10, 2.15, 2.19, 2.20, 2.24, 2.26, 2.29, 2.32 and 2.34. Not all ad hominem bias subtype cases involve an allegation of a shift to interest-based bargaining (usually financial interests of some sort are involved), but many do. Such instances include cases 1.8, 2.2, 2.6, 2.7, 2.15, 2.19, 2.20, 2.24, 2.26, 2.29, 2.32 and 2.34. It is difficult to judge, in many of these cases, however, whether or not the ad hominem attack is fallacious, for not much context is given.

In deciding whether allegations of bias are justified, careful attention to the language of an argument and the precise form in which conclusions are expressed can require judicious analysis of discourse. Blair (1988) has argued that not all bias is bad bias, subject to negative criticism. By analyzing several case studies of imputations of bias,

Blair has shown how to look for biased language that violates norms of fairness and honesty in a dispute. Often, bias takes the form of misrepresentation of an opponent's position aimed at discrediting it. In other cases, bias is associated with an advocacy that is too strenuous and results in a loss of critical doubt appropriate for a dialogue. In a critical discussion, it is important to advocate your partisan point of view as aggressively as you can, at some stages of a dialogue. But at other stages, it is important to suspend that advocacy attitude and instead adopt an attitude of *critical doubt* that considers the evidence and possible arguments against your own point of view. The confusing of these two attitudes, especially the suppressing of critical doubt (when critical doubt is appropriate), is associated with bias.

It is not the present goal to try to give a full analysis of the concept of biased argumentation It is enough to see that the bias type of ad hominem argument typically involves a dialectical shift, of the kind analyzed as being harmful to argumentation—in the sense that it obstructs constructive dialogue—as in Walton (*One-Sided*, 1998).

For these reasons analysis of arguments against the person is basically a practical or pragmatic undertaking, as a part of logic. The practical task is to read off the given circumstances of the arguer from the context of dialogue to tell what her commitments may be taken to imply in light of her argument. The task is to make this distinction in a fair and reasonable way according to the given discourse and the appropriate rules of the dialogue. In practical terms, the effect of personal attack is usually to shift the burden of proof, and therefore it most often functions as a form of presumptive argumentation. The job of the evaluator of the argument against the person is to judge whether a strong enough case for a circumstantial inconsistency, direct personal attack, or allegation of bias has been built up by the attacker to shift the burden of proof toward a continuation of the dialogue by the arguer who has been criticized.

Bias is not a kind of commitment, in the sense in which this term is defined in Hamblin (1970) and meant in AC. It follows that the bias subtype of ad hominem argument is not a subspecies of the Lockean ex concessis type of argument and not a subspecies of argument from commitment. If the bias ad hominem is to be included as a subtype of ad hominem argument, the Lockean analysis of ad hominem simply will not work (to cover all three basic subtypes).

9. Ad Hominem Attacks and Defenses

Some arguments, as Fitch noted, are inherently more open to ad hominem attack than are others. If a person is arguing passionately for moral convictions to the effect that everyone ought to follow certain principles, then she can be very vulnerable to ad hominem attack if she herself does not follow those principles in her own private life. The ad hominem criticism in such a case can be devastating, for it can suggest that this person's argument is internally inconsistent or that she is hypocritical or insincere. What is suggested is that she has no right to tell others how to act because she cannot even follow her own convictions on how people should act.

In political argumentation, ad hominem attacks can be devastating because, in principle, they are often reasonable arguments. A person who opts for political office should do so on the basis of a political position—that is, on the basis of personal convictions about how concerns ought to be handled. By taking up office or campaigning for it, such a person puts herself in a high profile position in which her ideas and her capability to implement those ideas become proper subjects for public debate. In theory, as will be demonstrated in detail in chapter 5, the ad hominem argument is a reasonable argument in political discourse.

It is possible to defend against ad hominem attacks, in some cases. Indeed, in some, they can be shown to be fallacious. The fundamental nature of the argumentum ad hominem as an argument can be brought out by considering the nature of argumentation as used in dialogue. Basically two kinds of uses are evident—attacking and defending. Of the former kind, there are two subkinds. First, you can attack your opponent's argument externally (called *ad judicium* by Locke, and *ad rem* by Whately) by citing objective evidence to bear against his arguments. External attacks can also show why an opponent's argument lacks evidence to support it, for example, because its premises are weak. Second, you can attack your opponent's argument internally, by showing that it conflicts with his own prior commitments. The internal attack tends to be more powerful—if successfully mounted—because it shows that the opponent's position is inconsistent. It is not just that his argument conflicts with or is unsupported by external evidence. The internal attack shows that his argument conflicts with itself. Broadly speaking, this second kind of (internal) attack may be identified with the argumentum ad hominem because, as shown in section 2 above, it raises questions about the person's internal consistency of commitments as a well-organized, coherent reasoner who stands behind (in his principles) what he advocates at the moment.

The Lockean conception of the argumentum ad hominem also clearly identifies it as a species of internal argumentation. To attack an arguer on the internal basis is to press him with the logical consequences of his concessions, in Locke's view of ad hominem.

In our view, however, this type of argumentation is not ad hominem unless it is used ultimately to show that these consequences lead to a contradiction or otherwise to attack the respondent personally.

According to Locke's description, the ad hominem argument is essentially argument from commitment: pressing a person "with consequences drawn from his own principles or concessions" (Hamblin, 1970, p. 160). As shown in section 1, argument from commitment is inherently a reasonable type of argumentation (at least in many cases). Indeed, in a critical discussion, the goal of argumentation is precisely to prove your thesis as a consequence drawn from your opponent's concessions (commitments) in the discussion. This too was the goal for the Socratic *elenchus*, so one can see how the argumentum ad hominem was built into the Greek idea of dialectical examination.

Indeed, Johnstone (1978, p. 53) defines argumentum ad hominem in this Lockean manner as arguing to what a man is bound to admit relative to his own commitments; Johnstone argues that it is, in principle, a reasonable kind of argumentation. According to Johnstone, the argumentum ad hominem is a relative kind of argumentation that refers to the internal consistency of an arguer's position. By contrast, what Johnstone called (after Whately) the argumentum ad rem "establishes, or at least claims to establish, an absolute and general conclusion, of the form 'such and such is the fact' " (p. 53). The difference is the key to understanding the basic difference between internal and external uses of arguments.

In practice, however, what has been identified by the logic textbooks traditionally as the argumentum ad hominem is somewhat narrower than this Lockean conception, and it also has a more pragmatic flavor. Typically, according to the conception of the texts, the argumentum ad hominem is not just trapping the opponent in a logical contradiction per se but trapping him or finding him in a conflict between what he says (his verbal argumentation) and what he does or is (his circumstances, situation, actions, previous commitments, and so forth), thus revealing (subject to clarification or rebuttal) confusion or dishonesty. These circumstantial and personal factors make the argumentum ad hominem a personal attack or argument against the person.

The personal attack cases of the argumentum ad hominem have been especially identified by the logic textbooks, given their practical bent. Such identification has led us in the twentieth century to look at the ad hominem in a highly pragmatic way as a special kind of argument that cites personal characteristics, circumstances, and so forth of an arguer as the object of the attack. To be sure, this pragmatic character of the ad hominem is important. Looked at from a broader perspective as a type of argumentation in general, the ad hominem is really a species of internal, attacking argumentation that is used to throw doubt on an arguer as a personal advocate of his own argument, consistent in his commitments. Small wonder then that it is both a powerful and common form of argumentation tactic in politics and other everyday forms of persuasion dialogue. It is a basic argumentation method, and it is not inherently fallacious as an argument.

The best practical advice on how to use and respond to ad hominem argumentation in dialogue depends on the type of argumentation that is used. It can be personal (abusive), circumstantial, or the bias type of attack. With the personal type of attack, it is important to be sure that character (or the personal aspect cited) is relevant to the issue and that your personal allegation can be supported by some evidence. It is often a good idea for the proponent to pose the argumentation in the form of a question. This shifts the burden of proof just as strongly as a more categorical speech act and leaves you more open to retractions if the argumentation goes badly (as in the smoking and sportsman's rejoinder cases).

The defender against the personal ad hominem has many ways out. He can challenge the evidence for the allegation or the relevance of the allegation. If these defensive tactics are weak or not available, he can claim to be "born again" and beg his audience for forgiveness (see the argumentation tactics used for excuses and image restoration analyzed in Benoit, 1995).

The circumstantial argument is trickier. First, the proponent needs to pin down the inconsistency as tightly as she can by citing specific propositions alleged to be inconsistent and backing this up with careful evidence. The vehicle for this task, as shown in chapter 5, is practical reasoning. Moreover, the proponent should think out, in advance, why she considers the attack to be relevant to the issue of dialogue.

Once again, various possible lines of responding to argumentation are available, and the respondent must think out which of these he needs to emphasize. He can argue that no inconsistency is present because his personal conduct is a different matter from his group affiliations or public convictions about what is good for everyone. He can dispute the relevance of the attack, calling it "mudslinging." If none of these responses is successful, and the attack is strong, the respondent might find it better to apologize or otherwise try to retract commitments or give some reasons for observers to conclude that his (current) position is not as inconsistent as it may appear. Because the circumstantial ad hominem attack, if mounted strongly, carries with it a powerful shift in burden of proof, it demands a response. Lack of an effective response implies (concedes) guilt.

The proponent is well advised to work on this guilt-implying aspect of the circumstantial argument, suggesting that the pragmatic inconsistency implies hypocrisy or illogicality on the part of the defender. The proponent can slide from the circumstantial to the personal ad hominem, citing the alleged inconsistency as evidence of hypocrisy, dishonest opportunism, or other faults of moral character, thus combining the two argumentation schemes in the same theme.

The usual and most obvious form of the bias type of ad hominem argument is to accuse the opponent of having the prospect or motive of financial gain in supporting his side of the argument. See, for example, case 1.8, in which Bob accused Wilma of this motive. If the relationship implying gain has been concealed by the respondent, or at any rate, not announced at the opening stage, this type of ad hominem criticism can be powerful and difficult to respond to effectively (as in case 1.8, for example).

Nevertheless, if the financial interest of the party to be criticized has not been concealed or is evident to everyone at the outset, pinning down a substantial criticism of bias generally takes more work. What the proponent has to do is look at the text of the respondent's discourse in detail, showing why its claims are exaggerated or one-sided in a way that indicates a lack of balance or neutrality appropriate for the context of argument. This task requires a careful analysis of the argumentation theme in relation to a dialectical shift.

An excellent example of a well-documented criticism of bias is a case in which Blair (1988) criticized a tobacco company for producing a biased argument on the health effects of second-hand smoking inhalation. Blair did not just make the obvious attack that the tobacco company had something to gain by pushing for its side of the argument. In addition, he mounted a carefully documented criticism of bias by examining the specific wording of the argumentation theme in relation to the evidence offered for its claims. This well-documented thematic type of criticism of bias is much more damaging to an argument and also much harder to defend against.

In general, well-documented criticisms of bias are hard to defend against because to admit bias is to weaken one's credibility and integrity as an arguer, whether or not the bias was intentional. In fact, weak criticisms of bias can often be brushed aside by strenuous avowals of a sincere intent to be willing to look at both sides of the issue.

In a case in which an argument is vulnerable to ad hominem criticism, this form of argumentation is the most powerful kind of attack that exists in a critical discussion or inquiry. If the ad hominem attack is inappropriate in a context of dialogue, however, it may rebound on the attacker, undermining her own motives and character as a serious and honest participant in reasoned dialogue.

10. Prospects for Further Progress

A central remaining problem is that the gap between the Lockean and personal attack conceptions of ad hominem has not been bridged. It has been shown how the circumstantial ad hominem can be analyzed as a subspecies of argument from commitment, but the gap remaining is that between the direct (abusive) ad hominem argument and argument from commitment. Ethotic argumentation is based on the arguer's character. Here 'bad person' means that a person taking part in an argument has (or is perceived to have) a morally bad character (particularly for veracity) that justifies a lowering of credibility for that person as a contributor to an argument.

But what is the connection here? Maybe there is a connection between character and commitment (in the Hamblin-type sense of commitment in dialogue). But what is it? The scholarly literature on the ad hominem argument and the resources available in the field of argumentation theory give us no direction on how to analyze the concept of a person. Here it is difficult to know where to turn, except to analyze the concept of character insofar as it is involved in the case studies of ad hominem argument examined so far. This task will be the main subject of chapter 5, which has a unified account of the concept of the character of a person suitable for analysis and evaluation of ad hominem arguments.

What about the bias type of ad hominem? Is bias connected to commitment? Once again, the connection seems oblique and tenuous. Commitment, as defined in Hamblin, means going on record in a dialogue as having asserted a proposition or otherwise having made some kind of move in the dialogue in such a way that a particular proposition is inserted into one's commitment set. In the sorts of dialogue that Hamblin, Lorenzen, Barth and Martens, and van Eemeren and Grootendorst have in mind, commitment in this sense means that a participant in the dialogue is obliged by the rules to give evidence or reasons to support this proposition, if challenged to do so by the other party (or alternatively to retract commitment from the proposition in question).

The problem posed by the bias type of ad hominem attack is that the attacked party is allegedly committed to what she advocates in an entirely different sense. She is "committed" in the sense that it represents an interest for her—it is alleged that she has an interest (usually financial) in advocating the particular proposition at issue. This is an entirely different meaning of 'commitment' from the idea of "principle" or "concession" in the Lockean account of ad hominem. In fact, it involves a dialectical shift out of the critical discussion dialogue to an entirely different type of goal-directed conversational exchange. The bias type of ad hominem argument, like the circumstantial, is a kind of implied personal attack that indirectly suggests a kind of dishonesty, concealment, or insincerity in an argument. But it seems to take us quite far away from the Lockean conception of ad hominem because bias or having something to gain is not a type of commitment in the sense of 'commitment' defined in Hamblin (1970) and Walton and Krabbe (1995).

Of the three basic types of ad hominem recognized so far, the circumstantial is the most promising to try to reduce to argument from commitment. What the typical circumstantial ad hominem attacks (of the kinds studied in this chapter and previously) is that some personal circumstances—often some cited personal actions of the arguer—are taken to express commitments of the arguer that clash with (are pragmatically inconsistent with) her argument. This type of ad hominem argument is definitely a subspecies of argument from commitment. It does not seem to be identical to the form of argument from commitment AC. But it is a subspecies of AC that essentially involves the additional elements (a) that the argument is based on an allegation of pragmatic inconsistency and (b) that this allegation is used as a basis for the kind of personal attack in the form GENERIC AH. Typically, the thrust of this circumstantial type of ad hominem is to the effect that the arguer is a *hypocrite*, in the sense that his deeper (covert) commitment, representing his "real" or underlying commitment, clashes with the overt commitment expressed in his argument. The implication is that one should not accept or give credibility to his argument because it does not express what the arguer is actually (or really) committed to. The expression of this implication is: "His actions speak louder than his words." It would seem that the circumstantial ad hominem represents by far the most promising avenue for extending the Lockean conception to cover the kinds of cases emphasized by the textbook treatments.

As we saw in section 7, however, the context sensitivity of real cases of the circumstantial ad hominem argument seems to provide plenty of obstacles. Do actions really speak louder than words? Well, sometimes they do, as cases reveal. But other cases seem to have plenty of relatively convincing defenses against this type of allegation of circumstantial conflict. To explore this territory further, one may turn to a more realistic case study of the circumstantial ad hominem (chapter 4).

The general points that indicate the way to a solution of the ad hominem fallacy can be summed up as follows. First, the legitimacy of an ad hominem attack depends upon the role an arguer is playing in a conventional framework of dialogue exchange in a given case. Second, this role goes beyond the commitments of the arguer (in the technical sense of 'commitment' defined in this chapter). But third, a person's role in a dialogue does carry with it certain obligations a person will have in a dialogue; if he falls short of these obligations, he will reasonably be taken to be less credible as a person; consequently, it could be a reasonable move (in some cases) for the other participants in the dialogue to assign his argument less plausibility or value as an argument carrying weight in the dialogue. Fourth, this assessment will be a function of theory if that role in dialogue is defensible. For example, the role of a politician who is taking part in group deliberations, as in an election campaign, might be different, in this respect, from the role of a private citizen who is discussing a political issue.

A final general comment that points the way toward the analysis of the ad hominem fallacy given in chapter 7 concerns the general concept of a fallacy. Blair (1995, p. 333) distinguishes between two views of fallacy that have been taken in the literature on fallacy theory. According to the *injury view*, a fallacy is any shortfall of cogency in an argument, that is, a logical weakness or flaw in the argument. According to the *fatality view*, the claim that an argument commits a fallacy is quite a serious charge, implying that the argument is more than just weakly supported or insufficiently substantiated but is quite badly wrong in its underlying structure in such a way that it is tricky and deceptive. In Walton (*Pragmatic Theory*, 1995) a distinction is made between two kinds of fallacies—the error of reasoning type and the sophistical tactics type.

In our subsequent analysis of the ad hominem fallacy, we will be leaning more toward what Blair calls the fatality view, implying that the ad hominem is generally more of the sophistical tactics type of fallacy. At any rate, it will be important to distinguish between two kinds of cases. First, there are the weak or insufficiently justified ad hominem arguments in which the premises of the ad hominem argument have not been adequately supported. Second, there are the fallacious ad hominem arguments in which, possibly in addition to this first fault, a more serious kind of failure generally involving deceptive tactics or moves in a dialogue is involved.

4

A Longer Case Study

It was the contention of chapter 3 that in order to understand how ad hominem functions as a fallacy in argumentation, you have to understand how it is used and misused as a technique of argumentation. To have a theory of ad hominem as a fallacy is not enough just to say that it is a type of argumentation that violates a rule of a critical discussion. Undoubtedly, if a particular use of an ad hominem argument in a critical discussion is fallacious, it violates some rule of critical discussion. It could be a failure of relevance or a failure of burden of proof, for example. That claim is not enough to pin down this particular case as a fallacy, for the ad hominem could violate either of these rules and yet be a weak argument and not a fallacy. Also, the case could be one in which the argument was put forward as part of some other type of dialogue, such as an interest-based negotiation. To pin down an argument in a particular case as an instance of the ad hominem fallacy, one has to be able to understand and show how the violation was executed and why it is such a serious and systematic abuse of the technique of ad hominem argumentation that it can justifiably be judged fallacious, in the context of dialogue of that case.

The pragmatic view of the ad hominem fallacy advocated in chapter 3 contends that it is not so easy generally to pin down a charge of fallacy as would appear to be presumed by the standard treatments of the textbooks, which often dismiss ad hominem arguments as transparently or obviously fallacious. To illustrate this contention, it is worthwhile to look at a longer case study than would be normal—much longer than would be normal in the textbook treatment, for sure—and to examine the difficulties of pinning down such a charge.

The basic problem of evaluation of ad hominem arguments is posed by the fact that these types of arguments are not always fallacious. In some cases, the ad hominem is a reasonably used technique of argumentation (in context). At least, this is the contention on which the pragmatic view of chapter 3 is based; from the point of view of this approach, it would appear to be quite a likely outcome that comparable questions can be raised for most or even all of the other cases covered in chapters 1 and 2. So much depends, in these cases, on how one construes the context of dialogue.

Suppose the ad hominem argument was used to attack an opponent in argumentation in a case in which the outcome was important, but that opponent (contrary to the textbook treatment cases) is actually around to dispute the point. The opponent is, of course, going to meet the attack by describing it as fallacious, as "muckraking," "irrelevant," "character assassination," and so forth. Who would really be in the right then—the attacker or the defender? And how could he or she prove it? The problem is that, in the textbook accounts, there are no prima facie, applicable, right answers to all the questions raised. One must look at each individual case carefully to see how the technique of ad hominem argumentation was advanced and defended against. It could even result that the ad hominem attack was a reasonable argument, in the circumstances, and the responses to it were not. The proof or disproof of fallaciousness lies buried in the context of dialogue, in the particulars of how the argument was used in the given case.

Suppose an arguer is fairly accused of committing a circumstantial inconsistency. If the case is made completely enough, can the argument of this arguer be refuted, or does the arguer always have a way out, a reasonable reply that would defend his argument? Are there critical questions that could be asked, which would cast doubt on the ad hominem argument? If a reply, a critical question that would shift the burden of proof, is always available in principle, then it would seem to follow that the ad hominem argument is always defeasible by the respondent against whom it had been directed. But what are these "ways out" or critical questions?

Some of the most subtle but effective "ways out" of an ad hominem attack are illustrated by the longer case study of this chapter. In the kind of case illustrated here, the problem is one of "pinning down" or carrying forward an ad hominem argument that is basically reasonable in the given tactical situation but is effectively repelled by some clever and subtle distinctions that are basically reasonable, at least as underlying techniques of argumentation. But are they used reasonably in this case? Addressing this question requires looking carefully at the cut and thrust of the text of dialogue in the case study. The attacks and defenses need to be evaluated together as tactics used as dynamic moves in a larger sequence of dialogue. This specific problem has to do with what Hamblin called the "nailing down" of a fallacy. If a circumstantial ad hominem argument can only be finally "nailed down" against an arguer in a context of dialogue that allows for "ways out," what does this modification tell us about the concept of fallacy as a working concept of informal logic? It would seem that the concept would need to be more subtle, dialectical, pragmatic, and nonmonolectical in nature than indicated in the textbook accounts of the ad hominem (chapter 2).

1. Problem of Fixing Ad Hominem Criticisms

The most devastating type of criticism or refutation generally of an arguer in dialogue is for the critic to find that the arguer has committed himself deeply to a particular proposition but has also shown indications of having committed himself to the opposite proposition or to some commitment that runs contrary to the first one. Such a finding of inconsistency in an arguer's position may suggest that the arguer is confused or illogical, especially if he has not realized that the contradiction exists. In addition, such an inconsistency is likely to suggest in many instances that the arguer is a liar, seems hypocritical, or lacks integrity. In either event, doubt has been cast on the trustworthiness, capability, or sincerity of the arguer so criticized in entering into reasoned, cooperative dialogue. Such an ad hominem argument is therefore potentially serious in dialogue and can destroy an arguer's credibility altogether, undermining his case and concluding the dialogue against it.

Characteristically, however, this type of refutation is not a finding of logical inconsistency but something different (though related). It is typically a kind of practical or personal inconsistency alleged between what the person says or "preaches" and what he does or "practices." Condemnations citing a failure to practice what a person has preached go back to ancient times. It has been reported by Aulus Gellius (165 B.C.) that Epicurus criticized certain would-be philosophers for being persons who preached but did not practice. According to Gellius (translation Rolfe, 1928, vol. III, p. 265), Epicurus criticized these individuals: "I heard Favorinus say that the philosopher

Epictetus declared that very many of those who professed to be philosophers were of the kind *aneu tou prattein mecri tou legein,* which means "without deeds, limited to words"; that is, they preached but did not practise." This censure could be taken as a form of criticizing a failure of actions to be consistent with a person's professed views on how one's life should be lived. Indeed, it strongly implies or suggests that the criticism of circumstantial inconsistency characteristic of this subtype of ad hominem attack can be a reasonable type of argument against a philosopher, at least in some instances. Epictetus appears to have professed the view that a philosopher's personal actions and biographical circumstances are relevant to judging the worth of his philosophy.

Often it is not outright logical inconsistency that is involved in the circumstantial ad hominem argument, however, and therefore it is sometimes problematic to make the criticism stick. There are many ways a defender can try, often with considerable success, to wriggle out of the attack. The following case illustrates precisely this difficulty of pinning down the circumstantial type of ad hominem criticism.

The difficulty of this type of case was brought to my attention as early as 1982 when Krister Segerberg related to me the story of a Swedish woman who had made a real estate investment that enabled her to take advantage of a tax loophole, even though she had previously gone on record as arguing for the elimination of this loophole in the tax laws. Nevertheless, the woman argued that she was being reasonable and consistent in arguing for the general removal of this tax regulation, although personally taking advantage of it while it was still on the books. Segerberg seemed to think, as I remember, that this woman might have a prima facie reasonable case to be made for the logicality of her position, and if so, that this posed a significant problem for the analysis of the ad hominem argument.[1] For if the criticism does not stick in this case, why should it stick in any case?

At the time, this seemed an important problem for the analysis of ad hominem argumentation, but as I could see no fully adequate solution to it at once, it was bypassed except for a brief mention in Walton (*Logical Dialogue,* 1984, p. 74). The only answer that seemed hopeful was the suggestion that a kind of equivocation of the sort mentioned by Hamblin (1970, p. 292) might be involved: the possible presence of a distinction between what is legally obligatory for everyone or for a group and what is personally obligatory or ethical, on grounds of morality or personal conscience. On this basis, perhaps a case could be made for explaining the apparent tenability of the woman's position in the argument by seeing that the inconsistency was only an appearance created by the equivocality of the use of the term 'obligation' in the argument.[2]

Whether this case can be made is open to further argument, but enough has been said to reveal that the problem of pinning down an ad hominem criticism in dialogue and of getting it to stick to an arguer (like Velcro instead of Teflon) who is determined to refute the charge is a nontrivial difficulty.

The following case exhibits the same difficulty, but in this one the individual who was the object of the ad hominem criticism fought back and resisted the attack with unusual determination and ingenuity. The argumentation presented is an invention, but it is based on transcripts of discourse of a real case, collected from televised speeches, newspaper accounts, and transcripts of political debates in a government assembly. Names are not given, and details have been changed to preserve anonymity, but the substance of some of the main arguments pertaining to the ad hominem objections and replies in the controversy has been preserved through reconstruction of the points taken to be most important to the argument as a whole. Through following the lines of argumentation in this case, the reader can come to realize the fuller dimensions of analysis of an ad hominem argument in a practical manner.

Many interesting features of ad hominem argumentation are revealed by this case. One is the tactical continuity of use between the circumstantial and personal forms of argument.[3] An attack on a person's alleged circumstantial inconsistency is often used to lead into an attack on the person's integrity and moral values. Another is the tactic of portraying the ad hominem argument by the defending arguer, as "muck-raking" and "character assassination," and the replies to these defenses by the attackers. Yet another important feature is the evolution of the sequence of ad hominem argumentation as a dynamic but unified tactic of attack from the initial confrontation through to the closing stages of the argument.

2. Framing the Issues of the Dialogue

In this case, the newspapers reported that a member of the state government had admitted making a substantial profit by investing his money in a "quick-flip" tax deduction scheme that he condemned. This man belonged to the socialist party that had often gone on record denouncing the use of tax avoidance schemes by business and corporate investors. He argued, however, that the particular tax scheme he had invested in was perfectly legal and therefore he was operating within the legal system. Although he condemned the system, saying it should be changed, he felt that he had no qualms personally about taking advantage of the program. He argued that he did not personally develop this tax scheme and that the persons who designed the scheme and made it into law at the federal level of government are the ones who should feel uncomfortable.

The question at issue was whether this man was guilty of a personal inconsistency between his private conduct and the public principles he advocated through his political convictions. Initially, he was put on the defensive by newspaper reports that described his activity as "cashing in on a tax dodge" through taking advantage of a scheme that he condemned. His critics in the opposition conservative party soon took up the line of argument that this man's personal integrity as a politician and member of the government was made questionable by his illogical and inconsistent position, citing a clash between his principles and his actions. This man himself, whom we shall call Mr. S., and his party supporters defended his conduct as consistent and tenable. As the debate wore on, the attacks became more severe, and the defenses against those attacks became more subtle.

The sequence of argumentation began by Mr. S. defending his position as consistent and not incongruous. This initial defense already presupposed a confrontation stage (see van Eemeren and Grootendorst, 1984, p. 154) during which the story of the tax return had been made public, and Mr. S. felt defensive. He attempted to justify his position by personally advancing the following arguments in the media, in response to stories that had already appeared in the news.

In the sequel, we will number the arguments presented for ease of subsequent reference. Defending arguments will be prefaced with a *D*. Attacking arguments will be prefaced by an *A*.

First, Mr. S. argued that from his point of view as an investor, nothing was incongruous about his position.

Argument D1

As an investor, you have to look at the rate of return and the risk. From this point of view, there is nothing incongruous about arguing for tax reform while making an investment allowed by the tax law you are criticizing.

Opposition critics responded that you must also look at the argument from the point of view of a politician because the person involved is a politician.

Argument A1

Politicians who criticize tax loopholes and then take advantage of them create cynical attitudes and loss of credibility by the general public. These investors are operating within the bounds of the law, but they leave ordinary taxpayers with a cynical attitude.

Mr. S. continued to maintain that his stance was consistent and within the law.

Argument D2

You cannot condemn anyone for taking advantage of the law. You can rightly argue that questionable tax laws should be abolished, but nothing is wrong with using them if they exist.

He concludes that what he did is not wrong. Nevertheless, the opposition critics continued to insist that what he did is a kind of reversal that involves S. in saying one thing but then turning around and doing something contrary to what he said.

Argument A2

Mr. S. is a member of a party that has denounced this type of tax-avoidance scheme long and hard. But then he turns around and personally invests in such a scheme. It attacks his credibility as an elected official. It rightly offends the public.

This criticism attacks Mr. S.'s conclusion that he did nothing wrong. It concludes that what he did is offensive to the public. It brings in his party affiliation as part of the reason for the culpability of what he did and cites the failure as one of credibility as an elected official. The suggestion is that it is not just anybody whose conduct is at issue here. This person is a public official and therefore has certain standards to maintain. Hence the criticism truly is an ad hominem attack or "argument against the person."

An interesting point is that Mr. S. is trying to portray himself as an ordinary citizen who is looking at the situation from the "point of view of an investor." However, the critics argue at A1 and subsequently that Mr. S. is not just anybody, he is a politician. This point will turn out to be of increasing significance to the dispute as it evolves.

The ad hominem argument is, in other instances as well, not merely an argument against this particular person but also an argument against a person in some particular role. And roles may require commitments to certain forms of conduct. In such a case, personal matters may legitimately be at issue.

In their next move, S. and his defenders use the tactic of shifting the line of argument away from the personal element.

> *Argument D3*
>
> The problem is with the system, not with the individual, of any party affiliation, who participates in a tax shelter. All citizens are entitled to use tax laws. It is the law that creates an unfair tax burden that one should take a stand against.

Mr. S.'s defenders claim that he should have the same right as any citizen to take advantage of tax laws and that the "problem" is with "the system." This is a continuation of the tactic of framing the issue of the dialogue in such a way that personal matters and party affiliations are not to be taken as the real issue of concern. As a counter tactic, the opposition critics insist that such matters are a primary concern in this case because the issue of the discussion is one of personal integrity.

> *Argument A3*
>
> You cannot judge a public official's conduct only on the basis of whether it is strictly legal. An elected official must maintain a position for which his or her integrity cannot be open to serious challenge.

Each side has adopted a tactic of framing the issue differently to this point. S. and his defenders see the two questions of law and personal or party integrity as different issues, and they insist that the primary issue should be the fairness of the tax law. The critics keep trying to frame the issue as one of personal integrity or as a question of conduct that is contrary to party affiliations and principles. The critics see a conflict that is evidence of moral error on the part of S. The defenders refuse to acknowledge a conflict or try to present the matter in such a way that no serious conflict exists. These are opposed tactics of shifting the issue of the dialogue.

3. The Main Argumentation Stage

At the next stage of the development of the argument, the attacking tactics focus on a criticism that becomes more pointed, and the defense tactics become more subtle and deep. As the critics move more seriously to the attack, the contention that there is a basic conflict of moral import is developed by the attackers.

Argument A4

Mr. S. sees nothing wrong in benefiting from laws with which he disagrees. This rigorous logic could be used in the same way to justify his conscience if he had been an ardent abolitionist in the South in the last century and had continued to own slaves and profit from their labor, as long as the law allowed it.

The analogy made in this argument between slavery and tax evasion is perhaps excessive and unjustified as a fair parallel. But the basic point made here by the critics is that a serious moral error has been made by Mr. S. It is a conflict between words and actions that is so serious that it cannot be overlooked or set aside as a nonissue. Mr. S. will have to answer for his actions. The tactic of using the analogy emphasizes the seriousness of the charge maintained by the attackers.

At this point Mr. S.'s party has to concede that a serious problem does exist here that requires some sort of concession, excuse, reply, or explanation. They now adopt the tactic of admitting that S.'s actions have contradicted the party philosophy and that this contravention is a serious problem.

Argument D4

We of Mr. S.'s party concede that his actions have contradicted the party philosophy and therefore have jeopardized the need for national tax reform. But where do you stop with your moral judgments? This is a matter for the church, a matter of individual conscience. We in the party cannot play God and judge people on matters of personal conscience and religious belief.

The next stage of the evolution of the tactics of argumentation was an acknowledgment of the problem by Mr. S. personally and his announcement of his regrets for his actions.

Argument D5

Mr. S. made an announcement going on record as saying that he regretted that his actions may have diminished the support for his party's stand on tax reform. He asked those who would criticize him to join in the campaign to make the system fair to all.

Although S. has now been forced to a position in which he has, in effect, tendered an apology, he is still using the tactic of framing the issue in a way that is designed to contain the damage. He frames the question as one of party credibility rather than one of personal ethics. In addition, he uses the tactic of posturing in such a way as to appear to be on the side of right by appealing to his critics to join him in a "campaign to make the system fair for all." The tactic here is to paint the error in as minimal a way as possible while still making an apology that might take off the heat of the personal attack without being too potentially damaging or without conceding too much.

Needless to say, the opposition was not at all satisfied with the description of the error as only a fault of damaging his own party's credibility. This error could be construed as a simple strategic lapse rather than as a serious ethotic shortcoming that would challenge Mr. S.'s sincerity as a participant in political dialogue. One critic, in particular, rose to the attack.

Argument A5

A critic alleged that Mr. S.'s explanation of his conduct was weak and inappropriate when he claimed he had only made a political mistake as opposed to a moral error. This critic contradicted Mr. S.'s claim that what he did was not unethical or immoral, adding that Mr. S.'s questionable circumstances are a moral issue that he is trying to evade.

The critic's reply keeps the heat on by refusing to acknowledge S.'s description of his error as a purely strategic mistake rather than a moral error that would challenge S.'s honesty as a participant in political dialogue. The critic replies that S.'s "explanation" was inadequate and that S. is still trying to evade the real issue of his immoral circumstances.

Now S. has adopted a tactic of trying to end the argument by making a concession that, he hopes, will close the issue or make it seem as though it has been resolved. The critics refused the concession offered, however, claiming that it was not adequate to conclude the argument. So the argument continued at the insistence of the critics who decline to close off the dialogue.

At the next stage, the defending arguments took up a counter-attacking tactic of appearing to be the object of injury or unfair tactics by the other side. This tu quoque type of tactic deployed a line of argument that became more aggressive and took the initiative, mounting positive attacks by suggesting that the critics themselves were doing something culpable and unreasonable in attacking the character of S.

Argument D6

This personal attack that imputes immoral motives to a member of the government is muckraking. This questioning of the character of the opposition does not throw any light on the real issues, like taxation. It just makes the discussion of these issues more emotional, political, and difficult. This sort of character assassination does not address the real issue at hand and should be ruled out as irrelevant, and not useful.

This argument is a continuation of the defenders' tactic of trying to reframe the issue away from personal matters. It is an interesting and important type of new tactic in its own right, for it attempts to discredit the ad hominem criticism generally as a low and suspicious form of attack identified with "muckraking" and "character assassination." The defenders are hereby bringing out the so-called abusive aspect of ad hominem criticism and claiming that this abusive kind of argument is a "fallacy" that leads to or is associated with emotional discussion and is an obstacle to serious discussion of the issue.

The defending argument *D6* is a tactic of questioning the ad hominem criticism as a valid kind of argument. Responding to this challenge to its methods, the criticizing side of the argument deepened its criticism by providing a general type of justification of the ad hominem criticism as a legitimate type of argument.

Argument A6

Members of the government have to enter into serious financial commitments and multimillion-dollar ventures on behalf of the people. A member of government must be trusted by the people to put their interests before his own self-interest. How can we keep someone in government who must be trusted to act on financial matters like tax reform when he is the kind of person who says "Do as I say, not as I do"? Such a person cannot be trusted to act with integrity, and should not be in government as a political leader.

This argument is a deep one, of fundamental interest in relation to the ad hominem argument generally and also to democratic politics and debate. The argument cites the premise that a member of government must be trusted, and therefore such a person's personal integrity is an important issue of public affairs, should integrity be brought into question by his actions. The conclusion is that personal matters can be a legitimate issue in such a case and that therefore the ad hominem criticism can be a legitimate and valid type of argument and not just "muckraking" or the like.

Nevertheless, there are limits to how far a political discussion should go into personal matters, for even politicians have a right to some privacy. Spending too much time in political debate on purely personal matters, as opposed to such matters of state as economic issues, can be a sign that all is not well with the quality of the debate.

The next tactic of the defenders' argument was to insist that Mr. S.'s personal matters were not suitable for discussion in the political arena. Following up this line with a positive attack, the defenders expressed their confidence in S.'s past performance and contributions.

Argument D7

The issue of Mr. S.'s character is a personal matter that is not within the administrative competence of the government to discuss in the political arena. We in Mr. S.'s party have confidence in the work that he has done and expect him to continue this successful work in the future. Despite the efforts of the opposition to discredit his efforts to contribute to the economy of the state, we have no doubts about Mr. S.'s capability and efficiency as a member of the government.

The argument *D7* is a continuation of the strategy of insisting that S.'s character should not be an issue. But here the claim is backed up more positively by reaffirming the party's confidence in S. and citing S.'s past record.

In such an ad hominem argument, there is room for debate on how far questioning of a person's character, motives, and personal conduct should go. The case of Gary Hart's alleged personal misconduct so widely reported by the U.S. news media raised this question. Standards of privacy in this regard have clearly changed in the United States since the Kennedy era, when similar personal matters were not reported in the media.[4] It is always a question of judgment what types of personal matters are relevant in a particular issue and how much time in a discussion should be spent on them.

In this instance, the critics responded to defense *D7* using the tactic of another argument that reinforces their contention of the relevance of personal actions made in *A6*. In this new argument following, the critics come back to the alleged pragmatic inconsistency between the party platform and the actions of Mr. S. Their new line of argument is that this inconsistency raises a "cloud of suspicion" and doubt that requires clarification and discussion.

This issue of Mr. S.'s actions is relevant because it has raised a cloud of suspicion over the integrity of the whole party to which Mr. S. belongs. This party in the past has often argued for national tax reform in order to prevent quick-flip tax arrangements from shifting the tax burden from the wealthy to working people. Mr. S.'s party even raised this issue in the last election campaign and tried to blame tax abuses on the opposition party. Hence the question of the party's credibility is relevant.

This argument responds neatly to *D7* by concurring that the issue should not be the purely personal or individual character of S. alone and takes the discussion to a more general level by bringing into it the socialist party's policies on national tax reform. According to *A7*, it is the conflict between this platform and S.'s personal actions that have made the question of integrity relevant in this case.

4. Closing Stages of the Argument

The ad hominem argumentation outlined above was part of the larger sequence of ongoing contestive disputation between the two opposing political parties that were the primary participants in the discussion. This particular ad hominem interlude came to a close as the news media and political speeches went on to other topics. The conservatives had made an issue of S.'s tax returns, and the socialist party's participation in the dialogue was of a defensive sort, in the sense that it clearly preferred not to raise or discuss the issue if possible. Once the issue was raised by the opposition, however, the government was obliged to respond and to defend itself in some fashion.

The concluding shot by the critics consolidated the argument, posing it as a loss of credibility by the government.

Argument A8

It is the whole government that has lost the trust of the people on grounds of questions about honesty and personal ethics, not just Mr. S. This government claims to be the champion of the "little guy" and has long inveighed against tax dodges. Yet it has been first at the trough to take advantage of tax loopholes, taking money from the needy. By defending S., the whole government party has destroyed the credibility of its platform. This is not only a matter of individual character but also a question of party position and principle that has been revealed.

The opposition has two connected goals in mounting this type of ad hominem criticism. One is to cause the offending individual to have to resign his position. The other is to discredit the whole opposition party and to attack its position generally.

As this particular dialogue turned out, the critics were not successful in forcing S. to resign, and in their concluding argument *A8* above, they concentrated on using the ad hominem criticism to attack the credibility of the party position of the socialists. It would be hard to measure the success of this argument in attaining its objective because much success depends on how public opinion has been influenced by the government, but the argument does not seem to be an extremely powerful one.

By forcing the government onto the defensive on the question of income tax reform, an issue on which the socialists have traditionally been vocally on the offensive, the conservatives would appear to have gained high ground. Having attacked the credibility of the government on this issue with some success in this instance, when the topic arises again, this earlier victory could be referred to and exploited once more. On the whole, therefore, it would seem that the ad hominem criticism in this instance has been carried forward with at least a partial success in reaching its goal. Thus the concluding argument *A8* summarizes the attack, consolidating its gains by emphasizing once again the ethotic questionability of the alleged conflict between the socialists' party philosophy and their personal performance.

Once the socialist party stuck to the tactic of remaining solid in its continuing support of S., closing ranks instead of abandoning S., the best tactic for the critics was to concentrate on their goal of discrediting the whole party rather than concentrating on trying to unseat S. in particular. Hence the concluding attack centers on "party position and principle" using the colorful phrase "first at the trough" to add punch to the attack.

Following the analysis of van Eemeren and Grootendorst (1984, pp. 85–86), it is possible to look over the whole sequence of argument as a critical discussion and classify it into four main stages. The confrontation stage of a critical discussion (p. 85) is the stage where the participants identify a dispute. The opening stage is the stage in which they decide to try to resolve the dispute by means of a discussion. The argumentation stage is the stage in which they attempt to resolve the dispute by putting forward arguments that cast doubt on the viewpoint of the other side and support their own viewpoint. At the concluding stage, the question is answered whether or not the dispute has been resolved.

The case study in this chapter is, of course, not exactly a critical discussion. It often shifts into an eristic dialogue. But even so, it can be viewed as having distinct stages, which correspond to the sequence represented by van Eemeren and Grootendorst's four main stages (with intervals and substages). The opening stage of identifying the dispute was already set by the media reporting of the facts of Mr. S.'s tax returns and the charge of apparent inconsistency of conduct implicit in the accounts of S.'s actions. The confrontation stage was composed of *D1–D3* and *A1–A3*, the initial moves during which the participants tried to frame the issues of the dialogue and enunciate their points of view. At this stage, S. was trying to neutralize the serious aspects of the charge already posed by the reports of his actions. The critics tried to formulate the charge more pointedly and explicitly but were at best only partially successful against Mr. S.'s persistent defenses.

The argumentation stage initially centered on S.'s attempt to close the argument by making a concession. This attempt failed, and the second stage advanced both the attack and defense arguments, making each more pointed. The next part of the argumentation stage was the intensification and deepening of the argument on both sides, arriving at the core of the ad hominem argument as a type of criticism and showing the real nature of the room for argument on both sides. Finally, the closing stage of the argument was the parting shot of the critics, consolidating and summarizing their whole attacking strategy.

5. Analysis of the Opening and Confrontation Stages

What is especially important about the opening phase is that the issue is raised by the newspaper reports of the "facts" of Mr. S.'s tax arrangements. The reported facts "make the issue public" and create a climate of opinion that raises a question of personal responsibility. This setting already tilts a burden of presumption toward accountability that requires further explanation or discussion. Hence it is not an arguer that poses the issue of the dialogue initially. The issue arises out of a given situation. Then the two sides of the argument arise as responses to this initial situation. (See figure 4.1.)

In this particular argument, it is not a case of two arguers sitting down and deciding that such-and-such will be the agenda of their discussion. Instead, the issue is forced into the arena of debate by the surfacing of the reported facts. The facts then provide a setting that creates the issue or leads to it in a sequence of four phases.

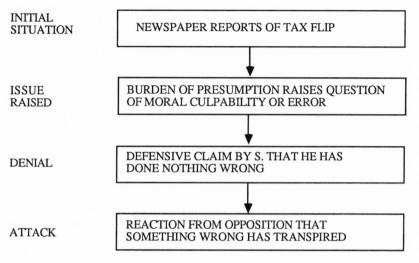

INITIAL SITUATION — NEWSPAPER REPORTS OF TAX FLIP

ISSUE RAISED — BURDEN OF PRESUMPTION RAISES QUESTION OF MORAL CULPABILITY OR ERROR

DENIAL — DEFENSIVE CLAIM BY S. THAT HE HAS DONE NOTHING WRONG

ATTACK — REACTION FROM OPPOSITION THAT SOMETHING WRONG HAS TRANSPIRED

Figure 4.1. Opening Stages of Dialogue

Once the opening phase of the dialogue has raised the question of personal error or fault, then the confrontation stage goes on to dispute about (a) the type of alleged error or fault, and (b) whether personal matters are a legitimate issue. The confrontation has already begun, to some extent, during the opening stages in which there is already an opposition between the denial of any wrongdoing and the initial attack on this denial.

Note that this opening phase already tilts the burden of proof strongly against Mr. S. to defend himself against the presumptive inconsistency already implicit in the description of his actions and position as a socialist political leader. Even at this point, Mr. S. would lose heavily in political credibility if he were not to respond at all and simply let matters stand.

Of course, the subsequent stages showed that S.'s critics still had a lot of work to do. But mainly what they had to do was to respond effectively to S.'s defenses, in order to execute a successful ad hominem attack. The presumptive inconsistency was already made obvious in the newspaper reports, to anyone with an understanding of the background of the story. Thus the burden was on S. to explain or deal with the inconsistency.

Much of the general lines of strategy in the confrontation and argumentation stages were already shaped by the opening situation. Mr. S. was already in a vulnerable position, and if he could contain the damage, that outcome would be reasonably successful for him.

In the confrontation stage of the dialogue, the first three attacks and defenses, the problem is whether there is a presumption of incongruity or inconsistency of some sort involved in S.'s conduct that makes S.'s position open to criticism. Looking at *A1*, an initial pass at formulating both sides of the apparent incongruity could be formulated below.

P1

S. criticized tax-avoidance program T and argued that T should be abolished.

S. personally took advantage of program T and made a profit from it.

Is this a contradiction? Not according to *D1*: "there is nothing incongruous about arguing for tax reform while making an investment allowed by the tax law you are criticizing." This point seems inherently plausible, for it is not evident that there is any logical contradiction in *P1*, and intuitively, it seems plausible that the two propositions on either side of the broken line can be maintained consistently with each other.

Perhaps this appearance of consistency can be explained as the failure of the following argument to be deductively valid.

P2

T should be condemned as a policy [law] that applies to everyone.

Everyone who takes advantage of T should be [morally] condemned.

The argument *P2* is not deductively valid because there might be good reasons for acting in accord with a law with which one personally or morally disagrees. But it seems reasonable that law and morality are two different matters (except perhaps for legal positivists). Why then would the critics press forward on the presumption that some sort of incongruity or inconsistency is evident in this case?

One explanation might be the following reconstruction of an argument that connects principles and actions, in which the first premise is taken as the statement of a personal commitment to a general policy.

P3

Nobody should ever do action A, I maintain.
But, I am now doing A.
I am a person.

Therefore, I should not do A.
So, I am doing something I should not do.
Hence [barring some good explanation of my action], I am culpable of violating a moral principle.

This type of argument would presumably be applicable to the case of S., according to S.'s critics, because S. is maintaining a general principle as stated in the first premise, yet S.'s admitted conduct violates this same principle. Hence S. does not "practice what he preaches." By trying (illicitly) to make an exception of himself, S. is being illogical or perhaps deceitful. So runs the tactic of criticism, according to this first pass at reconstructing it, at any rate.

But of course S. has an excellent defense tactic against this version of the charges against him. For S. maintains that the deduction *P3* does not go through as a valid argument if the first premise is changed to a legal prescription rather than a moral requirement. In other words, S. transforms *P3* into a counterpart inference that he claims is the real argument at issue, and it is an invalid argument.

> *P4*
>
> Nobody should ever be allowed *legally* to do *A*, I maintain.
> But, I am now doing *A*.
> I am a person.
> Therefore, I should not do *A*.
> So, I am doing something I should not do.
> Hence [barring some good explanation of my action], I am culpable of violating a moral principle.

The first premise in *P4* is a statement of what the law should *ideally* be like, even if in fact the actually existing law to which I am subject is quite different.

Is *P4* valid or not? The point made by S. is that even if *P3* is valid, it does not necessarily follow that *P4* has to be valid for that reason. And when S. argues in *D3* that the problem is with the (legal) system, not with the individual's (personal, moral) conduct, he could be interpreted as blocking the move from accepting the plausible validity of *P3* to accepting the (implausible) validity of *P4*.

In a nutshell, S.'s arguments in phase one suggest that his critics are equivocating between moral obligations and legal requirements. He seems to have a good point. His defensive tactic pits a charge of equivocation against the ad hominem attack pressed against him.

Despite the inherent plausibility of S.'s objections in phase one, it also seems that the critics are trying to enunciate a different criticism from the one S. is (reasonably) refuting. At some points, it seems as if the critics are trying to express the idea that it is not a logical contradiction that they are criticizing but some other sort of incongruity or lapse. For instance, argument *A1* says that S.'s actions and words lead to "cynical attitudes and loss of credibility by the general public." What does this tactic of argumentation amount to? It seems not so much an attack on S.'s illogicality per se but more an attack on his sincerity as a credible advocate of a position on tax issues.

Perhaps the argument could be reconstructed as follows.

P5

A sincere person should practice what he preaches.
S. did not.

Therefore, S. is not a sincere person.

This reconstruction seems to come closer to the mark. But S.'s reply at *D3* would still appear to be an effective rebuttal to it. S., in effect, replied at *D3:* "I did practice what I preach because the problem is with the [legal] system, and my own investment did not violate or support the system." Here S. is making a plausible distinction between an act in accord with a law and an act of supporting (or taking a stand against) a law. Once again, he could be suggesting that using an argument such as *P5* against him is based on a questionable equivocation.

Round one seems to have moderately well left S.'s position standing because S.'s critics cannot seem to formulate their argument in a perspicacious way, even though they do seem to be generally occupying the higher moral ground. They seem to have the germ of a good criticism but cannot seem to utilize the tactic of attack in such a way that it is not blocked by S.'s defenses. At the closing part of this first phase however, the critics' move at *A3* seems to be bringing out a key tactical element that holds a good deal of promise for the critics' line of advance. At *A3*, it is emphasized that S. is a public official and that therefore his moral integrity is at issue. The suggestion seems to be that somehow the equivocation defense can be waived aside because personal morality, not legality, is the issue. Legality of S.'s actions aside, *A3* suggests that somehow S.'s personal conduct is out of line with his moral commitments as a public official. But what is the personal incongruity or inconsistency involved at this purely moral or personal level? So far, the critics have not formulated this technique of attack explicitly enough to penetrate S.'s defenses persuasively.

6. Analysis of the Argumentation and Closing Stages

At the argumentation stage, both sides open with arguments that are strong and aggressive. And the arguments of both sides are also open to some serious objections. The argument *A4* compares S.'s situation to that of an abolitionist slaveowner in the nineteenth century. As are all arguments from analogy, this one has its stronger and weaker points. Most noticeable, however, is the aggressiveness of the argument. Comparing Mr. S. to a slaveowner is to make him look intolerably bad in the eyes of a contemporary audience. The vehemence of this argument is an indicator that S.'s critics feel that they have a strong moral backing for their criticism.

The defending arguments *D4* and *D5* try to react to the growing momentum of the attack by making a concession to the attack while at the same time exploiting this concession to suggest that the attacking arguments are improper and outside the proper arena of discussion. Conceding that S. has damaged the party's credibility, S.'s defenders go on to suggest that the issue of his actions is a private, religious matter, which is not a proper topic for political debate. This argument is introduced by the slippery slope question: "But where do you stop with your moral judgments?" The argument goes on to conclude that the party "cannot play God." The suggestion is that the issue of S.'s personal conduct should not be a proper subject of discussion in the public arena of political debate and that therefore the whole issue is closed. Mr. S.'s party has conceded his political error, and all else is now declared closed from discussion.

This juncture of the argument is interesting because usually it is the ad hominem attacker who adopts the tactic of trying to close off the argument by declaring that his opponent is unreliable, untrustworthy, biased, or mentally disturbed, and so forth and therefore unfit to carry the argument any further. This is the familiar poisoning the well type of ad hominem argument.[5] In this case, however, the defenders are trying to close off the ad hominem attack against them by attempting to declare that further argument is inappropriate and pointless.

An interesting feature of the whole line of argumentation in this case is that the defenders keep trying to close off the issue of personal integrity. Therefore, to a considerable extent, even in the preargumentation stages and continuing through the argumentation stage, the strategy of the defending side is to reach the closing stage as soon as possible. They are clearly hoping that the issue will dry up or go away, and the thrust of their general argument strategy is directed toward trying to close off and conclude the dialogue as abruptly as possible. The attackers, however, are trying to open up a personalized line of argument by attacking the integrity of the opposition. Their strategy is a continued attempt to keep opening up the issue of S.'s character and actions in connection with his tax returns. Thus the whole sequence of argument is a seesaw between the one side's tactics to reach the closing stage as soon as possible and the other side's tactics to keep the issue open enough to develop the momentum of the attack.

Another overlap is the strategy of the defending arguments D6 and D7, attempting to revert to the confrontation stage by arguing about what the issue of the argument should properly be. The defenders contend that character should not be an issue because it is a personal matter not fit for political debate and because attacks on character are "muckraking." Arguments A6 and A7, however, give persuasive reasons why character should be relevant in political debate. Curiously, then, these attacks and defenses straddle the confrontation and argumentation stages. To a considerable extent, the issue is "What is the issue?" At the same time, however, powerful argumentation is also being brought forward. In A6, the opposition finally gets to the crux of the ad hominem argument by squarely accusing S. as a political leader who lacks integrity because he does not practice what he preaches. Following that move, a powerful ad hominem argument is advanced in A7 by the contention that S.'s quickflip tax arrangement is directly contradictory to his party platform that has so often condemned this type of abuse in order to maintain their goal of helping "the working people."

One could perhaps say that by mounting powerful ad hominem arguments, the critics are opening up the issue further. By moving to the attack, the critics are overcoming the dual strategy of the defenders either (a) to avoid serious confrontation on the issue of personal integrity in relation to the question of S.'s tax return or (b) to close off the argumentation in the hope that it will cease to be an item of interest or further scandal.

In this case, the critics should be judged successful in having carried out a sufficient ad hominem attack. The concluding arguments A7 and A8 are the consolidation of this attack and the expansion of it from a personal attack on S. to an attack on the credibility of the whole government party to which he belongs. In evaluating the outcome, the defensive side must be credited with some clever and appropriate moves, but the initial situation left them in a highly vulnerable position that was, eventually, fully exploited by the critics' tactics of pressing forward the attack.

The cleverness of the defensive arguments D4 and D5 are noteworthy. Also, the seriousness of the concessions made by these arguments indicates the power of the ad hominem criticism as a form of attack. It seems to be a serious error for a politician to have put himself in a position in which it appears that he has not "practiced what he preaches" on an issue. The ad hominem attack against this position is a serious criticism that seems to carry great weight in political debate. But why? Is it a rhetorical matter? Is it that the electorate is, for whatever reasons, powerfully impressed by and attracted to this sort of personal criticism? Or is it that the ad hominem criticism of this sort does really have an important logical basis indicating a real deficiency in an arguer's position or political stance? This is not an exclusive disjunction—the answer to both questions could be yes.

The evolution of the argument indicated that, despite the defenders' attempts to evade the problem, a serious charge remained to be answered. In the end, the defending arguments could not withstand the full assault of the ad hominem argument.

In evaluating the closing stages, we can see a certain ambiguity present in the conclusion of the ad hominem argument. Was the argument directed toward attacking S. personally, or was it the whole position of the government socialist party that was being attacked? Indeed, the closing arguments *A7* and *A8* are an expansion of the personal attack on S.'s integrity to an attack on the position of the whole governing party as socialists.

A noteworthy problem in sorting out the rights and wrongs of ad hominem criticisms in political argumentation is that of potential conflict for a politician between his own personal position on an issue and the official position of his party on the issue.[6] He might be criticized by an ad hominem argument on the basis of either position. Moreover, it is quite possible, in some instances, that a politician might be reasonably able to defend himself from an alleged ad hominem inconsistency by differentiating his personal position and the party position. Even so, of course, in many cases this tactic of defense has sharp limits because a politician, in western democratic political systems at any rate, is expected to take on commitments both in regard to personal and party positions. To belong to a party or to support it is generally to create a presumption that, broadly speaking, one has taken on some measure of commitment to the main outlines of the party platform and philosophy. You can disagree on specific issues and even criticize your own party on occasions, but if such disagreements become too deep or extensive, the rationale behind your membership in or support of this party can be brought sharply into question on grounds of consistency of your reasoning and commitments.

In this case, S. made no attempt to identify or justify his own personal stance on the issue of fair taxation as a position that differs significantly from that of his party. Hence, the attackers' expansion of the ad hominem criticism from the personal level to the level of party position seems to be not only a successful attack but also, in principle, a reasonable kind of criticism to raise.

Another crucial aspect of this case, pointed out by Frans van Eemeren in discussion,[7] is that the arguments on both sides are really directed toward a third party—the audience. The arguments of S.'s defenders and critics appeared in newspapers, televised speeches and political debates, all media of argument directed to the public. Therefore, in a sense, the public is the real arbitrator of who won or lost the argument, according to the goals of the arguers. The debate is a public one, and the purpose of each of the participants is not simply to refute the contentions of the other side but to do so in such a way that will make political gains in winning over the electorate. As critics, however, we can still evaluate the strengths and weaknesses of the participants' argument from a more removed or "logical" point of view.

Yet another curious aspect of this case is the absence of a particular thesis at issue or agenda of the discussion, other than tax reform and S.'s alleged misdemeanor. Although the defenders do argue that the real issue should be the fairness of tax laws, for the critics the primary issue is the attack on the person and circumstances of S. and his party. From their point of view, integrity is the primary issue. This view is different from many other cases of ad hominem attacks in which a definite agenda of the debate is present, and an ad hominem may be sharply questioned concerning whether it is relevant to the issues of the agenda.

The success of the ad hominem attack in the closing stage should be judged against the background that S.'s reported conduct in the opening stage of the argument left his party highly vulnerable, and in fact the public, even at this stage, would no doubt draw their own ad hominem conclusions. In view of S.'s defending argumentation, the ad hominem argumentation of the critics should be judged on the criterion of how well it refutes these defending moves, thereby restoring or even advancing the allegation of pragmatic inconsistency implicit in the opening situation of the argument.

7. Panoramic View of the Argument

Of the individual stages of the evolution of the strategy of each side as revealed in each of their main moves, five especially important stages of argument stand out, outlined below.

Various ways can be used to look at the challenge and response rhythm of the sequence, but because the defense takes the initiative

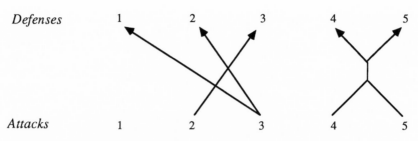

Defenses 1 2 3 4 5

Attacks 1 2 3 4 5

Figure 4.2. Argument Structure

in making explicit moves at the beginning, it is especially useful to view each of the attacks as a response to individual defense moves. This rough pattern is outlined in figure 4.2.

Normally, it would make more sense to view the defending arguments as responses to individual attacking moves. In fact, to some extent, the present argument could be viewed that way, but this particular argument is a little different in that the initial reports of the "facts" by the news media, in effect, constituted a threat or attack to the position of the defendant, Mr. S. Therefore, before his political opponents even began to articulate and advance specific attacks against him, S. took the initiative and staked out a preemptive rebuttal, defending the consistency of his position.

The other factor in this case that distinguishes the flow of the argument is the initial inability of the attacking side to articulate the thrust of its argument in a pointed way. Only in the later stages of the attack do the arguments of the attacking side become more powerful and focused. At first, they seem to be groping. Their later tactics are developed in response to the rebuttals of the defending side.

In a panoramic overview, the most important stages of argument in the defending sequence fall into five propositions.

Defending Tactics

1. My critics are equivocating. There is no real inconsistency.
2. The public issue of tax reform is really the problem.
3. Mr. S. apologizes for damaging the party platform.
4. Personal matters are not appropriate for political debate.
5. This abusive "character assassination" is irrelevant.

The defense arguments each time revert to the underlying thread of maintaining that personal matters are not relevant. The attack evolves toward showing why personal matters should be held relevant.

Attacking Tactics

1. Mr. S.'s "turnaround" has led to public cynicism.
2. S.'s apology is not good enough. The error is moral, not just political.
3. Integrity, not just legality, is at issue.
4. Government members must be trusted. So personal integrity is an issue.
5. The integrity and philosophy of the whole party is at issue.

The attacks start out being nonspecific, citing public cynicism about an error or "turnaround" on the part of S. But the attack is blunt and inchoate because the exact error that is supposed to be blameworthy is not specified clearly or precisely. It is more a presumption of some error or fault that is brought forward. As the attack unfolds, it develops the contention that personal integrity, not just legality, is an issue, in response to Mr. S.'s disclaimers and rebuttals. Finally, the key point is made that personal integrity is an issue because government members must be trusted. A secondary attack on the integrity of the whole party and its platform is then mounted. The attack builds up a mounting momentum from steps 1 through 5, as it responds to the defense moves.

The attacks can be viewed as responses to the defense positions, especially in regard to the relationships pictured. Attacking move 2 is a reply to defending move 3. Attack 3 can be viewed as an attempt to overcome the defense put up by moves 1 and 2 of the defenders. And attacks 4 and 5 function jointly as a rebuttal of the defense moves at 4 and 5 to exclude integrity and personal conduct as legitimate topics of the discussion.

Whether the ad hominem criticism should be evaluated as successful or correct in this case is a judgment that should be made in relation to the evidence of the overall dialogue from its initial situation to its closing stage. It is a question of how the individual attacking and defending moves as techniques of argumentation fit into the larger pragmatic context of dialogue.

The initial situation was highly favorable for deploying the tactic of an ad hominem criticism because a particular member of a socialist party (who had often condemned tax flips and evasions) had in fact personally engaged in a tax flip of the very sort he would personally condemn because of his political philosophy. In this situation, it was relatively easy for a critic to advance successfully a circumstantial ad hominem criticism. There were no problems of failure of being parallel, comparable to such cases as the situation in the sportsman's rejoinder case. Therefore, all the critics had to do was to fill in certain gaps in the sequence of ad hominem argumentation opened up by the defenders' arguments. Although the process of filling in these gaps proved slow in gaining momentum, ultimately it was completed in the closing stage of the argument, effectively enough to raise serious questions about the consistency of the socialists' position.

In fact, the critics may have had specific goals in mind in mounting this attack. They may have wanted to force Mr. S. to resign his seat. They may have wanted to attack the government on the issue of tax reform as a kind of hedge against future attacks by the government party on the critics' party. Or they may have wanted to discredit the governing party in the eyes of the voters generally. Whether these specific objectives were in fact achieved in this case do not matter significantly from a logical point of view of analyzing the normative worth of the ad hominem argumentation. What does matter is that the sequence of argumentation did present enough of the right sort of evidence to raise a strong presumption of circumstantial inconsistency to question seriously the personal integrity of S. and by inference, the collective sincerity of his party in relation to tax reform. A key requirement was showing the relevance of character as an issue.

8. Personal Conduct and Character of Political Officeholders

In recent years, public discussion of the "character issue" and the issue of "ethics in government" has followed the Gary Hart case through a sequence of other cases to the John Tower case, the Jim Wright case, and so on. Evidently a change in public standards has taken place concerning which "private" matters of personal and sexual conduct and of personal financial affairs of political officeholders have been considered relevant as issues for public discussion. During the Kennedy era "womanizing" and sexual conduct generally was regarded as, for the most part, off limit to reporters. Now such questions have routinely become matters for intense public scrutiny and discussion. Similarly, personal financial affairs of politicians have come under much greater scrutiny and surveillance. Conflict of interest has now become a common subject of political argumentation.

A TIME/CNN poll taken by Yankelovich Clancy Shulman (Walter Shapiro, "Drawing the Line," *Time*, March 13, 1989, 34–35) gives an indication of attitudes of the time on the various categories of situations that have been subjects of controversy.

Note that none of the categories in table 4.1 applies to the case of Mr. S. In particular, he was not accused of "cheating" on his income tax. The real issue in the case study of Mr. S. was not whether his profiting from a tax dodge was in itself unethical but whether this conduct is consistent with his condemnation of similar conduct on the part of his political opponents. One of the major tactics used by Mr. S. was to try to frame the discussion in such a way that questions of character could be excluded as "irrelevant" and as "mudslinging." But what should be said about this tactic?

The use of this tactic is reasonable in some cases, not reasonable in others, depending on the extent of the use of it in a particular dialogue. Evaluation of the reasonableness or fallaciousness of this tactic is a question of judgment that should take into account how the original ad hominem technique was used in the dialogue. The defending tactic should then be judged in relation to the original attack and the context of the dialogue. Generally, it needs to be emphasized that a presumption is present that personal conduct and character are relevant subjects for political debate if political officeholders or candidates for political office are concerned.

Character is bound to be a relevant consideration in political argumentation, for various reasons. One important reason is that the is-

Table 4.1. TIME/CNN Poll

Should people in high government offices be required to:	YES	NO
Publicly disclose income from outside jobs	67%	28%
Publicly disclose all their financial assets	49%	42%
Not accept income from speeches to business or other private groups	40%	51%
Put their stock holdings in a blind trust	37%	46%
Not accept income from any other job source	35%	57%
Sell all their holdings in the stock market	26%	60%
Should any of the following actions disqualify someone from holding a high position in government?	YES	NO
Cheating on their income taxes	86%	12%
Being drunk in public	68%	29%
Being a high-paid business consultant in an area related to their government job	43%	48%
Having an extramarital affair	31%	64%

From a telephone poll of 504 adult Americans taken for TIME/CNN on March 2 by Yankelovich Clancy Shulman. Sampling error is plus or minus 4.5%.

sues, on such complex matters as economic and foreign affairs, are inherently difficult for most voters to have much of a thorough knowledge of them. Nobody can be an expert on everything. Inevitably, a voter will be inclined to choose a candidate who appears to stand for the voter's values and viewpoint generally, and the best way to make this choice is to try to form some estimate of the candidate's character and personality. Moreover, making such judgments on the basis of character is, to some extent at least, a reasonable way of going about making a decision in the absence of firm or comprehensive knowledge of the issues of a political contest.

Another element of character is the factor of judgment that enters into political reasoning through the importance of a politician's perceived competence, as shown in the way she manages affairs and handles problems. Does she show firmness in standing up to the country's opponents? Does she show good business and management skills in dealing with economic problems? Does she show compassion to the less fortunate? And how does she respond to stress and handle difficult situations? These kinds of questions are important, and they do seem to have a place in a reasonable assessment of the capabilities of political aspirants or leaders.

These questions are appropriate because the issues are constantly changing, whereas a politician is likely to be in power for an extended period, when new issues and developments will have to be confronted. A candidate's position on a set of specific issues at any given point is therefore only a partial measure of the person's underlying, deeper position or philosophical approach as a whole. The person's general outlook is as important as his proclaimed stand on this or that specific issue. But general outlook is related to a person's dispositions, judgment, and personal style. Issues are essentially related to values, and values are related to character.

For example, confidence and decisiveness can be important values for a politician to have. According to political commentators, southern white males in the United States are especially disappointed by lack of confidence or decisiveness in a political leader (Tamar Jacoby, Howard Fineman, and Vern E. Smith, "Going After White Males," *Newsweek*, September 14, 1987, p. 40). Criticisms of President Clinton in late 1994 (see case 5.5) were based on public perceptions that he lacked a consistent set of values because of his many policy reversals. Lack of consistency is not the same as indecisiveness, but perceptions of lack of consistency can have implications for a candidate's inferred character or personal "image." " 'It has less to do with issues,' explains Democratic campaign consultant David Doak, 'than with the image of the candidate that flows from them: weakness versus strength, character versus lack of character, family values versus non-traditional ones.' "

According to campaign consultants, southern men believed that Reagan had qualities of confidence and decisiveness that Carter lacked and therefore thought that Reagan stood for important values. These values were not expressed by a specific issue but were perceived as a matter of character by the voters who expressed their preferences (p. 39). While voters may lay stress on different aspects of character, it seems hard to deny that these judgments of character can and should have a proper role to play in a democratic, political, decision-making process. The connection between character and political discourse in a democratic system will be precisely established in chapter 5.

The following case can be used to indicate how ad hominem argumentation can be a legitimate part of an election campaign.

Case 4.1

A cartoon that appeared in *Newsweek* in 1995 (Mike Luckovich, *Atlantic Constitution, Newsweek*, November 6, 1995, p. 35) shows two identical Bill Clintons in a speechmaking pose. One says, "I regret raising taxes," while the other says, "Raising taxes was a good thing." The caption under the cartoon reads, "With Clinton in the race, who needs other candidates?"

This cartoon is a legitimate political comment, in the context of the election campaign reporting, even though it definitely poses a circumstantial ad hominem attack against Clinton's political arguments by implying that Clinton lacks a consistent set of values because of his many policy reversals.

Other editorial commentators have defended Clinton's policy stands and character from such ad hominem attacks. Michael Kinsey in an editorial in *Time* ("Everybody Does It," *Time*, April 29, 1996, p. 108) asked, "Why is Clinton's character such a liability when he is no worse than other pols?" The voters may have agreed with this view of the matter. With less than three weeks to go in the presidential election, Bob Dole tried to make the character issue a central one by using the ad hominem argument against Clinton, "Never has America seen a politician who brags so freely about promises he never kept, votes he hasn't earned, goals he never accomplished or virtues he never displayed" (Richard Stengel, "The Trouble with Character," *Time*, October 28, 1996, 38–40; quoted from p. 38). This attack, when used by Dole in a speech, drew little response from the audience (p. 38) and evidently did not turn out to influence voters to swing to Dole's side in the election.

It follows that ad hominem argumentation, which brings in considerations of individual character and personality of an arguer in weighing his arguments, should not be excluded from political debate on a set of issues. It follows too that the personal or character-centered type of ad hominem attack on an arguer should not always be declared "abusive" or, at any rate, fallacious. In some political arguments, character is relevant.

Indeed, ad hominem attacks clearly can be unjustifiably abusive in some cases and logically open to criticism and condemnation on various grounds. When purely ad hominem matters of character and personal conduct dominate a debate, at the expense of serious consideration of the designated issues of an agenda, it is clear that something has gone wrong. For example, serious decisions may be inadequately reasoned through if too much time is given in congressional or parliamentary debates to personal attacks on members' alleged misconduct, moral transgressions, or faults of character. If the news media give in to the temptation to sell stories by pandering to an excessive and unjustified interest of the public in the private lives and personalities of individuals rather than giving factual coverage or explanations of important events and issues, then the whole process of political reasoning in a democracy is short-circuited. The dangers of excessive and fallacious ad hominem argumentation in political debates should not be underestimated. It is a form of argument that can and often does go badly wrong because it is so powerful as an attack.[8]

In the case of Mr. S., however, character clearly should be regarded as relevant and his defensive argument D6 attributing "muckraking" and "character assassination" to his attackers should be discounted. Note, however, that D6 is based on an underlying technique of defense that is, in principle, legitimate. Therefore, it is up to the attackers to deal with D6 if their ad hominem argument is to be successfully advanced. This task was carried out effectively by the subsequent argument A6 at the next move.

In general, this form of attack and defense on the relevance of "the character issue" should be duly noted as an important part of the use of the ad hominem technique. Any use of ad hominem argumentation is based on a presumption that character or the personal conduct of the individual in question is a relevant consideration in the discussion. Anyone attacked by an ad hominem argument has a way out and can argue that considerations of character or personal conduct are not relevant. This defense, however, is more tactically appropriate in some cases than in others. Some cases will require careful judgment to evaluate in this regard.

9. The Equivocation Defense

Right at the outset, Mr. S. counterattacked by claiming that as an investor he was acting as a private citizen and not in the capacity of a political officeholder (argument *D1*). Mr. S. claimed that his attackers were equivocating and that a distinction must be drawn between matters of personal conduct and matters of public policy. Using this argument, he claimed to show that no inconsistency was implicit in his personal conduct of taking advantage of the tax dodge while decrying the use of tax dodges by his opponents in politics.

This defense did not turn out to be entirely plausible in his case in the end and was effectively countered by his attackers. It is interesting to note that the technique used by this defense is a reasonable kind of argumentation tactic. In principle, it is possible for a political officeholder to distinguish between his private sphere of conduct based on his personal morality or religious point of view and his public sphere of action as an officeholder or member of a political party.

An issue that was prominent in 1984 political campaigns concerned Democrats who supported the party line of freedom of choice but also claimed as Catholics that they personally opposed abortion. The controversy was heightened in two instances in particular. Vice-presidential candidate Geraldine Ferraro defended her support of "reproductive freedom" as consistent with her personal commitment to the Catholic religion, which is against abortion, on grounds of separation of church and state.

This argument was attacked by Bishop James W. Malone, president of the National Conference of Catholic Bishops, who rejected it as "simply not logically tenable," writing that it would be as unacceptable as the case of an officeseeker who puts forth his personal views but has no proposals for implementing them. Although he acknowledged that Catholics can legitimately disagree on how moral principles are applied to public policies, he stressed the church's opposition to the direct taking of human life, as in the case of abortion.[9]

Governor Cuomo responded to this criticism by a speech "Religious Belief and Public Morality," given to the Department of Theology at the University of Notre Dame on September 13, 1984 (Cuomo, 1984). In this carefully reasoned and judicious exposition of his position, Mr. Cuomo argued that the Catholic who holds political office in a pluralistic democracy in which other religious points of view must also be represented and respected must pay attention to the "complex interplay of forces and considerations" that go into the making of laws and policies (p. 32) and that a certain "latitude of judgment" (p. 34) must be allowed. As a result, when translating Catholic teachings into public policy, a degree of "realism" does not necessarily mean that a policymaker is being a hypocrite. In the "application of [church] teachings"—he argued—"[in] the exact way we translate them into action, the specific laws we propose, . . . there [is] no one, clear absolute route that the church says, as a matter of doctrine, we must follow" (p. 34).

On the question of abortion, Mr. Cuomo argued that he did not believe that a constitutional amendment is the best way for Catholics to seek to deal with the question in a realistic way.

With regard to abortion, the American bishops have had to weigh Catholic moral teaching against the fact of a pluralistic country where our view is in the minority, acknowledging that what is ideally desirable isn't always feasible, that there can be different political approaches to abortion besides unyielding adherence to an absolute prohibition. This is in the American-Catholic tradition of political realism. In supporting or opposing specific legislation the Church in this country has never retreated into a moral fundamentalism that will settle for nothing less than total acceptance of its views.[10]

What Mr. Cuomo was arguing is that a Catholic politician who signs a bill for funding of abortion is not necessarily being illogical, inconsistent, or hypocritical in the sense that would support an ad hominem attack against his position.

The right way to respond in any particular case of this sort requires a degree of judgment and balance. A Catholic political officeholder who signs a bill to support abortion funding is definitely putting himself in a potentially vulnerable position that is rightly open to critical questioning on grounds of ad hominem consistency. Yet such a presumptive inconsistency can, in principle, be defended against—and there should be a right to reply to such charges. As Mr. Cuomo's speech made clear, in such cases, there is, in general, room to reply.

Mr. Cuomo differs with the bishops in that he thinks their view of the matter requires too tight or too strict a relationship between an officeholder's political or legislative actions and religious (personal) views on morality. In fact, it seemed to some commentators that the arguments of Ms. Ferraro went to the opposite extreme and that she at some point denied that her religious beliefs were even relevant to her political actions. Joseph A. Califano, Jr., in an essay in *The Wash-*

ington Post (Califano, 1984) agreed with Cuomo's views, but he also agreed, to some extent, with the point of view advocated by the bishops that those who oppose abortion "have an obligation to fight for their convictions."[11] It is, however, a question of how this obligation is to be interpreted or judged in a particular case.

Mr. Califano argued that, as he saw it, Ms. Ferraro had taken a stronger position in that she had perceived the ad hominem attacks on her consistency as being, in general, based on irrelevance.

What strikes me as the difference between Geraldine Ferraro's position and that of the bishops is this: The bishops are saying that public officials who consider abortion morally wrong have an obligation to espouse their view, to battle in the political arena for their position. Mrs. Ferraro seems to be saying that she has no obligation as a public official to argue for what she believes as a private person about abortion. Indeed, at some points she seems to be saying that her personal convictions about abortion are irrelevant to her role as a member of Congress; that she can support public funding of abortion in circumstances where she personally considers abortion wrong.[12]

Whether this interpretation of Ms. Ferraro's response is accurate or justified is an open question, but it does raise an interesting point. It indicates that one tactic available to someone who has been attacked by a circumstantial ad hominem argument of this sort is to respond by arguing that the cited incident of personal (in this case religious) commitment is not relevant to an assessment of the political action carried out as an officeholder. The response, in other words, is to argue that the ad hominem attack is based on an irrelevant alignment of two matters that should really be kept separate.

This type of response is the opposite extreme of the tactic used in the original attack of the bishops. It did not allow for enough latitude for judgment or explanation of a presumptive ad hominem inconsistency. This response allows too much latitude: it claims that the presumptive inconsistency can simply be dismissed or ignored, as based on irrelevance, without any explanation or intervention of questions of judgment in applying the presumptive inconsistency to a particular case.

Although Mr. Cuomo's speech given on September 13, 1984, at the University of Notre Dame took a moderate and measured approach to the issue, his earlier response to the attack of Archbishop John J. O'Connor of New York was more peremptory. In a *Newsweek* article (Kenneth J. Woodward, "Politics and Abortion," *Newsweek*, August 20, 1984, p. 66), it was reported that in the escalating debate with O'Connor, Cuomo responded strongly to a statement issued by Bishop James W. Malone, president of the National Conference of

Catholic Bishops. As noted above, Malone had put forward a strong ad hominem attack to the effect that any candidate who says that his personal views should not influence his policy decisions would be on ground that is "simply not logically tenable." Cuomo replied by calling this a straw man attack.

"Straw Man": Last week in his Albany office, Cuomo reviewed Malone's statement and concluded that "there isn't a line I can disagree with. The bishops are saying they won't take positions on candidates and that office-holders should make decisions based on conscience." As Cuomo saw it, the bishops "outlined a straw man" in describing candidates who take personal positions but do not act on them. "It certainly doesn't apply to me," he insisted. "I don't think it's good that society aborts its young," he declared, "but for a public official, the question is where you draw the line between the beliefs you hold personally and those you pursue in public policy."[13]

This response to the ad hominem criticism is interesting because it rebuts one attack of fallacy by posing another charge of fallacy in reply. As applied to his own case, Mr. Cuomo criticized Mr. Malone's argument as use of the straw man fallacy, imputing to him (Mr. Cuomo) a position he had not adopted. Or as Mr. Cuomo himself concisely put it, he does not disagree with any line of Mr. Malone's statement, but he thinks that the statement does not apply to his own case.

In general, we have discovered another "way out" that is systematically available to anyone who is attacked by an ad hominem argument. If you can claim that you were acting in some official capacity or in some other role, say, as a member of a group or organization, then you can claim no inconsistency (as alleged) between these actions and others that you carried out on the basis of your personal or private morality.

As in the defense based on relevance (in section 8), however, this technique works very well in some cases and not at all well in others. It did not work well for Mr. S. in the end. It seemed to work well at first, but under pressure from the attacks, the exponents of Mr. S.'s side of the argument were forced to concede that his actions had "contradicted the party philosophy." Yet, even at this point, they dug in for a partial defense by asking about the limits of moral judgments in "a matter of individual conscience." In principle, here was a way out for Mr. S., and he took full advantage of it, even up to Argument *D7* in which character was said to be "a personal matter that is not within the administrative competence of the government to discuss." Just as it was difficult to define the exact scope and limits of these private and public spheres in the cases of Ms. Ferraro and Mr.

Cuomo, so here too, the lack of precise guidelines to fit the particular case appears to leave room open for defense.

At argument *A8*, however, the attackers argued effectively that this case is "not only a matter of individual character but also a question of party position and principle that has been revealed." Mr. S. and his defenders are vulnerable to this attack, given that they have placed such emphasis in their political platform on how bad it is to take advantage of tax dodges available only to "the rich" to take money from "the little guy." Because this emphasis is an important part of the political platform of Mr. S.'s party and not an incidental issue involving division of opinion, argument *A8* is on a strong basis.

10. Evaluating a Case

In this case, the use of the ad hominem argument to attack Mr. S.'s actions was basically reasonable and legitimate, even though it was pressed forward firmly, persistently, and even aggressively in places. But the defenses used were also in principle reasonable arguments and were used to good effect in this case. The defenses enabled the defenders to contain the damage of an ad hominem attack to which they were extremely vulnerable. These defenses themselves are interesting tactics as responses to an ad hominem argument, and they are, in fact, themselves associated with baptized fallacies—equivocation, irrelevance, and straw man.

An ad hominem attack is always by its nature a defeasible type of argument that works by shifting presumptions, but it can be replied to and even refuted by raising considerations special to a particular case. It can be defended against effectively in some cases by the tactics of arguing that character is not relevant or that private morality must be adjusted to the realities of public politics. Just how successful either defense is, in a given case, always needs to be evaluated in relation to the sequence of dialogue in which the attack was advanced. By the same token, an evaluation of the ad hominem attack as strong or weak, reasonable or fallacious, should be judged in relation to the text of discourse that includes the defenses of the party attacked, should these be available.

Whether such an ad hominem argument is fallacious is not, therefore, exclusively a question of who is breaking a rule of the dialogue. It should be a question of how the attack was carried out and how it was defended against. Critics who are supposedly making a nonbiased evaluation should ask: Are the sequences of moves in context reasonable, or are they excessive ways of responding to the moves of the other side, given the initial situation of the dialogue? Evaluating "excessiveness" requires judgment of how the technique of argumentation was used or misused in the dialogue.

The context of dialogue in this case is a form of public debate in which one politician has taken the initiative of attacking another politician of an opposed party. The dialogue was carried back and forth in newspaper reports, speeches, and other releases to the media. Clearly the dialogue contains a strong adversarial (eristic) element, but even so, the debaters adhere fairly well to rules and conventions of critical discussion. Some of these conventions and standards of discussion (for example, which questions about "personal" matters are acceptable to ask) are themselves in a process of change and adjustment as the dialogue proceeds (see table 4.1).

The fourth critical question in the set of critical questions for the circumstantial ad hominem (chapter 6, section 3) is really two questions. The second one asks whether the person attacked could resolve or explain the alleged circumstantial inconsistency. This question reveals the essential defeasibility of ad hominem as a technique of argumentation, for it shows how such an attack is always (in principle) open to rebuttal. It also reveals the dialectical nature of the job of evaluating an ad hominem argument, especially if the arguer attacked by this technique is available to dispute the attack.

Any theory of fallacy that holds promise of being a useful theory must be able to take into account this dialectical sensitivity of the uses of the ad hominem technique to tactics of attack and defense. In this case, the dialectical framework is different from what we have been led to expect in the standard examples of ad hominem arguments. It is considerably more complex, and the argument is a lot more difficult to "pin down" or prosecute against a determined respondent than the textbook treatments would indicate. In this case, the leader of the opposition had to prove that his ad hominem argument was not fallacious, by showing the relevance of character and personal conduct to the discussion in the given case. We see then two sides to the ad hominem argument.

5

Character, Deliberation, and Practical Reasoning

This chapter breaks new ground by defining the elements of character most important in direct (abusive) ad hominem arguments and by showing how character is linked to commitment by practical reasoning in ad hominem arguments. A goal-directed normative model of dialogue called deliberation is outlined.[1] Using this model, it is proved, along Aristotelian lines, that ad hominem arguments centered on the ethos (character or personality) of a speaker (Braet, 1992, p. 311) are not only relevant in political argumentation but are an important and even fundamental part of it.

The biggest gap in the literature on ad hominem is that of defining the concept of character in the abusive subtype. In this chapter, an Aristotelian definition of *character* as a speaker's set of core convictions or personal goals is given. What is referred to in this definition is a person's character (ethos), representing the core principles, values, or goals that he or she stands for, in a relatively consistent pattern of action and argumentation over a prolonged period during which personal choices are made. Through the Aristotelian notion of practical reasoning, this chapter reveals the connection between commitment and character, laying the groundwork for a solution to the dilemma posed by chapter 3.

1. What Is Character?

Character is the habit or disposition of a person to act in certain relatively consistent ways, over a lifetime. These habitual, preferred ways of acting are revealed in responses to crises, challenges, or problems that occur in a person's lifetime. Character, as a practical concept, has to do with responding well or badly to such challenges. The terms 'well' and 'badly' are meant here in a practical (pragmatic) sense in that certain qualities (or traits) of character of a person are generally presumed to be morally positive, and others are revealed by the actions they carry out and the goals they profess or are committed to, as revealed by their words and arguments. Whether a person's character is deemed "good" or "bad" is judged in this theory as a function of the role that person is supposed to be playing in a given case in point. A role defines certain commitments and obligations in a dialogue in which the person takes part.

These traits of character are qualities of a person exhibited in the actions of that person when confronted with practical choices. Nussbaum (1992, p. 131) offers the following definition of 'character':

A person's character is a group of relatively stable traits connected with practical choice and action. These traits—such as, for example, courage, moderation, and justice—are usually taken to involve a complex interweaving of beliefs, motivational desires, and emotional responses. They are considered to be not arbitrary personal idiosyncrasies, but traits that any normal human being can cultivate, given an appropriate moral education and personal effort.

Nussbaum's definition is expressed in terms of beliefs and desires. A comparable, but significantly different definition of 'character' is given by Kupperman (1991, p. 17): "X's character is X's normal pattern of thought and action, especially with respect to concerns and commitments in matters affecting the happiness of others or of X, and most especially in relation to moral choices." Kupperman's definition is expressed in terms of concerns, commitments, and normal patterns of thought and action. For Kupperman (p. 17), "normal pattern" is taken as a "shorthand" for "what is normal (or at least not distinctly abnormal) for X in various circumstances, especially including highly unusual circumstances that we might regard as moral test cases." Kupperman sees concerns and commitments as the linkage between a person's internal thoughts and feelings and her externally evident choices and actions. What is especially interesting about Kupperman's definition, in light of our study in chapter 3 of the problem of analyzing ad hominem argumentation, is that commitment is taken to be an essential part of character. But does 'commitment' here mean the same thing as in the argument from commitment (chapter 3), or does it refer to ethical commitment to actions or ways of conducting oneself in making personal choices?

The word 'character' itself, as Kupperman (p. 3) notes, is said by the *Oxford English Dictionary* to come from the Greek word for "instrument for marking and graving, impress, stamp, distinctive mark, distinctive nature." Nussbaum (1992, p. 131) gives a revealing account of the Greek origins and etymology of this word.

The word "character" is derived from the Greek *charakter,* originally a mark impressed upon a coin, later, more broadly, of a distinctive mark by which a thing is distinguished from others. The philosophical use of the English word "character," however, usually translates the Greek word *ethos* (importantly distinct from *ethos,* "habit"). And the expression "excellence of character" renders the Greek expression *ethike arete* (sometimes also translated as "moral virtue").

The equation of excellence of character with moral virtue in the Greek philosophical lexicon is a good indication that character is not the same thing as personality. As Kupperman (1991, p. 5) puts it, "the word *character* has moral overtones the word *personality* lacks." Character is an ethical concept, closely related to the concept of virtue in ethics, as opposed to an empirical term in psychology or a medical term in psychiatry.

The preeminent account of excellence of character is that of Aristotle. Aristotle defines *excellence of character* (*Nicomachean Ethics* 1106 b 36–1107 a 2)—translated in Ross (Oxford) edition as "virtue" and translated by Nussbaum as a settled state concerned with choice (Nussbaum, 1992, p. 137): "Excellence of character is a settled state *(hexis)* concerned with choice, situated in a mean relative to us, this being determined by reasoning, the reasoning that a person of practical wisdom would use to determine it." This definition makes it clear that for Aristotle, character is concerned with deliberation or choice of actions and is closely connected to reasoning—in fact, what is usually called practical reasoning or practical wisdom *(phronesis).*

An example of a character trait is *good character for veracity,* which is generally presumed to be a good quality—a positive character disposition. But character for veracity is expressed in the allegation that a person has shown a pattern of being a "liar" or in the allegation that a person is a hypocrite (or shows a pattern of being insincere in advocating policies she does not believe in personally), and such traits are generally presumed to be negative qualities. In fact, calling someone a liar or a hypocrite is a generally accepted method of personal attack.

Character is supposed to be a long-term quality, something that even lasts over a lifetime. Hence evidence of someone's good or bad character may come from a report of an alleged personal action in the past. Character could change, but the general presumption is that it tends to be relatively stable (with explainable deviations and alterations of course) over a long period in an individual's life.

This aspect of presumed stability is important in evaluating ad hominem arguments because evidence of bad character may come from an incident reported by someone else as having occurred long ago in the past. So the evidence for or against a character allegation may often involve alleged facts that are external to the situation, the given discussion in which the allegation is being made. If someone is alleged to be a liar, for example, the allegation may be on the evidence of something that he is reported to have said long ago, in quite a different situation from that of the present discussion.

A key difference between the abusive and circumstantial ad hominem arguments is that the circumstantial attack generally centers on a single action or connected sequence of actions, and an inference is drawn from this action concerning the arguer's commitments. With the abusive ad hominem argument, the arguer's character as a long-term settled state is the focus of the attack. This type of argument uses a different kind of evidence and inference because a person's character is internal and is a settled disposition or attitude that involves interpreting how the person has acted in many different situations and what these actions may, over a prolonged period, be judged to imply about his goals and virtues or vices. Actions (or the events associated with them) can be directly observed by witnesses, but character is more difficult to judge because it involves long-term extrapolations that are biographical in nature. Character is part of the person.

2. Place of Character in Critical Discussion

As noted in chapter 3, section 4, the concept of a person, over and above being a participant in a dialogue exchange of speech acts, seems to have little or no place of importance in the argumentation in a critical discussion. What seems to matter in a critical discussion is not the character of the arguer per se but the kinds of moves made by a participant and the commitments inserted into a participant's commitment store, in virtue of the kinds of moves she makes in the dialogue. 'Commitment' here is used in Hamblin's sense of going on record as having accepted a proposition in a dialogue exchange of arguments. If a place for character issues exists in a critical discussion, it would seem to lie in a participant's commitment set, as somehow expressing his or her character.

But does commitment in a critical discussion imply a certain type of character on the part of a participant? Nothing rules out that it might, in some cases. But there is no necessary connection, and nothing we have examined so far implies that there is generally some connection of any kind yet identified.

A critical discussion is about an *issue*, meaning that one participant supports a proposition called her *thesis*, and the other participant either doubts that thesis (in the weaker type of conflict of opinions) or supports the opposite proposition as his thesis (in the stronger type of conflict of opinions). In a critical discussion the argumentation is supposed to be directed toward a resolution of this conflict of opinions by rational means (van Eemeren and Grootendorst, 1984). Hence any argument or other move made in the critical discussion is relevant only to the extent that it contributes to the resolution of this originating conflict of opinions. Other arguments, like personal attacks, if they do not bear on the issue, are irrelevant (in the critical discussion).

Is an attack on the character of a participant relevant if cited as an argument or the basis of an argument in a critical discussion? *Prima facie*, the answer seems to be "no" because in a critical discussion the arguments are supposed to present evidence, on one side or the other, that is used to prove or justify that the proposition at issue is true or false. Attacking the other party's character, in the form of honesty, sincerity, reliability for veracity, and so forth, would not seem to be relevant evidence of the kind generally required in a critical discussion.

Under the surface of these initial expectations, however, the character of a participant could be relevant in a critical discussion. As applied to real cases of conversational argumentation, the rules of a critical discussion exist in the form of implicit, Gricean maxims of politeness.[2] These maxims require a collaborative participant to take turns in the dialogue exchanges and to contribute to the dialogue in accord with reasonable expectations of seriousness, clarity, sincerity, honesty, relevance and informativeness. In such a situation, if one participant finds evidence from the previous dialogue exchanges to show that the other party is not seriously contributing to the dialogue or is being dishonest in a way that contravenes one of the maxims of the conversation, then citing each evidence should be a relevant part of the dialogue. Such a charge of dishonesty or insincerity could amount to an ad hominem personal attack on the other party's character. Still, it would be a relevant argument because (or to the extent that) it could function as a legitimate contribution to the goal of the dialogue. The reason it would contribute is that it would be useful to get the dialogue back on track, by citing a violation of a maxim and calling for the deviation to be corrected. The challenge would call into question the person's attitudes as deemed appropriate for a collaborative critical discussion requiring a certain amount of sincerity and good faith on both sides.

In a critical discussion, a participant is supposed to be an advocate for her thesis and support it as strongly as possible by proargumentation. In doing so, a participant is also supposed to show balance and restraint by exhibiting five characteristic attitudes at appropriate points (Walton, *One-Sided*, 1998, chapter 1):

1. *Flexible Commitment.* An arguer must generally stick to her commitments, but she must also be ready to retract them (in the appropriate circumstances).
2. *Empathy.* An arguer must base her arguments on the commitments of the other party, portraying these commitments accurately, perceptively and fairly.
3. *Open-mindedness.* An arguer must be willing to consider the arguments of the opposed point of view and weigh them on their merits, instead of just rejecting them out of hand.
4. *Critical Doubt.* In considering objections to her own arguments, an arguer must be able to suspend her own commitments (hypothetically).
5. *Evidence Sensitivity.* An arguer must react by retracting or modifying commitments when confronted by an argument based on evidence of the type generally appropriate for the type of dialogue.

These five characteristics define who is a "good person" or a participant who has favorable and constructive attitudes in a critical discussion.

For example, if one participant is quarreling or shows evidence of clearly contravening earlier commitments he had advocated, it could be appropriate for the other party to reply, "Be serious!" or "You are not really honestly and sincerely taking part in the critical discussion here!" Then these ad hominem critical reactions could be relevant replies in the critical discussion. Such a reply could be regarded, in the appropriate case, as a kind of procedural or meta-dialogue move that tries to get the dialogue back on a constructive track and thus serves as a collaborative move that contributes to the goal of the critical discussion.[3]

Although it may appear initially that personal attack, of the ad hominem sort of argument, has no place in a critical discussion, once we probe beneath the surface, it appears that such arguments could, in some cases, have some secondary but legitimate place in such a discussion. The key to understanding this place lies in the distinction, noted in chapter 1, section 9, between rigorous persuasion dialogue (RPD) and permissive persuasive dialogue (PPD), analyzed in Walton and Krabbe (1995). In the permissive type of persuasion dialogue, moves are not exactly specified in a rigorous way, allowing room for flexibility but, at the same time, making successful dialogue dependent on Gricean maxims of politeness. This permissive aspect leaves some room for moves that question an arguer's sincerity in meeting the Gricean cooperative principle (CP) that requires a participant to make the right sort of move, at any particular stage of a dialogue, that will contribute to the dialogue.[4]

Hence there would seem to be some room in a critical discussion for arguments that would question a participant's sincerity or cooperativeness in contributing to the dialogue as a constructive process requiring polite collaboration. But even this aspect would not appear to leave as much latitude for an attack on a person's character of the kind typically found in abusive ad hominem attacks. These attacks are, very often, not of a procedural kind, concerning a participant's cooperativeness in following maxims of politeness for dialogue, but are full-blown allegations that this person has a bad moral character generally in his or her personal life.[5]

To get a better idea of how personal attack is an effective and powerful type of argument, we need to examine types of dialogue other than critical discussion.

3. Deliberation As a Type of Dialogue

The characteristics of deliberation, as a type of goal-directed dialogue in which argumentation occurs, are outlined in Walton (*New Dialectic*, 1998, chapter 6).[6] As typified by this account of its normative framework as a type of dialogue, deliberation involves discussion of different points of view that represent proposed solutions to some practical problem. In this section, the main characteristics of deliberation that are important with respect to the ad hominem argument are outlined.

Deliberation as a type of dialogue has the goal for the participants of coming to some agreement on an action or policy that can be pursued as a solution to a practical problem. The initial situation prompting a deliberation is a practical conflict or problem that requires a choice to be made between or among two or more mutually exclusive courses of action.

A typical example of a deliberation is a town hall meeting, called by a group of concerned citizens who have to decide whether or not to go ahead with the project of installing a new sewer system in their community. Proponents for the two sides of the issue—to keep the old system for the time being or to go ahead with the project of installing a new system—present their arguments.

Of course, in a town hall meeting, many participants are involved in the argument. But from a point of view of the normative model of deliberation as a type of dialogue, the argumentation is seen as having two sides—one for keeping the old sewage system and one for going to a new system. In a case of a solitary process of deliberation—for example, when I decide (by myself) what kind of cereal to have this morning, bran flakes or cornflakes—only one person is involved. But we can look at such a case as an instance of argumentation in a deliberation framework by postulating two sides to the issue, the pro bran flakes side versus the pro cornflakes side. Assuming that I do not want to have a mixture of the two cereals, the exclusive disjunction involves a choice between these two courses of action.

In still other cases of solitary deliberation, a person who advocates one course of action can also play "devil's advocate" by trying to think up and consider the strongest arguments for the opposed point of view.

In a typical case of deliberation dialogue, the participants share common goals (for the most part or to a large extent) and have a common perception of many of the circumstances of the situation in which they must make a choice. In deliberation, both parties have many common interests and are trying to work together to carry out their goals jointly. In this respect, deliberation is less adversarial than the critical discussion as a type of dialogue.

The argumentation in a deliberation takes the form of one party claiming to the other that if she wants to achieve her goals she should carry out certain actions. Typically, the argumentation takes the form of arguments from consequences, in which the good (bad) consequences of some contemplated course of action are cited as reasons for (or against) it.

It does not seem that Aristotle thought of deliberation as a normative model of dialogue to evaluate argumentation, in the same way proposed here.[7] Nevertheless, Aristotle in the *Nicomachean Ethics* (1112 a 20–1113 b 25) gave a clear and self-contained account of deliberation that is useful for this purpose. According to his account, we deliberate about things that are in our control and are attainable by action (1112 b 8). Also (1112 b 9), we deliberate about matters that are not eternal or firmly fixed as principles but that are subject to change and uncertainty. Aristotle also thought about deliberation as a kind of orderly or rational thinking because it contains reasoning, of a kind he called practical reasoning (phronesis).

Deliberation seems initially as if it could be a critical discussion, but the two types of dialogue are essentially distinct. The goal of a critical discussion is to resolve a conflict of opinions. Critical discussion is a subtype of persuasion dialogue, in which each party tries to convince the other side that a particular proposition, representing her point of view in the discussion, can be justified as true, based on evidence brought forward to support it. Deliberation, in contrast, is a much more collaborative (less adversarial) type of dialogue, in which the goal is for the two participants to reason together to seek out the most prudent line of action that would satisfy both their goals.[8] The dialogue in deliberation is on formulating goals, on how to realize these goals, starting from a given set of circumstances as perceived by both parties, and on discussing the possible long-term consequences of the possible courses of action being considered. Deliberation involves weighing one possible course of action against another, sometimes making a choice and in other cases making a compromise that provisionally represents the most prudent course of action. The factor of safety or following a procedure that has proved to be safe in the past often tilts the burden of proof toward one side.

Brinton (1995, p. 220) agrees that deliberative rhetoric represents a distinctive framework of argumentation in its own right and is a context in which ad hominem arguments are frequently used. Brinton also agrees that ethotic ad hominem arguments in deliberation can be nonfallacious in some cases. Garver (1994, p. 188) argues that rhetorical argument "*qua* argument, is necessarily ethical, because it requires deliberation, and deliberation requires the habits of desire and perception that contribute character." But how is character connected to the kind of commitment one finds in deliberation?

In deliberation, commitment is expressed in two ways—in the goals or principles one professes and holds and in the actions carried out as the ways and means of realizing these goals. The kind of thinking or reasoning used in deliberation works by combining goals and actions in a sequence of inferences used by an agent making choices in given circumstances, guided by her knowledge of those circumstances, representing her external situation. The internal aspect is the *agent* herself, a person or active entity who can influence her external environment.[9]

One important aspect of deliberation with respect to ad hominem argumentation is that a person who advocates a particular course of action as the right path for a whole group (the community or the audience) to take is herself a member of that community of persons who are involved. If the speaker argues, "Everyone ought to do such-and-such," but she herself does not do such-and-such, then she is open to the criticism that she does not "practice what she preaches." This form of ad hominem argument will be identified as the universal pragmatic subtype of the circumstantial ad hominem in section 4.

This kind of criticism can be devastating in a deliberation because it can suggest the speaker is illogical and confused, or even worse, is deceptively advocating something as a policy for others that she does not really believe in herself. Such a person has adopted the role of "leader" but is evidently pointing others toward a path that she does not sincerely believe in herself—for, after all, actions speak louder than words. So if her advocacy of a policy or course of action is not one she chooses for herself, an element of hypocrisy or duplicity is revealed.

This aspect of personal consistency in words and deeds is not so crucial in a critical discussion, especially if the issue is some matter for which objective or factual considerations are of most significance.

In some cases, however, elements of deliberation can be mixed in with a critical discussion. For example, a critical discussion on the abortion issue is likely to involve policies and laws that affect the whole community.

4. Practical Reasoning

Practical reasoning is a chaining together of a sequence of practical inferences. In the simplest type of case, a practical inference is based on two premises. One premise states that an agent a has a goal G. The other premise states that the agent thinks that carrying out an action A is a means of her realizing G.

PI

G is a goal for a.
a thinks that bringing about A is a means to bring about G.
Therefore, a concludes that bringing about A is a practically reasonable course of action.

A simple example would be an inference like the following case.

Case 5.1

I want to satisfy my thirst. Drinking this glass of water would be a way to satisfy my thirst. Therefore, I conclude that the practically reasonable thing for me to do is to drink this glass of water.

Other cases are given by Aristotle (see, for example, *De Motu Animalium* 701 a 19). Garver (1994) has shown how Aristotle's notion of practical reasoning (phronesis) is a kind of instrumental reasoning that requires not only prudent decision making but also good habits of thinking based on good character. The modern literature on practical inference as a distinctive type of reasoning includes studies by Anscombe (1957), Diggs (1960), von Wright (1963; 1972), Clarke (1985), Audi (1989), and Walton (*Practical Reasoning*, 1990; *Plausible Argument*, 1992). Practical reasoning involves an agent's use of practical inferences in a particular situation in which the agent is aware of her circumstances and can steer her way through these changing circumstances by recognizing the likely consequences of her actions in altering these circumstances.

Typically, practical reasoning works by fitting abstract goals together with specific courses of action. For example, a physician's goal may be to maintain the health of her patient. But 'health' is a highly abstract concept. So when considering possible courses of treatment, there may be many intervening steps of practical inference linking a specific course of treatment action with the general goal of health. In the joint deliberation between the physician and the patient, the physician provides knowledge about the expected consequences of the various alternatives.[10] This type of talk exchange is a species of advice-giving dialogue in which the physician is a source of expert advice. Practical reasoning can be used in different types of dialogue, but the most typical and common context of its use is in deliberation dialogue.

Farrell (1993, p. 98) emphasizes that according to Aristotle's account, practical wisdom (phronesis) is cultivated by deliberation about choice and action. In Aristotle's theory, practical wisdom is an acquired trait of character that is cultivated in what Farrell (p. 98) calls "deliberative civil conduct." In other words, practical reasoning is especially used and revealed in a context of deliberation such as a town hall meeting in which a participant's character plays a key part in his reasoning. Practical reasoning has a structure as a kind of inference used in a dialogue exchange of viewpoints.

In a dialogue framework, when the proponent puts forward a recommendation in the form PI, the respondent can shift the weight of presumption back to the other side by asking any one of four appropriate critical questions (Walton, "Practical Reasoning," 1992, p. 999).

CQ

1. Are there alternative means of realizing G, other than A?
2. Is it possible for a to do A?
3. Does a have goals other than G, which have the potential to conflict with a's realizing G?
4. Are there negative side effects of a's bringing about A that ought to be considered?

According to the account given in Walton (*Practical Reasoning*, 1990), practical reasoning is characteristically used to shift a burden of proof back and forth in a dialogue exchange. The circumstances of the proposed actions are not generally known as exact knowledge. Indeed, the probable or possible consequences of contemplated courses of action are at stake in the issue of the dialogue. Hence an inference of the form PI is generally a kind of plausible reasoning or guessing, subject to default as new information comes into the dialogue. If both premises of PI are reasonably supported by the proponent's argument in a given case, a tentative weight of presumption is placed against the respondent's side. If the respondent asks any one of the four critical questions (CQ), the weight of presumption shifts back to the other side, until the question is adequately answered.[11]

Not all types of advice-giving dialogue that contain practical reasoning are cases in which the one party in the dialogue is an expert and the other is a layperson in a field of knowledge or practical skill. In some cases, the advice giver is in a special position to know about some subject because of familiarity with it, even though she is not an expert. An example of this sort, given by Diggs (1960), concerns the asking of directions.

Case 5.2

A visitor to campus walks up to a young person carrying books down the hallway and asks: "Excuse me. Can you tell me how to get to the Registrar's Office?" The respondent replies: "Certainly. Go down to the first floor, walk straight ahead through three sets of doors. After the third set, you need to go down the stairwell past the stained glass window, and then you'll see the door to the Registrar's Office. You could also go outside, but I think the inside way is better."

In this case, the visitor presumes that the other party is a student, who is probably familiar with the campus. The student is not an expert on campus buildings but is in a position to give informed advice because of familiarity with services located on the campus.

This case would be an information-seeking type of dialogue, except that the visitor did not ask for the location of the Registrar's Office by asking "Where is it?" Instead, she asked how to get there, so she is asking for advice on the kinds of actions needed to get there. The student notes in his answer that alternative routes are available but indicates what is, in his opinion, the best one for the visitor to take.

To carry out the task of getting to the Registrar's Office, the visitor will have to undertake a whole series of subactions that are part of a long sequence, beginning by moving her feet and turning to the nearby elevator or stairwell that leads to the first floor. The student has sketched only the key points needed to orient the visitor to make the correct turns needed.

In a case of advice-giving dialogue of this sort, the one party states a goal, and the other party provides advice, in the form of practical reasoning, on how to achieve that goal by a series of proposed actions.

Practical reasoning is the framework for proving or disproving the existence of a pragmatic inconsistency in cases of the circumstantial ad hominem such as the smoking case (1.5), the sportsman case (1.18), and the tree hugger case (1.6). Actions express commitments to other actions, which can then be related, by a sequence of practical reasoning, to an arguer's other commitments as expressed by his goals or principles in such statements as "Smoking is bad for your health."

5. Character and Practical Reasoning

What does character have to do with practical reasoning? Answering this question is the key to understanding the nature of ad hominem arguments, particularly the abusive or direct subtype. Some clues to the answer have already been made evident. The ethotic ad hominem, in many cases, has been relevant because the context is that of deliberation, in which prudence in making choices for solving practical problems is a key skill of character. Also, on the Aristotelian theory of character, a close connection indeed is present between character and practical reasoning. According to Sherman (1989, p. 1), character for Aristotle has to do with a person's enduring states (as also noted by Nussbaum, 1992) that will explain "why someone can be *counted on* to act in certain ways." In other words, character has to do with a person's accountability, in a sense implying stable commitment to certain patterns of action. As Sherman (1989, p. 5) states, this connection may not be immediately apparent to readers of the *Nicomachean Ethics*, but it is implicit in Aristotle's argument.

The inseparability of character and practical reason is often inadequately appreciated by readers of the *Nicomachean Ethics*. The reason may be Aristotle's own classification of virtue or excellence *(arete)* into that of character *(ethikes)* and intellect *(dianoetikes)* in *NE* II. I, and his announced plan of treating each separately. But while he offers some sort of sequential treatment, with the excellence of intellect the special focus of *NE* VI, and to some extent *NE* X. 6–8, the descriptions of the virtues of character are in all cases descriptions of character states which are at once modes of affect, choice, and perception. The definition of virtue makes this painfully clear: to have virtue is to be able to make the choices characteristic of the person of practical wisdom.

Aristotle in fact defines 'virtue' (*NE* 1107 a I) as "a character state concerned with choice, lying in the mean relative to us, being determined by reason and the way the person of practical wisdom would determine it" (trans. given by Sherman, 1989, p. 5).[12] Aristotle also writes (*NE* 1144 b 31–32) that practical wisdom is impossible without excellence of character. This summary of the main line of argument in the *Nicomachean Ethics* makes it very clear that character, in Aristotle's sense, is inextricably tied to practical reasoning and incomprehensive without it.

Practical wisdom for Aristotle is the faculty or ability possessed by the practical person who is excellent at skills of deliberation that utilize practical reasoning. But precisely what are these specific skills or abilities that enable their possessor to excel in practical affairs? According to Hamblin (1987, p. 206), Aristotle is "distressingly abstract" on this question, "juggling with twenty or so nouns denoting agglomerate mental faculties or abilities whose overlaps, interconnections and shades of meaning must have been obscure even to his Greek readers." But "regrettably or otherwise," Hamblin adds (p. 206), "it is not clear that matters have advanced much in the 2300 years since he [Aristotle] wrote." According to Hamblin's summary (p. 206) the ingredients of practical wisdom, in Aristotle's view, can be classified into four groups of qualities of character: (1) a knowledge group, containing knowledge gained by sense perception as well as scientific knowledge *(episteme)* and knowledge by intuitive reason *(nous)*; (2) art or skill *(techne)*, including cleverness; (3) a group concerned with the weighing of ends, including deliberative excellence, understanding, and judgment; (4) moral virtue *(arete).* It is important to note that for Aristotle philosophical (theoretical, scientific) wisdom *(sophia)* is not the same as practical wisdom *(phronesis).*

We need not delve any further into the particulars of Aristotle's ethics and his theory of character to see how, at least broadly speaking, a close connection is apparent between practical reasoning and character. Character has not only to do with abstract goals (principles) a person may have or profess but also with how those goals (presumed goals) are translated into actions, in a reasoned way.

Aristotle's group of ingredients of practical wisdom, as described by Hamblin, fit fairly well with the kinds of aspects of character characteristically attacked in the use of the abusive type of ad hominem argument.

1. *Honesty—a* is a liar, *a* has no regard for the truth.
2. *Judgment Skills—a* has poor judgment, shown by his having made foolish mistakes. This aspect has to do with judging the "mean" in a situation, a sensible (prudent) course of action that is balanced to multiple considerations relevant to the issue.[13]
3. *Realistic Perception of Situation—a* ignores the facts, is not aware of relevant changing developments in the situation, pretends to be well-informed but is not.
4. *Cognitive Skills—a* is illogical, has commitments to inconsistencies, and commits elementary logical errors; in extreme cases *a* is insane, has psychological problems (fantasizing, delusions), or is mentally imbalanced, resulting in cognitive impairment in rationally comprehending his circumstances.[14]
5. *Personal Moral Standards* (on some grounds other than 1–4 above)—*a* lacks moral virtue, as shown, for example, by criminal convictions, marital infidelity, etc.

Use of any of these five bases for an abusive ad hominem has force as an effective argument in a context of dialogue in which two parties are engaged in deliberation. In particular, in advice-giving dialogue (for example, in the smoking case) in which the one party is purportedly giving advice to the other on how to act prudently in personal deliberations, the other party can raise questions under any of the five categories above, and the resulting ad hominem argument will be relevant in that context. Of course such an argument could be fallacious, if used to dismiss peremptorily the other party's argument or to ignore the good objective evidence presented. But if used as a defeasible argument to question the other party's credibility or sincerity, it could be an appropriate move.

In a deliberation type of dialogue a speaker is advocating a particular course of action or policy not just as the prudent choice for herself but as a course of action that she is advising the other party (or parties, if a group or community is involved) on the prudent path to follow. If it is revealed that the speaker has poor judgment skills or does not have a realistic grasp of the circumstances surrounding the choice or is a hypocrite, in the sense of advocating one policy for the group and following a different path herself, these are good reasons for the audience (or the other parties involved) to reduce the credibility it gives to the speaker. Consequently, by the ad hominem argument, it is a good reason for the audience not to accept her argument—that is, to assign it a lesser plausibility than before.

Finally, the connection between character and reasoned argument has been established through the medium of practical reasoning. Attacks on an arguer's character are powerful, relevant, and effective because they raise legitimate critical questions about the practical reasoning of that arguer as a participant in deliberation. At the same time, as noted in section 4, practical reasoning exhibits the connection needed between actions and commitment in circumstantial ad hominem cases.

6. Making Circumstantial Charges Stick

The problem of evaluating circumstantial ad hominem arguments is typically one of judging what to conclude from a pragmatic inconsistency, as in the case of Mr. S., whose personal actions seemed to conflict with his professed political principles.[15] A better grasp of this inconsistency can be achieved by seeing the case as containing a sequence of practical reasoning in which Mr. S.'s personal actions imply personal commitments of his that are in conflict with his political goals. Because the context is at least partly one of deliberation, Mr. S.'s personal standards of morality are relevant to judging his recommendations for legislation and public policy guidelines. Now that this connection of practical reasoning between political goals and personal actions has been revealed, Mr. S. cannot get around the ad hominem so easily.

The problem with many circumstantial ad hominem arguments is that they are weak or thinly substantiated allegations that, at best, shift the burden of proof by suggesting a cloud of suspicion over the opposition in an argument. Nevertheless, such arguments, though weak, are typically not totally worthless or baseless. To dismiss these ad hominem arguments as "fallacies" in a line or two, as the textbooks have too often done, is equally weak and inadequately substantiated, from a logical point of view. As we have repeatedly seen, if the person criticized is available to dispute the point, making an ad hominem criticism stick is not a trivial job of argumentation. In fact, many ways are available for responding to an ad hominem attack and for rebutting or refuting it. In reasonable dialogue, the person criticized should have the right to such a defending reply, or if he is not present to defend himself, a representative of his side of the argument should be able to take up his case.

The problem for the logic of the circumstantial ad hominem argument is posed, however, by the availability of so many defenses or "loopholes" that allow a way out for someone who wants to defend himself against an ad hominem criticism (see chapter 3, section 7). One may begin to wonder, therefore, whether all ad hominem arguments are, by their nature, tentative, provisional, and inconclusive. If so, the worry is possibly that circumstantial ad hominem argumentation never really settles anything conclusively and only escalates a dispute by leading to further charges or abusive personal recriminations. In fact, good evidence supports this suspicion. In political debates, one ad hominem attack often leads to another in reply. Notoriously, in such debates, the resulting abusive attacks evade and obscure the issue, instead of resolving it by reasoned argument.

The general problem for ad hominem argumentation posed by these observations could be described as the problem of pinning down a circumstantial ad hominem argument or of making a charge stick in circumstantial ad hominem criticisms. We have already seen a number of goals one needs to achieve, gaps to plug, in order to make an ad hominem argument at least well enough set up to avoid the counter-rebuttal of being an ad hominem fallacy. As shown in the sportsman's rejoinder as well as the case of Mr. S., even if a circumstantial inconsistency in an arguer's position is clearly nailed down, in principle there can be room for escape. Even if, for example, the critic decries the sportsman's hunting game for pleasure, yet acknowledges he himself has hunted game for pleasure, he may have a good argument that his actions should be treated under a special exception to his professed principle. But actions do sometimes speak louder than words. To the extent that his act of hunting for sport may be reasonably interpreted in the circumstance as reflecting a commitment to the policy of hunting game for sport, the critic's position becomes increasingly difficult for him to maintain with much credibility. The reason is that his admitted act of hunting puts into place by a practical inference a presumptive conclusion that when it comes down to his own personal deliberations, he really is committed to hunting, in a way that makes it seem unconvincing for him to profess to be against this practice as a goal.

As in any presumptive argument, however, the ad hominem does leave ways to reply and rebut the argument. The following case is given by Hughes (1958, p. 112).

Case 5.3

> During the course of a conversation, Jones remarks, "It's wrong to join the army." However, the next morning, Jones is observed at a recruiting office enlisting in the army. Wondering whether he really meant what he said, we ask Jones: "We thought you said it was wrong to join the army."

Although Hughes's discussion of this case has a different focus from ad hominem criticisms, the circumstantial inconsistency in case 5.3 is typical of the type associated with ad hominem argumentation. Among the responses open to Jones catalogued by Hughes's article are the following: (1) Jones could have changed his mind; (2) Jones could admit a lack of "moral fiber"; or (3) Jones could plead that his case is a special one. Each of these types of responses could be a reasonable "way out."

Hughes's discussion of this third type of response is especially revealing in relation to ad hominem criticisms, for a case is made that it could be consistent for Jones to maintain that *in general* it is wrong to join the army while still maintaining that his own case is a special one. According to Hughes (p. 173), Jones could reasonably claim that the principle he adheres to is of the form, "It is wrong to do [action] X except in certain specific types of circumstances." Jones's case could be reasonable if his own circumstances fall under those covered among the admissible exceptions.

This type of case is especially interesting because it shows that many ad hominem circumstantial criticisms are essentially open rather than closed inasmuch as they can admit of exceptional pleading for certain circumstances or individuals. Thus the form of generalization that binds an individual's conduct to a class of individuals or to a general rule or policy is neither universal nor statistical but based on a kind of presumptive (defeasible) commitment that may admit of justifiable exceptions in some cases. Enunciation on the principle by an individual incurs a certain commitment to the principle on the part of the individual, but it is a kind of commitment based on burden of proof that may be overturned in exceptional cases, a species of nonmonotonic reasoning, subject to default.

An excessive insistence to the letter of a general principle in the face of legitimate exceptions is the kind of practice associated with the traditional *secundum quid* fallacy. According to the analysis given in Walton ("Ignoring," 1990), citing Hamblin (1970, p. 28), fallacies secundum quid involve the neglect of necessary qualifications. However the secundum quid is ultimately to be analyzed, note that the type of default reasoning it uses is related closely to the problem of evaluating the uses of circumstantial ad hominem arguments.

Given this open-ended and defeasible nature of presumptive circumstantial ad hominem criticisms, how can they ever be "nailed down" or closed? Can the arguer so criticized always wriggle out of the criticism? This possibility seems inherently open, depending on the circumstances of a particular case. Indeed, the very nature of the ad hominem criticism as a form of questioning an arguer's position, by shifting the burden of proof onto the arguer, is tied up with its inherent defeasibility in argument. This defeasibility stems from the use of parallel cases in the circumstantial ad hominem, which is a form of argument from analogy, as noted in chapter 1, section 7. Because of the form of argument from analogy characteristically involved in such criticisms, the type of argument involved is that of plausible reasoning. It is situationally open-ended and nonmonotonic in nature because of the many ways that two parallel cases can be compared as sharing or failing to share relevant characteristics. New relevant information can always come in.

Note the presence of a variability in the susceptibility of different ad hominem arguments to the ease with which exceptions can be argued for.

Case 5.4

A critic argues that reporters are circumstantially inconsistent when they criticize the free lunches, air trips, and other "free benefits" that people in the public service are often said to receive by reporters. For, the critic alleges, these reporters themselves are often the recipients of these same benefits.[16]

One way a defender against this tu quoque criticism could argue (comparably to the case of Mr. S.), would be to claim that the situation of public servants is different from that of reporters in one key respect. Public servants' salaries are paid through government taxes, whereas reporters are private sector employees. Much more could be said about the pros and cons of the argument of case 5.4. But one can see that the alleged parallel between the two cases of public servants versus reporters at least could be supported or refuted in any number of ways that might be relevant to the criticism. The key to this support lies in a sequence of practical reasoning, as analyzed in detail in the study of this case in Walton (*Arguer's Position*, 1985), joining up the reporter's personal actions in taking part in these free benefits.

Comparing case 5.4 to the smoking example of case 1.5, we can see that the smoking case allows for somewhat less scope for exceptions. If the smoker concedes that smoking is unhealthy for everyone and that her goal is to avoid being unhealthy, it is difficult for her to make a plausible exception of her own case. But, as noted in chapter 1, it can be done. She might claim to have quit smoking or to have tried. She might even argue, for example, that because she is already suffering from terminal cancer of the colon, in her case smoking now will not significantly affect her health. Although this sort of defense could conceivably be plausible in an unusual set of circumstances, the scope for escape by exceptions appears somewhat narrower than that admitted by case 5.4. The practical reasoning in each case must be analyzed on the basis of what can be inferred from the admitted actions and professed goals of the arguer.

The key to the problem of pinning down an ad hominem argument is to realize that a pragmatic inconsistency is not a logical inconsistency—although it may be reducible to one given set of commitments to propositions—and therefore it depends on the reading off or interpretation of a set of circumstances relative to a particular case in contention. But each set of circumstances is unique and can potentially be described in an indefinitely large number of respects. Because commitments must be read off from what is known about a particular case, and what is known may be partially encoded in the script or implicit "common-sense" knowledge of the participants in the argument, most ad hominem pragmatic inconsistencies are based on a comparison between two cases alleged to be parallel.

Hence most ad hominem criticisms are really forms of the argument from analogy. Because of the case-oriented nature of arguments from analogy, ad hominem arguments are instances of presumptive reasoning in a dialogue and best treated as inherently defeasible. Perhaps this conclusion should not be too distressing, if the real function of an ad hominem criticism is to shift the burden of proof toward an opponent's position in a dialogue, for that result can be accomplished very well by a reconstruction of the sequence of practical reasoning linking circumstances to commitments of an arguer in a given case.

7. Character in Political Discourse

It is not possible to pin down argumentation in political discourse as occurring within one normative framework of dialogue because elements of several types of dialogue are involved—critical discussion, negotiation, deliberation, information-seeking dialogue, and eristic (quarrelsome) dialogue.[17] It would be naive to view political debate generally as a critical discussion and to dismiss ad hominem arguments as irrelevant or fallacious in political discourse, judging the argumentation from the viewpoint of a critical discussion. In political discourse (for example, in argumentation in an election campaign), the participants generally have a financial stake in the outcome; they may belong to or be influenced by advocacy groups in particular. It would be naive to presume that interest-based bargaining is not involved at all.

Aristotle's theory of political argumentation was based on practical reasoning, adopting the viewpoint that political discourse is concerned with deliberations on how to proceed in situations requiring choices among different possible courses of action. Within the Aristotelian framework of political deliberation, Brinton (1986, p. 246) sees ethotic argumentation, in which the character of a speaker is "invoked, attended to, or represented in such a way as to lend credibility to or detract credibility from conclusions that are being drawn," as a legitimate part of the argumentation. According to Aristotle's theory of political discourse, the ad hominem argument that centers on the speaker's character as the principal focus of the argument is in principle a reasonable and appropriate type of argument.

Aristotle's proof of the relevance of character is broken down into five steps in Walton (*Place of Emotion*, 1992, p. 201):

1. Speech event of deliberation—practical reasoning.
2. Variable circumstances produce uncertainty.
3. Experienced counsel of the wise could be relevant.
4. Presumption of honesty, sincerity, and judgment skills.
5. Therefore, the character of the speaker is important.

The basic premise of Aristotle's proof is that political discourse, as a species of deliberation about practical concerns in matters that are highly variable and do not admit of answers based on exact (scientific) knowledge, needs to be decided by practical reasoning. Accordingly, the best person to give advice on how to proceed is a practically wise person of good character (ethos). Following this line of argument through leads to the conclusion that character is a legitimate issue in political discourse, especially, say, in an election campaign during which the electorate is trying to elect a person who will have good moral values (or at least share the values thought of as good).

Critics will say that political debate is nothing like a rational deliberation based on practical wisdom, that this is too "rational" a view of it, and that real political discourse (in the current context) is more like a quarrel or negotiation between dominant, vocal advocacy groups. Of course, as noted, political discourse does inherently have elements of negotiation and eristic dialogue. However, it is also difficult to deny that political discourse does have and ideally should have elements of deliberation. Thus, at least to some extent, it is justifiable to evaluate the argument in a case of political discourse from the viewpoint of deliberation as a normative model of dialogue. If so, following Aristotle's five-step proof, the ad hominem argument should not be immediately rejected as fallacious in every case.

Ethotic argument is centrally important even in the present political discourse because voters rightly want to know a candidate's core convictions that represent his or her ethos or moral character for values. In fact, it can be a problem for a political officeholder if her or his character is elusive—if there appears to be no consistent set of values she or he stands for on a long-term basis. In late 1994, the public perception was that President Bill Clinton had lost public confidence because too many of his policy reversals had made his character seem elusive (Fraser, 1994, p. A7).

Case 5.5

Part of the problem is the sense that his character is elusive; that there is little he will draw a line on and fight for.

David Gergen, who is leaving the Clinton administration, said recently that U.S. voters want to know what Mr. Clinton's "core convictions" are as he faces the next two years.

"Bill Clinton . . . has few core values on which his presidency is built," said James Lake, a former communications adviser to Presidents Reagan and George Bush. "Ted Kennedy—I never agree with him, but he stands for something, he's consistent, you know where he stands. Ronald Reagan—people disagreed with him, time after time, but you knew where he stood. No one can say that they know what Bill Clinton stands for."

Privately, many Democrats say the same thing and fear that, as a result, the Clinton presidency cannot recover.

In political deliberations, one can see how character and commitment are connected. With Reagan, it was said, "you knew where he stood." His commitments were consistent and could be rationally perceived to be so, once you got a grasp of his character or core values. Because his actions were consistent, insofar as they expressed a stable set of commitments that made sense as core values or an identifiable character, one could clearly agree or disagree with what he "stood for." Because Clinton's positions seemed to admit of so many pragmatic inconsistencies, the report in Fraser (1994, A7) concluded that Clinton's greatest problem is that "too many Americans do not believe that he has a basic set of inner values." Hence character or ethos in the sense of a person's core moral values is not only a legitimate issue in political discourse; it is also a central and fundamentally important aspect of a speaker's credibility on political issues in a democratic system.

Character in political argumentation can be attacked in a number of ways. If a politician changes his commitments too often, he is said to lack "a basic set of inner values." But if he does not retract his commitments or change them often enough, he can be criticized as being inflexible, dogmatic, insensitive, or "out of touch with the changing times."

Furthermore, these kinds of attacks on the stability or instability of commitments can easily be followed up by using the initial attack as evidence to argue that the person lacks character for veracity, claiming that he has no regard for the truth. In 1995, Democrats feared that Bill Clinton might betray Democratic principles by coming to a budget agreement with the Republicans. When Clinton aides said he was "rethinking" his support for a Senate welfare bill, both sides began to attack Clinton's character in their discussions of the issue (Will, 1995, p. 94).

Case 5.6

Today's bipartisan consensus is that Clinton is neither bad nor dangerous, just silly. Plainly put, almost no one thinks he believes a word he says. Or, more precisely, he believes everything he says at the moment he emphatically says it, and continues to believe it at full throttle right up to the moment he repudiates it. He has the weird sincerity of the intellectual sociopath, convinced that when he speaks, truth is an option but convenience is an imperative.

This ad hominem argument is definitely an attack on Clinton's character for veracity, claiming that for him "truth is an option" and even calling him an "intellectual sociopath," someone who has no intellectual conscience and consistently lies and cleverly deceives those around him. The upshot is that Clinton is claimed to have exhausted his credibility: "almost no one thinks he believes a word he says." Here we see how the ad hominem criticism of a person's political deliberations can lead to a direct ad hominem attack on that person's character for veracity.

8. Aristotle on Ethotic Argument

Aristotle in the *Rhetoric* (1355 b 35) distinguished between two types of proof in the kind of argumentation that would be used, for example, in a legal trial. One of these he called *nonartistic (inartificial) proof* is direct evidence that is "not the product of the speaker's art" (Kennedy, 1963, p. 88). According to Kennedy (p. 88), such direct evidence would include "laws, witnesses, testimony extracted from slaves under torture, contracts, and oaths." In the fourth century B.C., the custom in the courts was to secure such evidence before the trial, write it down, put it in a sealed urn, and read it aloud during the trial procedure (p. 88). But the Greeks quickly learned that this kind of evidence, by itself, could be highly unreliable. In Athens, outside the courts, people even gathered to offer to bear false testimony on behalf of litigants going to court, for a fee.

To deal with this kind of problem posed by assessing direct evidence, something called "argument from probability" *(eikos)* was introduced, a kind of argumentation frequently mentioned by the sophists in their rhetorical handbooks (Kennedy, 1980, p. 21). The classic example of this kind of argumentation is mentioned by Socrates in the *Phaedrus* (273 a–c) and also by Aristotle in the *Rhetoric* (1402 a 17ff.): a weak man is accused in court of assaulting a stronger man, and his defense is that it is not "probable" that he would attack the stronger man. However, the reverse argument from probability could also be used if the stronger man were to be accused of assault. He could argue, "the crime is still not probable for the very reason that it was bound to appear so" (Kennedy, 1963, p. 31). In other words, he could argue that it is improbable that he would attack such a weaker man, for he would realize that he could easily be convicted for such an assault.

Argument from probability (eikos) does not mean "probability" in the modern sense of statistical reasoning. It means arguing from what is generally accepted as true because of the way things normally happen or are done in common practice or experience. For this reason it would be better for argumentation theory to translate "eikos" in modern English as "plausibility" rather than probability. At any rate, it is easy to see how argument from plausibility is fundamental in cross-examination of a witness in court.

To accommodate argument from probability, Aristotle introduced another category of proof. *Artificial* proof, in contrast to the kind of proof furnished by such direct evidence, is the kind of proof that is constructed by the art of the orator. In the *Rhetoric* (1356 a 1), Aristotle distinguishes three types of artificial proof (Loeb Edition, p. 17): "Now the proofs furnished by the speech are of three kinds. The first depends upon the moral character of the speaker, the second upon putting the hearer into a certain frame of mind, the third upon the speech itself, in so far as it proves or seems to prove." The first type of proof, based on the character of the speaker, is called "ethos," a term used by Aristotle to refer to character, but especially to the moral character of a person.

Character was used in persuasive argumentation by Greek orators in different ways, according to Kennedy (1963). One way is the use of arguments from "probability" or eikos (plausibility, in the sense of Rescher [1976] would probably be a better word here). The best example of this use of character in argument is in the first of thirty-four speeches of Lysias (Kennedy, 1963, p. 136):

Case 5.7

In the first speech, for example, the defendant is old-fashioned and blunt in his ways; one might not choose him for a friend or even much respect him, but because of Lysias' portrayal it is difficult to believe that he has laid a subtle trap for his wife's lover and very easy to believe that he killed the lover when taken in the act of adultery.

The argument used in this kind of case has the following form.

ARGUMENT FROM CHARACTER

Person a has character trait ψ.
Carrying out action A is not the sort of thing a person with trait ψ would normally be expected to do.
Therefore, person a (probably, or plausibly) did not carry out action A.

This form of argument is defeasible or *eikotic,* in the sense that it provides only a weight of presumption as supporting a tentative conclusion that is subject to rebuttal. It is possible that a carried out A, but producing a justified argument of the form ARGUMENT FROM CHARACTER makes it "improbable" or implausible (subject to doubt).

The other way that character was used to support an argument in Greek oratorical practices was for the speaker to represent his own character in a favorable way, within the fabric of his speech: "Usually, like Socrates in the *Apology,* the speaker claims to be unskilled in speaking, simple, honest, deserving, but caught up in circumstances; his opponent is sly, cunning and worthless" (Kennedy, 1963, p. 91). This type of character-based argument is different from the use represented by the eikotic argument ARGUMENT FROM CHARACTER. Instead, it has a form more like, "I (the speaker) am a person of good character; therefore you should accept my argument as (more) credible (than you otherwise might)."

Aristotle elaborates on ethotic argument at several places in the *Rhetoric*, where he presents it as a distinctive type of proof or argument that is made in a speech. He defines *ethotic argument (Rhetoric* 1356 a 4) as a kind of proof furnished by an orator in a speech, for which the proof depends on the moral character of the speaker (Loeb Edition, p. 17): "The orator persuades by moral character *(ethos)* when his speech is delivered in such a manner as to render him worthy of confidence; for we feel confidence in a greater degree and more readily in persons of worth in regard to everything in general, but where there is no certainty and there is room for doubt, our confidence is absolute." Aristotle emphasizes that in this type of ethotic argumentation, it is not just our preconceived idea of the speaker's character that convinces an audience, but how that character is conveyed in the speech. The audience, to grasp the argument in this type of speech, according to Aristotle *(Rhetoric* 1356 a 7), must be capable of understanding the kind of logical reasoning *(syllogismos)* that is concerned with character and virtues.

Although a good character is conveyed in an ethotic argument of the kind Aristotle has in mind, for such an argument to be successful a requirement is that the speaker be perceived or presumed by the audience to have a good character. For Aristotle *(Rhetoric* 1361 a 8), this requirement means that the speaker must have a good reputation (Loeb Edition, p. 53): "A good reputation consists in being considered a man of worth by all, or in possessing something of such a nature that all or most men, or the good, or the men of practical wisdom desire it." It is not ruled out that a speaker with a bad reputation could make a speech containing ethotic argumentation, but the success of the argument would be very much influenced by that preexisting reputation (as considered by the audience). The character most likely to persuade a given audience *(Rhetoric* 1366 a 6) is one that is presumed by that audience to have a good reputation, the kind of character they approve.

Aristotle makes it clear, at the beginning of Book II of the *Rhetoric* (1377 a 3–4), that in ethotic argumentation both the speaker and the audience have to be disposed in a certain way toward each other (Loeb Edition, p. 169): "For it makes a great difference with regard to producing conviction—especially in demonstrative, and, next to this, in forensic oratory—that the speaker should show himself to be possessed of certain qualities and that his hearers should think that he is disposed in a certain way toward them; and further, that they themselves should be disposed in a certain way toward him." The three qualities needed by an orator to achieve successful ethotic proof, according to Aristotle (*Rhetoric* 1378 a 5) are practical wisdom or prudence (phronesis), virtue (arete), and good will (eunoia).

Certainly we can see that the perceived character of a speaker by his audience is of the highest rhetorical importance in many kinds of oratory. Aristotle went so far as to claim (*Rhetoric* 1356 a 13) that in cases in which there is "not exact knowledge" character is almost the "controlling factor in persuasion" (translation of Garver, 1994, p. 176). It does not follow that ad hominem arguments are nonfallacious, from these observations, but it is shown that the character of the speaker does have a legitimate and important place in certain kinds of discourse, especially in speeches relating to public affairs, ethics, and political deliberations.

Garver (p. 176) has emphasized that Aristotle's justification of the fundamental need for ethos in evaluating arguments is based on the assumption that an audience has to trust a speaker in order to judge the worth of his argument. Having to deal with the problem of responding to practical situations in which the audience cannot have determinate knowledge of the situation yet may have to make a decision on how to proceed gives rise to the need for trust and the consequent need for reliance on the ethos of the speaker, according to Garver (p. 177). For their evaluation, not all arguments need to depend on ethos, but a significant number of cases will have to depend on ethotic considerations for their proper evaluation—especially in political deliberation and in legal arguments in a trial.

It is interesting to note that according to Garver (p. 188), citing the *Rhetoric* (1417 a 19–1417 a 21), Aristotle took the view that arguments in a scientific inquiry (for example, in a treatise on mathematics) do not have ethos because they do not show deliberative choice, whereas the arguments used in a Socratic dialogue do speak of matters related to moral purposes. So the kinds of argumentation used in a Socratic dialogue (which would most likely be classified as a type of persuasion dialogue or critical discussion on our view) do properly have ethos as a relevant aspect.

9. Ad Hominem in Legal Argument

As noted in chapter 2, the most widely recognized type of exception to classifying ad hominem as a fallacy in the standard textbook treatments was the use of an ad hominem argument to cross-examine a witness in court. In fact, character is very important in legal trials, particularly in criminal cases, in which the attorney's basic line of argument is often framed around the character of the defendant as a good (or bad) person. In specific cases, the judge is supposed to rule whether or not an attack on a person's character is relevant.

Questions of the character or previous conduct of a participant in a legal trial are sometimes judged relevant. But as an *Encyclopaedia Britannica* article (11th ed., 1960) by Sir Courtenay Ilbert indicated, not all evidence of character and conduct have been regarded as admissible in legal argumentation. According to Ilbert (p. 16), "Evidence is not admissible to show that the person who is alleged to have done a thing was of a disposition or character that makes it probable that he would or would not have done it." Generally, arguments of the form ARGUMENT FROM CHARACTER are not admissible in law. Nevertheless, Ilbert also cited several exceptions: for example, a defendant charged with rape has been allowed to give evidence of the immoral character of the plaintiff (p. 16). This sort of question (for example, whether criminal convictions of a witness can be cited in questioning the honesty or veracity of the witness) has been subject to considerable debate.

One of the most interesting uses of the ad hominem argument in legal cases is in cross-examination of an expert witness. The cross-examining attorney can attack the expert witness testifying for the other side as being a dishonest person or an incompetent practitioner in his field, whose methods are out of date or who is in low standing in reputation with other experts. In such a case, the context of dialogue involves not only the two opposing attorneys but also the expert witnesses and the jury or judge who decide the outcome.

Cross-examination of an expert witness can be viewed as a form of persuasion dialogue in which the proponent is the cross-examining attorney and audience to be persuaded is the jury. The expert being interviewed is the third party in the dialogue. He is a participant who is (in theory) supposed to be neutral; in fact, the reasonable presumption is that he is on the opposite side to that of the cross-examining attorney.

According to Weber (1981, p. 299) an "impartial" expert may be defined as "one who will testify not less than 75% in favor of the party who hires him." The expert is supposed to be an impartial witness and should be perceived to be impartial as one of his qualifications as a persuasive witness. In reality, according to Weber (p. 299), "the cross-examiner usually is facing a skilled advocate masquerading as a high-minded trained specialist whose principal purpose is to use his expertise to "aid the jury." Thus the role of the expert in the dialogue is somewhat ambivalent.

Theoretically, the expert is an impartial source of skilled knowledge, but the cross-examiner had better assume that the expert is a kind of opponent. According to Weber (p. 304), "[t]he jury recognizes the two as antagonists even though a harsh word may never be exchanged." In effect, then, the cross-examiner and the expert are engaged in a kind of persuasion dialogue against each other, to see whose point of view will persuade the jury.

The situation of the dialogue in expert cross-examination is therefore quite complex. Of the three participants, the role of at least one is highly ambivalent. Moreover, there is a superimposing of one type of dialogue on another. Superficially cross-examination may appear to be a kind of information-seeking dialogue in which the questioner (the attorney) is trying to bring to light knowledge to which the expert has special access. Indeed, in theory, in a kind of ideal postulated by the law, that is or should be the type of dialogue involved. In more practical and realistic terms, however, everyone knows that the question-reply dialogue is really a kind of contest in which the attorney is trying to discredit the testimony of the expert and neutralize it as an argument that will support the opposing attorney's case in the trial.

In these types of cases, the kinds of tactics used to attack and defend an expert's opinion can be highly complex and sophisticated. One might think that the expert (being an expert) would be in a dominant position to express his point of view, but attorneys can become highly skilled at techniques of cross-examining experts. The attorney actually can exert a good deal of control because he knows the rules of dialogue of the court and is free to ask any questions he thinks relevant. The expert, like any witness, is obliged to give direct answers to these questions. A skilled lawyer can "lead" the expert witness in one direction while effectively preventing him from going in other directions.

Lawyers can spend a lot of time preparing and researching elaborate strategies and tactics of presenting expert opinions. At the same time, the tactics for attacking an expert appeal can be carefully prepared.

Appeal to expert opinion in argumentation is characteristically a form of plausible reasoning that shifts a burden of presumption in one direction or another. Argumentation here is most often a form of practical reasoning that becomes a basis for goal-directed deliberation when access to direct information or evidence, of the sort Locke calls the "argumentum ad judicium" and others call "argumentum ad rem," is not ready to hand. Therefore, in many cases, a decision may be made to act in accord with an expert opinion, or not, on the basis of only slight knowledge of the expert's credentials, the reasoning behind his conclusion, and other relevant considerations. Hence questions of style, appearance, and perceived reputation of the expert may in fact be important in persuading a respondent to accept an appeal to expert opinion.

In practice, the use of expert opinions in argumentation is often a short-cut method of making a decision or carrying out a course of action when there is little time to look into the facts first-hand. For these reasons, in practice, what the expert says may be less important in matters of persuasion than how he says it. This observation leads to another main area that requires a dialectical analysis of the argumentation, the dialogue between the alleged expert and his audience. In these types of situations, the audience could be the user or the recipient of the user's appeal to expertise in an argument or both. It is clear that the expert is taking part in a kind of advice-giving dialogue that is supposed to assist the deliberation of the jury by providing facts and expert opinions.

From the cross-examining attorney's point of view, however, the dialogue is seen as adversarial. Hoffman (1979, p. 318) suggests that the cross-examiner should devise a plan of attack, based on advanced preparation of the dialogue used to realize a clearly understood purpose of the cross-examination. Such a plan should use questions likely to have favorable consequences, in two respects especially. First, Hoffman (p. 319) advises never to ask the expert to "explain" or "say why" he has given an expressed opinion, for this may give him an opening to divert your ultimate line of argument. Second, Hoffman (p. 320) advises the use of yes-no questions that may trap the expert witness in an unguarded moment and create an impression of weakness in his veracity. For example, "Do you agree that appraising property is an inexact science?" or "Do you agree that responsible appraisers may and do differ as to the value of a particular tract of land?" could be good questions to ask an expert property appraiser, who will normally be compelled to answer affirmatively.

Here the astute attorney can take advantage of the rules of dialogue imposed by the court, which require a witness to give a direct yes or no answer to a question. An attempt by the expert witness to thwart this strategy by giving an explanation or "narrative" reply can be dealt with by the attorney by asking that the reply be "struck" as not responsive to the question.

Legal uses of the appeal to expert opinion can be on a razor's edge, from a logical point of view. On the one side, the expert is supposed to be a neutral source of advice, and that is the source of the plausibility of his opinions to the jury. On the other hand, it is clear to all the participants that the expert is not really neutral and is testifying for one side.

Normally, in advice-giving dialogue, the functions of the expert to provide in-depth answers to questions and to give explanations of arcane matters are important to the reasonableness of the appeal to his opinion. Yet, in court, the cross-examining attorney may be clearly adopting a tactic of frustrating and sealing off such replies, if they might be inimical to his case.

Hence the complex nature of the persuasion/advice-giving dialogue context in these legal cases makes understanding the argument tactics a complex and subtle matter. All kinds of tactics can be used, including ad hominem attacks, loaded and leading questions, and other tricks, and they can be combined in elaborately prepared strategies of argumentation, which can then be applied as tactics in the presentation and argumentation of a case. Therefore, when an ad hominem argument is used in a trial and allowed as admissible by the judge, it does not necessarily follow that this argument is nonfallacious, in a general or absolute sense. The same can be said of ad hominem arguments used in a political debate. In the context of the debate, the ad hominem argument may have a legitimate place rhetorically in persuading the audience to have doubts about the credibility of an opponent's argument. Yet if either of these arguments were to be looked at from the viewpoint of a critical discussion, each might correctly be judged inappropriate and even fallacious.

10. Actions, Commitments, and Character

So is the abusive (direct, ethotic) subtype of ad hominem argument well analyzed by the Lockean type of argument of "pressing" an arguer with the consequences of his concessions? Basically, the answer is no because the ad hominem personal attack on an arguer's character is not the same as the argument from commitment. However, it has emerged that the two types of argument are indirectly related. It seems fair to conclude that the direct ad hominem, which attacks a person's character to detract from his argument, can be partly modeled as a subspecies of argument from commitment. At least this turns out to be the case if we adopt the technical method of bringing character into the dialogue structure of argument through the commitment set of a participant, instead of trying to build up the concept of a participant so that it begins to approximate or take on characteristics of a person (with a character, having traits and long-term properties that can be defined as part of the person-participant). This latter approach does not seem promising or useful, in modeling the dialogue structure of the type of conversational exchange called the critical discussion. For, as we saw, character does not play much of a role there (except at the secondary level of the Gricean maxims) unless the subject matter of the discussion is in fact about the participants' characters. In such a case, the commitments in the dialogue would be related to character only accidentally because the propositions in the dialogue happen to be about character. On balance, then, there seems to be little or no point in enriching the concept of participant in a critical discussion so that it includes character or other person-related notions.

In deliberation dialogue, however, the participants are agents who have goals that express their commitments. The concept of an agent does quite appropriately include the concept of character—or can properly be extended in that direction—especially if character is thought of along Aristotelian lines, as being closely tied to practical reasoning. Once character is defined in relation to practical reasoning, in Aristotle's way, then an important link between the direct and the circumstantial ad hominem subtypes is brought out perspicuously.

What is suggested as a possible new avenue of research is to enrich the concept of a participant in a dialogue (whether it be deliberation, critical discussion, or any type of dialogue) by thinking of a participant as being an *agent*, in a new sense of this term coming into use in artificial intelligence. An agent, so conceived, is not just a repository of a set of commitments in a dialogue but is regarded as an entity that is aware of the moves of the other party in a dialogue and can react to those moves in an autonomous way. For example, if one agent in a dialogue acts in a way that is contrary to the collaborative principles for contributing to the goals of the dialogue, the other agent can rate the first agent as less credible than before. In this way, an agent can be seen as having certain properties of character that are relevant to the collaborative conduct of a dialogue.

What could turn out to be extremely useful for this purpose is a new development in computer science—multiagent software systems in which intelligent agents reason with each other (Wooldridge and Jennings, 1995). Multiagent systems provide a new framework to study how the credibility function can be modeled in ad hominem arguments. According to Wooldridge and Jennings (p. 116), an agent is an autonomous unit that can carry out actions, be aware of the effects of these actions, and can interact with other agents, both reactively and proactively. Another characteristic of an agent (p. 117) that is particularly relevant to the credibility function and ad hominem arguments is the property of veracity, meaning that an agent will not knowingly communicate false information. According to this model of how agents engage in collaborative argumentation with each other in dialogue exchanges, each agent is seen as an entity that has certain qualities of character; if the other agent perceives a failure of this quality exhibited in a dialogue, then this failure would be taken as grounds for lessening the credibility extended to that agent.

This new development is too recent to follow up here in depth. But it does provide an avenue of new possibilities for enriching the structure of formal dialogue theory to model an agent as having qualities of character relevant to an evaluation of that agent's argumentation in a dialogue with another agent.

Most important, in this chapter character has been linked to actions, and actions to commitments. All three elements are connected by the thread of practical reasoning. Actions express commitments because, in the right context, they imply that the agent has certain goals that express her loyalties, principles, and convictions. Practical reasoning, in a context of dialogue such as deliberation, expressed by an agent's actions and arguments (or assertions, concessions, questions) in a given case, enable another rational agent who plays the role of a critic to read off or to infer by implicature the presumed commitments of the first party, judging what to infer from the text of discourse in the case. Hence, in the right context of dialogue and particular circumstances, an action of an agent may be taken to express the agent's commitment to a certain proposition, which may be pragmatically inconsistent with the conclusion of an argument this agent has advocated in the same case. The whole package is tied together by the thread of practical reasoning.

Character, according to the definition given by Kupperman, is a normal pattern of thinking and acting relating to a person's commitment, especially in his or her moral choices. This definition is highly compatible with Aristotle's account of character, in which good moral character (ethos) is seen as a kind of excellence of practical reasoning used to make choices in intelligent deliberation "situated in a mean relative to us" (translations of Nussbaum, cited in section 1, above, and Sherman, cited in section 5). Thus, for Aristotle, excellence of character is connected to reasoning. It involves a kind of thinking or inferring called practical reasoning. Hence an attack on a person's ethos or character (of the direct or abusive ad hominem type, in particular), in Aristotle's account, is a kind of criticism of that person's reasoning.

Using the group of ingredients of practical wisdom in Aristotle's theory identified by Hamblin (section 5, above), we have identified five aspects of character in particular that are the focus of direct ad hominem attacks: honesty, judgment skills, cognitive skills, perception of one's circumstances, and personal moral standards.

The task of evaluating ad hominem arguments, of judging whether or not a given ad hominem argument in a particular case is fallacious, is left for chapter 7, but some of the essential requirements of this task have now been set in place by chapter 5. It has been shown how attacks on a person's character have an understandable and in principle legitimate place in argumentation in a kind of dialogue exchange called deliberation. Hence we can understand why and how such arguments are powerful, effective, and legitimate in political rhetoric. In addition, we can see from the viewpoint of deliberation as a normative model of dialogue in which argumentation can be evaluated, with respect to whether or not it contributes to the goal of the dialogue, that ad hominem arguments do have a distinctive structure as uses of practical reasoning. Of course, the same ad hominem argument that might contribute to a deliberation in one case might be irrelevant, obstructive, or fallacious in another case, in which the context of dialogue is that of a critical discussion and the issue of the discussion is not one of character.

Forms and Classification of Subtypes

This chapter presents a classification of subtypes of ad hominem arguments. For each subtype an argumentation scheme is given that represents the form of argument of the subtype so that in a particular case the form can be applied to identify the type of ad hominem argument in the case. Corresponding to each argumentation scheme is a set of appropriate critical questions.

Three species of ad hominem arguments are recognized as basic or primary subtypes: the direct (or so-called abusive), the circumstantial, and the bias arguments. The circumstantial is characterized primarily as an allegation of pragmatic inconsistency between the arguer's personal circumstances and his argument. The direct and bias arguments do not rest directly on any claim of inconsistency. The direct form characteristically is a direct attack on the person's character, and the focus of the attack is often the person's honesty and trustworthiness as a reliable and collaborative participant in a dialogue exchange of arguments. The bias criticism also questions veracity and trustworthiness, but by the particular means of suggesting that the arguer criticized is secretly engaged in advocacy dialogue or even interest-based negotiation rather than truth-directed persuasion dialogue. The tu quoque, guilt by association, and poisoning the well ad hominem arguments are included also as subtypes, and some additional subtypes are recognized.

Most often (but not always) and typically, in circumstantial ad hominem arguments, it is not logical inconsistency that is alleged but a kind of pragmatic inconsistency—usually it is a perceived conflict between the arguer's statements and his actions: he does not "practice what he preaches." In the tu quoque form of the argument, the criticism is made: "You criticize me [or someone else] for doing [action] α, but then you yourself do α." Any such circumstantial, person-relative form of criticism is effective in reducing support for a person's argument because, as Govier (1983, note 20, p. 24) has pointed out, when someone fails to practice what he preaches, his credibility is undermined. The assumption that makes this argument work is that what the arguer personally practices may be a better indication of his sincere or wholehearted[1] commitment than the argument he "preaches." This is the connection whereby the allegation of pragmatic inconsistency shades into the personal attack argument.

But is it not also true, in some cases, that logical inconsistency could work the same way as an allegation on which to base an ad hominem argument? If a person is logically inconsistent, in the sense that he advocates both a proposition and its negation, could not this contradiction also be used as the basis of an ad hominem argument against him, by suggesting he is either confused or dishonest? As shown in chapter 6, the answer to this question is yes, and therefore several classification problems are posed, with respect to the circumstantial ad hominem. How can we distinguish between an allegation of inconsistency, used to question or criticize someone, and an ad hominem argument against that person? Or are the two kinds of arguments really both the same type of ad hominem argument? According to Krabbe (1990) inconsistency in argument is not necessarily fallacious, although it can certainly be used as a basis for posing critical questions about an arguer's commitments.

A system of classification of the subtypes of ad hominem argumentation is given below, in section 10 (figure 6.2), at the end of this chapter. In figure 6.2, all the various subtypes are pictured, showing the names given to each subtype and the relationships of the various subtypes. Each subtype represents a particular form of argument, the structure of which as a form of inference is defined in this chapter.

In addition, figure 6.1 shows how all the various forms of ad hominem argumentation (argumentation schemes) are related to each other as subspecies and to certain other general forms of argument that are often associated with the argumentum ad hominem but are not (in our analysis) ad hominem arguments.

The topic of when ad hominem arguments are fallacious is reserved for chapter 7. The basis for evaluating ad hominem arguments is set in place in this chapter, however, by the argumentation schemes and set of critical questions for the various subtypes. In this analysis all three of the basic subtypes of ad hominem criticism are best regarded as inherently weak and fragile presumptive forms of argument that rely on questioning an arguer's integrity, veracity, sincerity, or balance. Such an argument can be appropriate in contexts of opinion-based reasoning on a controversial issue for which knowledge is difficult to achieve, and personal integrity, balance, or veracity can properly come into play as useful considerations of evidence. Paradoxically, this weak presumptive type of argumentation can often be extremely powerful in persuasion dialogue because it can shift a burden of proof and refute a presumption of collaborative reliability.

1. Form of the Direct Subtype

The argumentation scheme for the direct (purely personal) argument against the person (the so-called abusive ad hominem) is the following.

ETHOTIC AH

a is a person of bad (defective) character.
Therefore, a's argument α should not be accepted.

The upshot of this type of argumentation, which could be called the negative ethotic (direct, abusive) ad hominem argument, is that the person a is said to be not a person of good character, and therefore a's argument should not be accepted (or, at any rate should be evaluated as less plausible than before).

An argument of the form ETHOTIC AH is called a *negative ethotic argument*, and that is the best name for it, following Aristotle's observations in the *Rhetoric* (1377b) about appeal to ethos as a mode of argument. It is clear from Aristotle's account that he would have accepted a positive version of ethotic argument of the following form as a (generally) reasonable argument.

POSITIVE ETHOTIC ARGUMENT

a is a person of good character.
Therefore, a's argument α should be accepted.

This positive version does not qualify as an ad hominem argument in the sense studied here, however, in which ad hominem is essentially use of personal attack to discredit a speaker's argument. It could be called the positive ethotic argument.

Now, one should ask, is the negative ethotic argument generally a reasonable argument, in the sense that if a rational participant in argument accepts the premise, she should also accept the conclusion? Because ETHOTIC AH is not generally a reasonable argument of this sort, in general, it could be in many instances that a particular argument is quite good (based on strong evidence) even though the person who put forward that argument really does have a bad character, and his having a bad character can be proved quite convincingly by good evidence. Cohen and Nagel (1934), cited in chapter 2, show how in a case of a scientific argument, for example, the character of the arguer would not be a good basis for rejecting the argument.

What is revealed by these observations is that an implicit premise needs to be added to ETHOTIC AH to bridge the gap between the premise and the conclusion. The need for such a premise was already indicated in chapter 3, section 3, where the conditional WPP was used in conjunction with the basic ad hominem form of argument GENERIC AH. This implicit premise (Walton, *Argument Schemes*, 1996, p. 86) has the form of a conditional: if *a* is a person of bad character, then *a*'s argument should not be accepted. Whether or not this conditional is true in a given case depends on the dialectical context in which ETHOTIC AH was used as an argument. The key factor is that of relevance—dialectical relevance, as defined in Walton (*Pragmatic Theory*, 1995, chapter 6)—leading us to a consideration of the critical questions appropriate for the negative ethotic argument. The second critical question below (CQ2) matches the implicit conditional premise of ETHOTIC AH.

Three kinds of critical questions are appropriate for this argumentation scheme. The first relates to the premise, the second to the type of dialogue in which the argument of the form ETHOTIC AH was used, and the third relates to the conclusion. The three critical questions matching ETHOTIC AH are the following.

CQ1

Is the premise true (or well supported) that *a* is a person of bad character?

CQ2

Is the issue of character relevant in the type of dialogue in which the argument was used?

CQ3

Is the conclusion of the argument that α should be (absolutely) rejected, even if other evidence to support α has been presented, or is the conclusion merely (the relative claim) that α should be assigned a reduced weight of credibility, relative to the total body of evidence available?

There are five subtypes of the abusive subtype of ad hominem argument, corresponding to the five aspects of character relating to practical reasoning given in chapter 5, section 5. These five variants are represented in the following argumentation schemes.

Negative Ethotic Ad Hominem Argument from Veracity

VERACITY AH

a has a bad character for veracity.
Therefore *a*'s argument α should not be accepted.

Negative Ethotic Ad Hominem Argument from Prudence

PRUDENCE AH

a has a bad character for prudent judgment.
Therefore, *a*'s argument α should not be accepted.

Negative Ethotic Ad Hominem Argument from Perception

PERCEPTION AH

a has a bad character for realistic perception of his situation.
Therefore, *a*'s argument α should not be accepted.

Negative Ethotic Ad Hominem Argument from Cognitive Skills

COGNITION AH

a has a bad character for logical reasoning.
Therefore, *a*'s argument α should not be accepted.

Negative Ethotic Ad Hominem Argument from Morals

MORALS AH

a has a bad character for personal moral standards.
Therefore, *a*'s argument α should not be accepted.

The last argumentation scheme MORALS AH refers to bad character for personal moral standards, other than the more specific kinds of failures of practical wisdom represented by the other four schemes. The critical questions for the five schemes are comparable to those given for ETHOTIC AH as a general type of argument.

The critical questions for the five variants are the same as the critical questions CQ1, CQ2, and CQ3, except that in CQ1 the specific aspect of character is cited. For example, the first critical question for VERACITY AH is: 'Is the premise true (or well supported) that a is a person who has bad character for veracity?' In some cases, merely asking this question is enough to defuse the charge and rebut an ad hominem attack. Of course, in other cases, the premise can be plausible enough to sustain the ad hominem argument, and so a critic may need to ask one of the other two questions.

The negative ethotic argument from veracity typically takes the form "a is a liar" or other forms of speech suggesting the accused person is dishonest or has no respect for the truth of a matter. The negative ethotic argument from cognitive skills typically takes forms of speech suggesting that the accused person is irrational or "crazy" or that he is "stupid" or is logically confused.

One of the big problems with the ad hominem argument generally is that the negative ethotic argument from morals is such a bombshell that the audience loses all track of its relevance to the issue of a case, and the attack may stick even though unsupported.

The negative ethotic argument from perception is not just an accusation that an arguer is biased or ignorant but that he has failed to take the kind of information into account that is needed for intelligent and informed argument in the type of dialogue he is supposed to be taking part in.

The kind of ad hominem attack that centers on the arguer's failure to take relevant evidence into account and to be aware of factual information centers on the arguer's obligation or burden of proof in a particular type of dialogue exchange. For example, Johnson (1988, pp. 68–71) argues that Karl Marx, who wrote many books on economic matters and advocated social policies based on his economic findings was not only badly informed but also lazy in collecting facts and even dishonest in reporting them. Johnson writes that Marx "can never be trusted" because his use of evidence "forces one to treat with skepticism everything he wrote which relies on factual data" (p. 68). Supporting this ad hominem argument against Marx with many examples of citations from his works, Johnson even argues that Marx did not understand how industry worked because he failed to take into account or to use the factual evidence in an objective way (p. 69):

Case 6.1

What Marx could not or would not grasp, because he made no effort to understand how industry worked, was that from the very dawn of the Industrial Revolution, 1760–90, the most efficient manufacturers, who had ample access to capital, habitually favored better conditions for their workforce; they therefore tended to support factory legislation and, what was equally important, its effective enforcement, because it eliminated what they regarded as unfair competition. So conditions improved, and because conditions improved, the workers failed to rise, as Marx predicted they would. The prophet was thus confounded. What emerges from a reading of *Capital* is Marx's fundamental failure to understand capitalism. He failed precisely because he was unscientific: he would not investigate the facts himself, or use objectively the facts investigated by others. From start to finish, not just *Capital* but all his work reflects a disregard for truth which at times amounts to contempt.

This particular ad hominem argument is part of Johnson's larger ad hominem attack that accuses Marx of other defects of character. But the focus of this particular attack is Marx's alleged failure to base his social and economic recommendations for action on an informed appreciation of the real facts. This ad hominem argument can be related to the bias type of attack, but the central focus of it is the failure to be aware of or to gather the true facts that are the real circumstances of a deliberation.

Generally, the abusive ad hominem argument is fairly easy to recognize as an argument because of two requirements. First, there must be an attack on a person's character. Second, the attack on character must be used to criticize some particular argument that the person has advocated. The inference is that the person's argument should be rejected because of his bad character. The reader should be careful to note that it is a consequence of this definition that not all attacks on a person's character (mudslinging, etc.) are ad hominem arguments.

The more subtle problem of identification comes in distinguishing between the abusive subtype and the circumstantial subtype because the latter can in many cases (and even typically does) involve an attack on the arguer's character. This problem casts doubt on the approach found in many of the textbook treatments in chapter 2, of distinguishing between the abusive and nonabusive categories.

The root of the problem is that quite often, in ad hominem arguments in everyday conversation and even typically, an allegation of practical inconsistency is a lead-in to an abusive type of ad hominem attack. This allegation typically occurs in a kind of case in which a circumstantial attack is made, and then it is argued on this basis of alleged conflict that the person attacked is a hypocrite. The next step is to say that because this person is a hypocrite, he is a sort of liar and has a bad character for veracity, and one cannot believe what he says, and so forth. In such a case, there is a lead-in from the circumstantial type of attack to the abusive. That is why we think that defining the ad hominem as an exclusive subcategory of either abusive or non-abusive, in which the circumstantial is defined as the leading type of nonabusive argument or perhaps as the only type of nonabusive argument of the ad hominem category, is not a good way of proceeding. We ought not try to define the circumstantial or the other categories as being somehow nonabusive or even as being defined as exactly the nonabusive categories. The abusive subtype does have its own characteristics, but the circumstantial subtype can be partly abusive as well. Therefore, whatever the defining character of the circumstantial ad hominem argument, it must have some other distinguishing feature such as the existence of a pragmatic inconsistency, which is needed to define this type of ad hominem argument.

This theoretical problem of classification is one of the reasons why the negative definition of the circumstantial ad hominem as being "nondirect" will not work and is not a good idea. Instead, it is necessary to define the circumstantial type of ad hominem itself in a positive way. The same point applies to the bias type. All three main subtypes must have distinctive argumentation schemes with positive features of identification for each.

What distinguishes the circumstantial from the abusive (direct, ethotic) type of ad hominem argument is that in the circumstantial type the primary focus of the attack in the argument is not on character but on the external circumstances of person, primarily on an inconsistency that is alleged. Then this attack on an arguer's consistency of commitments may lead to an attack on character.[2] Certainly, if it is to be an ad hominem argument, the allegation of inconsistency must be used as the basis for a personal attack on the arguer.

2. Form of the Circumstantial Subtype

The most prominent kind of circumstantial attack cited as an ad hominem argument in the textbook treatment is the type for which some action or actions attributed to an arguer (as his personal circumstances) are cited as being in conflict (pragmatic inconsistency) with the argument he advocates. The smoking case is of this type. The argumentation scheme for this type of argument is the following.

PRAGMATIC INCONSISTENCY

a advocates argument α, which has proposition A as its conclusion.
a has carried out an action or set of actions that imply that a is personally committed to $\neg A$ (the opposite, or negation of A).
Therefore a's argument α should not be accepted.

The word 'imply,' in the second premise of PRAGMATIC INCONSISTENCY refers to defeasible implicature by practical reasoning, judged by the description of the action(s) in question, which bring a weight of presumption against a's side of a dialogue. A good label for this type of argument is YOU SAY ONE THING, DO ANOTHER.

The initial problem with PRAGMATIC INCONSISTENCY is that it does not (at least clearly or explicitly) seem to be a true ad hominem argument because it lacks the personal attack element of GENERIC AH. As it stands, PRAGMATIC INCONSISTENCY could be based on the rationale that an inconsistent set of propositions cannot all be true. It seems that this version makes it seem more like simply an argument from pragmatic inconsistency of an arguer's commitments, one that need not be a subspecies of ad hominem argument in a sense implying personal attack.

To represent this fuller idea of the circumstantial ad hominem argument we need to add an additional premise guaranteeing that PRAGMATIC INCONSISTENCY is really an ad hominem argument. For example, to represent many typical cases, we could add a premise stating that a's action(s) represent his true (underlying) commitment(s) more than or as opposed to his explicitly advocated commitment to A, the conclusion of his argument α. Once this additional premise is added to the existing two premises of PRAGMATIC INCONSISTENCY, the subconclusion would be implied that a is a hypocrite, a person who is deceiving us about his real (true) commitments and is therefore a dishonest or deceptive person. This conclusion, in turn, implies that a is morally bad, and that implication is the basis for not accepting his argument. Hence the supplemented version of PRAGMATIC INCONSISTENCY, so expressed, would be a genuine ad hominem argument. Let us call this form of argument CIRCUMSTANTIAL AH, which combines GENERIC AH and PRAGMATIC INCONSISTENCY to produce a complex (two-stage) argumentation scheme.

CIRCUMSTANTIAL AH

1. a advocates argument α, which has proposition A as its conclusion.
2. a has carried out an action or set of actions that imply that a is personally committed to ⅂A (the opposite, or negation of A).
3. Therefore, a is a bad person.
4. Therefore, a's argument α should not be accepted.

Conclusion 3 is generated from premise 2, typically on the grounds that a is a hypocrite, a specific type of morally bad person. Then in a second subargument of the form GENERIC AH, conclusion 4 is generated from premise 3. A good general name for this type of argument is YOU DON'T PRACTICE WHAT YOU PREACH, the word 'preach' suggesting that the arguer strongly advocates a code of conduct as right or wrong for a person to follow.

The conclusion of CIRCUMSTANTIAL AH is the same as that of PRAGMATIC INCONSISTENCY, and the former is a subspecies of the latter. The distinction is that not all instances of PRAGMATIC INCONSISTENCY are ad hominem arguments. It is the distinction between these two types of argument that was part of the problem in case 3.2. In this case, Bob cited an inconsistency in Ed's set of commitments, replying, "Come on, Ed. You can't have it both ways!" Now the question was whether this was an ad hominem attack on Ed or just a citing of the inconsistency of Ed's commitments as a basis for raising doubts about his argument (either in the form of requesting clarification or in the form of making the proposal that Ed's argument should not be accepted).

So now we are confronted with a choice. Which form better represents the circumstantial ad hominem, PRAGMATIC INCONSISTENCY or CIRCUMSTANTIAL AH? Judging from the textbook accounts in chapter 2, either could fit. But in keeping with the general viewpoint implicit in the examples used in the textbooks, ad hominem should be a personal attack type of argument. Hence, CIRCUMSTANTIAL AH is the better general representation of the circumstantial subtype.

One of the major questions (from chapter 3) that has plagued the analysis of the ad hominem historically is the relation of the forms of argument PRAGMATIC INCONSISTENCY and CIRCUMSTANTIAL AH to the form of argument from commitment (AC), representing the Lockean ex concessis concept of the ad hominem argument. The answer to this question is revealed by considering a form of argument intermediate between AC and PRAGMATIC INCONSISTENCY, called *argument from inconsistent commitment* or the *you contradict yourself* type of argument. The ⌐ is the conventional symbol for negation.

INCONSISTENT COMMITMENT

a is committed to proposition *A* (generally, or in virtue of what she said in the past).
a is committed to proposition ⌐*A*, which is the conclusion of the argument α that *a* presently advocates.
Therefore *a*'s argument α should not be accepted.

INCONSISTENT COMMITMENT is the same form of argument as PRAGMATIC INCONSISTENCY except that PRAGMATIC INCONSISTENCY refers explicitly to commitments incurred in virtue of *a*'s actions. So pragmatic inconsistency (inconsistency of actions and commitments) is an essential aspect of PRAGMATIC INCONSISTENCY and CIRCUMSTANTIAL AH. In contrast, INCONSISTENT COMMITMENT is meant to cover the kind of case in which a's verbal moves in a dialogue exchange (moves in the dialogue or speech acts) are what commit him to the proposition A. The critical questions for INCONSISTENT COMMITMENT are comparable to those for CIRCUMSTANTIAL AH, except they relate to the avowed opinions of a only and not a's acts (as expressing commitments). What is characteristic of INCONSISTENT COMMITMENT is a conflict between two of an arguer's "avowed opinions," to use Whately's phrase (from chapter 1, section 1).

Now that we have made the distinction between PRAGMATIC INCONSISTENCY and INCONSISTENT COMMITMENT, we can see that it is more likely the latter that represents the form of the argument in case 3.2. The reason is the presumption, as applied to case 3.2, that Ed's strong support of communism in the past, as cited by Bob in his argument, is being based on what Ed said in the past. Perhaps it could have been such remarks as "Power to the people!" or "Workers, cast off your chains!" However, if Bob's argument was based on Ed's actions, as opposed to his verbal declarations of support for communism, then the form of Bob's argument in case 3.2 would be PRAGMATIC INCONSISTENCY.

Having clarified these forms of argument, we can now see a connection between the Lockean ex concessis type of argument represented by ETHOTIC AH, the form of argument from commitment, and the circumstantial type of ad hominem argument, CIRCUMSTANTIAL AH. But the two types of argument are by no means identical, and their relationship is indirect and subtle. INCONSISTENT COMMITMENT is a special subtype of AC but has a different sort of conclusion from AC and is different also in respect to its introducing the idea of a pair of conflicting commitments. In AC the proponent tries to get the respondent to accept her view by showing it to be a logical consequence of her commitment set. In contrast, in INCONSISTENT COMMITMENT, in which the proponent also argues from the respondent's commitment set, the thrust of the argument is to reject the respondent's argument on the grounds that his commitments are inconsistent.

Now PRAGMATIC INCONSISTENCY is really a more specialized or at any rate different variant on INCONSISTENT COMMITMENT that bases the argument not just on the respondent's verbal commitments (what Whately called his "avowed opinions") but specifically on his actions and what they imply. Finally CIRCUMSTANTIAL AH is a subtype of PRAGMATIC INCONSISTENCY that adds an additional premise.

Another type of argument that could be called the *double standard argument* is related to and similar to the circumstantial ad hominem argument, but it is not quite the same. An example of the double standard argument is the following case (Mittelstaedt, 1995, A3), which arose from a comment by the premier of Ontario that it is "human nature" to cheat on taxes.

Case 6.2

Liberal finance critic Gerry Phillips accused the government yesterday of a "double standard" because it has launched a major effort to stem welfare cheating, including a toll-free provincial fraud hotline, while taking a sympathetic view of tax evasion.

"On the one hand, people who cheat on welfare are crooks and you have to prosecute them, but if you're just cheating on taxes, it's human nature," Mr. Phillips said of the government.

Tax fraud is likely 10 times larger than welfare fraud, he said, and the government should make "the same concerted effort" tracking it as has been put in place for social-assistance cheating.

Mr. Phillips is accusing the government of having a double standard, by taking a hard line against welfare cheats and a softer line with tax evaders.

This type of argument can be said to have the following general form, where *a* and *b* are actions or types of actions or situations.

DOUBLE STANDARD

The respondent has one policy with respect to *a*.
The respondent has another (different) policy with respect to *b*.
a is similar to *b* (or comparable to *b* in some relevant respect).
Therefore, the respondent is using a double standard.

The conclusion is meant to convey the idea that the use of one policy for one type of case and a different policy for another is an inappropriate (illogical and/or unfair) position for the respondent to take. Hence the double standard argument is frequently used to lead into an ad hominem attack by following up with drawing the conclusion that the respondent is a bad person in a role in dialogue, that is, the respondent is a hypocrite amd is dishonest or biased.

Even so, although the double standard argument is closely related to the ad hominem argument and is often used to lead into an ad hominem attack, it is a different type of argument (in general) from the ad hominem argument. It is similar to the *you contradict yourself* type of argument, except that it is based on an analogy or comparison between two actions or situations and is a pragmatic type of argument using practical reasoning.

3. Critical Questions for the Circumstantial Subtype

Presenting the best set of critical questions to be used in replying to a circumstantial ad hominem argument turns out to be a complex task for several reasons. First, as clearly shown by the case of Mr. S., in chapter 4, there are many different ways to respond effectively to a circumstantial ad hominem argument. Second, because the circumstantial ad hominem type of case is based on a sequence of practical reasoning, as shown in chapter 5, what really needs to be brought into consideration are the critical questions for practical reasoning, in chapter 5, section 4. Hence, no complete set of critical questions match the circumstantial ad hominem argument that is reasonably short. Ten critical questions for the circumstantial ad hominem are given in Walton (*Informal Logic,* 1989, pp. 164–65), listed as critical questions 8 through 17 inclusive in *Informal Logic.* The reader should begin by examining this list, quoted below.

8. In evaluating any circumstantial argument against the person as a reasonable or unreasonable criticism, one must first of all attempt to identify the propositions that are alleged to be inconsistent. What are these propositions? Clearly identify them from the given corpus of the argument.

9. Are the given propositions logically inconsistent? Collect together the set of propositions alleged to be inconsistent, and investigate whether they are logically inconsistent as they stand. To show that they are logically inconsistent, you must deduce a contradiction from them by valid arguments. If this cannot be done, go on to critical question 10.

10. Are the given propositions circumstantially inconsistent? If there is no logical inconsistency, then evaluate whether there are reasonable grounds for the claim that there is a circumstantial inconsistency in the defender's position. What sort of evidence does the given corpus offer for a claim of circumstantial inconsistency? Is the case strong or weak? Who is alleged to have committed the inconsistency? Often a group is referred to in an *ad hominem* allegation, for example a profession or a political party. If some members of the group have engaged in certain practices, it need not follow that the defender is one of those members or accepts all their policies.

11. How well specified is the defender's position? Could further dialogue spell out that position more specifically in relation to the conclusion at issue? Does the defender's position commit him to certain propositions that could lead to a propositional inconsistency, even if he has not explicitly accepted these propositions in his argument?

12. If the allegation of inconsistency is weak, what is the connection be-

tween the pair of propositions alleged to be the basis of the conflict in the defender's position? If the parallel is weak, or nonexistent, does that mean that the personal attack can be classified as erroneous?

13. If there is an inconsistency that can be established as part of the defender's position, how serious a flaw is this contradiction? Can the defender explain or resolve it very easily without destroying his position? What could be a plausible reply for the defender?

14. Does the defender have a legitimate opportunity to reply to the personal attack? Most arguments against the person can be answered by further dialogue, so it is important not to allow the criticism to be a conversation stopper if the accused party could respond. Remember that most arguments against the person are not conclusive refutations, but they can reasonably shift the burden of argument onto the defender to reply.

15. Could the arguer who has been attacked by a circumstantial argument against the person cite a relevant difference in the two sets of personal circumstances alleged to be parallel in the attack?

16. If the defender has in fact replied to an *ad hominem* attack with another *ad hominem* attack in reply, is there enough of a parallel to justify shifting the burden of proof back onto the attacker? In such a case, has a question been evaded or the issue avoided?

17. If a defense against an *ad hominem* attack involves a denial of inconsistency by taking a hard or dogmatic stance on the language used to describe the situations at issue, ask whether the terms used are being defined in a one-sided manner. Is the defender being consistent in his use of terms?

These critical questions are the appropriate ones to be asked in circumstantial ad hominem cases such as the sportsman's rejoinder (case 1.18) and the tree hugger (1.6).

To offer more concise guidance in evaluating arguments of the form CIRCUMSTANTIAL AH, the following short list of first priority critical questions is given. This set of six items concentrates on the most important or central critical questions that need to be asked in a typical and common type of circumstantial ad hominem that the reader is most likely to encounter. The first four questions, which focus on the alleged pragmatic (practical) inconsistency, are quoted from Walton (*Pragmatic Theory,* 1995, p. 145). The fifth and sixth are newly formulated additions.

CQ1

What are the propositions alleged to be practically inconsistent, and are they practically inconsistent?

CQ2

If the identified propositions are not practically (pragmatically) inconsistent, as things stand, are there at least some grounds for a claim of practical inconsistency that can be evaluated from the textual evidence of the discourse?

CQ3

Even if there is not an explicit practical inconsistency, what is the connection between the pair of propositions alleged to be inconsistent?

CQ4

If there is a practical inconsistency that can be identified as the focus of the attack, how serious a flaw is it? Could the apparent conflict be resolved or explained without destroying the consistency of the commitment in the dialogue?

CQ5

Does it follow from a's inconsistent commitment that a is a bad person?

CQ6

Is the conclusion the weaker claim that a's credibility is open to question or the stronger claim that the conclusion of a is false?

This is not the end of the problems with defining the argumentation scheme of circumstantial ad hominem and its set of matching critical questions. According to the account given in Walton (*Pragmatic Theory*, 1995, pp. 144–45), the argumentation scheme for the circumstantial argument against the person is the following. It is named SCHEME 95 for the year it was published.

SCHEME 95

a has advanced the contention that everyone in a certain reference class C ought to support proposition A and be committed to A.
a is in the reference class C.
It is indicated by a's own personal circumstances that he is not committed to A (or even worse, is committed to the opposite of A).
Therefore a's commitment to A is open to doubt.

There are two problems with this scheme. One is how 'reference class' ought to be defined. The other is the universal aspect of the scheme. This analysis of the circumstantial ad hominem argument applies very well to cases like 5.4, in which it is not the respondent herself who has allegedly carried out the action or supported the policy in question, but it is her membership in a group (profession, association, etc.) that has done so (collectively) that is the focus of the attack. For example, in case 5.4, the politician attacked the reporter for being a reporter, that is, for belonging to a group (profession) that has often taken advantage of free travel benefits offered by politicians. This argument is presumed to work because the reporter's ad hominem argument supposedly makes the claim that everybody who takes free benefits from corporations or other parties that offer them has committed some morally blameworthy action. This is the universal aspect of the scheme. In passing, note that a reply is open to the reporter. The reporter could argue that such benefits are only culpable if the benefactor is a public servant, and because reporters are not public servants or elected officials, they are not on the same footing with politicians in this regard.

From the universal aspect, in the smoking case, the child is not claiming that the parent is claiming, as a premise or conclusion of her argument, that everyone should not smoke. Rather, the child is simply puzzled by the apparent inconsistency between the parent's smoking while at the same time arguing to the child that he should not smoke because it is unhealthy. Analyzing the argument, however, the parent could be construed as making the claim that everyone who wants to be healthy should not smoke. So there may be a universal element involved even here, but the universal element is not so central to the ad hominem argument, in the way it is in the reporter's case. It is dubious, or at least controversial, whether the smoking case is an argument of the type represented by SCHEME 95. The other problem is how to define the notion of a reference class in SCHEME 95. Is a reference class a group of individuals, or does it represent a broader criterion?

For these reasons, it is best to replace SCHEME 95 as a way of representing the circumstantial type of ad hominem and to replace it with the more finely discriminating analysis presented here, which distinguishes between the universal aspect and the circumstantial aspects more carefully.

Another more fundamental problem with SCHEME 95 is that it is really a subtype of PRAGMATIC INCONSISTENCY, rather than being a definite circumstantial ad hominem of the form CIRCUMSTANTIAL AH. What needs to be added is the required premise that the alleged inconsistency is being used as a basis for personal attack. Accordingly, we redefine this scheme so that it is refined to be distinctive between two subtypes of ad hominem argument, which we call the *universal circumstantial* ad hominem argument and the *group circumstantial* ad hominem argument.

1. *a* advocates argument α, which has proposition *A* as its conclusion, which says that everybody should be committed to *A*.
2. *a* is bound by the 'everybody' in premise 1.
3. *a* has carried out an action or a set of actions that imply that *a* is personally committed to ⅂*A*.
4. Therefore *a* is a bad person.
5. Therefore *a*'s argument α should not be accepted.

GROUP CIRCUMSTANTIAL AH

1. *a* advocates argument α, which says that everybody in group *G* should be committed to *A*.
2. *a* belongs to group *G*.
3. *a* has carried out an action or a set of actions that imply that *a* is personally committed to ⅂*A*.
4. Therefore *a* is a bad person.
5. Therefore *a*'s argument α should not be accepted.

The group circumstantial ad hominem argument, as shown in section 7 below, turns out to be a subspecies of the guilt by association type of ad hominem. A good example of the group circumstantial ad hominem argument is the case of the reporter (case 5.4). It was not just the personal action of his taking free benefits that formed the basis of the ad hominem attack on his argument but the fact that reporters as a group were known regularly to take advantage of these benefits.

Another interesting type of case is the ad hominem argument used against Mario Cuomo (and Geraldine Ferraro, as well) that even though, as a Catholic, he personally opposed abortion, as a Democratic politician he was a member of a party that officially supported the right to abortion. This type of case is analyzed in Walton (*Informal Logic*, 1989, p. 169) and more fully in Farrell (1993, pp. 213–29). Cuomo defended himself by drawing a distinction between his personal ethical choices and policies and the general policies that he supports as a member of a political party. Still, it seemed to many, as one might expect, that his position was inconsistent in some pragmatic way (based on the apparent inconsistency).

We can see also that UNIVERSAL CIRCUMSTANTIAL AH is related to the group attack or guilt by association type of ad hominem argument, in virtue of premises 1 and 2 of UNIVERSAL CIRCUMSTANTIAL AH. This connection may suggest that the guilt by association ad hominem argument should be classified as a subtype of the circumstantial ad hominem argument. As will be shown in section 7, the group attack or guilt by association type of argument is in fact connected to the abusive and bias subtypes as well.

4. Form of the Bias Subtype

It is possible for a critic to attack an argument as biased without making any reference to the person who is the proponent of that argument.[3] In other cases, however, the argument is criticized by attacking the proponent of that argument as a person who is biased. Only this latter type of argumentation should properly be classified as the bias type of ad hominem argument. For example, in cases 1.8 and 1.9, Bob's conclusion is that Wilma is biased. If, instead, he were to have examined the details of her argument and pointed out some bias in the phrasing of it, that would not be an ad hominem argument, unless he used the allegation of bias to attack Wilma personally.

Of course, to allege that someone has used a biased argument may, indirectly, be an attack on the honesty or fairness of that person. So allegations of bias do tend to lead naturally to ad hominem arguments. But strictly speaking, an allegation of bias should not be classified as a bias type of ad hominem argument unless the argument is a personal attack directed against the proponent of the argument that is criticized.

The argumentation scheme for the bias type of ad hominem argument is the following.

BIAS AH

1. Person a, the proponent of argument α, is biased.
2. Person a's bias is a failure to take part honestly in a type of dialogue D, which α is part of.
3. Therefore a is a bad person.
4. Therefore α should not be given as much credibility as it would have without the bias.

The argumentation scheme BIAS AH, especially the second premise, makes it clear that the argument α is being used in a given context of dialogue and must be evaluated in that context of use. If the argument α is part of an advocacy type of dialogue (for example, a sales presentation), then bias would be expected. In this type of partisan context, bias in favor of the product is normal, and it is no failure for the person advocating the product to be biased. However, if the dialogue is supposed to be a kind of advice-giving dialogue (for example, a *Consumers Report* article, giving advice on which product is a "best buy") then an allegation of bias would be a strong kind of attack, which would make the audience have serious reservations.

The critical questions for the bias type of ad hominem are the following.

cq1

What is the evidence that *a* is biased?

cq2

If *a* is biased, is it a bad bias that is detrimental to *a*'s honestly taking part in *D* or a normal bias that is appropriate for the type of dialogue in which α was put forward?

With respect to cq1, one of the most common kinds of evidence cited is that of financial interest (having something to gain), but that is not the only kind of relevant evidence. In the cases of the bias type of ad hominem argument in chapter 2, several of the allegations of bias related to the arguer's having adopted a particular position (being a Catholic). Ten different types of evidence on which charges of bias are based are studied in Walton (*One-Sided*, 1998).

The problem posed by cq2, as noted in chapter 3, section 8, is that not all bias is "bad bias." Bias is normal in advocacy argumentation (partisanship) and is not a basis for criticism of one's argument as critically defective, provided the proponent has made it clear at the outset that his argument is meant to advocate one point of view. Also, having a financial interest is normal if the dialogue is supposed to be a negotiation. Bias becomes a problem, however, if the advocacy or interest-based bargaining takes place in a type of dialogue that is supposed to be a critical discussion. In that type of dialogue, advocacy of your own point of view is appropriate, but in some instances, you are also supposed to take a balanced perspective, from which your opponent's arguments are considered on their merits, even if they go against your own point of view.

The problem is that the critical discussion is a delicate kind of dialogue to carry on successfully, requiring a balance between an adversarial partisan type of dialogue and a more cool-headed type of exchange in which one respects one's opponent and gives him the freedom to develop his own point of view, as much as one is inclined to dislike that point of view or find it wrong or even biased. See Walton (*Pragmatic Theory*, 1995, chapter 8, section 9) on this balancing function of argument. Learning the skill of maintaining this kind of balance in a hotly contested argument is no trivial matter. Even one who is professionally skilled in this kind of dialogue is often going to go wrong with it and perform poorly. The temptation to push ahead with promoting one's own point of view, especially for one deeply committed to a "cause" or deeply held position, is a strong force that is always present. The trick is to respond to this force with emotion and dedication, while at the same time maintaining an honest equilibrium that resists being overpowered by it. If this description resembles Aristotle's doctrine of the mean in ethical judgment, that is precisely how we should think of it. In the Aristotelian spirit, dialectical skills are comparable to the kinds of skills required by judgment in practical reasoning. A respect for one's opponent and honesty in following the collaborative maxims of discussion have to be balanced against an intense desire to win, translated coolly into one's performance in the changing situation one is confronted with during an argument.

The credibility an argument has for an audience or observer depends on this balanced presumption that the arguer has honestly considered the arguments available to her on both sides of the issue as a basis for her own argument. If the observer has reason to think that this basis of balance is lacking with respect to an argument—because the arguer is taking a one-sided approach of simply advocating one viewpoint and ignoring the evidence for the other side—then the observer will (rightly) give the argument less credibility than she normally would. In short, if evidence shows that the arguer is biased, an observer or audience will discount her argument, either not accepting it all or giving it less weight as evidence.

5. The Poisoning the Well Subtype

The bias subtype of ad hominem is addressed to a single argument α and has the conclusion that α is not acceptable (or is less credible) because the proponent *a* of α is biased. The poisoning the well subtype is an extension of the bias ad hominem that puts forward the stronger conclusion that every argument advanced by *a* in the critical discussion is not acceptable. The reason given is that *a* has a fixed bias, so whenever any argument comes up, she always advocates a particular point of view and is never really open to the arguments on both sides.

The poisoning the well subtype of ad hominem has the following argumentation scheme.

POISONING THE WELL AH

1. For every argument α in dialogue D, person a is biased.
2. Person a's bias is a failure to take part honestly in a type of dialogue D, that α is part of.
3. Therefore a is a bad person.
4. Therefore α should not be given as much credibility as it would have without the bias.

POISONING THE WELL AH is an even more extreme type of ad hominem attack than BIAS AH because it condemns any and all arguments that a person may put forward. The first premise means that any argument that a has put forward or will put forward in the dialogue shows a's bias. Typically, this type of argument is put forward, as well, in virtue of some fixed attribute an arguer has: for example, "You can never believe or take seriously anything she says on the abortion issue because, as a woman, she will always take the feminist point of view, which supports her own interests as a female" (compare case 2.23). The force of this argument is stronger than that of the simple bias ad hominem because it permanently shuts out the person attacked as a credible participant in a balanced discussion of an issue. In effect, it shuts down the discussion.

When it is claimed that a is a "bad person" in an argument of the form POISONING THE WELL AH, it should be recalled from section 1 above that this charge does not necessarily mean that a is a morally bad person (unless the argument specifically also has the form of the negative ethotic ad hominem argument from morals). It needs to be kept in mind that, at least in the reasonable type of ad hominem arguments coming under the GENERIC AH type, the expression 'bad person' stands in for a deficiency of the person's role as a participant in a type of dialogue in which there are obligations. In a critical discussion, for example, certain attitudes are required for a person who is honestly and collaboratively taking part in the discussion.

The kind of balance required by a participant in a critical discussion involves not only raising critical questions about the opponent's arguments but also being able to consider objections to your own arguments by suspending your commitment temporarily. Critical doubt requires a suspension of one's pro-attitude toward one's own point of view in argumentation temporarily. Some say that critical doubt entails having a neutral attitude—one that is neither pro nor contra with respect to the issue of the discussion. But nothing is quite this simple. One is generally biased to accepting one's own point of view, but bias is not in itself inherently bad.

Suppose there is a border dispute between two countries, and you are not a citizen of either of these countries, nor do you have any close relationship with either of them or anything at stake in the dispute, as far as you know. Then you can be neutral with respect to this argument. But on most issues of ethics or public policy that affect you, you are not going to be neutral, whether or not you think you are. You are going to have bias, one way or the other, even if you are not aware of this bias.

With respect to many arguments in everyday controversies, you are not going to be neutral, even if you try to be or if you think you are. However, it is still possible for you to have critical doubt with respect to such an argument. How is this possible?

It would seem that this critical doubt is possible because you can temporarily suspend your pro attitude or contra attitude and by such an act of suspension of commitment put yourself in the frame of mind of someone who has the opposed point of view, while at the same time seeing the issue from your own partisan point of view. By such an act, to the extent that it is successful, you can discover what the strongest arguments against your own position must plausibly be, as well as being aware of the arguments in its favor. To carry out this act of looking at the issue from your opponent's point of view, you do have to adopt an attitude of removal from pushing ahead for your own partisan viewpoint. This position does involve a suspension, but it does not yet involve the step of taking up a neutral attitude.

To find a way in which critical doubt can involve a neutral attitude, in some cases it is useful to look at your own argument or one you support from the point of view of the "neutral observer," a person who has no strong opinion on the issue of the discussion at all or who is not committed to the conclusion of the argument in question, one way or the other.[4]

This so-called neutral observer is a hypothetical construct except that he is a particular type of average person who is not either strongly pro or contra on the proposition in question. Nevertheless, this person is not entirely a hypothetical construct; he must also share some features of the average person who is likely to be taking part in this discussion. This average person can be taken to have a lot of general knowledge about familiar issues related to the subject of the discussion, but he has no strong, special, or unusual commitments one way or the other on the proposition at issue.

To function well in a critical discussion, an arguer needs to be able to play several roles. Sometimes she must push ahead with the strongest arguments she can find or articulate from her own point of view. At other times, she must enter into the spirit of her opponent's position well enough to appreciate and anticipate the arguments her opponent is likely to use and to find credible for defending that position. Still, at other times, she must try to adopt a neutral point of view, to the extent possible, in order to try to see how others—an audience—would react to these opposed arguments. The skills and abilities demand a certain amount of flexibility and openness (see the set of attitudes for a critical discussion given in chapter 5, section 2).

So if one party in a critical discussion accuses the other of lacking the balance and flexibility characteristic of the proper exercise of critical doubt, this type of criticism has much force. It suggests that the other party is not sincerely taking part in the critical discussion and is instead simply engaged in advocacy of his own point of view or interests. As such, his argument is not worthless, but we pay less attention to it or take it in a different way, once we see that he is biased to the one side.

Hence both BIAS AH and POISONING THE WELL AH are subspecies of GENERIC AH, but they both introduce, as an additional subargument, the allegation that the person is biased. This allegation of bias is used to support the contention that the arguer is a morally bad person, insofar as he lacks the appropriate collaborative attitudes of honesty and balance necessary to take part properly in a critical discussion.

6. Tu Quoque and Two Wrongs

The main problem with the textbook treatment of the tu quoque ad hominem fallacy is that according to the way it is most often defined, it becomes essentially the same type of argument as that in the two wrongs make a right fallacy. For example, in case 1.11, cited as an example of the tu quoque by Kaminsky and Kaminsky (1974, p. 46), one student accuses the other of copying an exam answer, and the other accuses the first one of handing in a term paper he did not write. This counterblaming, instead of directly confronting an allegation of morally wrong action—which is the essence of this supposed fallacy or type of argument—is identical, as a species of argumentation, to what is usually called the two wrongs fallacy, in other textbooks (see, for example, the treatment of case 1.13 by Groarke,

1982, p. 10). In this case, one government accuses another of torture or other human rights abuses, and the second government replies by accusing the first of using similar or worse practices. Groarke calls this example a case of the two wrongs fallacy, but clearly the identical type of argument used in case 1.13 is called the tu quoque.

The second problem with this way of proceeding, aside from the terminological confusion, resides in the question of whether the supposed fallacy or type of argument in these cases is really an ad hominem argument at all. The answer is that it is not, in many of the textbook cases cited in chapter 2, or that at any rate the evidence in these cases is insufficient for us to conclude that it is, given the criteria for what constitutes an ad hominem argument laid down in chapters 3 and 4. If it is an argument, it is not one used to attack the other party's argument by attacking that party personally. By our criteria, an ad hominem argument must be use of personal attack on a participant in a dialogue in order to claim that his argument is wrong (or to claim that it should be given reduced credibility as an argument).

Cases 1.11 and 1.13 did not seem to be ad hominem arguments in this sense, as far as the given evidence in the texts of these cases indicates, according to the analysis of that evidence given in chapter 1, section 5. In case 1.11, the first student is not attacking an argument of the second student (as far as we are told). The first student is simply accusing the second student of having committed a morally wrong action. This accusation could be put in the form of an argument, 'You copied your exam answer. Copying an exam answer is cheating. Cheating is wrong. Therefore, you did something wrong.' This sequence of propositions is an argument because the last one is a conclusion based on the prior three propositions that are used as premises to support the conclusion. But is this argument an ad hominem argument? The answer is that it is not (as things stand, as far as we can judge on the given evidence). This argument could be justified by citing objective observations that support the premises. It is not appealing to evidence that the first student is a bad person to support those premises.

What about the reply of the second student? It is on a different footing; it does allege that the first student is a bad person as a key premise. The argument of the second student could be classified as an ad hominem because it is used to attack the first student's argument (outlined above) that the action of the first student was morally blameworthy. Similar comments apply to the argument in case 1.13.

The best way to rectify the problem of distinguishing between the tu quoque and two wrong subtypes is to require, as part of the definition of the tu quoque subtype of ad hominem argument, that the first argument of the pair must be an ad hominem argument itself. Hence what is characteristic of the tu quoque subtype is that the proponent attacks the respondent with an ad hominem argument, and the respondent in reply (at the next move) attacks the proponent's ad hominem argument by advancing another ad hominem argument against her.

In this account, the tu quoque argument has the following form: the proponent accuses the respondent of some character fault or blameworthy action (of being a bad person), using that accusation to attack an argument put forward by the respondent; the respondent then makes the same type of accusation (that the proponent has also committed a wrong action or is a bad person) in reply, using that accusation to throw doubt on the proponent's argument against him. In this account, the tu quoque subtype always involves one ad hominem argument used to reply to a prior ad hominem argument. The two wrongs argument is different and begins with an accusation by the proponent that has the form of an argument, generally to the effect that the respondent has committed a morally blameworthy act. But it is not an ad hominem argument. Then the respondent attacks the proponent's argument by claiming that the proponent has committed a comparably culpable act herself. The conclusion implied is that the proponent is not a credible or trustworthy person to make this kind of allegation. The tactic is used to shift blame away from the accusation against the respondent and back toward the side of the proponent, at the same time undercutting the proponent's credibility as a person to trust to make the original accusation.

A good example of a tu quoque used to reply to a circumstantial ad hominem attack is the following case (Anonymous, 1995).

Case 6.3

California Gov. Peter Wilson has made the crackdown on illegal aliens a key theme in his '96 Republican presidential bid. But the issue could backfire. *Newsweek* has obtained documents showing that in 1989, as a senator, Wilson wrote the Immigration and Naturalization Service on behalf of a long-time political supporter, Anne Evans, whose San Diego hotels had been raided on suspicion of employing illegals. Evans paid a $70,000 fine after being charged with 362 immigration-law violations. Meanwhile, following allegations that Wilson and his first wife hired illegals as household help, Democrats are placing ads in newspapers from Washington to Tijuana, seeking information from former Wilson employees. "These are cheap political games by people who got their butts kicked in the last gubernatorial campaign," said a Wilson spokesman.

In this case, Wilson was accused of circumstantial inconsistency: making cracking down on illegal aliens a key theme in his election bid, while at the same time hiring illegal aliens (compare cases 1.6 and 1.18). Then, using the tu quoque, Wilson accuses his critics of playing "cheap political games." His reply even suggests that his opponents probably learned how to use this type of argument when they themselves were defeated with it in the past.

The form of the tu quoque subtype of ad hominem is best exhibited as a *profile of dialogue,* a sequence of characteristic types of connected moves in a dialogue exchange.

TQ

Proponent: Respondent, you are a bad person (because you have bad character, are circumstantially inconsistent, biased, etc.), therefore your argument should not be accepted.

Respondent: You are just as bad, therefore your ad hominem argument against me should not be accepted as having any worth.

In effect, in the TU QUOQUE AH type of argument, the respondent is saying that the proponent has no right to make such an accusation or to take the high moral ground because her own moral standing as a serious or honest person is in doubt.

An interesting case in Farrell (1993, pp. 39–47) that is too long to describe fully here concerned the Army-McCarthy hearings of 1954. These hearings were convened to investigate charges that Senator Joseph McCarthy had used improper influence during his surveillance for communist activities and conspiracies in the U.S. Army. During one point in the hearings, McCarthy accused the lawyer representing the army, Mr. Welch, of having in his firm a young man who had at one time been a member of an organization that supported the Communist party. Welch counterattacked by sketching a sympathetic portrait of the young man in question and then attacked McCarthy for attacking him, arguing quite persuasively that McCarthy was a cruel and reckless person for injuring this young man with an ad hominem attack. Welch's counterattack was a tu quoque ad hominem argument that, according to Farrell's account, impressed the audience.

We leave the evaluation of the argument form TU QUOQUE AH for chapter 7, but it is appropriate to note that although TU QUOQUE AH seems generally to be taken in the textbook treatments as a fallacious form of argumentation, this view of the matter may be simplistic. To reply to an ad hominem with another ad hominem argument may not be entirely unreasonable, in all cases. It may, in fact, be a reasonable kind of argument with some worth, especially if the attack of the reply is comparable (by analogy), as a type of case, to the original ad hominem argument or if the attack of the reply reasonably argues that the original ad hominem attack was malicious and unfair. Too often such attacks are weak, however, because the two cases are not comparable. Moreover, another danger is that the original attack is not dealt with or responded to directly, and instead the dialogue degenerates into a quarrel.

Notice also that many circumstantial ad hominem cases (the sportsman's rejoinder, for example) are no longer classified as coming under the tu quoque category, but they would be placed (generically, though not as ad hominem arguments specifically) under the two wrongs category. As a general question of classification, it seems that the tu quoque ad hominem argument is a subspecies of the two wrongs ad hominem. In the two wrongs type of argument, the initial accusation can be any accusation of moral wrongdoing, and the accusation does not have to be used as an ad hominem attack. In the tu quoque type of argument, it has to be a case of one ad hominem attack used to reply to another one. So in the tu quoque type of case, the first accusation must not only be an allegation of moral wrongdoing by the other party; it must also be an allegation of moral wrongdoing specifically used as an ad hominem attack on that other party. Therefore all cases of tu quoque ad hominem arguments are also cases of two wrongs ad hominem arguments. But the converse implication is not necessarily true.

7. Guilt by Association

Many of the textbook cases of ad hominem arguments have an element of guilt by association, and the arguer is attacked on the basis of some group he belongs to or is associated with. In case 2.7, the proponent discounts a union official's argument for higher wages on the grounds that he is a member of a union. In case 2.11, an arguer who supports a proposal for birth control is attacked because he is a Catholic. In case 2.15, an arguer on smelter pollution is attacked on the grounds that he is on the board of a copper company, and in the similar case 1.8, Wilma is attacked because she is the president of a coal company. All these cases are also similar to case 2.19, in which the arguer is attacked on the grounds he is a member of the American Petroleum Institute. All three of these latter arguments are bias cases, but they do have an element of guilt by association. In cases 2.18 and 2.21 (like case 2.11) the ad hominem attack is based on the arguer's being a Catholic. Also, the famous poisoning the well case of Cardinal Newman (case 1.10) is based on Newman's being a Catholic. Finally, in the tree hugger case (1.6), the entire group of environmentalists are attacked because of their consumption of wood products.

At first, it might seem plausible that guilt by association could be classified exclusively as a subspecies of circumstantial ad hominem argument because the element of the arguer's group association could be thought of quite naturally as an aspect of his personal circumstances. What defeats this hypothesis is that the bias type of ad hominem (as indicated by many of the cases noted above) has an element of guilt by association. It is also quite possible for the abusive type of ad hominem argument to be based on an allegation that the arguer belongs to some group, for example, Satanists, that is presumed to be bad, showing he has a bad moral character.

For these reasons, it is best to define the argument from guilt by association as a sort of superargument scheme that is a complex form of GENERIC AH, joined to another subargument, defined as follows.

GUILT BY ASSOCIATION AH

a is a member of or is associated with group G, which should be morally condemned.
Therefore a is a bad person.
Therefore a's argument α should not be accepted.

The form GUILT BY ASSOCIATION AH, which defines the ad hominem argument from guilt by association as a distinctive subtype of ad hominem argument, is quite broad, in that, like GENERIC AH, it can include as subspecies all the other subtypes—the direct (abusive), the circumstantial, the bias. Nevertheless, the key difference between GENERIC AH and GUILT BY ASSOCIATION AH is that GENERIC AH defines the nature of ad hominem arguments generally. Thus every ad hominem argument (of any subtype) has the general form of GENERIC AH, as well as its more specific form as a particular subtype. In contrast, GUILT BY ASSOCIATION AH only applies to some but not all ad hominem arguments, those that base the attack on some sort of guilt by association basis.

In an earlier attempt at analyzing the guilt by association argument (Walton, *Place of Emotion*, 1992, p. 238), the author defined the guilt by association type of ad hominem argument in a broader way that discredits an argument by arguing that the arguer belongs to a group whose views are "not worth listening to as serious arguments." Within the new theory of the ad hominem argument now put forward GUILT BY ASSOCIATION AH is the preferred analysis of the guilt by association type of ad hominem generally. It should also be noted that a subtype of the guilt by association ad hominem argument called *poisoning the well by alleging group bias* GROUP BIAS AH is defined in Walton (*Place of Emotion*, 1992, p. 239).

GROUP BIAS AH

Person *a* has argued for thesis *A*.
But *a* belongs to or is affiliated with group *G*.
It is known that group *G* is a special-interest partisan group that takes up a biased (dogmatic, prejudiced, fanatical) quarreling attitude in pushing exclusively for its own point of view.
Therefore, one cannot engage in open-minded critical discussion of an issue with any members of *G*, and hence the arguments of *a* for *A* are not worth listening to or paying serious attention to in a critical discussion.

This extension of the bias subtype of ad hominem argument can be put forward in four ascending degrees of severity, depending on whether *a* is alleged to be (1) biased, (2) dogmatic, (3) prejudiced, or (4) fanatical.

Now we are in a position to solve the principal single problem with the textbook treatment of the guilt by association subtype, which is well indicated by case 1.14. In this case, Smith's claim that unemployment is a greater problem than inflation is discredited on the grounds that Smith is a communist. Rightly, this case is classified as an instance of guilt by association by Toulmin, Rieke, and Janik (1979, p. 173) because the claimant is associated with a discredited group.[5] But the way Toulmin, Rieke, and Janik describe the fallacy (confusingly, when it comes to keeping the subtypes clearly distinguished) comes out as a case of the poisoning the well subtype. That is, the fallacy is described by writing that if the claimant is a "Red" then "he or she cannot be trusted to tell the truth" because the opinions of communists "on such matters are always biased." This case is very confusing because it is supposed to be an instance of the guilt by association subcategory of ad hominem, yet its description by Toulmin, Rieke, and Janik clearly indicates that it falls under the bias subcategory. Which is it, then?

Analyzed in the framework of GUILT BY ASSOCIATION AH, the argument in case 1.14 is definitely a poisoning the well subtype of ad hominem, which in turn is a subspecies of the bias subtype. But as a bias ad hominem case, it is also quite possible for it to fall under the guilt by association category, defined by GUILT BY ASSOCIATION AH, as well. Generally, although a particular case must be classified as abusive, circumstantial, or a bias subtype, it can be classified as both abusive and guilt by association, or both circumstantial and guilt by association, or both bias and guilt by association.

8. The Situationally Disqualifying Subtype

In case 2.3, a student replied to a professor who argued in favor of a military draft in 1941 by saying "You favor the draft because you are in the higher age bracket and are not in danger of being drafted." Ruby (1950, p. 135) classified this ad hominem argument as a case of the tu quoque. It would seem to be legitimately classifiable as a tu quoque subtype, according to the analysis above, in which the tu quoque subtype of ad hominem has the form TU QUOQUE AH. It does not appear to fit into any of the other categories of ad hominem—the direct (abusive) circumstantial or bias types.

Ruby's case is interesting because it is similar to the kind of case used by Krabbe and Walton (1993, p. 79) to illustrate a special type of ad hominem argument called a "situationally disqualifying" ad hominem:

Case 6.4

[Holland, December 1990] A retired major general argues in front of his relatives that the Dutch government must give more substantial support to the allied efforts in the Gulf Area. "We ought to send ground forces," so he claims. His grandson retorts: "It's all very well for you to talk, grandpa! You don't have to go there."

The grandson's point, as explained in Krabbe and Walton (p. 79) in this case, is that the grandfather's actual situation—that of being a retired person who will not be sent to the Gulf war—disqualifies him morally as a defender of his point of view. It is as if he really has no right to advocate that point of view because it will be others, not he, who will suffer the consequences if his proposal is brought about. According to Krabbe and Walton, this is quite an unusual and specially distinctive type of ad hominem in its own right, and it does not fit clearly into any of the usual categories of the abusive, circumstantial, bias, tu quoque, or the poisoning well categories. So, it is interesting to see Ruby (1950) citing a comparable case and classifying it as an instance of the tu quoque type of ad hominem argument.

A significant difference is present between the two cases: the Krabbe and Walton case has just one ad hominem argument; in contrast, the Ruby case has a second ad hominem argument used by the older person to respond to the original ad hominem put forward by the younger person. So the Ruby case has a situationally disqualifying ad hominem argument used by the student and then another ad hominem used to reply to it. This other ad hominem argument does not appear to be a situationally disqualifying type. Perhaps it is best classified as a bias type. At any rate, case 2.3 can fairly be described as tu quoque because it is a case of an ad hominem argument being used to reply to another.

Is it possible for case 6.4 to be a tu quoque subtype as well as an instance of the situationally disqualifying subtype? Yes, it is, on the analysis of the tu quoque given in section 6 above, where generally the tu quoque does incorporate the other subtypes within its complex form of argument TU QUOQUE.

Another question about the situationally disqualifying subtype is whether it is a distinctive category in its own right or whether it should be a subtype of the circumstantial subtype. This problem led Krabbe and Walton (p. 87) to introduce a system of classification that distinguished between two meanings of 'circumstantial' as applied to ad hominem arguments. 'Circumstantial' in the narrower sense requires the existence of a circumstantial inconsistency—a conflict between the arguer and his personal circumstances—whereas 'circumstantial' in the wider sense requires no such inconsistency in a given case.

So then the question is posed: Should a case of the situationally disqualifying type of ad hominem argument, such as case 6.4, be also classified as a case of the circumstantial ad hominem, or not? Answering this question requires taking a closer look at case 6.4.

In this case, the grandson's point is that the grandfather is a retired person who will not be sent out to the Gulf war, and therefore this condition disqualifies him as a defender of the point of view he advocates. In this type of case, there is no circumstantial inconsistency, nor is the grandfather being accused of a bias by the grandson. Instead, the basis of the accusation is that something is present in the grandfather's situation (his not being eligible to be called up to be in the Armed Forces) that situationally disqualifies him from being a serious advocate of that point of view. Hence, Krabbe and Walton (1993, p. 80) see the situationally disqualifying type of ad hominem argument as being theoretically distinct from either the bias type of attack or the circumstantial type of attack (defined in the narrow sense as involving an allegation of circumstantial inconsistency on the part of an arguer).

The various aspects of the situational disqualification type of ad hominem argument can involve lack of concern and lack of insight, factors that are not well classified under the subtypes of bias or pragmatic inconsistency. Possibly lack of concern or practical insight could be classified as aspects of character under some category of the direct ad hominem cited in chapter 5. But the aspect of character is not the real focus of the attack. In case 6.4, it is not argued by the grandson that the grandfather has a bad character or is somehow inconsistent or is biased. The argument is rather that the grandfather does not really have a right to speak out on this issue with much credibility because he is not one of the people who will stand to lose if his argument is put into effect. Yet this argument does seem to be an ad hominem argument because it is a way of citing something about the personal circumstances of the arguer that is presumed to be a basis for reducing the credibility of his argument. The argument is saying he does not really have a right to talk about this subject so we do not need to take his argument seriously. His personal circumstances disqualify him from being a serious advocate on this issue. So, here is posed a general theoretical problem in the analysis of the argumentum ad hominem. On the one hand, it seems possible that, as well as the abusive, circumstantial, the bias type and the tu quoque type, there may need to be this other distinct category of the situational disqualification type of ad hominem argument that also needs to be taken into account as a separate subtype in its own right. Yet, on the other hand, it seems very natural to classify the situational disqualification ad hominem as a subtype of the circumstantial ad hominem.

This problem poses a serious dilemma for defining the ad hominem argument. Above, the narrower definition of 'circumstantial' has been advocated on the grounds that the most typical and common cases of the circumstantial type do essentially involve an inconsistency as the basis of the ad hominem attack. The inconsistency or alleged inconsistency is the core of the argument that critics need to pay most attention to in identifying and evaluating this type of ad hominem argument adequately. Yet a legitimate wider sense of 'circumstantial' in which the situationally disqualifying type of case can naturally be called a circumstantial ad hominem argument seems to be present.

Moreover, it is possible that future research will discover other kinds of ad hominem arguments that, as the situationally disqualifying type, seem to belong under the circumstantial heading even though they do not involve inconsistency. Instead, in Krabbe and Walton (1993, p. 86) several subspecies of the situational ad hominem are cited including the "discredit the nonvictim argument" and the "lack of insight" ad hominem.

Consequently, on balance, the policy proposed here is to recognize a separate subcategory of circumstantial ad hominem arguments that do not require a claim of inconsistency as part of the argument. Here 'circumstantial' is meant in the wider sense. Provisionally, the only type inserted under this heading will be the situationally disqualifying subtype, recognizing that other subtypes may be discovered in future research.

Whereas normally the allegation of pragmatic inconsistency is the leading indicator of the circumstantial type of ad hominem argument, the more unusual kinds of cases do exist and will also be included under this category—situational disqualification and logical inconsistency cases.

In Krabbe and Walton (1993, p. 86) the situationally disqualifying ad hominem argument is defined as "an argumentative move in a dialogue whereby one participant points out certain features in his adversary's personal situation that are claimed to make it inappropriate for this adversary to make a certain dialectical contribution." These objectionable features as defined in Krabbe and Walton (p. 86) may include such aspects of an adversary's situation as lack of concern for the issue of the dialogue or lack of insight into the issue, but they are specifically stated to exclude evidence for a pragmatic inconsistency or a bias. On the bias of this definition, the form of the situationally disqualifying ad hominem argument is now defined as follows.

SITUATIONAL AH

1. In dialogue D, a advocates argument α, which has proposition A as its conclusion.
2. a has certain features in his personal situation that make it inappropriate for him to make a dialectical contribution to D.
3. Therefore, a is a bad person.
4. Therefore, a's argument α should not be accepted.

In clause 3 of SITUATIONAL AH, the statement that a is a "bad person" is meant in a certain specific or qualified way: that because of features of a's personal situation, it has become open to question whether a is a sincere and honest participant in the dialogue, who can be relied on to make the kinds of contributions to the dialogue required by the maxims (rules) of good conduct for verbal exchanges in the dialogue. Thus the sense in which the arguer is said to be a "bad person" in SITUATIONAL AH is similar to the sense of the same expression in BIAS AH. The specific type of quality questioned is the arguer's meeting the requirements for fulfilling the role of a collaborative and reliable participant in a type of dialogue, such as a critical discussion, that requires him to have the appropriate attitudes reasonably expected in that type of dialogue.

9. Applying the Classification System to Cases

Is it possible for two types of ad hominem arguments (say, the abusive and the bias subtypes) to occur in the same case? Yes, the answer is that such instances in argumentation do occur and should be classified as mixed. But does not this possibility challenge the whole project of classifying ad hominem arguments into these distinct subtypes, as carried out above? The answer is that, no, it does not.

In fact, all the cases studied in chapters 1 and 2 can be clearly classified as falling into one of our subtypes. It is possible, particularly in a larger case, for two ad hominem subtypes to be present in the case. For example, in the case of Mr. S., the ad hominem argument was basically of the circumstantial type, but at some points during the sequence of argumentation, abusive personal attacks were made as well. In such a case, however, using our classification of the subtypes, it is possible to determine at what stage in this sequence the ad hominem shifted over from circumstantial to direct.

In some cases of ad hominem arguments, it is possible to observe a shift during the sequence of argumentation from one subtype to another. For example, a circumstantial ad hominem attack will often begin by an allegation of pragmatic inconsistency and then use the conflict cited as a springboard to attack the respondent who "does not practice what he preaches" using the direct ad hominem argument. Typically (as noted in section 1) this transition takes place through the allegation or suggestion that the person attacked is a hypocrite, meaning that his actions, revealing the true nature of his commitment, show that he is not following his own advice or is not sincere in following his own argument. Of course, once someone is said to be a hypocrite, it is implied that he is a dishonest and deceptive type of person—a dissembler who cannot be trusted for veracity. This type of argument is an abusive ad hominem attack. A shift has taken place internally, within the dialogue, from a circumstantial to a direct ad hominem argument.[6]

This same kind of shift can be evident in a transition from the bias type of ad hominem argument to the direct type, as the following case from Brinton (1985, p. 86) illustrates.

Case 6.5

The subject of a debate in the U.S. Congress in 1813 was the New Army Bill, a proposal to raise more troops for the war against England. The majority, led by Speaker of the House Henry Clay, argued that an invasion of Canada with these additional troops would help to win the conflict. Josiah Quincy, speaking for the opposition on January 5, 1813, argued that the additional troops would be insufficient, that an invasion of Canada would be unsuccessful and immoral, that a conquest of Canada would not force England to negotiate, and finally that the bill was personally motivated, "as a means for the advancement of objects of personal or local ambition of the members of the American Cabinet." (*Annals of the Congress of the United States, Comprising the Period from November 2, 1812 to March 3, 1813, Inclusive* [Washington, D.C., Gales and Seaton, 1853, pp. 540–70])

Quincy's last argument is different from his preceding arguments in that it is an ad hominem argument that questions the honesty and impartiality of the exponents of the New Army Bill. In his speech, Quincy cited facts to support his contention that the most outspoken supporters of the bill had much to gain by its passage. His charge that the supporters of the bill were motivated by personal ambition can, on the basis of the details of his argument given in the *Annals of the Congress*, be evaluated as a reasonable ad hominem argument.

At a subsequent point in his speech, however, Quincy went on to call his opponents "toads, or reptiles, which *spread their slime on the drawing room floor*" (p. 599). Here, it could be argued that Quincy has carried his ad hominem attack too far and gone over the borderline into a quarrelsome attack, using the abusive ad hominem. His attack is based on an odious and excessive analogy that would be extremely hard to justify as a reasonable criticism and should not reasonably be treated as relevant evidence against the New Army Bill. So, in this instance, we can see how a reasonable ad hominem criticism can degenerate into a direct ad hominem argument if it is carried further as an attack.

These types of cases, in which there has been a shift from one of the other types of ad hominem arguments to the abusive (direct) type, pose a problem for any attempt to provide a clear basis for differentiating between the subtypes. This problem is especially acute if the circumstantial subtype is defined broadly so that the arguer's character or financial stake in the argument can be included within the definition of "circumstances."

The existence of this problem is one of the reasons why it is better to define the circumstantial subtype of ad hominem argument more precisely, by requiring it to have the essential characteristic of an allegation of pragmatic inconsistency made by the attacker. This method of classification provides a clear basis for showing how and why the circumstantial type of ad hominem is different from both the bias type and the abusive type. We no longer need to rely on the distinguishing feature that a case of either the circumstantial or the bias type of ad hominem argument has to be nonabusive in nature (see section 1). It is much better to be able to say that the ad hominem can be partly abusive in some cases, but the distinguishing feature that marks off its circumstantial nature is the charge of pragmatic inconsistency. Then we can explain quite well how, during the sequence of argumentation in a given case, a shift can take place from the one subtype to the other. Now we can identify where and how the shift occurs.

The problem is that because we have admitted the situationally disqualifying subtype and the logical inconsistency subtype under the circumstantial ad hominem category, we can no longer claim that pragmatic inconsistency is the sole and exclusive criterion of the circumstantial type. We need instead to make a carefully qualified method of classification. According to this method, pragmatic inconsistency is normally the best indicator of a circumstantial ad hominem argument, but with two exceptions to this initial rule of thumb. One is that in some cases the inconsistency is not a pragmatic inconsistency (between actions and propositions advocated) but a logical inconsistency, in which two propositions in the form of commitments or "avowed opinions" of a person are the focus of the attack. The other is that in the situationally disqualifying type of case the circumstance cited is the arguer's nonvictim status that, it is argued, removes his right to be a credible advocate of his argument (because it will not apply to him personally). Although pragmatic inconsistency is the most usual sign of the circumstantial ad hominem, we have to be on guard to be aware of these two special kinds of cases for which this characteristic does not apply.

Accordingly, one more subtype of ad hominem is recognized, the *logical inconsistency* type, in which instead of a pragmatic inconsistency as in CIRCUMSTANTIAL AH, the basis of the allegation is an inconsistency in a set of propositions that are allegedly commitments of the arguer.

LOGICAL CIRCUMSTANTIAL AH

1. a advocates argument α, which has proposition A as its conclusion.
2. a is committed to proposition A (generally, or in virtue of what she said in the past).
3. a is committed to proposition ⌐A, which is the conclusion of the argument α that a presently advocates.
4. Therefore a is a bad person.
5. Therefore a's argument α should not be accepted.

There can be different types of inconsistent commitments and cases of commitment to inconsistencies, as catalogued usefully in Krabbe (1990). But the key feature of CIRCUMSTANTIAL AH, for our purposes, is that it is not a conflict between actions and propositions asserted that are the basis of the inconsistency. Instead, it is a conflict between a pair of propositions to which the arguer committed himself verbally.

Despite these complications, the circumstantial ad hominem is a clearly recognizable type of argument, according to the criteria proposed for it in this chapter, and the guidelines given here are workable and useful, as applied to the kinds of cases commonly encountered. They are not perfect, and future research may turn up still more subvarieties, but they are a clearer and more comprehensive set of criteria than have been available so far.

Finally, it is useful to add some clarification on how to classify the two wrongs type of ad hominem argument. This type of argument has an initial accusation by the proponent that the respondent has done something wrong, and then the respondent replies using an ad hominem attack, arguing that the proponent is a bad person who has no credibility and therefore that her initial argument is not plausible. As we saw in section 6, the tu quoque ad hominem is a special case of this type in which the initial accusation by the proponent was an ad hominem attack on the respondent.

A general problem with identifying the two wrongs type of ad hominem argument is that it is too easy to classify any counteraccusation, whether or not it really is an ad hominem argument (properly, in the sense defined in this book). Once a critic sees a case having an attack on a second party with the claim that this second party is blameworthy for some alleged act, and then a counterattack by the second party, who claims that the first party is also guilty of having committed some blameworthy act, the critic may be tempted to describe the case as an instance of the two wrongs type of ad hominem argument. But the case may not even be an ad hominem argument.

Quintilian, in the *Institutio Oratoria* (Book VII.IV.8–9) cites a kind of defense that the Greeks called counteraccusation, *antegklema* (literally, to accuse in turn), in which the argument consists in replying to the accusation by accusing the person the other side is trying to vindicate. Quintilian (VII.IV.9) gives two examples: "He was killed, but he was a robber; he was blinded, but he was a rapist." This type of argument, at least initially, looks much like a two wrongs subtype of ad hominem. But is it? Is it really an ad hominem argument at all? The answer is that it is not, as Quintilian's subsequent description of the argument (VII.IV.10) indicates—he calls the defense "defending the act *per se.*" In other words, the pleader is arguing that his act of killing, for example, was not really blameworthy because the person killed was a robber. The thrust of this argument is not to the effect that the person who died was a bad person and that therefore his argument (or the pleader's argument on his behalf in court) is a bad or implausible argument. The thrust of the argument is a denial of the accusation that the act in question was blameworthy.

The general problem posed by these remarks is that a good hard look needs to be taken at many of the cases classified by the textbooks (chaotically, as we saw in chapter 2) as being instances of the two wrongs type of ad hominem argument (sometimes also mistakenly, in our classification system taken to be instances of tu quoque arguments). Depending on how these examples are analyzed, many of them may not be ad hominem arguments at all.

10. Summary of the Classification System

For the reader's convenience, all twenty-one forms of argument that are significant for defining the various subtypes of ad hominem arguments, as well as other related forms of argument, like argument from commitment, are listed.

Argument from Commitment

AC

a is committed to proposition A (generally, or in virtue of what she said in the past).
Therefore, in this case, a should support A.

cq1

Is *a* really committed to *A*, and if so, what evidence supports the claim that she is so committed?

cq2

If the evidence for commitment is indirect or weak, could there also be contrary evidence or at least room for the rebuttal that this case is an exception?

cq3

Is the proposition *A*, as cited in the premise, identical to the proposition *A* as cited in the conclusion? If not, what exactly is the nature of the relationship between the two propositions?

Generic Ad Hominem Argument

GENERIC AH

a is a bad person.
Therefore *a*'s argument α should not be accepted.

Critical Questions (GENERIC AH)

cq1

Is the premise true (or well supported) that *a* is a bad person?

cq2

Is the allegation that *a* is a bad person relevant to judging *a*'s argument α?

cq3

Is the conclusion of the argument that α should be (absolutely) rejected even if other evidence to support α has been presented, or is the conclusion merely (the relative claim) that α should be assigned a reduced weight of credibility, relative to the total body of evidence available?

Negative Ethotic (Abusive, Direct) Ad Hominem Argument

NEGATIVE ETHOTIC AH

a is a person of bad character.
Therefore *a*'s argument α should not be accepted.

CQ1

Is the premise true (or well supported) that *a* is a person of bad character?

CQ2

Is the issue of character relevant in the type of dialogue in which the argument was used?

CQ3

Is the conclusion of the argument that α should be (absolutely) rejected even if other evidence to support α has been presented, or is the conclusion merely (the relative claim) that α should be assigned a reduced weight of credibility, relative to the total body of evidence available?

THE FIVE IMMEDIATE SUBTYPES OF NEGATIVE ETHOTIC AD HOMINEM ARGUMENT

Negative Ethotic Ad Hominem Argument from Veracity

VERACITY AH

a has a bad character for veracity.
Therefore *a*'s argument α should not be accepted.

Negative Ethotic Ad Hominem Argument from Prudence

PRUDENCE AH

a has a bad character for prudent judgment.
Therefore *a*'s argument α should not be accepted.

Negative Ethotic Ad Hominem Argument from Perception

PERCEPTION AH

a has a bad character for realistic perception of his situation.
Therefore *a*'s argument α should not be accepted.

Negative Ethotic Ad Hominem Argument from Cognitive Skills

COGNITION AH

a has a bad character for logical reasoning.
Therefore *a*'s argument α should not be accepted.

Negative Ethotic Ad Hominem Argument from Morals

MORALS AH

a has a bad character for personal moral standards.
Therefore *a*'s argument α should not be accepted.

Note: The critical questions for the five immediate subtypes are the same as the critical questions for NEGATIVE ETHOTIC AH, except that the type of character at issue is inserted.

Argument from Pragmatic Inconsistency (or, You Say One Thing, Do Another)

PRAGMATIC INCONSISTENCY

a advocates argument α, which has proposition *A* as its conclusion.
a has carried out an action or set of actions that imply that *a* is personally committed to ¬A (the opposite, or negation of *A*).
Therefore *a*'s argument α should not be accepted.

Critical Questions (PRAGMATIC INCONSISTENCY)

CQ1

Did *a* advocate α in a strong way indicating her personal commitment to *A*?

CQ2

In what words was the action described, and does that description imply that *a* is personally committed to the opposite of *A*?

CQ3

Why is the pragmatic inconsistency indicated by satisfactory answers to CQ1 and CQ2 a relevant reason for not accepting argument α?

Circumstantial Ad Hominem Argument (or, You Don't Practice What You Preach)

CIRCUMSTANTIAL AH

1. *a* advocates argument α, which has proposition *A* as its conclusion.
2. *a* has carried out an action or set of actions that imply that *a* is personally committed to ¬A (the opposite, or negation of *A*).
3. Therefore *a* is a bad person.
4. Therefore *a*'s argument α should not be accepted.

CQ1

What are the propositions alleged to be practically inconsistent, and are they practically inconsistent?

CQ2

If the identified propositions are not practically (pragmatically) inconsistent, as things stand, are there at least some grounds for a claim of practical inconsistency that can be evaluated from the textual evidence of the discourse?

CQ3

Even if there is not an explicit practical inconsistency, what is the connection between the pair of propositions alleged to be inconsistent?

CQ4

If there is a practical inconsistency that can be identified as the focus of the attack, how serious a flaw is it? Could the apparent conflict be resolved or explained without destroying the consistency of the commitment in the dialogue?

CQ5

Does it follow from *a*'s inconsistent commitment that *a* is a bad person?

CQ6

Is the conclusion the weaker claim that *a*'s credibility is open to question or the stronger claim that the conclusion of α is false?

Argument from Inconsistent Commitment (or, You Contradict Yourself)

INCONSISTENT COMMITMENT

a is committed to proposition *A* (generally, or in virtue of what she said in the past).
a is committed to proposition ⌐*A*, which is the conclusion of the argument α that *a* presently advocates.
Therefore *a*'s argument α should not be accepted.

Note: The critical questions for INCONSISTENT COMMITMENT are the same as those for CIRCUMSTANTIAL AH, except that they only relate to the avowed opinions of *a* (not as expressing *a*'s commitments).

The Double Standard Argument

DOUBLE STANDARD

The respondent has one policy with respect to a.
The respondent has another (different) policy with respect to b.
a is similar to b (or comparable to b in some relevant respect).
Therefore, the respondent is using a double standard.

Critical Questions (DOUBLE STANDARD)

cq1

What is the respondent's policy with respect to a?

cq2

What is the respondent's policy with respect to b?

cq3

How is the one policy different from the other?

cq4

How is a similar (or comparable) to b?

cq5

Can the differences in policies be explained, or is it significant as evidence that the respondent's policies are not consistent in some important way?

Universal Circumstantial Ad Hominem Argument

UNIVERSAL CIRCUMSTANTIAL AH

1. a advocates argument α, which has proposition A as its conclusion, which says that everybody should be committed to A.
2. a is bound by the 'everybody' in premise 1.
3. a has carried out an action or a set of actions that imply that a is personally committed to $\neg A$.
4. Therefore a is a bad person.
5. Therefore a's argument α should not be accepted.

Critical Questions (UNIVERSAL CIRCUMSTANTIAL AH)

cq1

Does a's argument conclude that everybody should be committed to A?

CQ2

Is there any basis for *a* being an exception to the commitment?

CQ3

Does the action, as described, imply that *a* is personally committed to the opposite of *A*?

CQ4

Why does it follow (if it does) that the alleged practical inconsistency shows that *a* is a bad person?

CQ5

Is *a*'s being a bad person a good reason for concluding that *a*'s argument should not be accepted?

Group Circumstantial Ad Hominem Argument

GROUP CIRCUMSTANTIAL AH

1. *a* advocates argument α, which says that everybody in group *G* should be committed to *A*.
2. *a* belongs to group *G*.
3. *a* has carried out an action or a set of actions that imply that *a* is personally committed to ⌐*A*.
4. Therefore *a* is a bad person.
5. Therefore *a*'s argument α should not be accepted.

Critical Questions (GROUP CIRCUMSTANTIAL AH)

CQ1

How exactly does the argument α state or imply that everybody in group *G* should be committed to *A*?

CQ2

Does *a* belong to group *G*?

CQ3

Does *a* belong to other groups that would have goals affecting *a*'s commitment to *A*?

CQ4

Does *a*'s action, as described, imply that *a* is committed to the opposite of *A*?

CQ5

Why does it follow (if it does) that the alleged practical inconsistency shows that *a* is a bad person?

CQ6

Is *a*'s being a bad person a good reason for concluding that *a*'s argument should not be accepted?

The Bias Ad Hominem Argument

BIAS AH

1. Person *a*, the proponent of argument α, is biased.
2. Person *a*'s bias is a failure to take part honestly in a type of dialogue *D*, which includes α.
3. Therefore *a* is a bad person.
4. Therefore α should not be given as much credibility as it would have without the bias.

*Critical Questions (*BIAS AH*)*

CQ1

What is the evidence that *a* is biased?

CQ2

If *a* is biased, is it a bad bias that is detrimental to *a*'s honestly taking part in *D* or a normal bias that is appropriate for the type of dialogue in which α was put forward?

The Poisoning the Well Ad Hominem Argument

POISONING THE WELL AH

1. For every argument α in dialogue *D*, person *a* is biased.
2. Person *a*'s bias is a failure to take part honestly in a type of dialogue *D*, which includes α.
3. Therefore *a* is a bad person.
4. Therefore α should not be given as much credibility as it would have without the bias.

*Critical Questions (*POISONING THE WELL AH*)*

CQ1

What is the evidence that *a* has been biased with respect to every argument in the dialogue?

Is the bias a normal partisan viewpoint that a has shown, or can it be shown to indicate that a is not honestly participating in the dialogue?

CQ3

In what respect is a a bad person, judging from the evidence of his participation in the dialogue that gives a reason for doubting his credibility?

The Two Wrongs Ad Hominem Argument

TWO WRONGS AH

Proponent: Respondent, you have committed some morally blameworthy action (and the specific action is then cited).
Respondent: You are just as bad, for you also committed a morally blameworthy action (then cited, generally a different type of action from the one cited by the proponent but comparable in respect of being blameworthy). Therefore, you are a bad person, and your argument against me should not be accepted as having any worth.

Critical Questions (TWO WRONGS AH)

CQ1

Is there evidence to support the proponent's allegation that the respondent committed a blameworthy act?

CQ2

If the answer to CQ1 is yes, then should the respondent's counteraccusation be rated as very credible?

CQ3

Is the respondent's counteraccusation relevant in the dialogue to the proponent's original allegation?

The Tu Quoque Ad Hominem Argument

TU QUOQUE AH

Proponent: Respondent, you are a morally bad person (because you have bad character and are circumstantially inconsistent, biased, and so forth), therefore your argument should not be accepted.
Respondent: You are just as bad, therefore your ad hominem argument against me should not be accepted as having any worth.

Critical Questions (TU QUOQUE AH)

cq1

Is the proponent's ad hominem argument a strong one (according to the criteria for whatever type it is)?

cq2

Is the respondent's ad hominem a strong one (according to the criteria for whatever type it is)?

cq3

If the proponent's ad hominem argument is strong, how much credibility should be given to the respondent, as an honest arguer who can be trusted to make such an allegation?

The Guilt by Association Ad Hominem Argument

GUILT BY ASSOCIATION AH

a is a member of or is associated with group G, which should be morally condemned.
Therefore a is a bad person.
Therefore a's argument α should not be accepted.

Critical Questions (GUILT BY ASSOCIATION AH)

cq1

What evidence is there that a is a member of G?

cq2

If a was not a member of G, but was associated with G, how close was this association?

cq3

Is G a group that should be morally condemned?

cq4

Is it possible that even though a is a member of G, a group that ought to be condemned, a is not a bad person?

The Poisoning the Well by Alleging Group Bias Argument

GROUP BIAS AH

Person a has argued for thesis A.
But a belongs to or is affiliated with group G.
It is known that group G is a special-interest partisan group that

takes up a biased (dogmatic, prejudiced, fanatical) quarreling attitude in pushing exclusively for its own point of view.

Therefore, one cannot engage in open-minded critical discussion of an issue with any members of G, and hence the arguments of a for A are not worth listening to or paying serious attention to in a critical discussion.

Critical Questions (GROUP BIAS AH)

cq1

Has a given any good reasons to support A?

cq2

What kind of bias has a exhibited, and how strong is it?

cq3

Is the kind of bias that a has exhibited a good reason for concluding that she is not honestly and collaboratively taking part in the dialogue?

cq4

Is there evidence of a dialectical shift in the case, for example, from a persuasion dialogue to a negotiation?

cq5

Is the bias indicated in cq2 of the very strong type that warrants the conclusion that a is not open to any argumentation that goes against her position (or seems to her to go against her position)?

The Situationally Disqualifying Ad Hominem Argument

SITUATIONAL AH

1. In dialogue D, a advocates argument α, which has proposition A as its conclusion.
2. a has certain features in his personal situation that make it inappropriate for him to make a dialectical contribution to D.
3. Therefore, a is a bad person.
4. Therefore, a's argument α should not be accepted.

Critical Questions (SITUATIONAL AH)

cq1

What features of a's personal situation make it inappropriate for him to contribute to D?

CQ2

Do the features of *a*'s situation cited give any good reason to make one conclude that it is inappropriate to contribute to *D*?

CQ3

Could *a*'s argument be worth considering on its merits, even though there is reason to think them inappropriate for *D*?

The Logical Inconsistency Circumstantial Ad Hominem Argument

LOGICAL CIRCUMSTANTIAL AH

1. *a* advocates argument α, which has proposition *A* as its conclusion.
2. *a* is committed to proposition *A* (generally, or in virtue of what she said in the past).
3. *a* is committed to proposition ⅂*A*, which is the conclusion of the argument α that *a* presently advocates.
4. Therefore *a* is a bad person.
5. Therefore *a*'s argument α should not be accepted.

Critical Questions (LOGICAL CIRCUMSTANTIAL AH)

The critical questions for the LOGICAL CIRCUMSTANTIAL AH are comparable to those for the CIRCUMSTANTIAL AH (given above), except that the phrase 'logically inconsistent' is to be substituted for every occurrence of the phrase 'pragmatically inconsistent.'

Once these forms of argument have been defined as above, it is possible to see that they do fit into a system of classification, shown in figure 6.1, which indicates how the more complex forms are made up from the simpler forms.

The upper left branches of figure 6.1 show how the circumstantial ad hominem argument is indirectly related to argument from commitment. This nesting of CIRCUMSTANTIAL AH into AC exhibits the real nature of the Lockean ex concessis conception of the ad hominem argument and the conception of ad hominem personal attack, represented by the generic ad hominem form BP, which we have chosen here.

Notably, in our analysis, none of AC, INCONSISTENT COMMITMENT or PRAGMATIC INCONSISTENCY counts as genuine ad hominem arguments. However, although we see CIRCUMSTANTIAL AH as being a subspecies of LOGICAL CIRCUMSTANTIAL AH, the latter is viewed as being a genuine type of ad hominem argument. So if the argument forms

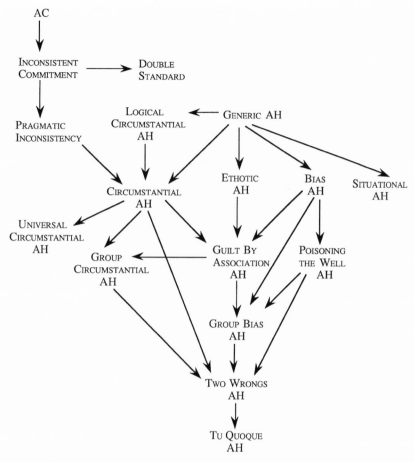

Figure 6.1. Classification of Argumentation Schemes

that are not genuine ad hominem arguments are to be excluded, that would mean erasing the three argument types at the top left of figure 6.1, namely AC, INCONSISTENT COMMITMENT, DOUBLE STANDARD, and PRAGMATIC INCONSISTENCY. None of these three forms is a subspecies of BP, and that is why they are excluded. When drawing up a system of classification of ad hominem that will be useful for teaching critical thinkers how to identify the various subtypes, it is best to alter somewhat the system of classification given in figure 6.1. The basic problem concerns the wider versus the narrower definitions of the circumstantial ad hominem.

Although the narrower definition certainly has strong advantages, which we have now advocated on numerous occasions, nevertheless the textbook treatments of the subject do suggest the practical and

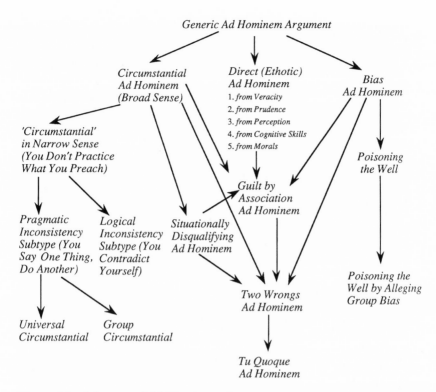

Figure 6.2. Subtypes of Ad Hominem Arguments

intuitive value of allowing the word 'circumstantial' to be used in a broader sense so that it can include ad hominem arguments, such as the situationally disqualifying kind, that are not based on a claim of inconsistency. Accordingly, in the classification scheme presented in figure 6.2, the situationally disqualifying type is included as a subtype of the circumstantial ad hominem (broad sense).

The guilt by association type of ad hominem argument is seen as a complex subtype involving a group attack. But since the core ad hominem argument around which the group attack is based can be any one of the following four kinds—circumstantial, direct, bias, or situationally disqualifying—we place the guilt by association type as a subtype of these four other types.

Similarly, the two wrongs ad hominem can incorporate any of these prior four types of ad hominem arguments, so it and the tu quoque are classified as derived categories. The three subtypes of the direct, circumstantial, and bias ad hominem arguments are given a special place of importance as the three basic or primary subtypes.

Many authorities portray the tu quoque as a third category of ad hominem argument in its own right. For example, van Eemeren and Grootendorst (1984, p. 190) classify the tu quoque as a separate category, identifying it with what is categorized above as the circumstantial ad hominem. However, the tu quoque is better classified as a derivative use of the abusive and the bias ad hominem and especially, in many cases, as the circumstantial ad hominem type of argument. It seems best, on balance, to construe the tu quoque type of ad hominem argument as an extension of the abusive, circumstantial, or bias categories of ad hominem argument.

The most important general (and philosophically controversial) decision in setting up the system of classification of argument types represented in figure 6.1 is whether ETHOTIC AH, as well as BIAS AH and SITUATIONAL AH could be brought under the umbrella of AC, making them species of Lockean ex concessis arguments. This significant move would vindicate the Lockean analysis of ad hominem, at least to a considerable extent, and make the historical ambiguity of ad hominem noted by Nuchelmans less of a wide gulf. On balance, it has seemed best not to bring these three types of ad hominem arguments under the umbrella of ASC, despite some evidence on both sides of the balance of considerations.

ETHOTIC AH, representing the direct (abusive) ad hominem type of argument, does seem to be related to AC, insofar as (especially as defined in this chapter) character is based on a person's commitments. But what is the exact nature of the relationship between an arguer's character and her commitments, in Hamblin's sense of commitment in dialogue as modeled by Walton and Krabbe (1995)? So far, this question has not been fully answered. But it can be shown on the Aristotelian analysis of character as relevant to one's role in a dialogue, given in this chapter, that character is a kind of long-term, stable commitment to certain attitudes, as revealed in a person's actions and goals (to the extent that the latter can be inferred from the person's words and actions, as known). In the structure of commitment in dialogue given in Walton and Krabbe (1995), then, such judgments about character of an arguer could be seen as based on inferences drawn concerning her dark-side commitments in a dialogue. But what needs to be kept in mind is that the character of an arguer is not (necessarily) the same thing as the arguer's commitments in a dialogue. While character is related to commitment, it also involves elements that go beyond commitment to a proposition, as determined by the speech acts or moves carried out in a dialogue in which one participant is engaged in argument with another.

Comparable questions can be raised about BIAS AH and SITUATIONAL AH as types of arguments. Although both may be related to commitment in some ways, both also appear to be distinctively different from AC as a general form of argument, and both involve special elements as forms of argument that are largely separate from AC.

Consequently, on balance of considerations, ETHOTIC AH, BIAS AH, and SITUATIONAL AH are not classified as subtypes of argument from commitment.

7

Evaluation of Ad Hominem Arguments

The problem with ad hominem arguments in political discourse is not that they are always fallacious. The problem is that character is a legitimate issue and that this legitimacy encourages a tendency to substitute soap opera for serious discussion of an issue. The all too frequent result is that excessive indulgence in ad hominem argumentation means that the underlying issue that is supposed to be discussed does not get an adequate examination. The problem is not that personal matters of character are irrelevant but that they get consideration out of proportion to the true weight that they merit, in the overall body of relevant evidence in a case.[1]

It is this observation that forms the basis of the explanation in this chapter of why and how ad hominem arguments are fallacious. It has been shown already, in chapter 6 especially, that many ad hominem arguments are not so bad that they should be judged as fallacious, and the schemes and critical questions in that chapter have furnished the basis from judging which ones are adequately justified, and which ones are not.

1. Fallacious and Inadequately Supported Arguments

The problem with most of the examples cited in the textbook treatments (chapter 2) as instances of the ad hominem fallacy, in retrospect, after our analysis of this type of argument, is that a lot of these ad hominem arguments seem as if they could be fairly reasonable. But a fallacious argument in a case is one that should be definitely and seriously wrong in its underlying structure of reasoning so that an evaluator of the case can say: "Yes, it is an incorrect argument because the evidence in the case shows that such-and-such an error was committed." Yet, typically, in the cases cited in chapter 2, there are two sides to the case—an ad hominem attack was made by one side, and from what we know of the case, a defense against it by the other side might or might not be justified. Indeed, the difficulty of pinning down such charges in a real example is illustrated by the case of Mr. S. in chapter 4.

It seems then that calling the cases in chapter 2 fallacious amounts to an exaggeration—a kind of black-or-white thinking that tries to pigeonhole complex arguments in a simplistic way, overlooking important qualifications.

It has been shown in Walton (*Informal Logic*, 1989; *Pragmatic Theory*, 1995; *Argumentation Schemes*, 1996) that often real arguments coming under the headings of informal fallacies have turned out to be not unreasonable arguments. They may not be deductively valid or inductively strong, but when they have been reasonable they tended to be presumptive arguments. When they are less than reasonable it is very often because they are weak, inadequately documented, or poorly supported. In such cases, the offending argument is open to reasonable criticism and should properly be criticized, but generally many of these arguments have been not altogether worthless. In many cases, they should be evaluated subject to correction, or as calling for a reply, rather than as being conclusively refuted in any absolute sense.

But to claim that an argument commits a fallacy is rightly taken as a strong form of criticism implying that the argument has committed a vitiating logical error, making it subject to refutation, even suggesting that the argument is misguided. To the contrary, however, although many of the cases studied could be called ad hominem arguments that commit a fallacy, many of the others do not seem to be quite so bad that they should be put in the category of fallacious.

In arguments on controversial subjects in natural language, often the most useful job of the reasonable critic is not necessarily to show that an argument criticized is inherently misguided and can be rejected completely. Such strong refutation is in many cases neither possible nor practical. More often, the most useful job of the critic is to show that an argument lacks needed support and is therefore open to reasonable questioning, for this weaker kind of criticism is often enough to reserve or withdraw the reasoned commitment of the audience to whom the argument was directed. Thus the exaggerated and too frequent use of the term 'fallacy' by the logic textbooks has engendered the unfortunate misconception that all kinds of arguments coming under the heading of a recognized type of "fallacy" are essentially worthless and should be completely refuted by the standards of logic.[2] Accordingly, this is a good time in the history of logic to pose the question, "What is a fallacy?" It is also a good time to reemphasize the distinction between a fallacy and an argument that is open to criticism.

One qualification, however, which is vitally important in evaluating particular cases, is that not all errors of reasoning are fallacies. Many errors in reasoning and argumentation are simply blunders, mistakes that are either not so serious or not results of underlying structural failures in an argument. Such mistakes do not properly deserve to be called fallacies. So errors of reasoning are fallacies only in some cases. Even so, some types of errors of reasoning are important to classify under the umbrella categories of the traditional types of fallacies because they characterize, give rise to, or lie at the bottom of kinds of arguments baptized as fallacies.

So the assumption that a fallacy is a purely logical error is misleading. Fallacies involve the use of logical reasoning in a communicative context of dialogue in which one party is putting forward an argument and the other party is asking critical questions in reply to that argument. The dialogue exchange between the two parties takes the form of a connected sequence of moves (speech acts) and replies. The actual dialogue that takes place needs to be evaluated using a normative model of argument that outlines, in general, the proper order such a sequence should take. Some deviations are relatively minor or can be repaired by simply filling a gap. But the sequences of moves found in some cases are sophistical tactics that are mixing up the right order of the question-reply sequence in order to interfere systematically with the proper realization of the goal of the dialogue. Such sophistical tactics fallacies are not purely logical errors, in the traditional sense of the logical failure of an inference.

The job of judging any individual argument as fallacious or not in a given case needs to be done at one or more of three levels—the local level, the expanded local level, and the global level—depending on the problems posed by the particular argument and on how much information is supplied by the text and context of discourse in the case. At the local level, what is important is identifying the argumentation scheme, investigating which critical questions have been asked or need to be asked, and seeing how well the premises for the argument (identified by its argumentation scheme) have been supported by appropriate evidence. At the expanded local level, the *profile of dialogue*—the sequence of moves in the exchange of argumentation on both sides—is used as the normative structure for evaluation. An example of such a profile would be the sequence of exchanges set out in case 1.17. What is important here is how each move is appropriate and adequate as a reply to the prior move by the other party. At the global level, the key question to be asked is "What type of dialogue are the participants supposed to be engaged in?" Once this question is answered, it can be determined whether the moves made in the argument are appropriate and useful contributions to that type of dialogue.

In some cases, an argument should be judged as weak or inadequate, but not fallacious, if insufficient evidence has been given to back up one of the premises or if a needed premise has been overlooked. Typically, however, in the fallacious cases, the fault is one of trying to block the asking of appropriate critical questions altogether by the opponent or even to shut the dialogue down (prematurely).[3] A pattern of overly aggressive and partisan argumentation characteristic of the committing of a fallacy will be revealed by the order of moves in the profile of dialogue. Generally, the job of evaluating particular cases is one of applying normative structures of reasonable argumentation to the particulars of a given case.

The tools for this job, in cases of ad hominem arguments, are the argumentation schemes (and accompanying sets of critical questions) for the various types of ad hominem arguments.[4] Identifying the type of dialogue is also critically important, however. An argumentation scheme can be used appropriately in one context of dialogue, but the same scheme can be inappropriate in another context of dialogue. For we have seen that personal matters of character and the like can be relevant in one context of dialogue but irrelevant in another. Thus, in many cases, it is vitally important to study how the argumentation profile has been continued in the context of dialogue, including the respondent's commitments, replies, and attitudes, as expressed in the discourse of the case.

The critical discussion and deliberation types of dialogue have proved to be important as normative models of argumentation, and it might be thought that fallacious ad hominem arguments occur only in these two types of talk exchanges. But ad hominem obstructions can occur in other types of dialogue, as well, like negotiations. For example, in Platiel (1995), a report by the Indian Commission of Ontario was cited, saying that millions of tax dollars were being wasted in negotiating native land claims in Ontario. Among the causes of fruitless delays and unnecessary and lengthy blockages, ad hominem arguments were cited (Platiel, 1995, p. A3): "Squabbling among negotiators is sometimes rooted in personality clashes, with the result that 'taxpayers' money is regularly diverted from problem solving to denigration of the other party's good faith.' " In such cases, excessive use of ad hominem arguments in quarrelsome verbal exchanges can be considered fallacious if it blocks or hampers the goals of the negotiation dialogue. Commenting on the quality of these negotiations, a government official called them "wasteful, inappropriate and aimless" (Platiel, 1995, p. A3). To control the problem, the Indian Commission asked for the power to limit unprofessional conduct in negotiations.

2. Dialectical Relevance

Many of the textbook treatments classify the ad hominem as a fallacy of relevance and invoke the concept of relevance in attempting to determine when ad hominem arguments are fallacious and when not. The problem is to define what 'relevance' means.[5] In Walton (*Pragmatic Theory*, 1995, chapter 6), the appropriate notion of relevance is defined as *dialectical relevance of argumentation*, meaning that an argument or other move made in a dialogue is said to be dialectically relevant to the extent that it functions as a contribution to the particular type of dialogue of which it is supposed to be a part. Six basic types of dialogue are defined in Walton (*Pragmatic Theory*, 1995, and *New Dialectic*, 1998)—persuasion dialogue (of which the critical discussion is a subtype), inquiry, information-seeking dialogue, deliberation, negotiation, and eristic dialogue (of which the quarrel is a subtype). This pluralism of normative frameworks of argumentation means that an argument could be relevant if it is supposed to be part of one type of dialogue, but that very same argument could be irrelevant in another context of dialogue. For example, the same appeal to a threat (*ad baculum* argument) that was appropriate in the context of a negotiation might be highly inappropriate and therefore irrelevant in the context of a critical discussion.[6] Because sometimes a *dialectical shift* in an argument—a move from one type of dialogue to another—can be concealed or illicit, fallacies of relevance can be deceptive.

According to the criteria given in Walton (*Pragmatic Theory*, 1995, pp. 192–93), in judging whether or not an argument is dialectically relevant in a given case, a critic should look at the evidence of six factors furnished by the text and context of discourse.

1. *Type of Dialogue.* What is the type of dialogue the participants are supposed to be engaged in? If it is a critical discussion, then the argument or

move in question should be judged as relevant or not, in relation to that type of dialogue. An argument that is relevant in a critical discussion might not be relevant, for example, if the dialogue is supposed to be an inquiry.

2. *Stage of Dialogue.* A speech act that was relevant at the confrontation stage of a dialogue, for example, may be irrelevant at the argumentation stage.

3. *Goal of Dialogue.* Relevance is always determined in relation to the goal of a dialogue. If the given dialogue is supposed to be a critical discussion to resolve a conflict of opinions between two opposed points of view, P_1 and P_2, then a subargument will be relevant insofar as it bears upon, or is related to, the resolution of the question of which is the stronger presumption, P_1 or P_2.

4. *Argumentation Scheme.* But how is the subargument related to some issue of a dialogue, like the opposition between two propositions P_1 and P_2? It depends on the type of argumentation scheme for that subargument. For example, if the subargument is an appeal to expert opinion, then whether that subargument is relevant depends on its argumentation scheme. And if a reply to it is to be judged relevant or irrelevant, the judgment depends on the types of critical questions that are appropriate for that argumentation scheme. For example, the reply, 'Is the authority you cited really an expert?' would be relevant.

5. *Prior Sequence of Argumentation.* Whether a subargument is dialectically relevant in an ongoing dialogue may depend very much on what sequences of argumentation have gone before in the dialogue. Any textual evidence of the prior sequence of argumentation in a dialogue, in a given case, is an important source of evidence in judging relevance of a new line of argumentation.

6. *Speech Event.* The given institutional setting or particular speech event may impose constraints and special rules that help to define relevance in a given case. For example, if the argument is taking place in a legal trial, specific legal rules will help to define kinds of moves that are judged to be relevant or irrelevant for that type of speech event.

Applying these six criteria of dialectical relevance to the ad hominem argument, several factors previously seen to be important can now be put in perspective. At the local level of argumentation, the critical questions given in chapter 6 for the various subtypes of ad hominem arguments serve to define what is or is not a relevant reply to an ad hominem attack. At the global level, a determination of the type of dialogue the participants are supposed to be engaged in has often proved a crucial factor in evaluating ad hominem arguments. The case studies have often shown, for example, that an ad hominem argument that raises issues of character and personal honesty might be irrelevant if the dialogue is supposed to be a critical discussion of some issue that has nothing directly to do with the persons of the participants. But the same ad hominem argument could be relevant if the context is one of deliberation, in which one party is giving some sort of personal advice to the other on how to live his life.

How relevance is to be determined in a particular case in which an ad hominem argument has been used is by the method of chaining the given sequence of argumentation (at the local level) in the case forward, to try to link it up with the issue of the dialogue (at the global level). At the same time, the argumentation can be chained backwards from the global level, to try to get it to meet up with the specific ad hominem argument used at the local level. This technique of forward and backward chaining of a sequence of reasoning is widely used in computer science (especially in artificial intelligence) and can be nicely adapted to determining relevance of argumentation in a given case. Relevance is a big topic in its own right, to be explored in the research program on fallacies in future work. It is enough to say that present here is a dialectical method for judging relevance of arguments used in a given context of dialogue.

The problem with many of the textbook cases cited in chapter 2 is that not enough of the text and context of discourse is given so that it can be absolutely pinned down whether or not the ad hominem argument is relevant. In other cases, however, as indicated below, there definitely is enough information given on how the argument is being used in a particular context of dialogue for an evaluator to determine clearly whether or not the ad hominem argument is relevant.

For example, Creighton (1904, p. 169) described the ad hominem as an argument that "has reference to a person or persons, not to the real matter under discussion," thus determining the ad hominem to be fallacious on grounds of irrelevance. Somewhat grudgingly, as noted in chapter 2, section 1, Creighton admitted that an ad hominem argument could be relevant in some cases, as in legal cases. The problem then is for an evaluator to determine by some criteria or clear evidence whether or not the ad hominem argument in a given case is relevant.

As noted in chapter 2, this tendency to emphasize relevance in judging ad hominem arguments continues right through, for example, to Johnson and Blair (1983) who advised their readers that whether an ad hominem argument is fallacious or not, in a particular case, depends on whether the personal aspect of character or circumstances cited is relevant. Relevance is rightly seen as an important concept for evaluating ad hominem arguments, but the problem so far has been the failure to define a useful notion of relevance clearly enough and to give a method for determining relevance in a particular case.

3. Subjective and Objective Evidence

Many of the textbook treatments surveyed in chapter 2 see the ad hominem argument as fallacious on the grounds that this type of argument concentrates on the subjective aspect of attacking a person, as opposed to considering the person's claim on the basis of the objective evidence for or against it. Having adopted this perspective, it is small wonder that so many of the textbook accounts treat the ad hominem argument as inherently fallacious.

For example, Rescher (1964, p. 81), as quoted in chapter 2, section 4, defined what we now call the circumstantial (and he calls tu quoque form of ad hominem) argument as occurring when an arguer "contends that the opponent has also on some other occasion held the view he now opposed or adopted the practice he now condemns . . . instead of trying to show by actual evidence that the view or practice is correct." Beardsley (1966, p. 216), as noted in chapter 2, section 4, describes the argumentum ad hominem as generally fallacious, on the grounds that "attention is no longer directed to the matter at hand *(ad rem)*, but to the person *(ad hominem)."* The fallacy cited by these textbooks is that of directing attention to subjective matters of the arguer's person instead of showing that the person's claim is true or false or that his argument is strong or weak by citing the "actual" or objective evidence that is relevant. What should we say about this kind of account of the ad hominem fallacy in light of our analysis of its forms as an argument, and our account of the appropriate critical questions in chapter 6? The first point to make is that if conflict exists between objective, for example, empirical or scientific evidence, and personal or subjective evidence, based on ad hominem arguments, then preference should be given to the objective evidence generally. This point seems to vindicate the analysis of the fallacy given by the textbook treatments, making the fallacy simply the using of subjective instead of objective evidence. But the matter is not that simple.

The problem is that in many cases the objective evidence is lacking or for various reasons is insufficient to prove or disprove the claim at issue. In many cases of practical deliberation, for example, conducting an inquiry to collect the relevant objective evidence would take so long or be so costly that the problem that is the issue of the deliberation would no longer be possible to solve in a prudent manner. Or on issues of controversial public policies, for example, in political or ethical argumentation, the issue may be so bound up with values that, although empirical facts are relevant, they are not sufficient to resolve the issue. In such cases, subjective evidence or ad hominem argumentation can be relevant. Moreover, if the objective evidence appears to support both sides, to some degree, then an ad hominem argument giving subjective evidence could function as the tie-breaker that shifts the burden of proof one way or the other in the balance of considerations.

For these reasons, it is an oversimplified and misleading account of many common arguments, of the kind that occur in everyday reasoning, to say categorically that the only kind of evidence that can be relevant is "actual" or objective evidence—what has been called ad rem or ad judicium argumentation. It is true, or at least it is recommended here, that objective evidence is generally preferable to subjective evidence because it can be reproducible to another observer in a way that subjective evidence is generally not. For subjective evidence is person-relative. Hence, according to the analysis put forward here, ad hominem arguments are best seen generally as defeasible and presumptive as inferences subject to critical questioning in a given case.

Since the enlightenment period, there has been an overwhelming preference for objective reasoning in Western culture, beginning with Pascal and Descartes, in particular, who expressed a strong preference for the axiomatic method of reasoning exemplified by Euclidean geometry. Since then the prevailing assumption in Western thinking is that the only kind of reasoning worth taking at all seriously, as pointing the way to discovering the truth of a matter, is the kind based on objective, impersonal evidence, that is, scientific reasoning. Practical reasoning based on subjective judgment and plausible inference has been cast aside as merely subjective and therefore worthless. This point of view, curiously, rejects character-based argumentation, of the kind that is so common both in the law and in everyday reasoning in the case studies of ad hominem arguments in the previous chapters, as worthless evidence. Small wonder, then, that in this cultural climate of opinion, it was an easy and natural step for the logic textbooks to take to presume generally that ad hominem arguments are fallacious. But this step overlooked the reality of argumentative practices in everyday life—especially in law and politics—that appealing to character is often not only your best attack when challenged but also your best defense when you are accused.

To conclude from this popularly presumed premise of the subjective and presumptive nature of ad hominem arguments that they are always fallacious because they fail to give objective evidence of a matter is too simplistic and categorical a view of evidence. Even though ad hominem arguments only give a kind of evidence that is person-based and therefore subjective, it would not be a cognitively useful standpoint on argumentation to reject them as inherently fallacious.

Of course, in the past, there has not been any structure or consistent method for evaluating ad hominem arguments or even for defining and identifying them as definite forms of argument. So the distrust of ad hominem arguments and the tendency to reject them categorically as fallacious were understandable. But now we can identify each of the subtypes as distinctive argumentation schemes, and we have a systematic grasp of what kind of evidence is needed to support them in particular cases. Through applying the matching set of critical questions for each scheme, the ad hominem argument can function as giving evidence that can be cited to support or detract from an argument that a view or practice is justified in a given case. To accommodate such evaluations, however, the conventional accounts of the formal structure of dialogue as a framework of reasoned argument needs to be modified and extended.

A participant in a dialogue needs to be seen not only as having a commitment store but also as having a credibility rating based on his "reputation," that is, a record of what is known about his attitudes, cognitive skills, and other aspects of character that are relevant in a given type of dialogue.

4. The Credibility Function

The best way to model ad hominem argumentation in the formal structures of dialogue, of the kind used by Hamblin (1970; 1971), Walton (*Logical*, 1984), and Walton and Krabbe (1995), is to assign a credibility function *cred* so that when you assign an input value (an ethotic rating) to the credibility of a participant as a person (which can be a positive or negative value) it gives an output value that raises or lowers the plausibility value of the proposition (or the argument) advocated by that person in a dialogue. The proposition (or argument) advocated will already have an initial, given value, as being highly plausible, not very plausible, and so forth.[7] Then once a credibility value is assigned to the person advocating that particular proposition in the dialogue, the initial plausibility of the proposition will be modified, upwards or downwards, depending on the credibility value of the person, one that is factored into our assessment of her claim or argument.

In the normal case of a critical discussion or other type of dialogue as modeled in the literature on formal structures of dialogue so far, the arguer is merely a "participant" who has a commitment store and who incurs or loses commitments depending on the type of moves she makes.[8] But to this basic structure, we now add the optional element that the participant is known as a *person*, an individual who, on the basis of what is known about her personal circumstances, character, knowledge, or status as a biased or unbiased spokesperson, has a certain ethotic rating. If the person is well respected with good character and credentials, she may be assigned a positive ethotic rating. If she is known to be a habitual liar or hypocrite or to have a bad character for veracity, she may be assigned a negative ethotic rating. In the first type of case, the plausibility value of the proposition she advocates will be raised. In the second type of case, it will be lowered. The ethotic rating can be fine-tuned as the aspect of ethos becomes particularized. Distinct judgments can be made about veracity, prudence, perception, and so forth.

The important consideration is that the value or ethotic rating of the person will affect the value or plausibility of the proposition (or argument) advocated by the person.

Another important consideration about using this credibility function in evaluating arguments in particular cases is that it does not always matter. In fact, as already noted several times, generally in a critical discussion a *participant* is merely a designated individual with an attached commitment set, and no knowledge is introduced about his or her character or other personal characteristics or biographical background. The same is true in an inquiry, normally, in which what is important is the objective evidence for or against a claim. Personal or biographical matters concerning the individual who made the claim are irrelevant in evaluating whether an argument for or against the claim is sufficient or inadequate to prove it.[9]

In some cases, however, the personal characteristics of the proponent of a proposition or argument, if known, can be important in evaluating the claim made. For example, in a criminal trial in which an accusation has been made, and there were no witnesses or hard circumstantial evidence to validate or refute the claim made in the accusation, the character (circumstances, bias, past actions, consistency of commitments, and so forth) of the person who made the claim can be vitally important in trying to judge the plausibility of the claim. In some cases, the credibility of the accuser may be the only evidence that the defendant has access to, in order to argue against the accusation. Otherwise the accusation would be irrefutable, once the person who made it testified that it was true.

In a case like this one, the context of dialogue makes it appropriate to introduce a credibility function so that the arguments are evaluated not just on the basis of the objective evidence for or against them (ad rem or ad judicium, to use the traditional terms). In addition to this evaluation, we must introduce subjective evidence, based on our evaluation of the persons who are taking part in the argument, as well. In most cases, this subjective or ad hominem evidence is not decisive by itself or perhaps not even very strong, when you sum up the whole body of evidence in the case. But, still, it can have a place in enhancing or detracting from the support already in place for or against a disputed proposition, provided by a mass of objective evidence. In some cases, subjective evidence based on credibility of persons can be decisive, especially in tilting the balance one way or the other in a balance of considerations.

In applying the credibility function to any particular case of an ad hominem argument, two main factors need to be separated. One is the claim that the arguer is a bad person, in the sense defined in chapters 3 and 5, meaning that he is deficient in his role in a dialogue. In some cases, for example, an ethical claim may be made that a is a morally bad person because he cheated on his income tax returns in 1976, or something of that sort. This ethical accusation can then be gone into, and evidence external to the case may be brought in. In other cases, a may be claimed to be a bad person because he "does not practice what he preaches" or is inconsistent in some way. This kind of circumstantial allegation can be sorted out using the critical questions outlined in chapter 6.

A case in point was the following use of the circumstantial ad hominem to attack politician Al Gore in 1996. In an editorial page called *Election Notebook* (November 18, 1996, p. 16), *Time* gave out "Campaign 96" awards for "outstanding achievement" by politicians, including the following one.

Case 7.1

The Slight-Inconsistency Medal: To Al Gore, who left not a dry eye in the house at the Democratic Convention as he described his sister's death from smoking-induced lung cancer. Gore failed to mention that for some years following her death, his family continued to grow tobacco and that he continued to accept campaign money from tobacco interests.

The argument used in this case, having the form CIRCUMSTANTIAL AH, attacks Gore's credibility by making him look hypocritical, and ridiculously so. Attacking Gore on the basis of something someone in his family allegedly did is a weak form of circumstantial ad hominem argument, but when combined with the allegation that he accepted money from tobacco interests and the aura of ridicule suggested by such apparent hypocrisy, the ad hominem argument is quite a powerful attack on Gore's credibility as a politician who can be trusted to tell the truth.

The second critical question is whether it follows from the claim that *a* is a morally bad person so that the plausibility of what he asserts should be reduced. This assessment depends very much on the context of dialogue. In some cases, plausibility should be reduced commensurately with the seriousness of the claim. In other cases, the plausibility of the person's assertion should not be reduced at all because a person's credibility is not a relevant factor in this type of dialogue or because her lack of credibility is not shown by the ad hominem argument used.

5. Relevance of a Person's Credibility

The general solution to the problem of applying normative models of dialogue to cases of ad hominem argumentation is to add the credibility function to the structure of a dialogue, but only in selective cases. If the type of dialogue is that of a critical discussion or an inquiry, then personal matters may not be relevant or appropriate to take into account in judging the arguments. However, if the context of dialogue is a criminal trial, for example, in which testimony is being cross-examined, then personal matters of the arguer's character for veracity and so forth may be vitally important. So in a critical discussion or inquiry, in which personal matters should not be considered when judging the argumentation, the participants are not modeled as "persons," except that they will have commitment sets of the usual kind. But in a dialogue in which personal matters should be considered, the credibility function should be applied to each of the participants. In such a case, an initial credibility value is attached to each person (participant), and then as matters of character, circumstances, or bias are introduced in the moves made in the dialogue, a participant's argument, whether it be strong or weak, will be modified in its strength or weakness, according to the credibility function applied to it, at that point in the dialogue.

If the context is that of a dialogue between two nuclear physicists in an exchange of arguments in a physics journal on some technical question about the existence of a subatomic particle, then an ad hominem argument would be outrageously out of place. The character of one of the physicists, her personal circumstances, or any biographical facts about her personal life would not be relevant as evidence that would count for or against her scientific arguments.

In the context of a scientific inquiry of this sort, ad hominem arguments would only have some relevance as evidence at a procedural or metadialogue level—for instance, if one of the physicists was accused of reporting biased results in his experiment in order to make the outcome look better to improve his chances of getting a better research grant. But in the original scientific exchange on issues of physics between the two scientists, personal, subjective, ad hominem arguments have no real place as relevant evidence. Thus, in the dialogue exchange of arguments, the credibility function would have no place.

Nevertheless, if one of the scientists were being asked to give her advice on questions of physics as part of a town hall meeting on the issue of building a nuclear reactor, questions of the personal credibility of the physicist as a contributor to these deliberations could be relevant. For example, suppose the physicist supported the point of view of building the reactor enthusiastically, but it was found that she was employed by the company that had been given the lucrative contract for building it. In this context—that of a deliberation—matters of the scientist's personal credibility would be relevant.

The question of the relevance of ad hominem arguments is a subject of some controversy in law. According to McElhaney (1993, p. 76), four basic ideas explain law of character arguments.

- When character is an issue in the case, almost any kind of character evidence is admissible.
- Character is generally not admissible to prove conduct.
- But character can be used as a defense in criminal cases.
- Character is admissible to attack or to support the credibility of a witness.

According to Rule 608 of the *Federal Rules of Evidence* (1987, p. 46), evidence in the form of an opinion about the character or reputation of a witness can be used to attack the credibility of that witness, under two conditions: (1) "the evidence may refer only to character for truthfulness or untruthfulness" and (2) evidence of truthful character is admissible "only after the character of the witness for truthfulness has been attacked by opinion or reputation evidence or otherwise." This ruling is an interesting limitation because it excludes attacks on character other than on character for veracity. These rulings on relevance seem simple enough, but difficult problems arise when it comes to ruling on particular cases.

One problem that has recently been the subject of controversy concerns the kind of case in which an accused murderer or rapist has had a prior conviction or in which evidence is on hand that would indicate that he is a violent and aggressive person, but it relates to a different case. Should this evidence be considered relevant? Judges have often ruled that it is not relevant evidence in the case being decided because it makes the defendant appear as such a bad person that it would "inflame" the jury. The objection made to allowing such evidence is that it is thought to be so damaging that if presented to the jury it would make them declare the defendant guilty.[10] The objection is that such ad hominem evidence of prior acts of the defendant would "prejudice" the jury.

But such evidence surely is relevant, from a nonlegal perspective, apart from the "artificial reason" of the law (Bickenbach, 1990). It has to be recognized then that a legal trial is a very special type of speech event (see section 2 above) that is governed by rules of procedure and evidence that may differ in what is judged relevant from nonlegal persuasion dialogue. Generally, then, judgments of when a claim about an arguer's character is relevant to judging the plausibility or implausibility of his or her argument should be determined by the purpose and structure of the dialogue of which the argument is a part.

6. Ad Hominem As a Reasonable Legal Argument

Whately saw the ad hominem argument (Hamblin, 1970, p. 174) as establishing a conclusion that is not "absolute" and "general" (ad rem) but true only relative to a person and what he concedes. Locke grouped ad hominem with ad ignorantiam and ad verecundiam together (Hamblin, 1970, p. 160), contrasting them with "proofs and arguments arising from" the "foundations of knowledge and probability" or "from the nature of things themselves." Both these accounts suggest an important idea—that all three of these types of argumentation are subjective in nature. Yet despite their so often having been discounted as fallacious precisely for that reason, they are (within limits) often reasonable arguments.

We already know that ad hominem can frequently be viewed as a species of argumentum ad ignorantiam. These two types of argumentation are closely connected in practice, in their uses as argumentation techniques. This connection exists because many of the techniques of ad hominem argumentation are methods of shifting the burden of proof in a dialogue, and the argumentum ad ignorantiam is essentially the expression of the concept of burden of proof in dialogue (Walton, *Arguments from Ignorance*, 1996).

But what about combining ad verecundiam and ad hominem? This combination seems also to be a practical possibility because in some cases—see the analyses of M. Salmon (1984) and W. Salmon (1984), as well as Woods and Walton (1977) and Walton (*Arguer's Position*,

1985, p. 78)—the ad hominem argument can be described as a kind of obverse ad verecundiam.

The connection of these two techniques of argumentation comes out most explicitly in legal argumentation in which an attorney in court may attack expert testimony by attacking the reliability, neutrality, or veracity of an expert witness, as noted in chapter 5, section 9.

The cross-examination of the expert witness by a lawyer in court is a specific type of argumentation that reveals interesting links between the argumentum ad verecundiam and the argumentum ad hominem. Initially, one may be inclined to think that cross-examination of an expert witness is a classic context of the ad verecundiam type of argumentation. The attorney is extracting expert opinions from the expert authority by question-reply dialogue, and at the same time, the attorney is directing this process of questioning toward her goal of winning this case by persuading the jury (or judge). Yet the characteristic means of carrying out this goal reveals strong elements of the argumentum ad hominem, for the method is to undermine or if possible refute the opposing expert's testimony by discrediting the expert herself as a reliable source of knowledge. According to Hoffman (1979, p. 313), "By cross-examination, you seek to impeach the expert's veracity, his capacity to observe, his lack of impartiality and consistency." And these four goals quite accurately characterize main objectives of the argumentum ad hominem. Surprisingly, then, in cross-examination as a type of argument, the ad hominem and ad verecundiam mechanisms of argument converge and mesh together as components in the same argumentation. This curious connection comes about because the interview with the expert in cross-examination dialogue has a negative objective of destroying the argumentative credibility of the expert's testimony.

In cross-examination, the lawyer is trying to attack, refute, or cast doubts on the testimony of an expert who has been brought forward to support the opposing side's argument. Therefore, the tactical approach of the cross-examination lawyer is essentially negative. According to Weber (1981, p. 299), the purpose of cross-examination is "to destroy the expert and/or to destroy his testimony." Interestingly, then, the methods of cross-examination take a form of argumentation that is clearly equivalent to the argumentum ad hominem. The lawyer's choice is either to let the expert's testimony stand or to attack the expert and his testimony as a credible package. Often the latter option comes down to tactics that try explicitly to make it appear to the jury that the expert is either dishonest or incompetent. Weber (p. 306), for example, gives the following advice to a cross-examiner: "If you cannot successfully prove that the witness is wrong, unfair, biased, ignorant, or not believable or that his theories are probably incorrect, either do not cross-examine at all or ask only a few harmless questions and pass him. If you have no ammunition do not fire blanks—shut up." This tactical advice clearly shows that the ad hominem argument is being proposed as a species of effective attack against an appeal to expert opinion in courtroom argumentation. What should be cited here as a particularly useful kind of tactic for attacking an appeal to expert opinion is the deployment of the bias type of ad hominem argument and the kind of attack on the person's abilities as an informed practical reasoner that were cited in chapter 5, section 5, as subspecies of the direct ad hominem argument. Weber's advice is based on the assumptions that such ad hominem arguments can be convincing if you have the evidence to back them up but that they can backfire if mounted unconvincingly.

Because it is subjective and dependent on an arguer's character being judged as good or bad, the ad hominem argument tends to be discounted as a type of evidence and generally degraded, in contrast to the kind of objective, more factual kind of evidence that might be provided by objective proof such as ballistics, fingerprints, DNA evidence, eyewitness testimony, and expert opinions. But it is possible to see, from the accounts we have given of how ad hominem arguments are used in the courts, that these arguments, despite their subjective aspect, can be important in providing evidence in a trial. For example, expert testimony facts such as DNA evidence can be subject to different interpretations by different experts. Who to believe? Such a question often comes down to the credibility of the expert as a trustworthy, honest person who makes careful judgments, of the kind that were associated in chapter 5 with skills of practical reasoning.

What the legal admissibility and use of ad hominem arguments shows is that reasoning from the personal credibility of a witness, to a conclusion to increase or decrease the credibility one attaches to the proposition asserted by the witness, can be a reasonable kind of argument in some instances. It is reasonable if such a conclusion is arrived at within the context of a larger body of evidence in a case. Especially in a case in which the more objective or factual kind of (ad judicium) evidence is lacking or is, by itself, insufficient to settle an issue, the ad hominem argument is useful to swing a balance of considerations one way or another. Because legal argumentation in a trial is based on burden of proof, such arguments can be useful and appropriate, despite their subjective and ethical aspect.

The subjective aspect of the ad hominem argument is both the source of its usefulness as a reasonable kind of argument that can be valuable in some cases and at the same time the source of its fallaciousness. As shown in section 10 below, the fallacy is committed when the impact of the ad hominem is out of proportion to its true weight and relevance as part of a larger body of evidence in a case.

7. Evaluating the Direct Type

In evaluating the direct or abusive ad hominem, the first question is whether the claim on which the allegation of bad character is made is true. But even more important is the second question of the type of dialogue. For in some contexts of dialogue, even if the premise that *a* has a bad character is true, it will not detract from what *a* asserts.

For example, in the kinds of cases cited by Cohen and Nagel (1934) in chapter 1, the context of dialogue is that of scientific inquiry. Personal characteristics and biographical information on how a person lived are not relevant: "The personal history of Gauss is entirely irrelevant to question of the adequacy of his proof that every equation has a root; and the inadequacy of Galileo's theory of the tides is independent of the personal motives which led Galileo to hold it." Not surprisingly, because the context of argument they are concerned with is scientific method, Cohen and Nagel see the argumentum ad hominem as fallacious.

A much more difficult case is the one given by Copi (1961)—case 1.1. It is true that Francis Bacon, at the age of sixty, was impeached as chancellor for having accepted a bribe from a litigant. Found guilty, he was "removed in disgrace from all his offices under the Crown" (Cranston, 1967, p. 236). But this was the only documented incident showing bad character for morality in an otherwise excellent personal life. Also, a good deal of intrigue was present in the court during Bacon's time, raising legitimate questions of whether Bacon was unfairly accused by those who intrigued against him. In addition, the fact that questionable payments of various sorts were common practices in the governing court circles at the time raises the issue of whether Bacon was unfairly singled out by opponents who stood to gain themselves. Thus the premise of whether Bacon could justifiably be said to be a person of bad moral character should be subject to considerable doubt, in context.

The other main question of the context of dialogue is also problematic. Bacon's philosophy was mostly about scientific method. Although not a scientist himself, Bacon was the "prophet of modern science" (Cranston, 1967, p. 235) and the "founding father of modern science in England." But, as a philosopher, Bacon did expound some ideas that would likely be categorized as coming within the area of ethics. So should the credibility function be judged as applicable in weighing the worth of Bacon's philosophy? By and large, it would seem that the weight of presumption is toward the negative here, but it is a difficult case to evaluate in a clean or absolute way.

On cases 1.2 and 1.3, concerning the dispute on feminism, nothing can be said about whether or not the charges are substantiated without examining the text of discourse in detail to bring forward the evidence of how certain "intellectual methods" were used wrongly in the prior argumentation in the cases.

It is possible, however, to make some comment on the context of dialogue in which these ad hominem arguments were used. Both arguers are taking part in a dispute on feminism. Both are professional philosophers, and the text of discourse of each argument is a long letter to the editor of the *Proceedings of the American Philosophical Association.* What is especially interesting about case 1.2 is that the critic accuses the other party of using "intellectual methods" that are "dishonest." The latter term indicates that the argument is an ad hominem; the former one suggests that the context of dialogue is that of a critical discussion, in which the one party is being accused of deviating from the collaborative rules of the dialogue.

In case 1.3, the arguer accuses the other party of committing a straw man fallacy in order to get false or misleading documentation for ad hominem charges. Again the word 'dishonest' is used. These cases are not very good ones to be used in an elementary textbook, which introduces readers to the ad hominem argument for the first time, because they require a detailed analysis of a much wider part of the discourse (in the letters to the editor) that is not printed in the textbook, in order for the cases to be adequately analyzed.

Case 1.4, the case of the ad about Goldwater and the bomb, illustrates the importance of the third critical question appropriate for the direct ad hominem argument. The problem here concerns how much weight in dispute should be given to an ad hominem argument. In case 1.4, the ad hominem argument was such a powerful attack on Goldwater's credibility and character for prudent judgment as a good candidate for the office of the president that it had a terrific impact on the election deliberations, far outweighing the merit as an argument that one might expect it to have. The problem here is that in affecting a balance of considerations in a dialogue an ad hominem argument can have an impact far out of proportion to the weight it should be given, as an inherently weak and subjective plausibilistic type of argumentation. Even an element of poisoning the well is present in this case because Goldwater was categorized as "crazy" and dangerous—a kind of person not to be trusted with the power to "push the nuclear button."

Another interesting aspect of case 1.4 is that the ad hominem argument is put forward purely on a basis of innuendo. The explicit premises of the ad hominem against his being a good candidate are never expressed in so many words. Instead, all the viewers see on the television screen are the pictures of the young girl, the flowers, the exploding bomb, the messages about world peace, and so forth. Because there is no explicit ethotic ad hominem argument expressed, a critic is hard pressed to attack the argument by posing critical questions or trying to refute the premises with relevant evidence. The ad hominem argument in this case has plausible deniability, meaning that the proponents of the argument, if confronted with reasonable demands to fulfill the burden of proof, can simply back off and claim they never really meant to attack the victim personally at all.

A general problem with the negative ethotic type of ad hominem argument is that people are so impressed by the personal attack on an arguer's character that they condemn the individual attacked as a bad person and reject any policy or argument associated with him, casting aside all objective evidence on the issue. But such an overreaction may not be warranted, for after all the ad hominem is an inherently weak plausibilistic type of argument that needs to be judged against a broader background of evidence on a balance of considerations basis in a given case.

As a parting shot on the question of terminology, there is room to question whether the category of the abusive ad hominem argument might be better named by calling it the direct ad hominem argument. The problem with the term 'abusive' is that it suggests that this type of personal ad hominem argument is always fallacious or unjustified. And, of course, that suggestion would be at odds with our general finding that ad hominem argument can be, at least in some cases, a reasonable kind of argument.

Nevertheless, one might argue that "abusive" does not necessarily imply "wrong" or "fallacious" because in some instances abusive argument, at least in the form of a personal attack—a negative type of argument—could be justifiable. Be that as it may, the term 'abusive' does strongly suggest an attack that is wrong or culpable. Because, as we have seen, questions of character and personal integrity are sometimes properly issues in argument, an attack on someone's argument that uses allegations about the character of the person argued against, of the ad hominem sort, is not always culpable or fallacious. Hence the term 'abusive' is bound to be somewhat prejudicial and misleading. Therefore we recommend the term 'ethotic (or direct)' ad hominem argument as the best name for this type of argument.

Another possibility would be to reserve the term 'abusive' for the fallacious misuse of the direct ad hominem. This narrower usage is, at any rate, better than the broad usage covering all direct cases. It has proved difficult to get the textbooks to deviate from the traditional and often misleading timeworn terminology of the past, and all that can be done is to make recommendations.

To sum up, then, basically three reasons indicate why a negative ethotic (direct) ad hominem argument is fallacious: (1) the premise that the arguer has a bad character is not supported (according to requirements of burden of proof appropriate for the case), and by using innuendo and "smear tactics" the burden of proof is avoided altogether; (2) the premise is not relevant to the conclusion, in the type of dialogue the participants are supposed to be engaged in; and (3) the attack on the arguer's character has such a "staining" effect that the audience "throws out the baby with the bathwater," that is, rejects any argument associated with such a bad person, giving the ad hominem attack much more weight as an argument than it really deserves.

8. Evaluating the Circumstantial Type

Case 1.5 (the smoking case) shows how much depends on identifying the argument in many ad hominem cases even prior to evaluating it. Is the child merely questioning the apparent pragmatic inconsistency cited or using it to argue that the parent is a morally bad person and then using this subconclusion as the basis of an ad hominem attack? And if the latter is the case, is the child using the parent's lack of personal credibility to lower the plausibility of her argument, or is he strongly and absolutely rejecting her argument against smoking? In this case, it is difficult to opt for one against the other of these interpretations exclusively, so any classification and evaluation of the argument as an ad hominem should be conditional in nature.

At least in the smoking case, the inconsistency cited is relatively direct and simple. The parent admits smoking but at the same time argues against smoking as a bad practice. In many other cases, such as the sportsman's rejoinder (case 1.18) and the tree hugger (case 1.6), an alleged parallel is present between two situations, but also there could be significant differences between the two situations. The parallel is based on a kind of connection or similarity between two situations, but the critical questions cited in chapter 6 can bring out differences and bring into question the seriousness of the parallel as indicating a weakness in the position of the arguer who is attacked.

Much can be said from a logical point of view about the sportsman case, but one of the most important things to be noted is how the parallel, alleged by the hunter between his own actions and that of the critic, fails. As DeMorgan (1847, p. 265) neatly put it: "The parallel will not exist until, for the person who eats meat, we substitute one who turns butcher for amusement." Here then is a distinctive type of ad hominem fallacy: the critic is not inconsistent, or not as close to inconsistency in what she practices versus what she preaches, as the hunter's rejoinder appears to imply. A logical gap exists between conceding eating meat and conceding barbarity for sacrifice of innocent animals for amusement. Concealing this gap, the sportsman's rejoinder puts his critic sharply on the defensive.

A comparable evaluation of the tree hugger case can be made. The critic alleges that the tree hugger consumes wood products. This premise is plausible, and not difficult to substantiate, for houses and many other familiar products we all use are made of wood. But is this premise a sufficient basis for arguing that the tree hugger who decries the cutting of trees is inconsistent? That is the key critical question in this case.

The answer is no. The tree hugger would be pragmatically inconsistent if he admitted having engaged in tree cutting, while at the same time he denounces tree cutting as being a bad activity that nobody should engage in. But that alleged inconsistency is not the situation in case 1.6. What is the situation is that the tree hugger is (plausibly) committed to using wood products. But using wood products is not the same as cutting down trees (or clear-cutting of forests). A logical gap is present between these two issues, just as between the two actions cited in the sportsman's rejoinder case.

The lesson of both these cases—compare Walton (*Informal Logic*, 1989, p. 164)—is that the first step in evaluating any circumstantial ad hominem argument is to attempt to identify and to state clearly the pair of propositions alleged to be inconsistent. The second steps are to evaluate whether or not they are really pragmatically inconsistent, and if they are not, to analyze the nature of the connection between them. If some sort of connection is present, then it needs to be established whether it provides any kind of a reasonable basis for claiming that the person attacked by the ad hominem is in a weak position that needs to be defended in order to restore his credibility.

The key in evaluating these cases is the set of critical questions for the circumstantial ad hominem given in chapter 6, section 3. But a circumstantial ad hominem is not to be judged as fallacious simply because one of the critical questions has not been answered adequately by the proponent, in a given case. The fallacy occurs when a systematic attempt is made to evade the burden of answering these questions. For example, in the sportsman's rejoinder case, the hunter tries to shift the burden of proof by making the critic appear to be a bad person, who, it appears, must answer to the charge of meat-eating, a practice he himself seems to condemn.

To sum up the general pattern, circumstantial ad hominem criticisms can be judged as reasonable or unreasonable (even fallacious, in some cases) in relation to an arguer's commitments, as implied by her circumstances and the specific statements (premises and conclusion) of her argument. Evaluation of each individual case should be made in relation to the corpus of argument and the context of dialogue. Practical reasoning is the thread that joins up the sequence of reasoning to fill the logical gaps between the commitments at issue.

When, then, does this basically reasonable kind of argumentation become fallacious? The answer is that, in different cases, it can become fallacious in a complex variety of ways, by falling victim to various faults and excesses. But, basically, the fallacy is the use of deceptive tactics to interfere with the asking of the appropriate critical questions in the proper sequence of dialogue surrounding the argument. In other cases, the circumstantial ad hominem can be merely a weak or badly supported argument, rather than being such a bad fault that it deserves to be called fallacious. In these cases, an appropriate question is not answered, but no attempt is made to interfere with the proper order of asking and answering critical questions in the dialogue.

Nevertheless, one particular kind of error is based on the confusion between ad rem and ad hominem argumentation, that is, the error of arguing that a person's conclusion she advocates is inconsistent with her other commitments (actions, personal situation, etc.), therefore the conclusion is demonstrably false (in itself). This fault can occur with arguments of the type PRAGMATIC INCONSISTENCY and INCONSISTENT COMMITMENT generally, so it is not exclusive to ad hominem arguments. But it is relevant to the smoking case. Suppose the child citing the parent's pragmatic inconsistency by observing her conduct of smoking, draws the absolute conclusion that the proposition 'Smoking is unhealthy' is false. In such a case, the child commits a fallacy in his argument by drawing an absolute conclusion (ad rem) from a premise of pragmatic inconsistency. If the child is concluding from the perceived inconsistency that the parent is a hypocrite, or is a bad person for veracity and not credible, his argument is an ad hominem.

This argument is in fact a case of the fallacy that van Eemeren and Grootendorst (1987, p. 291) call *absolutizing the success of a defense*—concluding that a thesis is true (or false) only because it has been successfully defended or attacked ex concessis in an argument. As noted in chapter 1, section 7, it is the kind of argument move also analyzed by Barth and Martens. It is one thing for a proposition to be criticized or defended in relation to an arguer's commitments and concessions, but it is quite another thing to declare that this proposition is absolutely true or false from evidence external to these commitments and concessions in a context of discussion. This fault can be a fallacy or simply an error, depending on the case. Although it can occur as part of an ad hominem argument, it can also occur in INCONSISTENT COMMITMENT arguments that are not of the ad hominem type.

Although this absolutizing type of fallacy, which is a failure to recognize the subjective nature of ad hominem argumentation, is an important type of error to be looked for in ad hominem arguments, it is by no means the only common source of fallaciousness. Another fallacy cited above (section 5), is the sophistical tactic of using the ad hominem attack as a diversion or distraction from the main issue (fallacy of relevance). Other errors and kinds of ad hominem fallacies have been noted in Walton (*Arguer's Position*, 1985, p. 90). Sometimes the proponent finds merely the appearance of inconsistency and does not prove it adequately but still presses a strong ad hominem attack, not warranted by the evidence, using the power of the attack to try to shift the burden of proof to the other side and shield off the need to reply to critical questions. Examples, as noted above, are the sportsman's rejoinder and tree hugger cases.

Clearly, each ad hominem argument has to be looked at on its own merits (or demerits). As a critic, you have to look carefully at the evidence from the text of discourse. What are the propositions alleged to be inconsistent, and if there is such an inconsistency, does it constitute evidence that the arguer is a morally bad person? To determine whether a pragmatic inconsistency exists and what it shows, you may have to study not only an arguer's explicit concessions in a dialogue but also what you can infer about his implicit commitments as expressed by his known behavior, personal situation, and other circumstantial evidence. These so-called dark-side commitments (Walton, *Informal Fallacies*, 1987, p. 125) may not be known directly to a critic, who has to try to extract them from an arguer by critical questioning. Also, evidence of past events alleged to have taken place may have to be questioned and evaluated.

Of an ad hominem argument in a given case, however, the evaluation of the argument as strong or weak should be made on a conditional basis relative to the evidence given in the case. It should be recognized that many real cases of ad hominem arguments are powerful precisely because the accuser shields off the possibility of collecting such evidence. Innuendo in the form of "smear tactics" is used in argumentation of the following form: "I have heard that *a* is a morally bad person, but I would deny this myself." Such a "plausible deniability" move entails that the proposition put forward is not a commitment of the speaker. Hence there is no need to prove it.

Critical questions are shoved aside, and the audience is invited to condemn the argument simply on the grounds that the arguer is a bad person.

The circumstantial type of ad hominem argument can fail for a great variety of specific reasons, and there does not need to be any single, generic name for weak or incorrect arguments of this type. The key difference between it and the direct (abusive) type is that the latter argument involves no allegation of inconsistency, at least directly, in the same way that the circumstantial variety does. The circumstantial has an affinity with the direct category, however, because both are arguments of the GENERIC AH type.

Both the circumstantial and purely personal (ethotic) arguments can be reasonable kinds of criticisms in some cases because it is legitimate to question another arguer's commitments or character in certain types of dialogue. In political debate, for example, an arguer's commitments represent his goals. Qualities of character such as integrity and good judgment are also important in evaluating a person's readiness, reliability, and competence to carry out these alleged goals. But a person's real commitments are often not stated, in so many words, in a manner that can cover every issue that might arise. Therefore, presumptions about an arguer's actions, previous statements, professional or group affiliations, and personal character can be relevant evidence in evaluating his deeper commitments and his strength of adhering to those commitments.

All these qualifications are not to deny, however, that circumstantial and direct ad hominem arguments are both powerful and dangerous tactics in argument and have a notorious way of going badly wrong or being abused. Many types of lapses, shortcomings, errors, and powerful but irrelevant attacks are involved. Much of the future work of argumentation analysis of the rhetorical power of the ad hominem argument lies in classifying and studying these violations of rules of reasoned dialogue in order to see why they are wrong moves and why they are so effective as sophistical tactics that can be used to defeat an opposed arguer.

9. Evaluating the Bias Type

Essentially the same kind of mechanism is involved in the fallacious use of the bias type of ad hominem argument. To say someone has a bias is often taken as an indictment of that person, suggesting that she is a bad person and that therefore her argument should be completely discounted as worthless. In fact, dialectical bias in argumentation in the sense of having a point of view or advocating a particular position is not (in itself) fallacious or even inappropriate generally. In a critical discussion, for example, one is supposed to advocate one's point of view as strongly as possible, in order to make the discussion move forward in a revealing way. But the problem is that an arguer's bias (especially if the arguer has evidently tried to conceal it) can be portrayed as evidence of his guilt or dishonesty, and then a wholesale rejection of his argument may (inappropriately) be counseled.

Determining exactly when a particular criticism that a person is biased in an argument is justified remains a practical or pragmatic problem of judging what the type of dialogue in the case is supposed to be. Again, nothing is wrong with taking up one side of an issue. To have a position in an argument is not necessarily to be a biased person in the argument, in a sense that requires rejection of that argument, contrary to what is sometimes maintained. To be a biased person, in the more extreme pathological sense, is to refuse to engage in reasoned argument according to the rules of the given context of dialogue and instead to slip over into another context of dialogue such as the personal quarrel or the interest-based negotiation. If such a shift occurs, especially if it is concealed or exploited, a bias type of ad hominem fallacy has occurred.

Thus advocacy may be quite all right if it is not concealed. But if an arguer is supposed to be giving balanced advice or engaging in a balanced critical discussion of an issue, then cleaving too strongly to a commitment or concealing a vested interest can be significant indicators of the kind of personal bias that is an obstacle to the realization of the goal of the original dialogue. Shifting from one type of dialogue to another is not necessarily bad, from a critical perspective, but if the shift is unilateral or deceptive, it can be a source of mischief associated with fallacies (Walton, *Pragmatic Theory*, 1995). The bias ad hominem argument can be a legitimate way of exposing such a shift.

One of the most important types of dialectical shifts in understanding and evaluating fallacies is the shift from some other type of dialogue to a quarrel. A shift to a quarrel is not always illicit, and indeed the critical discussion and the debate already have an adversarial element within the type of dialogue. But, in general, a shift to a quarrel can be dangerous, from a point of view of fallacies, because the quarrel is an unregulated and emotional type of dialogue—issues easily get out of hand when a participant starts to make a quarrelsome move like an aggressive ad hominem attack on the other participant.

An important skill needed in a critical discussion is the ability to let your opponent state her point of view freely, and, at times, even to encourage her to develop her point of view. To accomplish this goal successfully, an arguer must resist the temptation to press ahead too strongly with the partisan task of pushing for his own point of view. The dogmatic or fanatical arguer is unable to carry out this function well and lacks the skills needed to accomplish it. Such an arguer sees his opponent as being hopelessly dogmatic or fanatical, the kind of person who is so captivated by advocating her own point of view that she is unable to acknowledge or concede a really good argument even when she is presented with it explicitly. In such a case, the more extreme type of bias ad hominem argument, the poisoning the well subtype, could even be justified as a reasonable argument in some instances. In a quarrel, the well could even be poisoned on both sides.

The problem in such a case is that the critical discussion remains in a quarrelsome kind of state, or, if not there already, degenerates into a quarrel. This is exactly the kind of climate in which fallacies tend to be committed because the quarrel leaves no room for the kinds of open-minded attitudes necessary for a successful critical discussion to take place. The one party always presumes in advance that the other party is clearly in the wrong, shows no respect for the ability of the other party to respond to a good argument, attacks the other party as a person who has no regard for the truth, tries to browbeat the other party with aggressive appeals to expert opinion, and so forth. Such combative tactics, while not inherently wrong in themselves as argumentation tactics to use in some contexts, are pushed forward in such a heavy-handed, one-sided, and aggressive way that they become serious obstacles to the continuation of the critical discussion in a fruitful manner. Once both parties get carried away with this quarreling kind of exchange, each trying to top the other, the critical discussion of the original issue becomes hopelessly blocked.

So the bias type of ad hominem argument can, in many cases, properly deployed, function as an important mechanism for keeping a critical discussion on track and preventing this shift to the quarrel from blocking the goals of the dialogue. However, the bias type, like the direct and circumstantial types, can also be a powerful form of innuendo, if the evidence for the charge of bias is not given, or even worse, is shielded off by plausible deniability.

For example, in case 2.2, the arguer accuses his opponent of supporting a privatization of a municipal garbage disposal plant in order to "get in on a profitable little monopoly." Although the charge was put in the form of a question, it poses a powerful accusation. So if critically questioned, the accuser should be required to back up the allegation with sufficient evidence.

If, in fact, an arguer would benefit personally by the proposal she advocates, then she is vulnerable to the bias ad hominem attack. In such cases, she would be well advised to defuse the charge in advance, by disavowing a motive for personal gain, while acknowledging her personal interests that exist. Like all ad hominem arguments, the bias subtype is essentially subjective or person-relative in nature. Therefore, another possibility, illustrated in case 2.6, is to counterattack by accusing one's accuser of the opposite bias. This type of case is an instance of the tu quoque subspecies of the bias subtype.

In these cases, a poisoning of the well type of factor can set in, if the person has some sort of a group affiliation that makes him continually open to the charge of being self-serving. For example, in case 2.7, the union official is very vulnerable to this form of attack whenever he argues for higher wages because he is an "interested party."

The critical questions for the bias type of ad hominem argument (chapter 6, sections 5 and 6) indicate what kind of evidence is needed to back up this type of argument. First, evidence is needed to support the charge of bias, and second, that evidence must be shown to be of a kind that demonstrates the existence of a bad or counterproductive type of bias that justifies the conclusion that the arguer is a morally bad person for contributing to a dialogue such as a critical discussion. It is not necessarily a bad thing for a person in a critical discussion to have a bias or viewpoint, as noted many times already.

What type of evidence, then, is needed to support the charge that an arguer is a biased person in a way that makes his honesty and fairness in a dialogue open to doubt?

If an arguer always adheres closely to a particular position on every issue, he is open to a criticism of being a biased or even a dogmatic person. For example, a candidate for the supreme court who is conservative in his political views may be accused by his critics of having a "right wing bias," for, on many issues, this candidate may have taken up the conservative point of view on these issues, as shown by his voting record and court rulings. But is he biased in the sense necessary to support a bias type of ad hominem argument against him?

The only way to reply to this question would be to look at this individual's arguments on a specific issue or on a set of issues. If he always takes a rigid conservative stance on every issue, then that would be evidence of bias. If he takes a conservative stance on some but not all these issues, then that would be prima facie evidence for the case against bias. On any particular issue, much should depend on the quality of the individual's argumentation and how he responds to opposing arguments. For sticking to a position in argument is not inherently bad. Indeed, maintaining consistency and resolving criticisms of inconsistency are generally positive marks of good argumentation.

To evaluate such a charge, then, one would have to look at past cases of how a person has argued to see whether he always rigidly advocates the same point of view, or interest group, or whether he has been more flexible and open in taking arguments on the other side fairly into account, when they are good arguments.

Bias, of the bad kind that throws a participant's honesty and balance in a critical discussion open to doubt, is the rigid defensive posture of making commitments only to logical consequences of a very definite and fixed commitment-set, refusing to countenance any commitment that shows any plausibility of conflicting with that commitment-set and refusing to retract or reconsider commitments, even if the arguments for retraction are convincing. Such a pattern is revealed in a profile of dialogue, or in a global context of dialogue.

Charges of bias can be especially damaging if the critic can reveal a concealed bias or hidden agenda, as in the cases of Wilma and Bob. But charges of bias can be based on various sorts of evidence from a text of discourse or from alleged facts brought forth about an arguer's personal commitments. Each case needs to be studied on its own merits. Too often, allegations of bias are based on presumptions about an arguer's person or character that are not well enough substantiated to be any better than innuendo or slander. In these cases it can become especially appropriate to speak of the ad hominem being committed by an accuser.

10. Explaining the Fallacy

According to the pragmatic concept of fallacy expressed in the theory of fallacy in Walton (*Pragmatic Theory*, 1995), a fallacious argument involves an error of reasoning but also a misuse of reasoning, in many cases, as a sophistical tactic to try unfairly to get the best of a speech partner in a dialogue by deception. In the case of many informal fallacies—and this is especially true with the ad hominem— to understand the fallacy, you have to understand how a basically reasonable type of argument can be used in a tricky, deceptive way as a powerful tactic of persuasion.

Govier (1987, p. 177) has put forward a nicely expressed definition of the concept of a fallacy that captures what is worthwhile in the traditional ideas while at the same time suggests the dual nature of the concept. In this definition, we see the error of reasoning idea as the basis of the concept of a fallacy. But at the same time, we see the element of a deceptive tactic grafted onto the concept in a way that extends the notions of fallacy.

By definition, a fallacy is a mistake in reasoning, a mistake which occurs with some frequency in real arguments and which is characteristically deceptive. This means, not that a person who uses a fallacious argument necessarily intends to deceive his audience but that the fallacious argument itself is deceptive, in the sense that it strikes many people as cogent, though it is not. An arguer may recognize his fallacious argument as fallacious and intend to deceive others, or he may think that it is a cogent argument and use it in all sincerity.

Why then does the ad hominem argument so often "strike many people as cogent," even in cases when it is not? Now the conditions have been given (in chapter 6) to show when an ad hominem argument is "cogent," the framework for understanding how and why it can be fallacious has been set in place.

Several factors combine to explain why the ad hominem argument is a fallacy, in the sense of a powerful tactic of argumentation that can be used deceptively to persuade an audience or to trick a speech partner. One is that even though the ad hominem argument in a given case may be very weak, in the sense of not being supported by evidence to back up the charge, it can be swept ahead by suggestion and innuendo ("Where there's smoke there's fire.") to make the accused appear guilty, thus shifting a burden of proof. To deny the charge too strenuously or to try to give evidence to prove it false may make the accused party appear even more guilty because he appears to be on the defensive. In the case of Mr. S., for example, in argument A7, a cloud of suspicion was raised over the integrity of Mr. S.'s party by the circumstantial attack on him personally.

When such a cloud of suspicion is raised by an ad hominem attack, an audience may find this personal interlude highly entertaining and diverting. Even if the attack is not relevant, it may seem such a powerful and interesting charge to the audience that the person charged may feel obliged to try to rebut it, thereby making it seem relevant.

Another factor is that an ad hominem argument may seem relevant when it is not because of a dialectical shift or because of an initial failure to clarify what type of dialogue the exchange of arguments is supposed to be part of. This shift may mask the weakness and the irrelevance of the argument, by making it appear to be genuine, when really it is not.

Another factor is that an ad hominem argument always by its nature needs to be evaluated against the body of other relevant evidence in a case. Because of its impact on an audience, who may be more impressed by the personal titillation of subjective character evidence than by impersonal evidence, the ad hominem argument may have an impact far out of proportion to its real weight as evidence in the larger picture of a case. Thus the element of what is called in rhetoric "the opportune moment" *(kairos)* can be crucial in an ad hominem attack. Introduced at the right point in the sequence of argumentation in a case, an ad hominem argument can powerfully influence an audience with colorful allegations of a personal nature. Objective evidence may be difficult to understand or remember, while an ad hominem argument tends to have a vibrant and memorable persuasive impact.

What emerges most significantly and clearly is the thesis that the argumentum ad hominem, in all three of its main types, is not an inherently fallacious scheme of argumentation in itself. But it is an inherently defeasible type of argumentation coupled with critical questions that need to be answered by the person attacked, if she is to answer the charge posed by the attack. The ad hominem fallacy arises (in its various specific forms) when the proponent presses ahead too aggressively in the dialogue, adopting a tactic of preemptive suppression of critical questioning by the person who is attacked. The working of these mechanisms of attack and defense can only be understood by explicitizing the argumentation schemes for the argumentum ad hominem, in the given case.

The approach to evaluation defended here is that the argumentum ad hominem is an argumentation scheme that is subject to numerous faults in use, like many other kinds of argumentation. The argument can be too weak to sustain a burden of proof, it can get the conclusion wrong, it can fail to prove adequately a presumption of inconsistency, it can get an arguer's commitments wrong (straw man fallacy), and it can be an unduly coercive way of trying to close off dialogue and prevent the other arguer from asking further questions or advancing further arguments. It can be used to commit all of these abuses and more.

Van Eemeren and Grootendorst (1984, p. 191) describe the error of ad hominem as a violation of certain specific rules of argumentation. The thesis advocated by the present analysis, however, will suggest that this approach should be broadened. The errors of ad hominem arguments do include the faults cited by van Eemeren and Grootendorst but must also include numerous other faults of argumentation. No single rule or small set of rules is violated. Many abuses of personal attack argumentation techniques remain to be studied and catalogued. Our thesis is that the generally plausible types of personal credibility arguments defined by our argumentation schemes of the ad hominem are more appropriate in certain dialectical circumstances than in others, depending on the textual and contextual evidence given in the particular case.

Notes

Chapter 1

1. The opponent may be said to be a liar, to have no regard for the truth, to be "crazy" and irresponsible, or to have motives for being untruthful. The varieties of the abusive subtype are studied in chapter 6.

2. A case similar to this one was presented by David Hitchcock in discussion during the symposium "Walton on Informal Fallacies" at the Canadian Philosophical Association Meeting in Winnipeg, May 26, 1986.

3. These cases are based on a similar type of case first presented by Robert Binkley at the symposium mentioned above in note 2.

4. On these types of dialogue, see Walton, *Informal Logic,* 1989, chapter 1; Walton and Krabbe, 1995; and Walton, *New Dialectic,* 1998.

5. These quotes are taken from Hamblin (1970, p. 160).

Chapter 2

1. I would like to thank Victor Wilkes for photocopying the sections on the ad hominem fallacy in the textbooks in the University of Winnipeg library (financed by a SSHRC Research Grant). The remaining information came from the author's own personal collection of logic textbooks.

2. This example might be compared to case 1.1 on Francis Bacon's philosophy.

3. This case will be treated below, in chapter 6.

4. See the van Eemeren and Grootendorst classification cited at the end of chapter 1.

Chapter 3

1. It could be the source of our problem with case 3.2 that there is a third viewpoint that also needs to be considered. Perhaps Bob is requesting only that Ed clarify his commitments. We could say then that Ed is not really arguing against Bob, or against Bob's argument. Instead, he is trying only to get clarification from Bob on what Bob's argument is, prior to arguing against it. This interpretation makes case 3.2 different from the smoking case, with respect to the ad hominem.

2. See Walton (*Informal Logic*, 1989).

3. See the analyses given in Walton (*Arguer's Position*, 1985, and *Informal Logic*, 1989).

4. See R. Schank and R. Abelson, *Scripts, Plans, Goals and Understanding* (Hillsdale, N.J.: Lawrence Erlbaum Associates, 1977).

5. See "Overheard," *Newsweek*, March 31, 1986, p. 15.

6. "What Killed Jimmy Anderson?" *Sixty Minutes*, March 2, 1986.

7. This case is based on an exchange in the Oral Question Period of the Debates of the House of Commons (Canada) once heard by the author.

8. See Walton ("Bias," 1991).

Chapter 4

1. What clearly emerged was the possibility of the two sides to the case, and that is what made it an interesting problem.

2. On equivocation, see Walton (*Informal Fallacies*, 1987, chapter 10).

3. See also Walton (*Arguer's Position*, 1985, p. 203).

4. In the Hart case, a good deal of media attention focused on Hart's own reactions, whether or not he was contrite, and so forth. This attention on such matters could be defended as relevant, perhaps, on the grounds that what was at issue was Mr. Hart's commitments on the subject of marriage. It could be relevant on the grounds that voters could be said to have a legitimate interest in Mr. Hart's position on traditional family values.

5. See Walton (*Arguer's Position*, 1985, p. 49).

6. See also ibid., p. 256.

7. This discussion took place in Amsterdam on October 15, 1987, when the author gave an invited lecture on the ad hominem to the argumentation group at the University of Amsterdam.

8. Some of the material in this chapter was presented as a lecture to the Fellows, Visiting Scholars, and staff of the Netherlands Institute for Advanced Study in the Humanities and Social Sciences on October 1, 1987. Many useful suggestions were made during this presentation. Special thanks for comments are due to A. J. N. van Dongen, D. Handelman, J. Kmenta, E. Krabbe, P. van der Laan, J. Parry, L. Wegge, and D. van de Kaa.

9. Kenneth L. Woodward, "Politics and Abortion," *Newsweek*, August 20, 1984, pp. 66–67.

10. Cuomo (1984, p. 34).

11. Califano (1984, p. 164).

12. Ibid., pp. 164–65.

13. Kenneth J. Woodward, "Politics and Abortion," *Newsweek*, August 20, 1984, p. 66.

Chapter 5

1. Deliberation as a normative model of dialogue has been briefly outlined in Walton (*Pragmatic Theory*, 1995, 116–18) and more fully analyzed in Walton (*New Dialectic*, 1998, chapter 6). Helpful descriptions of deliberation as a type of dialogue can also be found in Walton (*Practical Reasoning*, 1990) and Walton and Krabbe (1995).

2. Grice (1975).

3. So the ad hominem argument, in such a case, would be a metalevel, procedural kind of move in the dialogue, meaning that it would take place outside the normal sequence of moves in the dialogue, regulated by the collaborative maxims. The ad hominem move could even be an appeal to try to get a third party, or referee, to condemn the offender's move as contrary to the maxims.

4. Grice (1975, p. 67).

5. In chapter 6, it will be revealed why the bias subtype and a new subtype (the situationally disqualifying subtype) of ad hominem arguments are particularly suited to this procedural kind of analysis.

6. See also note 1, above.

7. Aristotle treated deliberation as part of ethics, but he did not treat it as a framework in which to evaluate arguments in logic, broadly speaking. However, it is impossible to set down clear borderlines here, because, as noted just below, Aristotle did see deliberation (and political deliberation in particular) as based on a kind of reasoning called practical reasoning.

8. As noted above, deliberation could be one person who plays the role of two participants, by looking at the problem from two viewpoints. Empathy is a very important part of a critical discussion.

9. Walton (*Practical Reasoning*, 1990, chapter 5).

10. See Walton (*Physician-Patient*, 1985).

11. Walton (*Plausible Argument*, 1992).

12. See the translation quoted from Nussbaum in section 1.

13. Particularly interesting as a case of an ad hominem attack on a person's judgment skills is the essay of Johnson (1988, chapter 8) on Bertrand Russell. According to Johnson, Russell was "ignorant of how most people behave" (p. 202), his views and actions in his personal life were "as liable to be determined by his actions as by his reason" (p. 203), he treated the women in his life badly (pp. 214–18), he was impractical in matters of daily life and "detached from physical reality" (p. 202), and he was on social and political questions "an absolutist who believed in total solutions" (p. 204).

14. As part of his ad hominem attack on Rousseau, Johnson (1988, p. 16) cites the agonies in his personal life caused by a persecution complex dementia. Johnson writes that it is impossible to study the painful details of Rousseau's personal quarrels "without reaching the conclusion that he was a mentally sick man" (p. 14).

15. Chapter 4, above.

16. This case is based on an argument reprinted as Appendix I in Walton (*Arguer's Position*, 1985), where a detailed analysis of the argument can also be found.

17. Walton (*New Dialectic*, 1998, chapter 9) includes a study of political discourse as part of an analysis of mixed discourse, in which several types of dialogue coexist in the same case.

Chapter 6

1. See Hamblin (1987, pp. 158–59).

2. The inference from one to the other is very natural in everyday conversation. Alleging that a speech partner has contradicted himself verges on being impolite because it suggests that he is confused or, even worse, is not a very intelligent person or a careful and logical reasoner. Hence allegations of inconsistency tend to be put in a milder way that leaves room for an arguer to change her mind, for example, "Did you really mean what you said when you asserted *A* earlier?"

3. Walton (*One-Sided*, 1998).

4. See Walton ("Bias," 1991).

5. At least, the presumption is that communists are discredited, as a group, for the target audience of the argument that the textbook case has in mind.

6. See section 1, above.

Chapter 7

1. An excellent case study of how negative campaign tactics can blow questions of character out of proportion is case 3.5, in which the personality factor outweighed and overwhelmed the other issues in the campaign for governor of Illinois in 1982.

2. Hamblin (1970).

3. Walton (*Informal Logic*, 1989; *Pragmatic Theory*, 1995).

4. See chapter 6.

5. See the special issue (volume 6, no. 2) of *Argumentation* on 'Relevance,' edited by Frans van Eemeren and Rob Grootendorst, May 1992.

6. See Walton (*Place of Emotion*, 1992, pp. 183–89).

7. On assigning plausibility values to arguments, see Walton (*Plausible Argument*, 1992).

8. Hamblin (1970, 1971). Also see Barth and Krabbe (1982).

9. See Walton (*New Dialectic*, 1998).

10. A range of cases of this sort were presented in the program *Prime Time Live* on January 18, 1995 (ABC Network).

11. On the characteristics of the quarrel as a type of dialogue, see Walton (*Plausible Argument*, 1992, chapter 4).

12. See chapter 3, section 8, on the kind of balance required in argumentation in a critical discussion.

Bibliography

Anaximenes (?). 4th century B.C. *Rhetorica Ad Alexandrum*. Trans. H. Rackham. *Aristotle's Problems*. Vol. 2. Loeb Library. Cambridge, Mass.: Harvard University Press. 1965.

Annis, David B. 1974. *Techniques of Critical Reasoning*. Columbus, Ohio: Charles E. Merrill.

Anonymous. 1995. "Cheap Games," *Newsweek*, September 4:5.

Anscombe, G. E. M. 1957. *Intention*. Oxford: Blackwell.

Aristotle. 1915. *Ethica Nichomachea*. Translated by W. D. Ross. Vol. 9 of *The Works of Aristotle*. Edited by W. D. Ross. Oxford: Oxford University Press.

———. 1928. *On Sophistical Refutations*. Translated by E. S. Forster. Loeb Classical Library Edition. Cambridge, Mass.: Harvard University Press and London: William Heinemann.

———. 1937. *Rhetoric*. Loeb Library Edition. Translated by J. H. Freese. Cambridge, Mass.: Harvard University Press.

Audi, Robert. 1989. *Practical Reasoning*. New York: Routledge.

Barker, Stephen F. 1974. *The Elements of Logic*. 2d ed. New York: McGraw-Hill.

Barnes, Jonathan. 1980. "Aristotle and the Methods of Ethics." *Revue Internationale de Philosophie*. 34:490–511.

Barry, Vincent E. 1976. *Logic*. New York: Holt, Rinehart and Winston.

Barth, E. M., and E. C. W. Krabbe. 1982. *From Axiom to Dialogue*. New York: De Gruyter.

Barth, E. M., and J. L. Martens. 1977. "*Argumentum Ad Hominem*: From Chaos to Formal Dialectic." *Logique et Analyse* 77–78:76–96.

Bartky, Sandra Lee. 1992. "Letter to the Editor." *Proceedings and Addresses of the American Philosophical Association*. Vol. 65 (June), pp. 55–58.

Beardsley, Monroe C. 1950. *Practical Logic.* New York: Prentice-Hall.

——. 1966 [1950]. *Thinking Straight.* Englewood Cliffs, N.J.:Prentice-Hall.

Benoit, William L. 1995. *Accounts, Excuses and Apologies: A Theory of Image Restoration Strategies.* Albany: State University of New York Press.

Bentham, Jeremy. 1969. "The Book of Fallacies." [1984]. In *A Bentham Reader.* Edited by Mary P. Mack, 331–58. New York: Pegasus.

Bickenbach, Jerome E. 1990. "The Artificial Reason of the Law." *Informal Logic* 12:23–32.

Black, Max. 1946. *Critical Thinking: An Introduction to Logic and Scientific Method.* New York: Prentice-Hall.

Blair, J. Anthony. 1988. "What is Bias?" In *Selected Issues in Logic and Communication.* Edited by Trudy Govier, 93–103. Belmont, Calif.: Wadsworth.

——. 1995. "The Place of Teaching Informal Fallacies in Teaching Reasoning Skills or Critical Thinking." In *Fallacies: Classical and Contemporary Readings.* Edited by Hans V. Hansen and Robert C. Pinto, 328–38. University Park: Pennsylvania State University Press.

Blyth, John W. 1957. *A Modern Introduction to Logic.* Boston: Houghton Mifflin.

Bonevac, Daniel. 1990. *The Art and Science of Logic.* Mountain View, Calif.: Mayfield Publishing.

Braet, Antoine C. 1992. "Ethos, Pathos and Logos in Aristotle's Rhetoric: A Re-Examination." *Argumentation* 6:307–20.

Brennan, Joseph Gerard. 1957. *A Handbook of Logic.* New York: Harper & Brothers.

Brinton, Alan. 1985. "A Rhetorical View of the *Ad Hominem.*" *Australasian Journal of Philosophy* 63:50–63.

——. 1986. "Ethotic Argument." *History of Philosophy Quarterly* 3:245–57.

——. 1987. "Ethotic Argument: Some Uses." In *Argumentation: Perspectives and Approaches.* Edited by Frans H. van Eemeren, Rob Grootendorst, J. Anthony Blair, and Charles A. Willard, 246–54. Dordrecht and Providence: Foris Publications.

——. 1995. "The *Ad Hominem.*" In *Fallacies: Classical and Contemporary Readings.* Edited by Hans V. Hansen and Robert C. Pinto, 213–22. University Park: Pennsylvania State University Press.

Byerly, Henry C. 1973. *A Primer of Logic.* New York: Harper & Row.

Califano, Joseph A., Jr. 1984. "Moral Leadership and Partisanship." *America* (September 29): pp. 164–65.

Capaldi, Nicholas. 1971. *The Art of Deception.* New York: Donald W. Brown.

Carney, James D., and Richard K. Scheer. 1974. *Fundamentals of Logic.* 2d ed. New York: Macmillan.

Cederblom, Jerry, and David W. Paulsen. 1982. *Critical Reasoning: Understanding and Criticizing Arguments and Theories.* Belmont, Calif.: Wadsworth.

Chase, Stuart. 1956. *Guides to Straight Thinking.* New York: Harper & Row.

Clark, Romane, and Paul Welsh. 1962. *Introduction to Logic.* Princeton, N.J.: D. Van Nostrand.

Clarke, D. S., Jr. 1985. *Practical Inferences*. London: Routledge and Kegan Paul.

Cohen, Morris R., and Ernest Nagel. 1934. *An Introduction to Logic and Scientific Method*. New York: Harcourt, Brace.

Copi, Irving M. 1953. *Introduction to Logic*. 1st ed. [2d ed. 1961]. New York: Macmillan.

Copi, Irving M., and Carl Cohen. 1994. *Introduction to Logic*. 9th ed. New York: Macmillan.

Cragan, John F., and Craig W. Cutbirth. 1984. "A Revisionist Perspective on Political *Ad Hominem* Argument: A Case Study." *Central States Speech Journal* 35:228–37.

Cranston, Maurice. 1967. "Bacon, Francis." Vol. 1. *The Encyclopedia of Philosophy*. Edited by Paul Edwards, 235–40. New York: Macmillan.

Creighton, James Edwin. 1904. *An Introductory Logic*. 2d ed. 1st edition 1898. New York: Macmillan.

———. 1929. *An Introductory Logic*. 4th ed. New York: Macmillan.

Crossley, David J., and Peter A. Wilson. 1979. *How to Argue: An Introduction to Logical Thinking*. New York: Random House.

Cuomo, Mario L. 1984. "Religious Belief and Public Morality." *The New York Review of Books*. Vol. 31 (October 25), pp. 32–37.

Damer, T. Edward. 1980. *Attacking Faulty Reasoning*. Belmont, Calif.: Wadsworth Publishing.

Dauer, Francis Watanabe. 1989. *Critical Thinking: An Introduction to Reasoning*. New York: Oxford University Press.

Davis, Wayne A. 1986. *An Introduction to Logic*. Englewood Cliffs, N.J.: Prentice-Hall.

DeMorgan, Augustus. 1847. *Formal Logic*. London: Taylor and Walton.

Diggs, B. J. 1960. "A Technical Ought." *Mind* 69:301–17.

Eisenberg, Ann R. 1987. "Learning to Argue with Parents and Peers." *Argumentation* 1:113–25.

Emmet, E. R. 1960. *The Use of Reason*. London: Longmans.

Engel, S. Morris. 1982. *With Good Reason: An Introduction to Informal Fallacies*. 2d ed. New York: St. Martin's Press.

Evans, J. D. G. 1977. *Aristotle's Concept of Dialectic*. Cambridge: Cambridge University Press.

Farrell, Thomas B. 1993. *Norms of Rhetorical Culture*. New Haven: Yale University Press.

Fearnside, W. Ward. 1980. *About Thinking*. Englewood Cliffs, N.J.: Prentice-Hall.

Fearnside, W. Ward, and William B. Holther. 1959. *Fallacy: The Counterfeit of Argument*. Englewood Cliffs, N.J.: Prentice-Hall.

Federal Rules of Evidence, 1986–87 [no author given]. 1987. Binghamton, N.Y.: Gould Publications.

Finocchiaro, Maurice A. 1980. *Galileo and the Art of Reasoning*. Dordrecht: Reidel.

Fischer, David Hackett. 1970. *Historians' Fallacies: Toward a Logic of Historical Thought*. New York: Harper & Row.

Fitch, Frederic Brenton. 1952. *Symbolic Logic: An Introduction.* New York: Ronald Press.

Fraser, Graham. 1994. "Beleaguered U.S. Leader Can't Seem to Win for Losing." *The Globe and Mail* (December 28), p. A7.

Garver, Eugene. 1994. *Aristotle's Rhetoric: An Art of Character.* Chicago: University of Chicago Press.

Gellius, Aulus. 1928 [originally written around 165 B.C.]. *The Attic Nights of Aulus Gellius.* Translated by John C. Rolfe (3 volumes). London: William Heinemann, and New York: G. P. Putnam's Sons.

Govier, Trudy. 1983. "*Ad Hominem:* Revising the Textbooks." *Teaching Philosophy* 6:13–24.

———. 1987. *Problems in Argument Analysis and Evaluation.* Dordrecht and Providence: Foris Publications.

———. 1992. *A Practical Study of Argument.* 3d ed. Belmont, Calif.: Wadsworth Publishing.

Graham, Michael H. 1977. "Impeaching the Professional Expert Witness by a Showing of Financial Interest." *Indiana Law Journal* 53:35–53.

Grice, H. Paul. 1975. "Logic and Conversation." *The Logic of Grammar.* Edited by Donald Davidson and Gilbert Harman, 64–75. Encino, Calif.: Dickenson.

Groarke, Leo. 1982. "When Two Wrongs Make a Right." *Informal Logic* 5:10–13.

Guthrie, W. K. C. 1981. *A History of Greek Philosophy.* Vol. 6. Cambridge: Cambridge University Press.

Halverson, William H. 1984. *A Concise Logic.* New York: Random House.

Hamblin, C. L. 1970. *Fallacies.* London: Methuen. Reprinted in 1986. Newport News, Va.: Vale Press.

———. 1971. "Mathematical Models of Dialogue." *Theoria* 37:130–55.

———. 1987. *Imperatives.* Oxford: Blackwell.

Harrison, Frank R. III. 1992. *Logic and Rational Thought.* New York: West Publishing Company.

Hartman, Sylvester J. 1949. *Fundamentals of Logic.* St. Louis, Mo.: B. Herder Book.

Hoaglund, John. 1984. *Critical Thinking: An Introduction to Informal Logic.* Newport News, Va.: Vale Press.

Hoffman, Herbert C. 1979. "The Cross-Examination of Expert Witnesses." New York: *Planning, Zoning and Eminent Domain Institute* 3:313–49.

Holland, Bernard. 1919. *Memoir of Kenelm Henry Digby.* London: Longman Green.

Hughes, G. E. 1958. "Moral Condemnation." In *Essays in Moral Philosophy.* Edited by A. Melden, 108–34. Seattle: University of Washington Press.

Hughes, William. 1992. *Critical Thinking: An Introduction to the Basic Skills.* Peterborough: Ontario Broadview Press.

Huppé, Bernard F., and Jack Kaminsky. 1957. *Logic and Language.* New York: Alfred A. Knopf.

Hurley, Patrick J. 1994. *A Concise Introduction to Logic.* 5th ed. Belmont, Calif.: Wadsworth Publishing.

Ilbert, Sir Courtenay. 1960. "Evidence." *Encyclopaedia Britannica*. 11th ed. Vol. 10, 11–21.

Jamieson, Kathleen Hall. 1992. *Dirty Politics*. New York: Oxford University Press.

Jevons, W. Stanley. 1883. *The Elements of Logic: A Textbook for Schools and Colleges*. 2d ed. New York: Sheldon.

Johnson, Paul. 1988. *Intellectuals*. London: Weidenfeld and Nicolson.

Johnson, Ralph H., and J. Anthony Blair. 1983. *Logical Self-Defense*. 2d ed. Toronto: McGraw-Hill Ryerson.

Johnstone, Henry W., Jr. 1952. "Philosophy and *Argumentum ad Hominem*." *Journal of Philosophy* 49:489–98.

——. 1959. *Philosophy and Argument*. University Park: Pennsylvania State University Press.

——. 1978. *Validity and Rhetoric in Philosophical Argument*. University Park: Dialogue Press of Man and World.

Jungius, Joachim. 1638. *Logica Hamburgensis*. 2d ed. Hamburg: Bartholdi Offermans.

Kahane, Howard. 1969. *Logic and Philosophy: A Modern Introduction*. Belmont, Calif.: Wadsworth Publishing.

——. 1992. *Logic and Contemporary Rhetoric: The Use of Reason in Everyday Life*. 6th ed. Belmont, Calif.: Wadsworth Publishing.

Kaminsky, Jack, and Alice Kaminsky. 1974. *Logic: A Philosophical Introduction*. Reading, Mass.: Addison-Wesley.

Kelley, David. 1994. *The Art of Reasoning*. 2d ed. New York: W. W. Norton.

Kennedy, George. 1963. *The Art of Persuasion in Greece*. Princeton, N.J.: Princeton University Press.

——. 1980. *Classical Rhetoric and Its Christian and Secular Tradition from Ancient to Modern Times*. Chapel Hill: University of North Carolina Press.

Kilgore, William J. 1968. *An Introductory Logic*. New York: Holt Rinehart and Winston.

Kozy, John, Jr. 1974. *Understanding Natural Deduction: A Formalist Approach to Introductory Logic*. Encino, Calif.: Dickenson Publishing.

Krabbe, Erik C. W. 1990. "Inconsistent Commitment and Commitment to Inconsistencies." *Informal Logic* 12:33–42.

Krabbe, Erik C. W., and Douglas Walton. 1993. "It's All Very Well for You to Talk! Situationally Disqualifying *Ad Hominem* Attacks." *Informal Logic* 15:79–91.

Kreyche, Robert J. 1970. *Logic for Undergraduates*. 3d ed. New York: Holt Rinehart and Winston.

Kupperman, Joel J. 1991. *Character*. New York: Oxford University Press.

Lagerspetz, Eerik. 1995. "*Ad Hominem* Arguments in Practical Argumentation." *Argumentation* 9:363–70.

Latta, Robert, and Alexander MacBeath. 1956. *The Elements of Logic*. London: St. Martin's Press.

Little, J. Frederick, Leo A. Groarke, and Christopher W. Tindale. 1989. *Good Reasoning Matters!* Toronto: McClelland and Stewart.

Locke, John. 1961. [originally published 1690]. *An Essay Concerning Human Understanding.* Edited by John W. Yolton. 2 vols. London: Dent.

Lomasky, Loren E. 1992. "Person, Concept of." *Encyclopedia of Ethics.* Vol. 2. Edited by Lawrence C. Becker and Charlotte B. Becker, 950–56. New York: Garland.

Manicas, Peter T., and Arthur N. Kruger. 1968. *Essentials of Logic.* New York: American Book.

McElhaney, James W. 1993. "Understanding Character Evidence." *ABA Journal* (March): 76–77.

Mellone, Sydney Herbert. 1913. *An Introductory Textbook of Logic.* Edinburgh: William Blackwood and Sons.

Michalos, Alex C. 1970. *Improving Your Reasoning.* Englewood Cliffs, N.J.: Prentice-Hall.

Mittelstaedt, Martin. 1995. "Tories Accused of Double Standard." *Globe and Mail* (November 16), p. A3.

Moore, Kathleen Dean. 1993. *Reasoning and Writing.* New York: Macmillan.

Munson, Ronald. 1976. *The Way of Words: An Informal Logic.* Atlanta: Houghton Mifflin.

Nuchelmans, Gabriël. 1993. "On the Fourfold Root of the *Argumentum Ad Hominem.*" *Empirical Logic and Public Debate.* Edited by Erik C. W. Krabbe, Renée José Dalitz, and Pier A. Smit, 37–47. Amsterdam: Rodopi.

Nussbaum, Martha C. 1992. "Character." *Encyclopedia of Ethics.* Vol. 1. Edited by Lawrence C. Becker and Charlotte B. Becker, 131–34. New York: Garland.

Olson, Robert G. 1969. *Meaning and Argument: Elements of Logic.* New York: Harcourt Brace & World.

Perelman, Chaim, and L. Olbrechts-Tyteca. 1969. *The New Rhetoric: A Treatise on Argumentation.* Translated by J. Wilkinson and P. Weaver. Notre Dame: University of Notre Dame Press. [First published in 1958 as *La Nouvelle Rhétorique: Traité de l'Argumentation*].

Piaget, J. 1959. *The Language and Thought of the Child.* London: Routledge and Kegan Paul. [First ed., 1923].

Pirie, Madsen. 1985. *The Book of the Fallacy: A Training Manual for Intellectual Subversives.* London and Henley: Routledge & Kegan Paul.

Platiel, Rudy. 1995. "Millions Wasted on Native Land Talks, Report Says." *Globe and Mail* (January 19), p. A3.

Proctor, Robert N. 1995. *Cancer Wars: How Politics Shapes What We Know and Don't Know About Cancer.* New York: Basic Books.

Quintilian (Marcus Fabius Quintilianus). *Institutio Oratoria.* circa 95 A.D. trans. H. E. Butler. Loeb Library Edition (1936). Cambridge, Mass.: Harvard University Press.

Read, Carveth. 1901. *Logic: Deductive and Inductive.* 4th ed. London: Simpkin, Marshall, Hamilton, Kent.

Rescher, Nicholas. 1964. *Introduction to Logic.* New York: St. Martin's Press.
———. 1976. *Plausible Reasoning.* Assen: Van Gorcum.

Ruby, Lionel. 1950. *Logic: An Introduction.* New York: J. B. Lippincott.

Runkle, Gerald. 1978. *Good Thinking: An Introduction to Logic.* Chicago: Holt Rinehart and Winston.

Salmon, Merrilee H. 1984. *Introduction to Logic and Critical Thinking.* New York: Harcourt Brace Jovanovich.

Salmon, Wesley C. 1984. *Logic.* 3d ed. Englewood Cliffs, N.J.: Prentice-Hall.

Schank, R., and R. Abelson. 1977. *Scripts, Plans, Goals, and Understanding.* Hillsdale, N.J.: Erlblum.

Schipper, Edith Watson, and Edward Schuh. 1959. *A First Course in Modern Logic.* New York: Henry Holt.

Schopenhauer, Arthur. 1951. "The Art of Controversy" [1851]. *Essays from the Parerga and Paralipomena.* Translated by T. Bailey Saunders, 5–38. London: Allen and Unwin.

Sherman, Nancy. 1989. *The Fabric of Character.* Oxford: Clarendon Press.

Soccio, Douglas J., and Vincent E. Barry. 1992. *Practical Logic: An Antidote for Uncritical Thinking.* 4th ed. San Diego: Harcourt Brace Jovanovich.

Sommers, Christina. 1992. "Letter to the Editor." *Proceedings and Addresses of the American Philosophical Association* 65 (June):76–83.

Thomas, Stephen N. 1977. *Practical Reasoning in Natural Language.* Englewood Cliffs, N.J.: Prentice-Hall.

Toulmin, Stephen, Richard Rieke, and Allan Janik. 1979. *An Introduction to Reasoning.* New York: Macmillan.

van Eemeren, Frans H., and Rob Grootendorst. 1984. *Speech Acts in Argumentative Discussions.* Dordrecht: Foris.

———. 1987. "Fallacies in Pragma-Dialectical Perspective." *Argumentation* 1:283–301.

———. 1993. "The History of the *Argumentum Ad Hominem* Since the Seventeenth Century." *Empirical Logic and Public Debate.* Edited by Erik C. W. Krabbe, Renée José Dalitz, and Pier A. Smit, 49–68. Amsterdam: Rodopi.

Vernon, Thomas S. 1968. *Reflective Thinking: The Fundamentals of Logic.* Belmont, Calif.: Wadsworth Publishing.

Vernon, Thomas S., and Lowell A. Nissen. 1968. *Reflective Thinking: The Fundamentals of Logic.* Belmont, Calif.: Wadsworth.

von Wright, G. H. 1963. *The Varieties of Goodness.* London: Routledge and Kegan Paul.

———. 1972. "On So-Called Practical Inference." *Acta Sociologica* 15:39–53.

Waller, Bruce N. 1988. *Critical Thinking: Consider the Verdict.* Englewood Cliffs, N.J.: Prentice-Hall.

Walton, Douglas N. 1984. *Logical Dialogue-Games and Fallacies.* Lanham, Md.: University Press of America.

———. 1985. *Arguer's Position.* Westport, Conn.: Greenwood Press.

———. 1985. *Physician-Patient Decision-Making.* Westport, Conn.: Greenwood Press.

———. 1987. *Informal Fallacies.* Amsterdam and Philadelphia: John Benjamins.

———. 1988. "Burden of Proof." *Argumentation* 2:233–54.

———. 1989. *Informal Logic.* Cambridge: Cambridge University Press.

———. 1989. *Question-Reply Argumentation.* New York: Greenwood Press.

———. 1990. "Ignoring Qualifications *(Secundum Quid)* as a Subfallacy of Hasty Generalization." *Logique et Analyse* 129–30:112–54.

——. 1990. *Practical Reasoning.* Savage, Md.: Rowman and Littlefield.

——. 1991. "Bias, Critical Doubt, and Fallacies." *Argumentation and Advocacy* 28:1–22.

——. 1992. *The Place of Emotion in Argument.* University Park: Pennsylvania State University Press.

——. 1992. *Plausible Argument in Everyday Conversation.* Albany: State University of New York Press.

——. 1992. "Practical Reasoning." Edited by Lawrence C. Becker and Charlotte B. Becker, 996–1000. *Encyclopedia of Ethics.* Vol. 2. New York: Garland Press.

——. 1993. "Commitment, Types of Dialogue, and Fallacies." *Informal Logic* 14:93–103.

——. 1995. *A Pragmatic Theory of Fallacy.* Tuscaloosa: University of Alabama Press.

——. 1996. *Argumentation Schemes for Presumptive Reasoning.* Mahwah, N.J.: Lawrence Erlbaum.

——. 1996. *Arguments from Ignorance.* University Park: Pennsylvania State University Press.

——. 1998. *The New Dialectic: Conversational Contexts of Argument.* Toronto: University of Toronto Press.

——. 1998. *One-Sided Arguments: A Dialectical Analysis of Bias.* Albany: State University of New York Press.

Walton, Douglas N., and Erik C. W. Krabbe. 1995. *Commitment in Dialogue.* Albany: State University of New York Press.

Watts, Isaac. 1725. *Logick.* London: John Clark and Richard Hett.

Weber, O. J. 1981. "Attacking the Expert Witness." *Federation of Insurance Counsel Quarterly* 31:299–313.

Werkmeister, William Henry. 1948. *An Introduction to Critical Thinking: A Beginner's Text in Logic.* Lincoln, Neb.: Johnsen Publishing.

Whately, Richard. 1870. *Elements of Logic.* 9th ed. London: Longmans Green.

Wheelwright, Philip. 1962. *Valid Thinking: An Introduction to Logic.* New York: Odyssey Press.

Will, George F. 1995. "A Weird Sincerity." *Newsweek* (November 13), p. 94.

Wisse, Jakob. 1989. *Ethos and Pathos: From Aristotle to Cicero.* Amsterdam: Adolf M. Hakkert.

Woods, John, and Douglas Walton. 1977. *"Ad Hominem." Philosophical Forum* 8:1–20.

Wooldridge, Michael, and Nicholas R. Jennings. 1995. "Intelligent Agents: Theory and Practice." *Knowledge Engineering Review* 10:115–52.

Wright, Lynne. 1995. "Where Do Tree Huggers Live, Anyway?" *Globe and Mail* (November 7), p. A24.

Index

Argument against the person, 83
Argumentation schemes, 107, 269; classification of, 260
Argument from analogy, 17, 195–96
Argument from authority, 83, 84
Argument from commitment (AC), 23, 29, 105–6, 134, 137, 207, 248; critical questions for, 107, 249
Argument from consequences, 184
Argument from inconsistent commitment (INCONSISTENT COMMITMENT), 220, 252
Argument from pragmatic inconsistency (PRAGMATIC INCONSISTENCY), 251; critical questions for, 251
Argument from probability, 200–201
Argument from the other party's commitment, 41
Argumentum ad hominem, 8, 75; ambiguities of the expression, 40; defined, 47, 69; distinguishing between fallacious and nonfallacious, 51–52. *See also* Ad hominem argument
Argumentum ad ignorantiam, 278
Argumentum ad judicium, 23
Argumentum ad personam, 23
Argumentum ad rem, 23, 28, 134
Argumentum ad verecundiam, 8; obverse, 279
Aristotle, 21, 23–26, 38–41, 122, 124, 187, 213; analysis of character, 262; definition of character, 177, 179, 189, 191, 209; definition of virtue, 190; proof of relevance of character, 197–98; theory of political argumentation, 197; view of deliberation, 184
Assertions, 35–36, 74; attacked, 70
Associative ad hominem argument, 70
Assumption: conclusion from, 24
Attack: concluding, 154
Audience, 202; jury, 204; neutral observer, 232
Automobile insurance case (2.23), 78, 231

Bacon, Francis, case (1.1), 2, 3, 5, 59, 281–82
Barker, Stephen F., 62–63, 99
Barnes, Jonathan, 24
Barry, Vincent E., 19, 74, 92–94, 98
Barth, E. M., 29–30, 86, 111, 115, 119, 286
Bartky, Sandra Lee, case (1.2), 3

Beardsley, Monroe, 50–52, 64, 99, 271
Bias, 71, 72, 77, 93, 131, 211; accusation of, 51, 129; ad hominem criticism of, 14; allegation of, 14–15, 56, 57, 76, 131; arguer's, 289; as a failure, 228–29; bad, 229, 292; concealed, 115, 292; criticism of, 13, 136; deductivist, 46; expected, 228; misrepresentation of an opponent's position, 132; obverse bias type, 67; primary subtype, 211; problem of, 229
Bias ad hominem argument (BIAS AH), 2, 57, 130, 132, 228, 255; argumentation scheme for, 228; basis of, 14; critical questions for, 229, 255, 291; defined as circumstantial variant, 43–44, 60, 62, 69, 71, 79
Black, Max, 45, 48–49, 50, 53, 99
Blair, J. Anthony, 20, 81, 99, 131–32, 135, 139, 270
Blunders, 266
Blyth, John W., 56–57, 99
Bob/Ed cases (3.1, 3.2), 106–11, 220–21
Bob/Wilma cases (1.7, 1.8, 1.9), 12–14, 101–2, 131, 136, 228, 237, 292
Boethius, 24, 25
Bonevac, 87–88, 99
Brennan, Joseph Gerard, 57–58, 99
Brinton, Alan, 38–39, 41, 42, 122, 123, 185, 197, 245
Burden of presumption, 205
Burden of proof, 35, 216; altering, 124; deceptive, 289; powerful shift in, 136; shift, 8, 49, 126, 132, 135, 188, 192, 195, 224, 272, 278, 285, 287, 293; sustaining, 294; tilted, 156
Byerly, Henry C., 19, 70–72, 99

Carney, James D., 72, 99
Capaldi, Nicholas, 19, 70
Catholic bias (1.10), 15, 131, 238
Cederblom, Jerry, 80, 99
Chaining, 270
Character, 177; allegation of bad, 281; arguer's, 27; assassination, 142, 145; attacked, 96; competence, 168; defined, 178, 209; difficult to judge, 180; excellence of, 179; five aspects of, usually attacked, 191, 209; good character for veracity, 179; in law, 277; issue, 166; linked to actions, 209; of advice giver, 123–24; origins of term,

Dialectical shift, 120, 129, 130, 268; illicit, 130
Dialectic relevance of argumentation, 268; six factors of evidence, 268–69
Dialogue: advice-giving, 122, 187, 191, 206, 229; collaborative rules of, 282; confrontation stage, 156, 157; context of, 113, 123, 274; goal of, 131, 269; information-seeking type, 189, 205; opening stage, 156; profile of, 266–67; rules of, 175; type of, 268–69. *See also* Persuasion dialogue
Diggs, B. J., 188
Direct ad hominem argument. *See* Abusive ad hominem argument
Direct answers, 205
Direct attack, 6
Dishonesty: charge of, 181
Disputatio temptativa, 24
Dispute: adversarial, 14
Double blind hypothesis, 8
Double standard argument (DOUBLE STANDARD), 222, 253; critical questions for, 253

Eisenberg, Ann R., 8
Elenchus, 134
Emmet, E. R., 59, 99
Empathy, 182
Encyclopaedia Britannica, 204
Endoxa, 24
Engel, S. Morris, 18, 79–80, 86, 98
Enthymemes, 36
Epicurus, 143–44
Eristic arguments, 23, 198
Eristic dialogue, 268
Error of reasoning fallacy, 139
Ethics in government, 166
Ethos, 38–39, 177, 197–99, 200–201, 203
Ethotic ad hominem argument, 41, 124, 197–98, 283; based on arguer's character, 137; defined, 38, 202; dependence on context of dialogue, 123; negative use of, 122
ETHOTIC AH, 213, 262; critical questions for, 214–15; implicit conditional premise, 214; negative ethotic argument, 213
Ethotic rating, 274; negative ethotic rating, 274
Evaluator, 112
Evans, J. D. G., 25
Evidence, 7, 291; ad hominem, 278;

character as a type of, 123; defined, 27; direct, 200; external, 275; factual (ad judicium), 124, 280; independent, 15; objective, 271–72; personal-based, 272; prima facie, 291; relevant, 229; sensitivity, 182; subjective, 271–72
Excessiveness, 176
Ex concessis, 27, 111
Ex concessis argument, 22, 23, 25. *See also* Lockean
Exetastic, 23
Expert: impartial, 204

Fallacy: definition, 293; fatality view, 139; injury view, 139; overuse of term, 266
Fallacy of abusing the man, 68
Fallacy of ad hominem, 23
Fallacy of appealing to bad connections, 68
Fallacy of damning the origin, 79
Fallacy of faulty motives, 68
Fallacy of guilt by association, 74
Fallacy of irrelevance, 58, 59, 83, 86, 95, 97
Fallacy of poisoning the well, 72, 86
Fallacy of relevance, 59, 67, 77, 81, 84, 85, 88, 97, 268
Fallacy of the bad seed, 68
Fallacy of two wrongs (make a right), 19, 90–91, 93–94, 102
Fallacy of wishful thinking, 67
Farrell, Thomas B., 187, 236
Fearnside, W. Ward, 58, 79, 98, 99
Federal Rules of Evidence, 277
Ferraro, Geraldine, case, 171–75
Finocchiaro, Maurice A., 21–22
Fischer, David Hackett, 70
Fitch, Frederic Brenton, 53, 99, 132
Fundamentals of Logic, 53

Galileo, 22, 25, 48; definition of ad hominem argument, 22
Game of dialogue, 116
Garver, Eugene, 185, 187, 203
Gauss, 48
Gellius, Aulus, 143
Generalization, 107, 194; questionable, 3
Generic ad hominem argument, 249; critical questions for, 249
GENERIC AH, 112–14, 116–18, 138, 219, 233, 238, 249; conditional warrant, 113

argument (UNIVERSAL CIRCUMSTAN-
TIAL AH), 226, 253; critical questions
for, 253–54
Universal pragmatic subtype of the circumstantial ad hominem argument,
186

Van Eemeren, Frans, 28–30, 42, 62, 111,
116, 129, 130, 154, 163, 262, 286,
294; dialogue models, 117
Veracity, 106, 111, 120, 129, 211, 213;
arguer's, 6, 276; bad character for, 2–
3, 109, 125, 137, 215–17, 244, 250,
275, 286; character for, 38, 199, 206,
208, 211, 277; good character for, 122–
24, 179, 181; lacking, 112; witness,
204, 279
Vernon, Thomas S., 65–66, 98

Waller, Bruce N., 86, 99
Walton, Douglas N., 6, 31, 32, 35–36,
53, 65, 105, 116, 144, 240, 243, 262,
268, 273; analyzing secundum quid
fallacy, 194–95; argumentation

schemes, 107; commitment, 138; dis-
tinguishing meanings of circumstan-
tial, 241
Watts, Isaac, 25
Weber, O. J., 204–5, 279–80
Welsh, Paul, 61
Werkmeister, William Henry, 45, 99;
combines abusive and circumstantial
types, 49–50
Whately, Richard, 5, 28, 29–30, 46, 99,
133–34, 221, 278
Wheelwright, Philip, 20, 61, 98
Wilson, Peter A., 76–77, 98
Wisdom: as opposed to practical wis-
dom, 191, 209; practical, 187, 190
Wisse, Jakob, 38–39
Wooldridge, Michael, 208

You contradict yourself type of argument, 222
YOU DON'T PRACTICE WHAT YOU PREACH,
220. *See also* Circumstantial ad hominem argument

About the Author

Douglas Walton is Professor of Philosophy, University of Winnipeg. He received his B.A. from the University of Waterloo and his Ph.D. from the University of Toronto. His publications include many books and articles about argumentation. His book *A Pragmatic Theory of Fallacy* was published by The University of Alabama Press in 1995.

About the Series

STUDIES IN RHETORIC AND COMMUNICATION
Series Editors:
E. Culpepper Clark, Raymie E. McKerrow, and David Zarefsky

The University of Alabama Press has established this series to publish major new works in the general area of rhetoric and communication, including books treating the symbolic manifestations of political discourse, argument as social knowledge, the impact of machine technology on patterns of communication behavior, and other topics related to the nature or impact of symbolic communication. We actively solicit studies involving historical, critical, or theoretical analyses of human discourse.